# TAKING SIDES

Clashing Views on Controversial

# Issues in Physical Anthropology

D0062187

# TAKING SIDES

Clashing Views on Controversial

# Issues in Physical Anthropology

**Selected, Edited, and with Introductions by**

**Mary Courtis**
*Portland Community College*

**McGraw-Hill/Dushkin**
**A Division of The McGraw-Hill Companies**

*This book is dedicated to all my anthropology students at Portland Community College who have made me laugh, think and constantly revise what I think I know about physical anthropology.*

Photo Acknowledgment
Cover image: Photos.com

Cover Acknowledgment
Maggie Lytle

Manufactured in the United States of America

First Edition

123456789DOCDOC98765

0-07-313667-0
1554-6861

Printed on Recycled Paper

# Preface

**B**iological anthropology is one of the most exciting and thought-provoking fields in the social sciences. *Taking Sides: Clashing Views on Controversial Issues in Physical Anthropology* examines some of the issues that have been hotly debated by scholars over the years. A number of the issues—such as whether evolution is a rapid or gradual process—have been argued about since the concept of evolution was first introduced over a century ago. Other issues reflect more recent trends or concerns, such as the question of whether human cloning and genetic engineering pose any evolutionary dangers. Some selections also focus on the impact of evolution and biology on gender roles. Questions such as whether male aggression and competition are key to reproductive success, or are primate females naturally monogamous, are examined from opposing perspectives.

Many of the issues in this volume were also chosen to compliment the major topics covered in most introductory texts in physical anthropology. They are designed to encourage students to look more deeply into subject matter, such as genetics or evolutionary theory. Another goal is to help students understand the varied ways anthropologists approach their research and support their conclusions. This effort should stimulate critical thinking skills among students and provoke them to consider the comparative merits of different theories and explanations.

## Plan of the Book

This book is composed of 17 issues organized into three major sections. The first part deals with controversies in evolution and genetics. The next section examines controversies surrounding primates and the evolution of early hominids. The final section looks at controversies associated with the later stages of human evolution. Each issue begins with an introduction, which sets the stage for the articles of the yes and no selections. Following these articles is a postscript, which summarizes the main points of the issue, provides suggestions for further reading, and introduces alternative points of view. Students should remember that there are often other perspective on a topic besides the ones presented in the issue selections. Weighing the merits of alternative explanations can increase a student's understanding of the topic and the scientific process.

**A word to the instructor** An *Instructor's Manual With Test Questions* (multiple-choice and essay) is available through the publisher for the instructor using *Taking Sides* in the classroom. A general guidebook, *Using Taking Sides in the Classroom*, which discusses methods and techniques for integrating the pro-con approach into any classroom setting, is also available. An online version of *Using Taking Sides in the Classroom* and a correspondence service for *Taking Sides* adopters can be found at http://www.dushkin.com/usingts/.

*Taking Sides: Clashing Views on Controversial Issues in Business Ethics and Society* is only one title in the Taking Sides series. If you are interested in seeing the table of contents for any of the other titles, please visit the Taking Sides Web site at http://www.dushkin.com/takingsides/.

**Acknowledgments**   I would like to thank Jim Koch, sales representative at McGraw-Hill, for encouraging me to turn a good idea into a concrete reality. I also wish to thank my editors Nichole Altman, Larry Loeppke, and Ted Knight at McGraw-Hill and Dushkin for their insights and help in preparing this book for publication. I would also like to thank the students in my anthropology classes at Portland Community College for challenging me to think deeply about many of these issues. My heartfelt thanks go to the PCC library staff, especially Jane Rognlie and Keith Palmater for all their help finding and xeroxing articles.

**Mary Courtis**
*Portland Community College*

# Contents In Brief

# Contents

Douglas Futuyma discusses Charles Darwin and Alfred Wallace's ideas that evolution is responsible for physical and behavioral changes in all species and that this process is a gradual one. In contrast, Stephen Gould argues that evolution can occur quickly. He links speciation with environmental factors and suggests that intense selection pressure leads to either extinction or rapid evolutionary change.

Kenneth Kosik suggests that there are dangers and ethical issues inherent in genetic research and its results. In contrast, Robert Sapolsky stresses the importance of environment and social learning in determining how genes are expressed. He argues that individuals with the same biology do not necessarily develop the same personality.

Jared Diamond argues that the high incidence of the Tay Sachs gene among eastern European Jews was caused by cultural discrimination. He suggests that racial prejudice kept the Jewish population confined to urban ghettos. In these crowded conditions, the Tay Sachs gene may afford some protection against tuberculosis. Josie Glausiusz, on the other hand, believes that genetic drift alone is responsible for the presence of the gene in this population.

Craig Stanford argues that Gombe chimpanzees often hunt competitively in
open, woodland environments. He suggests that this sort of environment was
the one in which human hunting first evolved. Christophe Boesch and
Hedwige Boesch-Achermann contend that cooperative hunting works better
in a dense, rain forest environment. In their opinion, the hunting behavior of
the Tai chimps provides a better model of early human evolution.

Meredith Small suggests that homosexuality and bisexuality may have
important evolutionary advantages for bonobos. Although these behaviors do
not directly lead to reproduction, they do serve to increase social cohesion
and bonding among group members. In contrast, Melvin Konner suggests
that homosexuality is primarily the product of social conditioning and
enculturation and not biological factors.

Owen Lovejoy suggests that pair-bonding between males and females
insures greater reproductive success. Thus, sex is the main reason they
associate together. In contrast, Barbara Smuts argues that primate males and
females associate together for many other reasons besides reproduction.

Pete Wheeler contends that climatic changes in Africa forced early hominids
to walk upright in order to cope with the resulting heat stress. Pat Shipman
suggests that changes in diet rather than changes in climate were responsible
for the evolution of bipedalism. She suggests that scavenging may have been
the decisive factor leading to this change.

Meave Leakey and Alan Walker argue that there is good archaeological evidence to support the claim that later hominids evolved from *Australopithecus Africanus*. In contrast, Bernard Wood favors the idea that *Australopithecus Africanus* was an evolutionary dead end. In his view, *Africanus* should not be considered an ancestor of modern humans.

# PART 3  THE EVOLUTION OF LATER HUMANS  203

Kenneth Oakley suggests that the development of tools led to selection for intelligence among early hominids. Dean Falk opposes this perspective. Falk contends that hominid brain expansion is linked to the body's ability to effectively diffuse heat.

Sherwood Washburn and C.S. Lancaster propose that hunting stimulates cultural development among early humans. In contrast, Sally Slocum contends that gathering is just as important as hunting to cultural development. She cites male bias in anthropology as the reason that this factor has been often overlooked in the study of human evolution.

Ernestine Friedl argues that pregnancy and nursing young infants tends to limit women's ability to hunt effectively in hunting and gathering societies.

# Introduction

**W**e live today in a world that is a global community. People can travel and communicate with each other at a pace unheard of even a few years ago. Unfortunately, cultural tolerance has often lagged far behind technological innovation. Individuals and nations are confronted daily with other individuals and nations who see the world differently than they do. Living peacefully with these differences has not been easy. War, terrorism, racial prejudice, and many other problems that plague our planet are rooted in this sense of division. To see past all the disagreements and cultural diversity and embrace our underlying unity and common humanity is perhaps the most important task we face in the twenty-first century.

The discipline of physical anthropology provides a framework for achieving this goal. It reminds us that we are all biological beings who belong to one common species. Our shared history goes back thousands, if not millions, of years. Through mitochondrial DNA testing and archaeological investigation, we have been able to trace our origins back to Africa. We have also been able to understand how our species later moved out and populated the rest of the world. In this context, differences in height, skin color, and other characteristics are simply viewed as regional adaptations to different environments. Dark skin, for example, protects the body from overexposure to too much ultraviolet radiation in the tropics. Lighter skin similarly aids in vitamin D absorption in northern latitudes.

The study of physical anthropology also reminds us of our close connections with other species. As primates, human beings share many biological and behavioral characteristics with apes, monkeys, and prosimians. Chimpanzees, for example, share more than 97 percent of our genes. Research in the field has also revealed that they are capable of tool making, food sharing, and other cultural behaviors that we once attributed only to humans. Many primate groups also live in complex, social groups like humans do and are faced with similar challenges to defend their territories, cultivate allies, and protect their offspring. Primates also provide interesting insights into how much of our behavior is cultural rather than innate. For example, a popular belief in American culture is that males are naturally promiscuous and females are naturally monogamous. However, in many primate groups, females as well as males pursue sexual relationships with multiple partners. These "friendships" provide females and their offspring with many advantages (see Issues 6 and 9). Research on the bonobos—a subspecies of chimpanzee—also reveals that they use sex for many things besides reproduction, just like human beings. In the bonobo society, homosexuality and bisexuality are also adaptive behaviors, and these discoveries throw a new light on sexual orientation among humans (see Issue 8). Similarly, other studies suggest that males may increase their chances of passing on their genes by being cooperative rather than competitive. Among the Muriqui monkeys of Brazil, the males who can copulate the longest and the most frequently are the ones who stand the best chance of fathering offspring (see Issue 5).

Physical anthropology also highlights the importance of the environment and the decisive role it plays in evolutionary change and the survival of any species. By examining how the four forces of evolution—natural selection, mutation, gene flow, and genetic drift—have shaped animals and plant physiology over time, we can gain insight into our own evolutionary past. For most of our history, for example, human beings lived as nomadic hunters and gatherers. This style of life encourages people to live in balance with nature and share resources cooperatively. It is only in the last 10,000 years or so that human beings have begun to settle down and base their economies on saving rather than sharing resources. These changes have led to greater comfort and convenience for some people. However, they have also created problems such as social and class division, poverty, warfare, and environmental destruction. The wisdom of the past may help us to now go forward confidently into the future. By consciously deciding to align human values and society with nature, we can choose to live once again in balance with the environment rather than using culture and technology as a buffer against it. Otherwise, the human species may be selected out. Evolutionary history suggests that we are not special, but subject to the same laws as any other species. Unlike them, however, we are able to consciously choose our fate rather than having change forced upon us.

Another important question physical anthropology challenges us to examine is, To what extent does cultural values and beliefs aid or impede the scientific process? Although most scientists make an effort to be objective, there is ample evidence that personal bias and experiences can influence their work. For example, would Charles Darwin have arrived upon the theory of natural selection if he had not voyaged aboard the *Beagle*? How much did the fact that Darwin was a devout Christian affect his decision not to publish his findings until 1859? It is also interesting to speculate about how much the fact that Gregor Mendel was a monk may have influenced the scientific community of his day to reject his research on inheritance. It is important to think as critically about the context in which social discoveries are made as it is about the merits of the actual theories they propose. A number of the issues is this book explore this premise further by including original writings of the founding fathers of evolution and genetics (see Issues 1 and 2), or by examining instances in which cultural bias may have caused scientists to overlook important data (see Issues 14, 15, and 16).

Another intriguing area of investigation in physical anthropology is to explore how evolutionary ideas may be applied to help solve political or social problems. With the mapping of the Human Genome, will we be in a better position to prevent birth defects and hereditary diseases, or will we repeat the mistakes of social Darwinism and the eugenics movement? This question is examined in more detail in Issues 3 and 4.

Physical anthropology also helps us understand how the features that make us unique as humans evolved and were selected for over time. For example, we know that bipedalism or upright walking, first developed among our earliest ancestors 5 to 6 million years ago. Many ideas and theories exist, however, to account for why this change happened at this time and how bipedalism may have affected other aspects of our anatomy (see Issue 11). Our large and complex brains are another enigma. Why do we have brains three times the size of most other primates? Why did the human brain dramatically expand in size around 2 million years ago? Did our capacity for art develop from practical or spiritual concerns? These questions are explored in more detail in Issues 13 and 17.

As a reader, you are encouraged to think critically about each of the issues presented in this volume, and what value the questions have for you as an individual. You may find yourself drawn to certain theories or viewpoints just because they reflect or reinforce your personal beliefs and values. Try to be aware of this process and understand the way it predisposes you to reject other explanations. Then encourage yourself to stretch beyond your current assessment in order to see the situation or the data in a new way. Many scientific discoveries are made because a scientist is able to set aside his or her underlying presuppositions about the way the world works. Try to train yourself to see each issue or viewpoint from a fresh perspective.

The field of physical anthropology is a dynamic one. As scientists continue to probe into our past, they often unearth new evidence that alters our current understanding of human evolution. Therefore, contemporary debates may be resolved by future discoveries. So it is important to realize that none of the hypotheses or theories presented in this book are set in stone. Only time and further research will prove which viewpoints are enduring. It is best to keep an open mind and critically analyze each new idea as it arises. It is a skill that will serve you well in the classroom and in all other aspects of your life!

# On the Internet . . .

## Charles Darwin on Human Origins

This site contains the text of Darwin's classic work *The Origin of Species.*

http://www.literature.org/Works/Charles-Darwin/

## Human Genome Project Information

This site discusses the Human Genome project and provides information about ethical, legal, and social issues; support groups; and genetic information.

http://www.ornl.gov/TechResources/
Human_Genome/home.html

## OMIM Home Page—Online Mendelian Inheritance in Man

This database includes a catalog of human genes and genetic disorders and pictures, text, and reference information of interest to physical anthropology students.

http://www.3.ncbi.nim.nih.gov/omim/

# PART 1

# Evolution and Genetics

*E*volution has been a controversial topic ever since Charles Darwin published The Origins of the Species *in 1859. The theory of natural selection proposed a new paradigm of scientific understanding that was at odds with the popular view of divine creation. Although evolutionary ideas have gained strength and widespread acceptance over the last century and a half, creationist ideas still persist. The field of genetic research has also greatly expanded our knowledge of the laws of inheritance, and new insights have also been gained into the causes of ethnically related disease and genetic engineering. The issues covered in this section include:*

- Is Evolution a Gradual Process?

- Does Human Cloning and Genetic Engineering Pose Evolutionary Dangers?

- Is Culture Responsible for the Spread of Ethnically Related Disease?

- Should the Concept of "Intelligent Design" Replace Darwin's Theory of Evolution?

# ISSUE 1

# Is Evolution a Gradual Process?

**YES: Douglas J. Futuyma,** from *Science on Trial* (Pantheon Books, 1982)

**NO: Stephen Jay Gould,** from "What Is a Species?" *Discover* (December 1992)

## ISSUE SUMMARY

Douglas Futuyma discusses Charles Darwin and Alfred Wallace's ideas that evolution is responsible for physical and behavioral changes in all species and that this process is a gradual one. In contrast, Stephen Gould argues that evolution can occur quickly. He links speciation with environmental factors and suggests that intense selection pressure leads to either extinction or rapid evolutionary change.

Vast Chain of being! Which from God began
Natures aethereal, human, angel, man,
Beast, bird, fish, insect, what no eye can see,
No glass can reach; from Infinite to thee,
From thee to nothing.—On superior pow'rs
Were we to press, inferior might on ours;
Or in the full creation leave a void,
Where, one step broken, the great scale's destroy'd;
From Nature's chain whatever link you strike,
Tenth, or ten thousandth, breaks the chain alike.

—(Alexander Pope quoted in Futuyma, 2000:8)

One of the most influential ideas of the 1800s was the *scala naurae*, or the great chain of being. Originally a religious concept, it was also adopted by scientists to classify minerals, plants, and animals on a scale from the lowest and most material to the most complex and spiritual. As a result, scientists—like the clergy—tended to see all species as linked and codependent. Inherent in this view was also the notion of progression; species were classified from the simplest to the most complex. Change, if it did occur, occurred slowly and gradually and was always in one direction, or linear. This viewpoint is expressed perfectly by Jean Lamarck (1744–1829). In his essay on the inheritance of acquired characteristics, he noted that "Nature has produced all the species of animals in succession, beginning with the most imperfect or simplest, and ending her work with the most perfect, so as to create a gradually increasing complexity in their organization" (Lamarck, 2000:46). Lamarck's ideas had a profound influence on other scholars, including Charles Lyell. Lyell was mentor of Darwin's and a devout Christian. Lyell "was such a thorough uniformitarian that he believed in a steady-state world, a world that was always in balance between forces such as erosion and mountain building, and so was forever the same. There was no room for evolution, with its concept of steady change, in Lyell's world view, though he nonetheless had an enormous impact on evolutionary thought through his influence on Charles Darwin" (Futuyma, 2000:10).

Although Darwin is considered to be one of the co-discoverers of evolution today (along with Alfred Wallace), in his youth he was a devout Christian who did not doubt the literal truth of the Bible, and did not believe in evolution any more than did Lyell and the other English scientists of his day. It was only with time and the weight of accumulating evidence from his biological studies that Darwin began to embrace an evolutionary viewpoint. Although a ground-breaking theory, his concept of evolution and natural selection also encompassed the earlier religious notion of "the great chain of being" and Lyell's "steady state" view of geology. Consequently, Darwin saw change as always slow, linear, and progressive. Over time, successive and slight modifications in physiology led to the emergence of new species. This idea of gradualism and one slight evolutionary change building upon another and then another became one of the primary organizing principles of Darwin's system. Gradualism also guided Darwin's understanding of natural selection and its role in evolution.

Not all evolutionists agree, however, with Darwin's assessment. Thomas Huxley—even though he supported Darwin's theory of natural selection—felt that evolution did not have to be gradual. He believed that rapid changes in the environment could lead to rapid changes in animal and plant physiology or behavior. Therefore, new species could evolve almost overnight.

More recently, Stephen Gould and Niles Eldridge (1977) expanded upon Huxley's ideas and proposed the theory of *punctuated equilibrium*. According to this hypothesis, most species exist for long periods of time without appreciable change. This equilibrium is maintained not only by the size of the population—a large population makes it more difficult for new traits to spread and become fixed—but by the fact that the prevailing environmental conditions tend to select for the already established form rather than a new one. It is only when the environment changes drastically or rapidly and new selection pressures are introduced that this equilibrium is upset. At this point, a species may change rapidly. Gould and Eldridge also believe that speciation by *branching*, or the development of several new species from a common ancestor, is more likely to happen if the population size is small and isolated. Small populations that become isolated from the parental form are more likely to evolve quickly in response to new environmental pressures.

Is evolution gradual or rapid? Should we believe Darwin and Wallace, or their challengers? In the next section, we will consider this question in more detail by comparing articles written from these two competing perspectives. Futuyma's article outlines the development of Darwin and Wallace's ideas that evolution and speciation is gradual and progressive. On the other hand, Gould claims that the process is rapid and prolific.

Douglas J. Futuyma  **YES**

# The Growth of
# Evolutionary Science

Today, the theory of evolution is an accepted fact for everyone but a funda-
mentalist minority, whose objections are based not on reasoning but on
doctrinaire adherence to religious principles.

—James D. Watson, 1965*

In 1615, Galileo was summoned before the Inquisition in Rome. The guardians
of the faith had found that his "proposition that the sun is the center [of the
solar system] and does not revolve about the earth is foolish, absurd, false in
theology, and heretical, because expressly contrary to Holy Scripture." In the
next century, John Wesley declared that "before the sin of Adam there were no
agitations within the bowels of the earth, no violent convulsions, no concus-
sions of the earth, no earthquakes, but all was unmoved as the pillars of
heaven." Until the seventeenth century, fossils were interpreted as "stones of a
peculiar sort, hidden by the Author of Nature for his own pleasure." Later they
were seen as remnants of the Biblical deluge. In the middle of the eighteenth
century, the great French naturalist Buffon speculated on the possibility of cosmic and organic evolution and was forced by the clergy to recant: "I abandon
everything in my book respecting the formation of the earth, and generally all
of which may be contrary to the narrative of Moses." For had not St. Augustine
written, "Nothing is to be accepted save on the authority of Scripture, since
greater is that authority than all the powers of the human mind"?

When Darwin published *The Origin of Species*, it was predictably met by a
chorus of theological protest. Darwin's theory, said Bishop Wilberforce, "contra-
dicts the revealed relations of creation to its Creator." "If the Darwinian theory
is true," wrote another clergyman, "Genesis is a lie, the whole framework of the
book of life falls to pieces, and the revelation of God to man, as we Christians
know it, is a delusion and a snare." When *The Descent of Man* appeared, Pope
Pius IX was moved to write that Darwinism is "a system which is so repugnant
at once to history, to the tradition of all peoples, to exact science, to observed
facts, and even to Reason herself, [that it] would seem to need no refutation,

* *James D. Watson, a molecular biologist, shared the Nobel Prize for his work in discovering the structure
of DNA.*

did not alienation from God and the leaning toward materialism, due to depravity, eagerly seek a support in all this tissue of fables."[1] Twentieth-century creationism continues this battle of medieval theology against science.

One of the most pervasive concepts in medieval and post-medieval thought was the "great chain of being," or *scala naturae*.[2] Minerals, plants, and animals, according to his concept, formed a gradation, from the lowliest and most material to the most complex and spiritual, ending in man, who links the animal series to the world of intelligence and spirit. This "scale of nature" was the manifestation of God's infinite benevolence. In his goodness, he had conferred existence on all beings of which he could conceive, and so created a complete chain of being, in which there were no gaps. All his creatures must have been created at once, and none could ever cease to exist, for then the perfection of his divine plan would have been violated. Alexander Pope expressed the concept best:

> Vast chain of being! which from God began,
> Natures aethereal, human, angel, man,
> Beast, bird, fish, insect, what no eye can see,
> No glass can reach; from Infinite to thee,
> From thee to nothing.—On superior pow'rs
> Were we to press, inferior might on ours;
> Or in the full creation leave a void,
> Where, one step broken, the great scale's destroy'd;
> From Nature's chain whatever link you strike,
> Tenth, or ten thousandth, breaks the chain alike.

Coexisting with this notion that all of which God could conceive existed so as to complete his creation was the idea that all things existed for man. As the philosopher Francis Bacon put it, "Man, if we look to final causes, may be regarded as the centre of the world . . . for the whole world works together in the service of man . . . all things seem to be going about man's business and not their own."

"Final causes" was another fundamental concept of medieval and post-medieval thought. Aristotle had distinguished final causes from efficient causes, and the Western world saw no reason to doubt the reality of both. The "efficient cause" of an event is the mechanism responsible for its occurrence: the cause of a ball's movement on a pool table, for example, is the impact of the cue or another ball. The "final cause," however, is the goal, or purpose for its occurrence: the pool ball moves because I wish it to go into the corner pocket. In post-medieval thought there was a final cause—a purpose—for everything; but purpose implies intention, or foreknowledge, by an intellect. Thus the existence of the world, and of all the creatures in it, had a purpose; and that purpose was God's design. This was self-evident, since it was possible to look about the world and see the palpable evidence of God's design everywhere. The heavenly bodies moved in harmonious orbits, evincing the intelligence and harmony of the divine mind; the adaptations of animals and plants to their habitats likewise reflected the devine intelligence, which had fitted all creatures perfectly for their roles in the harmonious economy of nature.

Before the rise of science, then, the causes of events were sought not in natural mechanisms but in the purposes they were meant to serve, and order in nature was evidence of divine intelligence. Since St. Ambrose had declared that "Moses opened his mouth and poured forth what God had said to him," the Bible was seen as the literal word of God, and according to St. Thomas Aquinas, "Nothing was made by God, after the six days of creation, absolutely new." Taking Genesis literally, Archbishop Ussher was able to calculate that the earth was created in 4004 B.C. The earth and the heavens were immutable, changeless. As John Ray put it in 1701 in *The Wisdom of God Manifested in the Works of the Creation*, all living and nonliving things were "created by God at first, and by Him conserved to this Day in the same State and Condition in which they were first made."[3]

The evolutionary challenge to this view began in astronomy. Tycho Brahe found that the heavens were not immutable when a new star appeared in the constellation Cassiopeia in 1572. Copernicus displaced the earth from the center of the universe, and Galileo found that the perfect heavenly bodies weren't so perfect: the sun had spots that changed from time to time, and the moon had craters that strongly implied alterations of its surface. Galileo, and after him Buffon, Kant, and many others, concluded that change was natural to all things.

A flood of mechanistic thinking ensued. Descartes, Kant, and Buffon concluded that the causes of natural phenomena should be sought in natural laws. By 1755, Kant was arguing that the laws of matter in motion discovered by Newton and other physicists were sufficient to explain natural order. Gravitation, for example, could aggregate chaotically dispersed matter into stars and planets. These would join with one another until the only ones left were those that cycled in orbits far enough from each other to resist gravitational collapse. Thus order might arise from natural processes rather than from the direct intervention of a supernatural mind. The "argument from design"—the claim that natural order is evidence of a designer—had been directly challenged. So had the universal belief in final causes. If the arrangement of the planets could arise merely by the laws of Newtonian physics, if the planets could be born, as Buffon suggested, by a collision between a comet and the sun, then they did not exist for any purpose. They merely came into being through impersonal physical forces.

From the mutability of the heavens, it was a short step to the mutability of the earth, for which the evidence was far more direct. Earthquakes and volcanoes showed how unstable terra firma really is. Sedimentary rocks showed that materials eroded from mountains could be compacted over the ages. Fossils of marine shells on mountain-tops proved that the land must once have been under the sea. As early as 1718, the Abbé Moro and the French academician Bernard de Fontenelle had concluded that the Biblical deluge could not explain the fossilized-oyster beds and tropical plants that were found in France. And what of the great, unbroken chain of being if the rocks were full of extinct species?

To explain the facts of geology, some authors—the "catastrophists"—supposed that the earth had gone through a series of great floods and other catastrophes that successively extinguished different groups of animals. Only this, they felt, could account for the discovery that higher and lower geological strata had different fossils. Buffon, however, held that to explain nature we should look to the natural causes we see operating around us: the gradual action of erosion and the slow buildup of land during volcanic eruptions. Buffon thus proposed what came to be the foundation of geology, and indeed of all science, the principle of uniformitarianism, which holds that the same causes that operate now have always operated. By 1795, the Scottish geologist James Hutton had suggested that "in examining things present we have data from which to reason with regard to what has been." His conclusion was that since "rest exists not anywhere," and the forces that change the face of the earth move with ponderous slowness, the mountains and canyons of the world must have come into existence over countless aeons.

If the entire nonliving world was in constant turmoil, could it not be that living things themselves changed? Buffon came close to saying so. He realized that the earth had seen the extinction of countless species, and supposed that those that perished had been the weaker ones. He recognized that domestication and the forces of the environment could modify the variability of many species. And he even mused, in 1766, that species might have developed from common ancestors:

> If it were admitted that the ass is of the family of the horse, and different from the horse only because it has varied from the original form, one could equally well say that the ape is of the family of man, that he is a degenerate man, that man and ape have a common origin; that, in fact, all the families among plants as well as animals have come from a single stock, and that all animals are descended from a single animal, from which have sprung in the course of time, as a result of process or of degeneration, all the other races of animals. For if it were once shown that we are justified in establishing these families; if it were granted among animals and plants there has been (I do not say several species) but even a single one, which has been produced in the course of direct descent from another species . . . then there would no longer be any limit to the power of nature, and we should not be wrong in supposing that, with sufficient time, she has been able from a single being to derive all the other organized beings.[4]

This, however, was too heretical a thought; and in any case, Buffon thought the weight of evidence was against common descent. No new species had been observed to arise within recorded history, Buffon wrote; the sterility of hybrids between species appeared an impossible barrier to such a conclusion; and if species had emerged gradually, there should have been innumerable intermediate variations between the horse and ass, or any other species. So Buffon concluded: "But this [idea of a common ancestor] is by no means a proper representation of nature. We are assured by the authority of revelation that all animals have participated equally in the grace of direct Creation and that the first pair of every species issued fully formed from the hands of the Creator."

Buffon's friend and protégé, Jean Baptiste de Monet, the Chevalier de Lamarck, was the first scientist to take the big step. It is not clear what led Lamarck to his uncompromising belief in evolution; perhaps it was his studies of fossil molluscs, which he came to believe were the ancestors of similar species living today. Whatever the explanation, from 1800 on he developed the notion that fossils were not evidence of extinct species but of ones that had gradually been transformed into living species. To be sure, he wrote, "an enormous time and wide variation in successive conditions must doubtless have been required to enable nature to bring the organization of animals to that degree of complexity and development in which we see it at its perfection"; but "time has no limits and can be drawn upon to any extent."

Lamarck believed that various lineages of animals and plants arose by a continual process of spontaneous generation from inanimate matter, and were transformed from very simple to more complex forms by an innate natural tendency toward complexity caused by "powers conferred by the supreme author of all things." Various specialized adaptations of species are consequences of the fact that animals must always change in response to the needs imposed on them by a continually changing environment. When the needs of a species change, so does its behavior. The animal then uses certain organs more frequently than before, and these organs, in turn, become more highly developed by such use, or else "by virtue of the operations of their own inner senses." The classic example of Lamarckism is the giraffe: by straining upward for foliage, it was thought, the animal had acquired a longer neck, which was then inherited by its off-spring.

In the nineteenth century it was widely believed that "acquired" characteristics—alterations brought about by use or disuse, or by the direct influence of the environment—could be inherited. Thus it was perfectly reasonable for Lamarck to base his theory of evolutionary change partly on this idea. Indeed, Darwin also allowed for this possibility, and the inheritance of acquired characteristics was not finally proved impossible until the 1890s.

Lamarck's ideas had a wide influence; but in the end did not convince many scientists of the reality of evolution. In France, Georges Cuvier, the foremost paleontologist and anatomist of his time, was an influential opponent of evolution. He rejected Lamarck's notion of the spontaneous generation of life, found it inconceivable that changes in behavior could produce the exquisite adaptations that almost every species shows, and emphasized that in both the fossil record and among living animals there were numerous "gaps" rather than intermediate forms between species. In England, the philosophy of "natural theology" held sway in science, and the best-known naturalists continued to believe firmly that the features of animals and plants were evidence of God's design. These devout Christians included the foremost geologist of the day, Charles Lyell, whose *Principles of Geology* established uniformitarianism once and for all as a guiding principle. But Lyell was such a thorough uniformitarian that he believed in a steady-state world, a world that was always in balance between forces such as erosion and mountain building, and so was forever the same. There was no room for evolution, with its concept of steady change, in Lyell's world view, though he nonetheless had an enormous impact on evolutionary thought, through his influence on Charles Darwin.

Darwin (1809–1882) himself, unquestionably one of the greatest scientists of all time, came only slowly to an evolutionary position. The son of a successful physician, he showed little interest in the life of the mind in his early years. After unsuccessfully studying medicine at Edinburgh, he was sent to Cambridge to prepare for the ministry, but he had only a half-hearted interest in his studies and spent most of his time hunting, collecting beetles, and becoming an accomplished amateur naturalist. Though he received his B.A. in 1831, his future was quite uncertain until, in December of that year, he was enlisted as a naturalist aboard *H.M.S. Beagle*, with his father's very reluctant agreement. For five years (from December 27, 1831, to October 2, 1836) the *Beagle* carried him about the world, chiefly along the coast of South America, which it was the *Beagle's* mission to survey. For five years Darwin collected geological and biological specimens, made geological observations, absorbed Lyell's *Principles of Geology*, took voluminous notes, and speculated about everything from geology to anthropology. He sent such massive collections of specimens back to England that by the time he returned he had already gained a substantial reputation as a naturalist.

Shortly after his return, Darwin married and settled into an estate at Down where he remained, hardly traveling even to London, for the rest of his life. Despite continual ill health, he pursued an extraordinary range of biological studies: classifying barnacles, breeding pigeons, experimenting with plant growth, and much more. He wrote no fewer than sixteen books and many papers, read voraciously, corresponded extensively with everyone, from pigeon breeders to the most eminent scientists, whose ideas or information might bear on his theories, and kept detailed notes on an amazing variety of subjects. Few people have written authoritatively on so many different topics: his books include not only *The Voyage of the Beagle, The Origin of Species*, and *The Descent of Man, but also The Structure and Distribution of Coral Reefs* (containing a novel theory of the formation of coral atolls which is still regarded as correct), *A Monograph on the Sub-class Cirripedia* (the definitive study of barnacle classification), *The Various Contrivances by Which Orchids are Fertilised by Insects, The Variation of Animals and Plants Under Domestication* (an exhaustive summary of information on variation, so crucial to his evolutionary theory), *The Effects of Cross and Self Fertilisation in the Vegetable Kingdom* (an analysis of sexual reproduction and the sterility of hybrids between species), *The Expression of the Emotions in Man and Animals* (on the evolution of human behavior from animal behavior), and *The Formation of Vegetable Mould Through the Action of Worms*. There is every reason to believe that almost all these books bear, in one way or another, on the principles and ideas that were inherent in Darwin's theory of evolution. The worm book, for example, is devoted to showing how great the impact of a seemingly trivial process like worm burrowing may be on ecology and geology if it persists for a long time. The idea of such cumulative slight effects is, of course, inherent in Darwin's view of evolution: successive slight modifications of a species, if continued long enough, can transform it radically.

When Darwin embarked on his voyage, he was a devout Christian who did not doubt the literal truth of the Bible, and did not believe in evolution any more than did Lyell and the other English scientists he had met or whose books he had read. By the time he returned to England in 1836 he had made numerous observations that would later convince him of evolution. It seems likely, however, that the idea itself did not occur to him until the spring of

1837, when the ornithologist John Gould, who was working on some of Darwin's collections, pointed out to him that each of the Galápagos Islands, off the coast of Ecuador, had a different kind of mockingbird. It was quite unclear whether they were different varieties of the same species, or different species. From this, Darwin quickly realized that species are not the discrete, clear-cut entities everyone seemed to imagine. The possibility of transformation entered his mind, and it applied to more than the mockingbirds: "When comparing . . . the birds from the separate islands of the Galápagos archipelago, both with one another and with those from the American mainland, I was much struck how entirely vague and arbitrary is the distinction between species and varieties."

In July 1837 he began his first notebook on the "Transmutation of Species." He later said that the Galápagos species and the similarity between South American fossils and living species were at the origin of all his views.

> During the voyage of the *Beagle* I had been deeply impressed by discovering in the Pampean formation great fossil animals covered with armour like that on the existing armadillos; secondly, by the manner in which closely allied animals replace one another in proceeding southward over the continent; and thirdly, by the South American character of most of the productions of the Galápagos archipelago, and more especially by the manner in which they differ slightly on each island of the group; none of these islands appearing to be very ancient in a geological sense. It was evident that such facts as these, as well as many others, could be explained on the supposition that species gradually become modified; and the subject has haunted me.

The first great step in Darwin's thought was the realization that evolution had occurred. The second was his brilliant insight into the possible cause of evolutionary change. Lamarck's theory of "felt needs" had not been convincing. A better one was required. It came on September 18, 1838, when after grappling with the problem for fifteen months, "I happened to read for amusement Malthus on Population, and being well prepared to appreciate the struggle for existence which everywhere goes on from long-continued observation of the habits of animals and plants, it at once struck me that under these circumstances favorable variations would tend to be preserved, and unfavorable ones to be destroyed. The result of this would be the formation of new species. Here, then, I had at last got a theory by which to work."

Malthus, an economist, had developed the pessimistic thesis that the exponential growth of human populations must inevitably lead to famine, unless it were checked by war, disease, or "moral restraint." This emphasis on exponential population growth was apparently the catalyst for Darwin, who then realized that since most natural populations of animals and plants remain fairly stable in numbers, many more individuals are born than survive. Because individuals vary in their characteristics, the struggle to survive must favor some variant individuals over others. These survivors would then pass on their characteristics to future generations. Repetition of this process generation after generation would gradually transform the species.

Darwin clearly knew that he could not afford to publish a rash speculation on so important a subject without developing the best possible case. The world

*Figure 1*

Some species of Galápagos finches. Several of the most different species are represented here; intermediate species also exist. Clockwise from lower left are a male ground-finch (the plumage of the female resembles that of the tree-finches); the vegetarian tree-finch; the insectivorous tree-finch; the warbler-finch; and the woodpecker-finch, which uses a cactus spine to extricate insects from crevices. The slight differences among these species, and among species in other groups of Galápagos animals such as giant tortoises, were one of the observations that led Darwin to formulate his hypothesis of evolution. (*From D. Lack, Darwin s Finches [Oxford: Oxford University Press, 1944].*)

of science was not hospitable to speculation, and besides, Darwin was dealing with a highly volatile issue. Not only was he affirming that evolution had occurred, he was proposing a purely material explanation for it, one that demolished the argument from design in a single thrust. Instead of publishing his theory, he patiently amassed a mountain of evidence, and finally, in 1844, collected his thoughts in an essay on natural selection. But he still didn't publish. Not until 1856, almost twenty years after he became an evolutionist, did he begin what he planned to be a massive work on the subject, tentatively titled *Natural Selection*.

Then, in June 1858, the unthinkable happened. Alfred Russel Wallace (1823–1913), a young naturalist who had traveled in the Amazon Basin and in the Malay Archipelago, had also become interested in evolution. Like Darwin, he was struck by the fact that "the most closely allied species are found in the same locality or in closely adjoining localities and . . . therefore the natural sequence of the species by affinity is also geographical." In the throes of a malarial fever in Malaya, Wallace conceived of the same idea of natural selection as Darwin

### Figure 2

Processes of evolutionary change. A characteristic that is variable (1) often shows a bell-shaped distribution—individuals vary on either side of the average. Evolutionary change (2) consists of a shift in successive generations, after which the characteristic may reach a new equilibrium (3). When the species splits into two different species (4), one of the species may undergo further evolutionary change (5) and reach a new equilibrium (6). The other may remain unchanged (7) or not. Each population usually remains variable throughout this process, but the average is shifted, ordinarily by natural selection.

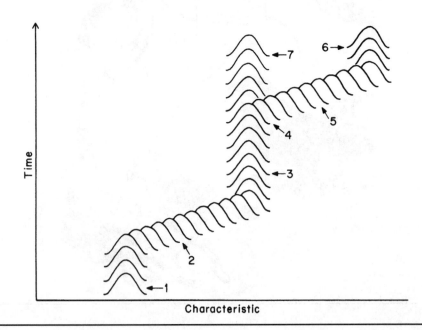

had, and sent Darwin a manuscript "On the Tendency of Varieties to Depart Indefinitely from the Original Type." Darwin's friends Charles Lyell and Joseph Hooker, a botanist, rushed in to help Darwin establish the priority of his ideas, and on July 1, 1858, they presented to the Linnean Society of London both Wallace's paper and extracts from Darwin's 1844 essay. Darwin abandoned his big book on natural selection and condensed the argument into a 490-page "abstract" that was published on November 24, 1859, under the title *The Origin of Species by Means of Natural Selection; or, the Preservation of Favored Races in the Struggle for Life*. Because it was an abstract, he had to leave out many of the detailed observations and references to the literature that he had amassed, but these were later provided in his other books, many of which are voluminous expansions on the contents of *The Origin of Species*.

The first five chapters of the *Origin* lay out the theory that Darwin had conceived. He shows that both domesticated and wild species are variable, that much of that variation is hereditary, and that breeders, by conscious selection of desirable varieties, can develop breeds of pigeons, dogs, and other forms that are more different from each other than species or even families of wild animals and plants are from each other. The differences between related species then are no more than an exaggerated form of the kinds of variations one can find in a single species; indeed, it is often extremely difficult to tell if natural populations are distinct species or merely well-marked varieties.

Darwin then shows that in nature there is competition, predation, and a struggle for life.

> Owing to this struggle, variations, however slight and from whatever cause proceeding, if they be in any degree profitable to the individuals of a species, in their infinitely complex relations to other organic beings and to their physical conditions of life, will tend to the preservation of such individuals, and will generally be inherited by the offspring. The offspring, also, will thus have a better chance of surviving, for, of the many individuals of any species which are periodically born, but a small number can survive. I have called this principle, by which each slight variation, if useful, is preserved, by the term natural selection, in order to mark its relation to man's power of selection.

Darwin goes on to give examples of how even slight variations promote survival, and argues that when populations are exposed to different conditions, different variations will be favored, so that the descendants of a species become diversified in structure, and each ancestral species can give rise to several new ones. Although "it is probable that each form remains for long periods unaltered," successive evolutionary modifications will ultimately alter the different species so greatly that they will be classified as different genera, families, or orders.

Competition between species will impel them to become more different, for "the more diversified the descendants from any one species become in structure, constitution and habits, by so much will they be better enabled to seize on many and widely diversified places in the polity of nature, and so be enabled to increase in numbers." Thus different adaptations arise, and "the ultimate result is that each creature tends to become more and more improved in relation to its conditions. This improvement inevitably leads to the greater advancement of the organization of the greater number of living beings throughout the world." But lowly organisms continue to persist, for "natural selection, or the survival of the fittest, does not necessarily include progressive development—it only takes advantage of such variations as arise and are beneficial to each creature under its complex relations of life." Probably no organism has reached a peak of perfection, and many lowly forms of life continue to exist, for "in some cases variations or individual differences of a favorable nature may never have arisen for natural selection to act on or accumulate. In no case, probably, has time sufficed for the utmost possible amount of development. In some few cases there has been what we must call retrogression of organization. But the main cause lies in the fact that under very simple conditions of life a high organization would be of no service. . . ."

In the rest of *The Origin of Species*, Darwin considers all the objections that might be raised against his theory; discusses the evolution of a great array of phenomena—hybrid sterility, the slavemaking instinct of ants, the similarity of vertebrate embryos; and presents an enormous body of evidence for evolution. He draws his evidence from comparative anatomy, embryology, behavior, geographic variation, the geographic distribution of species, the study of rudimentary organs, atavistic variations ("throwbacks"), and the geological record to show how all of biology provides testimony that species have descended with modification from common ancestors.

Darwin's triumph was in synthesizing ideas and information in ways that no one had quite imagined before. From Lyell and the geologists he learned uniformitarianism: the cause of past events must be found in natural forces that operate today; and these, in the vastness of time, can accomplish great change. From Malthus and the nineteenth-century economists he learned of competition and the struggle for existence. From his work on barnacles, his travels, and his knowledge of domesticated varieties he learned that species do not have immutable essences but are variable in all their properties and blend into one another gradually. From his familiarity with the works of Whewell, Herschel, and other philosophers of science he developed a powerful method of pursuing science, the "hypothetico-deductive" method, which consists of formulating a hypothesis or speculation, deducing the logical predictions that must follow from the hypothesis, and then testing the hypothesis by seeing whether or not the predictions are verified. This was by no means the prevalent philosophy of science in Darwin's time.[5]

Darwin brought biology out of the Middle Ages. For divine design and unknowable supernatural forces he substituted natural material causes that could be studied by the methods of science. Instead of catastrophes unknown to physical science he invoked forces that could be studied in anyone's laboratory or garden. He replaced a young, static world by one in which there had been constant change for countless aeons. He established that life had a history, and this proved the essential view that differentiated evolutionary thought from all that had gone before.

For the British naturalist John Ray, writing in 1701, organisms had no history—they were the same at that moment, and lived in the same places, doing the same things, as when they were first created. For Darwin, organisms spoke of historical change. If there has indeed been such a history, then fossils in the oldest rocks must differ from those in younger rocks: trilobites, dinosaurs, and mammoths will not be mixed together but will appear in some temporal sequence. If species come from common ancestors, they will have the same characteristics, modified for different functions: the same bones used by bats for flying will be used by horses for running. If species come from ancestors that lived in different environments, they will carry the evidence of their history with them in the form of similar patterns of embryonic development and in vestigial, rudimentary organs that no longer serve any function. If species have a history, their geographical distribution will reflect it: oceanic islands won't have elephants because they wouldn't have been able to get there.

Once the earth and its living inhabitants are seen as the products of historical change, the theological philosophy embodied in the great chain of being ceases to make sense; the plenitude, or fullness, of the world becomes not an eternal manifestation of God's bountiful creativity but an illusion. For most of earth's history, most of the present species have not existed; and many of those that did exist do so no longer. But the scientific challenge to medieval philosophy goes even deeper. If evolution has occurred, and if it has proceeded from the natural causes that Darwin envisioned, then the adaptations of organisms to their environment, the intricate construction of the bird's wing and the orchid's flower, are evidence not of divine design but of the struggle for existence. Moreover, and this may be the deepest implication of all, Darwin brought to biology, as his predecessors had brought to astronomy and geology, the sufficiency of efficient causes. No longer was there any reason to look for final causes or goals. To the questions "What purpose does this species serve? Why did God make tapeworms?" the answer is "To no purpose." Tapeworms were not put here to serve a purpose, nor were planets, nor plants, nor people. They came into existence not by design but by the action of impersonal natural laws.

By providing materialistic, mechanistic explanations, instead of miraculous ones, for the characteristics of plants and animals, Darwin brought biology out of the realm of theology and into the realm of science. For miraculous spiritual forces fall outside the province of science; all of science is the study of material causation.

Of course, *The Origin of Species* didn't convince everyone immediately. Evolution and its material cause, natural selection, evoked strong protests from ecclesiastical circles, and even from scientists.[6] The eminent geologist Adam Sedgwick, for example, wrote in 1860 that species must come into existence by creation,

> a power I cannot imitate or comprehend; but in which I can believe, by a legitimate conclusion of sound reason drawn from the laws and harmonies of Nature. For I can see in all around me a design and purpose, and a mutual adaptation of parts which I *can* comprehend, and which prove that there is exterior to, and above, the mere phenomena of Nature a great prescient and designing cause. . . . The pretended physical philosophy of

modern days strips man of all his moral attributes, or holds them of no account in the estimate of his origin and place in the created world. A cold atheistical materialism is the tendency of the so-called material philosophy of the present day.

Among the more scientific objections were those posed by the French paleontologist François Pictet, and they were echoed by many others. Since Darwin supposes that species change gradually over the course of thousands of generations, then, asked Pictet, "Why don't we find these gradations in the fossil record . . . and why, instead of collecting thousands of identical individuals, do we not find more intermediary forms? . . . How is it that the most ancient fossil beds are rich in a variety of diverse forms of life, instead of the few early types Darwin's theory leads us to expect? How is it that no species has been seen to evolve during human history, and that the 4000 years which separates us from the mummies of Egypt have been insufficient to modify the crocodile and the ibis?" Pictet protested that, although slight variations might in time alter a species slightly, "all known facts demonstrate . . . that the prolonged influence of modifying causes has an action which is constantly restrained within sufficiently confined limits."

The anatomist Richard Owen likewise denied "that . . . variability is progressive and unlimited, so as, in the course of generations, to change the species, the genus, the order, or the class." The paleontologist Louis Agassiz insisted that organisms fall into discrete groups, based on uniquely different created plans, between which no intermediates could exist. He chose the birds as a group that showed the sharpest of boundaries. Only a few years later, in 1868, the fossil *Archaeopteryx*, an exquisite intermediate between birds and reptiles, demolished Agassiz's argument, and he had no more to say on the unique character of the birds.

Within twelve years of *The Origin of Species*, the evidence for evolution had been so thoroughly accepted that philosopher and mathematician Chauncey Wright could point out that among the students of science, "orthodoxy has been won over to the doctrine of evolution." However, Wright continued, "While the general doctrine of evolution has thus been successfully redeemed from theological condemnation, this is not yet true of the subordinate hypothesis of Natural Selection."

Natural selection turned out to be an extraordinarily difficult concept for people to grasp. St. George Mivart, a Catholic scholar and scientist, was not unusual in equating natural selection with chance. "The theory of Natural Selection may (though it need not) be taken in such a way as to lead man to regard the present organic world as formed, so to speak, *accidentally*, beautiful and wonderful as is the confessedly haphazard result." Many like him simply refused to understand that natural selection is the antithesis of chance and consequently could not see how selection might cause adaptation or any kind of progressive evolutionary change. Even in the 1940s there were those, especially among paleontologists, who felt that the progressive evolution of groups like the horses, as revealed by the fossil record, must have had some unknown cause other than natural selection. Paradoxically, then, Darwin had convinced the scientific world of evolution where his predecessors had failed; but he had not convinced all biologists of his truly original theory, the theory of natural selection.

Natural selection fell into particular disrepute in the early part of the twentieth century because of the rise of genetics—which, as it happened, eventually became the foundation of the modern theory of evolution. Darwin's supposition that variation was unlimited, and so in time could give rise to strikingly different organisms, was not entirely convincing because he had no good idea of where variation came from. In 1865, the Austrian monk Gregor Mendel discovered, from his crosses of pea plants, that discretely different characteristics such as wrinkled versus smooth seeds were inherited from generation to generation without being altered, as if they were caused by particles that passed from parent to offspring. Mendel's work was ignored for thirty-five years, until, in 1900, three biologists discovered his paper and realized that it held the key to the mystery of heredity. One of the three, Hugo de Vries, set about to explore the problem as Mendel had, and in the course of his studies of evening primroses observed strikingly different variations arise, *de novo*. The new forms were so different that de Vries believed they represented new species, which had arisen in a single step by alteration or, as he called it, mutation, of the hereditary material.

In the next few decades, geneticists working with a great variety of organisms observed many other drastic changes arise by mutation: fruit flies (Drosophila), for example, with white instead of red eyes or curled instead of straight wings. These laboratory geneticists, especially Thomas Hunt Morgan, an outstanding geneticist at Columbia University, asserted that evolution must proceed by major mutational steps, and that mutation, not natural selection, was the cause of evolution. In their eyes, Darwin's theory was dead on two counts: evolution was not gradual, and it was not caused by natural selection. Meanwhile, naturalists, taxonomists, and breeders of domesticated plants and animals continued to believe in Darwinism, because they saw that populations and species differed quantitatively and gradually rather than in big jumps, that most variation was continuous (like height in humans) rather than discrete, and that domesticated species could be altered by artificial selection from continuous variation.

The bitter conflict between the Mendelian geneticists and the Darwinians was resolved in the 1930s in a "New Synthesis" that brought the opposing views into a "neo-Darwinian" theory of evolution.[7] Slight variations in height, wing length, and other characteristics proved, under careful genetic analysis, to be inherited as particles, in the same way as the discrete variations studied by the Mendelians. Thus a large animal simply has inherited more particles, or genes, for large size than a smaller member of the species has. The Mendelians were simply studying particularly well marked variations, while the naturalists were studying more subtle ones. Variations could be very slight, or fairly pronounced, or very substantial, but all were inherited in the same manner. All these variations, it was shown, arose by a process of mutation of the genes.

Three mathematical theoreticians, Ronald Fisher and J. B. S. Haldane in England and Sewall Wright in the United States, proved that a newly mutated gene would not automatically form a new species. Nor would it automatically replace the preexisting form of the gene, and so transform the species. Replacement of one gene by a mutant form of the gene, they said, could happen in two ways. The mutation could enable its possessors to survive or reproduce more effectively than the old form; if so, it would increase by natural selection, just as Darwin had said. The new characteristic that evolved in this way would ordinarily be considered an improved adaptation.

Sewall Wright pointed out, however, that not all genetic changes in species need be adaptive. A new mutation might be no better or worse than the preexisting gene—it might simply be "neutral." In small populations such a mutation could replace the previous gene purely by chance—a process he called random genetic drift. The idea, put crudely, is this. Suppose there is a small population of land snails in a cow pasture, and that 5 percent of them are brown and the rest are yellow. Purely by chance, a greater percentage of yellow snails than of brown ones get crushed by cows' hooves in one generation. The snails breed, and there will now be a slightly greater percentage of yellow snails in the next generation than there had been. But in the next generation, the yellow ones may suffer more trampling, purely by chance. The proportion of yellow offspring will then be lower again. These random events cause fluctuations in the percentage of the two types. Wright proved mathematically that eventually, if no other factors intervene, these fluctuations will bring the population either to 100 percent yellow or 100 percent brown, purely by chance. The population will have evolved, then, but not by natural selection; and there is no improvement of adaptation.

During the period of the New Synthesis, though, genetic drift was emphasized less than natural selection, for which abundant evidence was discovered. Sergei Chetverikov in Russia, and later Theodosius Dobzhansky working in the United States, showed that wild populations of fruit flies contained an immense amount of genetic variation, including the same kinds of mutations that the geneticists had found arising in their laboratories. Dobzhansky and other workers went on to show that these variations affected survival and reproduction: that natural selection was a reality. They showed, moreover, that the genetic differences among related species were indeed compounded of the same kinds of slight genetic variations that they found within species. Thus the taxonomists and the geneticists converged onto a neo-Darwinian theory of evolution: evolution is due not to mutation *or* natural selection, but to both. Random mutations provide abundant genetic variation; natural selection, the antithesis of randomness, sorts out the useful from the deleterious, and transforms the species.

In the following two decades, the paleontologist George Gaylord Simpson showed that this theory was completely adequate to explain the fossil record, and the ornithologists Bernhard Rensch and Ernst Mayr, the botanist G. Ledyard Stebbins, and many other taxonomists showed that the similarities and differences among living species could be fully explained by neo-Darwinism. They also clarified the meaning of "species." Organisms belong to different species if they do not interbreed when the opportunity presents itself, thus remaining genetically distinct. An ancestral species splits into two descendant species when different populations of the ancestor, living in different geographic regions, become so genetically different from each other that they will not or cannot interbreed when they have the chance to do so. As a result, evolution can happen without the formation of new species: a single species can be genetically transformed without splitting into several descendants. Conversely, new species can be formed without much genetic change. If one population becomes different from the rest of its species in, for example, its mating behavior, it will not interbreed with the other populations. Thus it has become a new species, even though it may be identical to its "sister species" in every respect except its behavior. Such a new species is free to follow a new path of genetic change, since it does not become homogenized with its sister species by interbreeding. With time, therefore, it can diverge and develop different adaptations.

The conflict between the geneticists and the Darwinians that was resolved in the New Synthesis was the last major conflict in evolutionary science. Since that time, an enormous amount of research has confirmed most of the major conclusions of neo-Darwinism. We now know that populations contain very extensive genetic variation that continually arises by mutation of pre-existing genes. We also know what genes are and how they become mutated. Many instances of the reality of natural selection in wild populations have been documented, and there is extensive evidence that many species form by the divergence of different populations of an ancestral species.

The major questions in evolutionary biology now tend to be of the form, "All right, factors $x$ and $y$ both operate in evolution, but how important is $x$ compared to $y$?" For example, studies of biochemical genetic variation have raised the possibility that nonadaptive, random change (genetic drift) may be the major reason for many biochemical differences among species. How important, then, is genetic drift compared to natural selection? Another major question has to do with rates of evolution: Do species usually diverge very slowly, as Darwin thought, or does evolution consist mostly of rapid spurts, interspersed with long periods of constancy? Still another question is raised by mutations, which range all the way from gross changes of the kind Morgan studied to very slight alterations. Does evolution consist entirely of the substitution of mutations that have very slight effects, or are major mutations sometimes important too? Partisans on each side of all these questions argue vigorously for their interpretation of the evidence, but they don't doubt that the major factors of evolution are known. They simply emphasize one factor or another. Minor battles of precisely this kind go on continually in every field of science; without them there would be very little advancement in our knowledge.

Within a decade or two of *The Origin of Species*, the belief that living organisms had evolved over the ages was firmly entrenched in biology. As of 1982, the historical existence of evolution is viewed as fact by almost all biologists. To explain how the fact of evolution has been brought about, a theory of evolutionary mechanisms—mutation, natural selection, genetic drift, and isolation—has been developed.[8] But exactly what is the evidence for the fact of evolution?

## Notes

1.  Andrew Dickson White, *A History of the Warfare of Science with Theology in Christendom* vol. I (London: Macmillan, 1896; reprint ed., New York: Dover, 1960).

2.  A. O. Lovejoy, *The Great Chain of Being* (Cambridge, Mass.: Harvard University Press, 1936).

3.  Much of this history is provided by J. C. Greene, *The Death of Adam: Evolution and its Impact on Western Thought* (Ames: Iowa State University Press, 1959).

4.  A detailed history of this and other developments in evolutionary biology is given by Ernst Mayr, *The Growth of Biological Thought: Diversity, Evolution, Inheritance* (Cambridge, Mass.: Harvard University Press, 1982).

5.  See D. L. Hull, *Darwin and His Critics* (Cambridge, Mass.: Harvard University Press, 1973).

6.  Ibid.

7.  E. Mayr and W. B. Provine, *The Evolutionary Synthesis* (Cambridge, Mass.: Harvard University Press, 1980).

8.  Our modern understanding of the mechanisms of evolution is described in many books. Elementary textbooks include G. L. Stebbins, *Processes of Organic Evolution,* (Englewood Cliffs, N.J.: Prentice-Hall, 1971), and J. Maynard Smith, *The Theory of Evolution* (New York: Penguin Books, 1975). More advanced textbooks include Th. Dobzhansky, F. J. Ayala, G. L. Stebbins, and J. W. Valentine, *Evolution* (San Francisco: Freeman, 1977), and D. J. Futuyma, *Evolutionary Biology* (Sunderland, Mass.: Sinauer, 1979). Unreferenced facts and theories described in the text are familiar enough to most evolutionary biologists that they will be found in most or all of the references cited above.

# NO ←

**Stephen Jay Gould**

# What Is a Species?

**I** had visited every state but Idaho. A few months ago, I finally got my opportunity to complete the roster of 50 by driving east from Spokane, Washington, into western Idaho. As I crossed the state line, I made the same feeble attempt at humor that so many of us try in similar situations: "Gee, it doesn't look a bit different from easternmost Washington." We make such comments because we feel the discomfort of discord between our mental needs and the world's reality. Much of nature (including terrestrial real estate) is continuous, but both our mental and political structures require divisions and categories. We need to break large and continuous items into manageable units.

Many people feel the same way about species as I do about Idaho—but this feeling is wrong. Many people suppose that species must be arbitrary divisions of an evolutionary continuum in the same way that state boundaries are conventional divisions of unbroken land. Moreover, this is not merely an abstract issue of scientific theory but a pressing concern of political reality. The Endangered Species Act, for example, sets policy (with substantial teeth) for the preservation of species. But if species are only arbitrary divisions in nature's continuity, then what are we trying to preserve and how shall we define it? I write this article to argue that such a reading of evolutionary theory is wrong and that species are almost always objective entities in nature.

Let us start with something uncontroversial: the bugs in your backyard. If you go out to make a complete collection of all the kinds of insects living in this small discrete space, you will collect easily definable "packages," not intergrading continua. You might find a kind of bee, three kinds of ants, a butterfly or two, several beetles, and a cicada. You have simply validated the commonsense notion known to all: in any small space during any given moment, the animals we see belong to separate and definable groups—and we call these groups species.

In the eighteenth century this commonsense observation was translated, improperly as we now know, into the creationist taxonomy of Linnaeus. The great Swedish naturalist regarded species as God's created entities, and he gathered them together into genera, genera into orders, and orders into classes, to form the taxonomic hierarchy that we all learned in high school (several more categories, families and phyla, for example, have been added since Linnaeus's time). The creationist version reached its apogee in the writings of America's greatest nineteenth-century naturalist (and last truly scientific creationist), Louis Agassiz. Agassiz argued that species are incarnations of separate ideas in God's mind, and that higher categories (genera, orders, and so forth) are therefore maps of the interrelationships among divine thoughts. Therefore, taxonomy is the most important of all sciences because it gives us direct insight into the structure of God's mind.

Darwin changed this reverie forever by proving that species are related by the physical connection of genealogical descent. But this immensely satisfying resolution for the great puzzle of nature's order engendered a subsidiary problem that Darwin never fully resolved: If all life is interconnected as a genealogical continuum, then what reality can species have? Are they not just arbitrary divisions of evolving lineages? And if so, how can the bugs in my backyard be ordered in separate units? In fact, the two greatest evolutionists of the nineteenth century, Lamarck and Darwin, both questioned the reality of species on the basis of their evolutionary convictions. Lamarck wrote, "In vain do naturalists consume their time in describing new species"; while Darwin lamented: "we shall have to treat species as . . . merely artificial combinations made for convenience. This may not be a cheering prospect; but we shall at least be freed from the vain search for the undiscovered and undiscoverable essence of the term *species*" (from the *Origin of Species*).

But when we examine the technical writings of both Lamarck and Darwin, our sense of paradox is heightened. Darwin produced four long volumes on the taxonomy of barnacles, using conventional species for his divisions. Lamarck spent seven years (1815–1822) publishing his generation's standard, multivolume compendium on the diversity of animal life—*Histoire naturelle des animaux sans vertèbres,* or *Natural History of Invertebrate Animals*—all divided into species, many of which he named for the first time himself. How can these two great evolutionists have denied a concept in theory and then used it so centrally and extensively in practice? To ask the question more generally: If the species is still a useful and necessary concept, how can we define and justify it as evolutionists?

The solution to this question requires a preamble and two steps. For the preamble, let us acknowledge that the conceptual problem arises when we extend the "bugs in my backyard" example into time and space. A momentary slice of any continuum looks tolerably discrete; a slice of salami or a cross section of a tree trunk freezes a complexly changing structure into an apparently stable entity. Modern horses are discrete and separate from all other existing species, but how can we call the horse (*Equus caballus*) a real and definable entity if we can trace an unbroken genealogical series back through time to a dog-size creature with several toes on each foot? Where did this "dawn horse," or "eohippus," stop and the next stage begin; at what moment did the penultimate stage become *Equus caballus*? I now come to the two steps of an answer.

First, if each evolutionary line were like a long salami, then species would not be real and definable in time and space. But in almost all cases large-scale evolution is a story of branching, not of transformation in a single line—bushes, not ladders, in my usual formulation. A branch on a bush is an objective division. One species rarely turns into another by total transformation over its entire geographic range. Rather, a small population becomes geographically isolated from the rest of the species—and this fragment changes to become a new species while the bulk of the parental population does not alter. "Dawn horse" is a misnomer because rhinoceroses evolved from the same parental lineage. The lineage split at an objective branching point into two lines that became (after further events of splitting) the great modern groups of horses (eight species, including asses and zebras) and rhinos (a sadly depleted group of formerly successful species).

Failure to recognize that evolution is a bush and not a ladder leads to one of the most common vernacular misconceptions about human biology. People often challenge me: "If humans evolved from apes, why are apes still around?" To anyone who understands the principle of bushes, there simply is no problem: the human lineage emerged as a branch, while the rest of the trunk continued as apes (and branched several more times to yield modern chimps, gorillas, and so on). But if you think that evolution is a ladder or a salami, then an emergence of humans from apes should mean the elimination of apes by transformation.

Second, you might grasp the principle of bushes and branching but still say: Yes, the ultimate products of a branch become objectively separate, but early on, while the branch is forming, no clear division can be made, and the precursors of the two species that will emerge must blend indefinably. And if evolution is gradual and continuous, and if most of a species' duration is spent in this state of incipient formation, then species will not be objectively definable during most of their geologic lifetimes.

Fair enough as an argument, but the premise is wrong. New species do (and must) have this period of initial ambiguity. But species emerge relatively quickly, compared with their period of later stability, and then live for long periods—often millions of years—with minimal change. Now, suppose that on average (and this is probably a fair estimate), species spend one percent of their geologic lifetimes in this initial state of imperfect separation. Then, on average, about one species in a hundred will encounter problems in definition, while the other 99 will be discrete and objectively separate—cross sections of branches showing no confluence with others. Thus, the principle of bushes, and the speed of branching, resolve the supposed paradox: continuous evolution can and does yield a world in which the vast majority of species are separate from all others and clearly definable at any moment in time. Species are nature's objective packages.

I have given a historical definition of species—as unique and separate branches on nature's bush. We also need a functional definition, if only because historical evidence (in the form of a complete fossil record) is usually unavailable. The standard criterion, in use at least since the days of the great French naturalist Georges de Buffon (a contemporary of Linnaeus), invokes the capacity for interbreeding. Members of a species can breed with others in the same species but not with individuals belonging to different species.

This functional criterion is a consequence of the historical definition: distinct separateness of a branch emerges only with the attainment of sufficient evolutionary distance to preclude interbreeding, for otherwise the branch is not an irrevocably separate entity and can amalgamate with the parental population. Exceptions exist, but the reproductive criterion generally works well and gives rise to the standard one-liner for a textbook definition of a species: "a population of actually or potentially reproducing organisms sharing a common gene pool."

⚬⟨◎⟩⚬

Much of the ordinary activity of evolutionary biologists is devoted to learning whether or not the groups they study are separate species by this criterion of "reproductive isolation." Such separateness can be based on a variety of factors, collectively termed "isolating mechanisms": for example, genetic programs so different that an embryo cannot form even if egg and sperm unite; behaviors that lead members of one species to shun individuals from other populations; even something so mundane as breeding at different times of the year, or in different parts of the habitat—say, for example, on apple trees rather than on plum trees—so that contact can never take place. (We exclude simple geographic separation—living on different continents, for example—because an isolating mechanism must work when actively challenged by a potential for interbreeding through spatial contact. I do not belong to a separate species from my brethren in Brazil just because I have never been there. Similarly, reproductive isolation must be assessed by ordinary behavior in a state of nature. Some truly separate species can be induced to interbreed in zoos and laboratories. The fact that zoos can make tiglons—tiger-lion hybrids—does not challenge the separate status of the two populations as species in nature.)

Modern humans (species *Homo sapiens*) fit these criteria admirably. We are now spread all over the world in great numbers, but we began as a little twig in Africa (the historical criterion). We may look quite different from one another in a few superficially striking aspects of size, skin color, and hair form, but there is astonishingly little overall genetic difference among our so-called races. Above all (the functional criterion), we can all interbreed with one another (and do so with avidity, always, and all over the world), but not with any member of another species (movies about flies notwithstanding). We are often reminded, quite correctly, that we are very similar in overall genetic program to our nearest cousin, the chimpanzee—but no one would mistake a single individual of either species, and we do not hybridize (again, various science fictions notwithstanding).

I do not say that these criteria are free from exceptions; nature is nothing if not a domain of exceptions, where an example against any clean generality can always be found. Some distinct populations of plants, for example, can and frequently do interbreed with others that ought to be separate species by all other standards. (This is why the classification of certain groups—the rhododendrons, for example—is such a mess.) But the criteria work in the vast majority of cases, including humans. Species are not arbitrary units, constructed for human convenience, in dividing continua. Species are the real and objective items of nature's morphology. They are "out there" in the world as historically distinct and functionally separate populations "with their own historical role and tendency" (as the other textbook one-liner proclaims).

Species are unique in the Linnaean hierarchy as the only category with such objectivity. All higher units—genera, families, phyla, et cetera—are human conventions in the following important respect. The evolutionary tree itself is objective; the branches (species) emerge, grow, and form clusters by subsequent branching. The clusters are clearly discernible. But the status we award to these so-called higher taxa (clusters of branches with a single root of common evolutionary ancestry) is partly a matter of human decision. Clusters A and B in the figure are groups of species with a common parent. Each branch in each cluster is an objective species. But what are the clusters themselves? Are they two genera or two families? Our decision on this question is partly a matter of human preference constrained by the rules of logic and the facts of nature. (For example, we cannot take one species from cluster A and one from cluster B and put them together as a single genus—for this would violate the rule that all members of a higher taxon must share a common ancestor without excluding other species that are more closely related to the common ancestor. We cannot put domestic cats and dogs in one family while classifying lions and wolves in another.)

The taxonomic hierarchy recognizes only one unit below species—the subspecies. Like higher taxa, subspecies are also partly objective but partly based on human decision. Subspecies are defined as distinctive subpopulations that live in a definite geographic subsection of the entire range of the species. I cannot, for example, pluck out all tall members of a species, or all red individuals, wherever they occur over the full geographic range, and establish them as subspecies. A subspecies must be a distinct geographic subpopulation—not yet evolved far enough to become a separate species in its own right but different enough from other subpopulations (in terms of anatomy, genetic structure, physiology, or behavior) that a taxonomist chooses to memorialize the distinction with a name. Yet subspecies cannot be irrevocably unique natural populations (like full species) for two reasons: First, the decision to name them rests with human taxonomists, and isn't solely dictated by nature. Second, they are, by definition, still capable of interbreeding with other subpopulations of the species and are, therefore, impermanent and subject to reamalgamation.

⋅✦⋅

This difference between species and subspecies becomes important in practice because our Endangered Species Act currently mandates the protection of subspecies as well. I do not dispute the act's intention or its teeth, for many subspecies do manifest distinctly evolved properties of great value and wonder (even if these properties do not render them reproductively isolated from other populations of the species). We would not, after all, condone the genocide of all Caucasian human beings because members of other races would still exist; human races, if formally recognized at all, are subspecies based on our original geographic separations. But since subspecies do not have the same objective status as species (and since not all distinct local populations bear separate names), argument over what does and does not merit protection is inevitable. Most of the major ecological wrangles of recent years—rows over the Mount Graham red squirrel or the Northern spotted owl—involve subspecies, not species.

These taxonomic issues were once abstract, however important. They are now immediate and vital—and all educated people must understand them in the midst of our current crisis in biodiversity and extinction. I therefore close with two observations.

By grasping the objective status of species as real units in nature (and by understanding why they are not arbitrary divisions for human convenience), we may better comprehend the moral rationale for their preservation. You can expunge an arbitrary idea by rearranging your conceptual world. But when a species dies, an item of natural uniqueness is gone forever. Each species is a remarkably complex product of evolution—a branch on a tree that is billions of years old. All the king's horses and men faced an easy problem compared with what we would encounter if we tried to reconstitute a lost species. Reassembling Humpty-Dumpty is just an exceedingly complex jigsaw puzzle, for the pieces lie at the base of the wall. There are no pieces left when the last dodo dies.

But all species eventually die in the fullness of geologic time, so why should we worry? In the words of Tennyson (who died exactly 100 years ago, so the fact is no secret):

> From scarped cliff and quarried stone
> She cries, "A thousand types are gone:
> I care for nothing. All shall go."

> (From *In Memoriam.*)

The argument is true, but the time scale is wrong for our ethical concerns. We live our lives within geologic instants, and we should make our moral decisions at this proper scale—not at the micromoment of thoughtless exploitation for personal profit and public harm; but not at Earth's time scale of billions of years either (a grand irrelevancy for our species' potential tenure of thousands or, at most, a few million years).

We do not let children succumb to easily curable infections just because we know that all people must die eventually. Neither should we condone our current massive wipeout of species because all eventually become extinct. The mass extinctions of our geologic past may have cleared space and created new evolutionary opportunity—but it takes up to 10 million years to reestablish an interesting new world, and what can such an interval mean to us? Mass extinctions may have geologically distant benefits, but life in the midst of such an event is maximally unpleasant—and that, friends, is where we now reside, I fear.

Species are living, breathing items of nature. We lose a bit of our collective soul when we drive species (and their entire lineages with them), prematurely and in large numbers, to oblivion. Tennyson, paraphrasing Goethe, hoped that we could transcend such errors when he wrote, in the same poem:

> I held it truth, with him who sings
> To one clear harp in divers tones
> That men may rise on stepping-stones
> Of their dead selves to higher things.

# POSTSCRIPT

## Is Evolution a Gradual Process?

**U**nderstanding evolution can be complex. It is clear that natural selection may be rapid in some circumstances and gradual in others. The key factor seems to be the role environment plays in the process. If the selective factors at work in the environment tend to promote gradual change, then the species in question may be more likely to evolve slowly and sequentially from one form to another. This process has been referred to as *phyletic transformation*. On the other hand, if selective factors are intense and severe, evolution is more apt to occur quickly and through *allopataric speciation*, or branching. Even in the case where speciation does not occur, natural selection may be rapid or gradual, depending on the environmental influences at work. In environments that are stable and constant, selection tends to favor individuals who show little variation from the current form (such as giraffes with the optimum neck length) and select against individuals who deviate from the norm (such as very long necked or very short necked giraffes). This process is called *stabilizing selection*. In contrast, environments that are changing rapidly and severely tend to favor individuals who possess characteristics that give them an advantage in adapting to the new conditions. Selection for these individuals is not only usually rapid but also directional, a process usually referred to as *directional selection*.

A good example of directional natural selection is provided by recent studies of ground finch populations on the small Galapagos Island of Daphne Major (Weiner, 1994; Grant, 1986). The researchers painstakingly captured, tagged, and released all the finches on the island so they could be identified in the field. This decision proved to be fortuitous when the island was stricken by drought. From mid-1976 to early 1978, no rain fell on the island. Due to the lack of water, fewer seeds were produced by plants. Those seeds that were produced also tended to be larger and harder than normal, making them difficult for the birds to eat. Birds with larger, more powerful beaks had a distinct advantage over the birds with smaller, weaker beaks. As the drought continued, more and more of the finches began to die from starvation. Of the 1200 finches that had been living on the island in 1977, only 180 remained by the end of that year. When the survivors were examined, it was found that all of them had larger, stronger beaks than was average for the finches prior to the drought. The larger beaks were also prevalent among the finches born after the drought began. Since natural selection favored large, strong-beaked individuals over smaller, weaker-beaked finches, only the segment of the population with the largest, strongest beaks were able to survive and reproduce under the severe conditions.

Similarly, adaptation to the environment may also mean that complex structures may be replaced by *simpler* ones. For example, a number of species such as whales, seals, and sea otters once lived on land and had more complex limbs for locomotion. Readaptation to life in the sea resulted in those structures becoming simplified (i.e., flippers instead of legs and paws). Therefore, it is clear that evolution may move directionally back and forth and not always in a linear or progressive way.

For more detailed descriptions of the gradualist position, see Charles Darwin's book *On the Origin of Species*, Darwin and Wallace's book *Evolution by Natural Selection*, and Wallace's book *My Life: A Record of Events and Opinions* (2 volumes). Another interesting read is *The Life and Letters of Charles Darwin* (2 volumes).

Important works on rapid evolution include *Man's Place in Nature* by Thomas Huxley, *Punctuated Equilibria: The tempo and mode of evolution reconsidered* by Stephen Gould and Niles Eldridge and Weiner's work *The Beak of the Finch*.

# ISSUE 2

## Does Human Cloning and Genetic Engineering Pose Evolutionary Dangers?

**YES: Kenneth S. Kosik,** from "The Fortune Teller," *The Sciences* (July/August 1999)

**NO: Robert Sapolsky,** from "A Gene for Nothing," *Discover* (October 1997)

### ISSUE SUMMARY

Kenneth Kosik suggests that there are dangers and ethical issues inherent in genetic research and its results. In contrast, Robert Sapolsky stresses the importance of environment and social learning in determining how genes are expressed. He argues that individuals with the same biology do not necessarily develop the same personality.

**I**n *The Origin of Species*, Darwin argues that English farmers and herders were able to produce different varieties of domestic plants and animals through selective breeding, and that nature acted in much the same way to produce different species over time. Darwin seemed to assume that because many of his readers would be familiar with selective breeding of domesticated animals and plants, this knowledge would serve as a conceptual bridge to allow them to grasp the significance of natural selection more easily.

Unfortunately, the close connection Darwin drew between selective breeding and natural selection led some readers to conclude that humans should also be bred selectively and for particular characteristics. In 1883, British naturalist and mathematician Francis Galton (1822–1911) coined the term *eugenics* to describe this process. The idea appealed to many doctors, lawyers, politicians, and other members of the elite who were concerned about the high reproductive rates among the lower classes and the influx of foreign immigrants endangering their social status and position.

The eugenics movement rapidly gained momentum in most of western Europe and America. Advocates of this approach campaigned to make abortion illegal in America in order to increase the birth rate among upper-class women. Eugenic supporters were also at the head of sterilization campaigns and anti-immigration laws; the purpose being to reduce the number of "unfit" individuals in society. Over 20 states passed laws to sterilize men and women in American mental hospitals and prisons (Horgan, 1998:212). "Through textbook and school curriculum revisions, fitter family and eugenic couple contests at state fairs, travelling exhibits and popular lectures, eugenicists in the United States managed to propagandize their cause to a large sector of the American public" (Allen, 1998:200).

Eugenic ideas also made inroads in academic fields such as anthropology and biology. Sociobiology, for example, suggests that human behavior is genetically determined and that there is "selection" for particular characteristics and traits that enhance their reproductive fitness. This approach has been used to suggest that gender roles are biologically determined or that societies evolve traditions over time which enhance reproductive rates.

Advances in medical technology—principally genetic engineering and cloning—have also paved the way for a resurgence of interest in "breeding a better human." The current Human Genome Project, for example, is committed to mapping gene sequences and locations of specific genes on human DNA. A complete map of this kind could lead to the improved diagnosis of hereditary diseases and their prevention. On the other hand, this sort of knowledge could also lead to new forms of prejudice and discrimination. As chillingly portrayed in the movie *Gattica*, individuals might be classified and stereotyped according to their genome. "De-gene-rates," or individuals with "inferior" or "undesirable" genes, might be barred from educational and occupational opportunities and considered second-class citizens.

Some scientists are confident that whatever the problems and ethical issues are, the potential benefits of human cloning and genetic engineering outweigh the potential costs. Others are not so sure. The following articles will examine different perspectives on this issue. Kosik suggests that advances in genetic research are often a double-edged sword. He questions whether or not it is ethical for scientists to reveal or conceal genetic information from people affected by it. In contrast, Sapolsky argues that advances in genetic engineering and cloning should not be feared. Genes are only part of the puzzle, he says. Environment plays just as large a role as heredity in determining personality, and the notion that genes determine behavior is overly simplistic.

# YES ↩

**Kenneth S. Kosik**

# The Fortune Teller

The locals of Medellín, Colombia, joke that when God created the world, one of the angels asked him why he was putting so many natural wonders in one place. God replied, "It will even out. Wait till you see the character of the people I'm going to put there." Self-effacement aside, among the people of Colombia there is a curious mixture of pride and bafflement, sorrow and theatricality, regret and resignation about their unusually bloody history—a history from which the country has not yet emerged. Violence and beauty intertwine in Colombia in complicated ways, just as the folk saying implies; that much I have learned during the many trips I have made there to conduct research and genetic testing on a rare form of Alzheimer's disease.

The lush valley of the Cordillera Central, the range of the Andes where Medellín is situated, is striking. From the airport, it is an hour-long winding descent to the city on a mountain road bordered by verdant slopes. At night, the soft lights in the valley suggest the mythical golden city of El Dorado, the way the first Spanish settlers must have pictured it some 400 years ago. But daylight exposes the urban sprawl that extends well up the sides of the surrounding mountains, and the cruel poverty that penetrates the choked streets. On the far outskirts of Medellín, a few swimming pools and enormous mansions dot the landscape. Some of them are the vast estates of the drug lords, who can be identified in the city by their powerful four-wheel-drive vehicles, and whose pursuits a few years ago gave Medellín one of the highest murder rates of any city not at war.

This highly insular world, where Internet access coexists with ancient folk beliefs, opened to me in 1991. A neurologist at Brigham and Women's Hospital in Boston, I visited Colombia that year with the support of the Fogarty International Center, a branch of the National Institutes of Health, to help develop neuroscience in Latin America. In October 1992 I traveled to the University of Antioquia School of Medicine in Medellín, where I gave a talk on the biology of Alzheimer's disease—the degenerative brain disorder that strikes so many people at the end of their lives. There I was introduced to the neurologist Francisco Lopera.

Lopera told me of a fascinating find he had made. About a decade earlier, while evaluating a forty-four-year-old man complaining of memory loss, he

From *The Sciences*, July/August 1999, pp. 13–17. Copyright © 1999 by New York Academy of Sciences. Reprinted by permission.

had been struck by how closely the man's symptoms resembled Alzheimer's disease, except for the patient's young age. More disturbing was the man's family history: he mentioned many relatives with similar problems back in his village. Beginning with mildly annoying symptoms such as asking the same question repeatedly, the affected people later developed personality changes, became disoriented, and about a decade later died, usually of pneumonia after a prolonged vegetative period.

Lopera began investigating, and by the time I met him he had developed a series of detailed genealogies that tracked twelve interrelated families. Intrigued by this mysterious early-onset form of dementia, I agreed to help Lopera try to find the gene mutation at work and unlock its secrets.

But genes are not isolated entities that live only in laboratory test tubes; they are part of the fabric of a person's individual and cultural identity. Thus our quest turned out to be more than a scientific search for a snippet of mutant DNA: it became, for me, an odyssey both geographical and personal. The work has connected me to people whose lives would otherwise be quite foreign— Spanish-speaking farmers who are provincial and unsophisticated, yet uncannily wise. Their fates are enmeshed in that microscopic skein of genetic material, the human genome—a tangled scroll that I know how to read, but whose dictates they will have to live with.

## A Definitive Diagnosis

Like many neurologists, Lopera brings a depth of scholarly and esoteric knowledge to his work, though his patients usually suffer from commonplace maladies such as headaches and epilepsy. He has a nearly fixed smile that conveys his genuine good nature, but that can shift with ease to an ironic grin. Our collaboration has included many earnest discussions over late-night bottles of wine, and has led to several articles written for professional journals.

The task that brought us together was a classic one. Geneticists are always on the lookout for inherited diseases that show up within a single extended family. Such case studies offer exceptional opportunities to isolate the faulty gene responsible, because family members tend to share certain idiosyncratic stretches of DNA that reappear through the generations. When investigators find that one of those unusual stretches of DNA always occurs in the family members who have the disease, but is not present in the other family members, they can assume the faulty gene is nearby, and zero in on it.

When Lopera and I began working together, our first task was to make certain the disease in question was Alzheimer's. A definitive diagnosis requires the microscopic study of brain tissue after death. But because funeral rites in Colombia invoke so many local traditions and superstitions, no one had yet been able to conduct a postmortem examination, even years after the afflicted families had come to light.

Nearly all the families live in a region of the country called Antioquia, of which Medellín is the capital, in a few rural pueblos: Angostura, Belmira, Caldas, Ituango, Sabanalarga, Santa Rosa de Osos and Sopetrán; San José de la Montaña, perched high in the mountains; and Yarumal—by far the largest, with paved streets and a sizable town square. About a year after I met Lopera, he learned that a middle-aged woman who had had early-onset dementia for eleven years had died in Angostura. Quickly he enlisted Juan Carlos Arango, a neuropathologist colleague at the University of Antioquia School of Medicine, to accompany him on the five-hour drive from Medellín.

When they arrived, the lloronas, professional mourners, had already joined family and friends around the body, which was laid out in the sitting room. People cried and talked, and some drank to excess through the night. Gradually one of the dead woman's sons became suspicious about why the city doctors wanted his mother's brain tissue. Perhaps they planned to sell it to the gringos. All the other children agreed to have the brain examined, but this son lent a sinister tone to the negotiations. People whispered that he was connected to the narcotraficantes as a sicario, or hit man, because he had been a member of the local police, a common route to the mafia. His gold chains, his remoteness from the townspeople and the bullyish way he carried himself enhanced that impression. He made the situation tense, and as he drank, the possibilities for trouble increased.

The mayor of Angostura came to the house, followed by the vaccine man, a village medical worker known to be very simpático, and both attempted to resolve the situation. Finally, with further entreaties from Lopera and other family members, the angry son relented. In a brief stop at the local infirmary on the way to the church, Lopera and Arango removed the dead woman's brain. Arango flew with it straight to Boston; there, in my laboratory, he proved the case was Alzheimer's disease.

Lopera, meanwhile, continued to labor over the genealogies. What had come to his attention as a few cases of early-onset dementia turned out to be a concealed epidemic involving nearly 4,000 people. Lopera's handwritten family trees began to fill large rolls of paper, enough to cover a huge wall. Each entry distilled an entire life story into a few spare symbols—age, gender, affected or non-affected, alive or dead. The names read like a dark, enchanted poem— Gilma, Resfa, María, Epifanía, Altagracia, Rosa, Fabiola, Lopera was struck by the inexorable appearance of the disease in one generation after the next. When one parent was affected, about half the children, regardless of gender, later developed the disease. In genetics that pattern of inheritance is called autosomal dominance, and it strongly suggested that a single mutation was responsible.

The gene involved was discovered—by someone else—a couple of years after we began the project. In 1995 the molecular geneticist Gerard D. Schellenberg of the Veterans Affairs Medical Center in Seattle identified an approximate site on chromosome 14 where one of the mutant genes for early-onset Alzheimer's resided. Within months the geneticist Peter St. George Hyslop of the University of Toronto zeroed in on the gene and named it presenilin 1.

When the presenilin 1 gene is intact, it causes no problems for its bearer. But more than fifty different mutations—misspellings of DNA—can exist in *presenilin 1,* and wherever they occur, they lead to early-onset Alzheimer's. (In addition to *presenilin 1,* two other genes are known to cause early-onset Alzheimer's, and workers think there are still others waiting to be found.) Later in 1995, I enlisted the help of Alison M. Goate, a geneticist at Washington

University in Saint Louis, and together we were able to identify the specific mutation responsible for the Colombian families' disease.

It is important to understand that Alzheimer's disease comes in two distinct flavors. The most common type, afflicting about four million elderly Americans, is not caused by a genetic mutation, though some people may have a gene that makes them more than usually susceptible. That form of Alzheimer's generally strikes people sixty-five or older; no one knows why. But in about 1 percent of cases—including those among the families in Colombia—Alzheimer's strikes the young and the cause is clearly a faulty gene. Both kinds of Alzheimer's leave the same telltale marks in the brain: knotty clumps of a protein called beta-amyloid. As investigators, we hope that an understanding of the relatively rare, genetic form of Alzheimer's will lead to a treatment for the more common type.

## Local Beliefs Clash With Genetic Principles

Shortly before our team learned the precise location of the Alzheimer's mutation, we invited the families involved to a meeting at the hospital in Yarumal. There we were greeted by the mayor, who assigned me two bodyguards: he said he had no fears about the people in his town, but could not be sure about people from other villages. Nearly a hundred people came—in donkey carts, on horseback and by bus. We gathered them together in an open auditorium, told them about our work and invited questions. They asked about a local superstition that the disease could be contracted by touching a tree, though they were unsure which tree was the contagious one. They also asked about marrying their first cousins. Although they were aware of the risk posed by intermarriage, still, the limited choice of a mate in their small villages meant that sometimes love outweighed more abstract concerns.

To the people gathered there, most of whom had no more than a first- or second-grade education, some genetic principles seemed to make intuitive sense, whereas others did not. No one had trouble, for instance, understanding that traits can be inherited. But the fact that the probability of inheriting a trait is unrelated to the previous births was more difficult to grasp. If one parent has the Alzheimer's mutation, there is a 50 percent risk that each child will have it too. But, just as parents who have had three girls in a row may expect their chance of having a boy to increase, the villagers endorsed a logical fallacy. One man announced to the assembled group: "We the families in which there are only a few affecteds must be grateful to those families with many affecteds." Local ideas of guilt and collective burden were deeply ingrained, and clashed with the principles of population genetics.

Where did the Colombian Alzheimer's mutation come from? *Paisas,* as the people of Antioquia call themselves, are generally regarded as different from other Colombians. Some say they are related to the Basques; others consider them a lost tribe of Israel. Various indigenous groups once ruled their land—principal among them the Chibchas, who originated the legend of El Dorado. Excellent goldsmiths, the Chibchas anointed their chiefs by rolling them in gold dust, which the new leaders then washed off in Lake Guatavita.

In the sixteenth century Spain conquered the area, and for three centuries governed it with a harsh grip.

Even tracing back seven generations, it is impossible to find a common ancestor who links any of the twelve extended families that carry the Alzheimer's gene. Yet undoubtedly they are all related to a single individual, the first person in whom the deadly mutation occurred. Perhaps that person was a pre-Columbian, whose own people are now extinct, and whose only legacy is the defective Alzheimer's gene propagating in retribution among the Spanish usurpers of her land. Or perhaps the curse originated with a Spaniard—a sailor whose forgettable fling left an indelible genetic memory. Indeed, the mutation may have spread by any of the myriad entanglements through which human beings accomplish genetic recombination.

After the discovery of the mutation it became possible to predict, from a simple blood test, who within the Colombian families would get Alzheimer's—even whether a pregnant woman's fetus would one day contract the disease. We then were ethically bound to find out how such powerful information, if made available, would affect the local people. There is no known way to dodge the illness or even to postpone it. If someone carries the mutation, early-onset Alzheimer's is inevitable—unless another cause of early death makes a pre-emptive strike.

The village of Caldas is not far from Medellín. To get there we turned off the road onto a dirt path that runs along an abandoned railroad track. Near the end of a row of houses a smiling señora, her face lined with creases, greeted us with a litany of salutations. Her middle-aged daughter, a ruddy, dough-faced woman, stood beside her. We sat in their simple living room while the daughter brought out the Colombian coffee they call *tinto*. After chatting a bit, the señora Autila asked whether we would like to see her son, Rodrigo.

She told us Rodrigo's disease had begun five years earlier, at age forty-four, when they had found him lost and wandering in a field. It was the same field where another of her sons had been shot dead. The murder was not unusual. Nearly every family we visited had been touched by the violence that permeates Colombian society, and often it struck me that the biological disease my colleagues and I were trying to defeat was dwarfed by another, equally deadly condition—one that had none of the predictability of an inherited gene defect, and about which we understood almost nothing.

In a small room next to the dining area, Rodrigo was neatly tucked into white sheets, unconscious and, except for his breathing, quite still. Occasionally this peaceful picture was interrupted by the gnashing of teeth and quick jerking movements that are typical of late-stage Alzheimer's. The room, bare of ornament, resembled a mortuary, with its white walls and the small cross at the head of the iron-railed bed—as if to ease Rodrigo's transition to the next world.

## To Know or Not to Know?

Our next stop was Manrique, a poor and violent barrio in Medellín. That was where Nubia lived with her demented mother and an unclear number of other family members. To reach the house we had to drive deep into what felt like a Brueghel painting. Blackened, distorted human faces looked out from dingy garages and the platforms of abandoned warehouses; vultures perched patiently overhead. Nubia's front door opened directly onto a busy street. Only a thin wall separated the inhabitants of the house from the noise and squalor outside.

Here was none of the tranquillity that surrounded Rodrigo in his white-washed room. Nubia's mama was on display, visible to every passerby through the open front door. Emaciated, she sat contorted, her hands gnarled and stuck in an unnatural position, a feeding tube protruding from her nose. Motionless except for her aimlessly roving eyes, she was a constant reminder to her children of the fate that lay ahead for those among them who carried the mutant gene.

I told the grown children that we could now determine which of them would get the disease, and I asked whether they would want to take the test. "Before answering," I told them, "remember that there is no treatment." All the children said they would want to take the test. What would they do differently, once they knew the result? I asked. At that point no one had an answer, except twenty-three-year-old González, who later told our nurse that if his test were positive, he would shoot himself.

Once the province of shamans and *curanderos,* revealing the future of an otherwise healthy person is a very modern responsibility for physicians. When the genes tell a cruel story, we must be prepared for the power and danger of that information. In the United States, genetic counselors are trained to help people make sense of such news. Faced with someone like González, a counselor would sympathize with his despair while reminding him that many more worthwhile years lay ahead. But Colombia has no genetic counselors, and so, adhering to well-established ethical guidelines, Lopera and I have decided that the gene test will be given for research purposes only: the results will not be made available to the person tested or to anyone else. I am not fully comfortable with that arrangement, however, because I know there are, among the Colombians, people who might limit the number of children they chose to have if they knew they carried the mutation.

## Delaying the Onset of Disease

Curiously, the *presenilin 1* mutation found among the Colombians does not strike all its victims at the same age. Some people with the mutation get Alzheimer's in their early thirties, and others are not stricken until their late fifties. The question is, Why? One possibility is that something in the environment triggers the disease. But if that were the case, one would expect family members with different onset ages to have divergent lifestyles. Instead, the affected people have similar habits and occupations: the men work on coffee plantations, and the women are housewives.

A more likely explanation, therefore, is a modifier gene—a second gene that controls when the *presenilin 1* mutation begins to do its damage. It is not unusual for two genes to work in tandem—one doing damage, the other dictating when the damage will occur and how bad it will be. Modifier genes are among a growing group of known "risk factor" genes, genes that increase a person's chances of getting a disease. For example, a specific variant of the *APOE* gene predisposes people to the more common kind of Alzheimer's (the kind that strikes elderly people), and may cause them to contract it earlier.

So the hunt is on among the Colombians. We have obtained blood samples from siblings who developed the disease at widely disparate ages, and we have begun the tedious search among the billions of nucleotides that make up the enormous stretches of human DNA. If a modifier gene exists, we will find it in two or three years. And the payoff could be enormous: if, for instance, a drug could be developed that inhibited the protein made by the modifier gene, physicians could delay the onset of Alzheimer's by as many as twenty years—not only in the Colombian families, but potentially also among the people who suffer from the more common version of the disease. Pushing back the age at which the widespread form of Alzheimer's strikes—from, say, age seventy to age ninety—would be nearly tantamount to a cure.

At one point in the novel *One Hundred Years of Solitude,* by the Nobel-prize-winning Colombian writer Gabriel García Márquez, the inhabitants of the fictional village of Macondo mysteriously begin to lose their memories. In a haunting parallel to the real disease that afflicts the families in Antioquia, the novel describes how the villagers first forget the names of objects, and then lose the ability to use them. The cure comes eventually in the form of "a drink of a gentle color," brought to town by a traveling gypsy.

Armed with the tools of modern genetics, are we biologists the gypsies who bring the campesinos the cure? Or are we dangerous intruders instead, one more band of exploiters in a long line of outsiders who, beginning with Cortés, have invaded and betrayed Latin America? Just as foreigners have historically plundered the continent's natural resources, so we, the prospectors of the late twentieth century, come to harvest genes.

Our work, however, has the feel of something predestined. Whether because of a Faustian pact or naive curiosity, knowledge cannot be denied. Sooner or later we will know our genes; if we do not, our children will. We stand poised to be expelled from an Eden of genetic ignorance into a society where every talent and weakness, every wrinkle and freckle may be predicted from our genomes. More disturbing is the possibility that our genomes will become public property, that employers and insurance companies will peer into our DNA and then discriminate against us as a result—that the knowledge of our genetic destiny will rob us first of opportunity, and later of all hope.

Like magical concoctions from a Márquez novel, geneticists' devices can predict a tragic fate for children playing along the railroad tracks of Caldas or in the sunny church square of Yarumal. I worry particularly about the impact of newfound genetic knowledge in a land far from the microtiter plates, DNA chips and fluorescent gel bands of my laboratory. Ultimately, however, such qualms are pointless.

Scientific revolutions derive from small, incremental discoveries. Lopera and I, and other neurologists, who contribute a jigsaw piece here or there, cannot envision the completed puzzle. My experiences in Colombia have helped me put the genetic enterprise in perspective. What I have learned in that colorful yet tortured land, where the threat of violence is constant and senseless murder is accepted as a fact of life, is that no matter how much progress we scientists make toward understanding the present and controlling the future, destiny will always hold the trump card. We cannot know, in advance, the eventual impact of genetic knowledge. We can only strive to untangle its secrets with a sense of responsibility toward the communities that hold the precious genetic clues.

# NO ↵

**Robert Sapolsky**

# A Gene for Nothing

**W**ell, these last six months have been an exciting time for the sheep named Dolly, ever since it was revealed that she was the first mammal cloned from adult cells. There was the night she spent in the Lincoln bedroom and the photo op with Al Gore; the triumphant ticker-tape parade down Broadway, the billboard ads for Guess Genes. Throughout the media circus, Dolly has been poised, patient, cordial, and even-tempered—the epitome of what we look for in a celebrity and role model. But despite her charm, people keep saying mean things about Dolly. Heads of state, religious leaders, and editorialists fall over themselves in calling her an aberration of nature and an insult to the sacred biological wonder of reproduction. They thunder about the anathema of even considering applying to humans the technology that spawned her.

What's everyone so upset about? Why is cloning so disturbing? Clearly, it's not the potential for droves of clones running around with the exact same renal filtration rate that has everyone up in arms. It's probably not even the threat of winding up with a bunch of clones who look identical, creepy though that would be. No, the real horror is the prospect of having multiple copies of a single brain, with the same neurons and the same genes directing those neurons, one multibodied consciousness among the clones, an army of photocopies of the same soul, all thinking, feeling, and acting identically.

Fortunately, that can't happen, as people have known ever since scientists discovered identical twins. Such individuals constitute genetic clones, just like Dolly and her "mother"—the sheep from which the original cell was taken. Despite all those breathless stories about identical twins separated at birth who flush the toilet before using it, twins are not melded in mind, do not behave identically. For example, if an identical twin is schizophrenic, the sibling, with the identical "schizophrenia gene(s)," has only about a 50 percent chance of having the disease.

A similar finding comes from a fascinating experiment by Dan Weinberger of the National Institute of Mental Health. Give identical twins a puzzle to solve and they might come up with closer answers than one would expect from a pair of strangers. While they're working on the puzzle, however, hook the twins up to a PET scanner, a brain-imaging instrument that visualizes metabolic demands in different regions of the brain. You'll find the pattern of activation in the pair differing considerably, despite the similarity of their solutions. Or use an MRI to get some detailed pictures of the brains of identical twins and start measuring stuff obsessively—the length of this part, the width of that, the volume of another region, and the surface area of the cortex—and those identical twins with their identical genes never have identical brains. Every measure differs.

The careful editorialists have made this point. Nonetheless, that business about identical genes producing identical brains tugs at a lot of people. Gene-behavior stories are constantly getting propelled to the front pages of newspapers. One popped up shortly before Dolly, when a team of researchers reported that a single gene, called fru, determines the sexual behavior of male fruit flies. Courtship, opening lines, foreplay, who they come on to—the works. Mutate that gene and—get this—you can even change the sexual orientation of the fly. What made the story front-page news, of course, wasn't our insatiable fly voyeurism. "Could our sexual behaviors be determined by a single gene as well?" every article asked. And a bit earlier, there was the hubbub about the isolation of a gene related to anxiety in humans, and shortly before that, a gene related to novelty-seeking behavior, and a while before that, a gene whose mutation in one family was associated with violent antisocial behavior, and before that . . .

Why do these stories command attention? For many, genes and the DNA they contain represent the holy grail of biology, the code of codes (two phrases often used in lay discussions of genetics). The worship at the altar of the gene rests on two assumptions. The first concerns the autonomy of genetic regulation: it is the notion that biological information begins with genes—DNA is the commander, the epicenter from which biology emanates. Nobody tells a gene what to do; it's always the other way around. The second assumption is that when genes give a command, biological systems listen. Genes, the story goes, instruct your cells as to their structure and function. And when those cells are neurons, their functions include thought, feelings, and behavior. Thus, the gene worshipers believe, we are finally identifying the biological factors that make us do what we do.

A typical example of the code-of-codes view recently appeared in a lead *New Yorker* article by Louis Menand, an English professor at the City University of New York. Menand ruminates on anxiety genes, when "one little gene is firing off a signal to bite your fingernails" (there's that first assumption—autonomous genes firing off whenever some notion pops into their heads). He asks himself how we can reconcile societal, economic, and psychological explanations of behavior with those ironclad genes. "The view that behavior is determined by an inherited genetic package" (there's the second assumption—genes as irresistible commanders) "is not easily reconciled with the view that behavior is determined by the kinds of movies a person watches." And what is the solution? "It is like having the Greek gods and the Inca gods occupying the same pantheon. Somebody's got to go."

In other words, if you buy into the notion of genes firing off and determining our behaviors, such modern scientific findings are simply incompatible with the environment having an influence. Something's gotta go.

Now, I'm not sure what sort of genetics they teach in Menand's English department, but the something's-gotta-go loggerhead is what most behavioral biologists have been trying to unteach for decades, apparently with limited success. Which is why it's worth another try.

Okay. You've got nature—neurons, brain chemicals, hormones, and of course, at the bottom of the cereal box, genes. And then there's nurture, all those environmental breezes gusting about. Again and again, behavioral biologists insist that you can't talk meaningfully about nature or nurture, only about their interaction. But somehow people can't seem to keep that thought in their heads. Instead, whenever a new gene is trotted out that "determines" a behavior by "firing off," they see environmental influences as the irrelevant something that has to go. Soon poor, sweet Dolly is a menace to our autonomy as individuals, and genes are understood to control who you go to bed with and whether you feel anxious about it.

Let's try to undo the notion of genes as neurobiological and behavioral destiny by examining those two assumptions, beginning with the second one—that cells, including those in our heads, obey genetic commands. What exactly do genes do? A gene, a stretch of DNA, does not produce a behavior. A gene does not produce an emotion, or even a fleeting thought. It produces a protein. Each gene is a specific DNA sequence that codes for a specific protein. Some of these proteins certainly have lots to do with behavior and feelings and thoughts; proteins include some hormones (which carry messages between cells) and neurotransmitters (which carry messages between nerve cells); they also include receptors that receive hormonal and neurotransmitter messages, the enzymes that synthesize and degrade those messages, many of the intracellular messengers triggered by those hormones, and so on. All those proteins are vital for a brain to do its business. But only very rarely do things like hormones and neurotransmitters cause a behavior to happen. Instead they produce tendencies to respond to the environment in certain ways.

To illustrate this critical point, let's consider anxiety. When an organism is confronted with a threat, it typically becomes vigilant, searches for information about the nature of the threat, and struggles to find an effective coping response. Once it receives a signal indicating safety—the lion has been evaded, the traffic cop buys the explanation and doesn't issue a ticket—the organism can relax. But that's not what happens with an anxious individual. Instead this person will skitter frantically among coping responses, abruptly shifting from one to another without checking whether anything has worked. He may have a hard time detecting the safety signal and knowing when to stop his restless vigilance. Moreover, the world presents a lot of triggers that not everyone reacts to. For the anxious individual, the threshold is lower, so that the mere sight of a police car in the rearview mirror can provoke the same storm of uneasiness as actually being stopped. By definition, anxiety makes little sense outside the context of what the environment is doing to an individual. In that framework, the brain chemicals and genes relevant to anxiety don't make you anxious. They make you more responsive to anxiety-provoking situations, make it harder to detect safety signals.

The same theme continues in other behaviors as well. The exciting (made-of-protein) receptor that apparently has to do with novelty-seeking behavior doesn't actually make you seek novelty. It makes you more pleasurably excited than folks without that receptor variant get when you happen to encounter a novel environment. And those (genetically influenced) neurochemical abnormalities of depression don't make you depressed. They make you more vulnerable to stressors in the environment, to deciding that you are helpless even when you're not.

One might retort that in the long run we are all exposed to anxiety-provoking circumstances, all exposed to the depressing world around us. If we are all exposed to those same environmental factors but only the people who are genetically prone to depression get depressed, that is a pretty powerful vote for genes. In that scenario, the "genes don't cause things, they just make you more sensitive to the environment" argument becomes empty and semantic.

The problems here, however, are twofold. First, a substantial minority of people with a genetic legacy of depression do not get depressed, and not everyone who has a major depression has a genetic legacy for it. Genetic status is not all that predictive by itself. Second, we share the same environments only on a very superficial level. For example, the incidence of depression (and its probably biological underpinnings) seem to be roughly equal throughout the world. However, geriatric depression is epidemic in our society and far less prevalent in traditional societies in the developing world. Why? Different societies produce remarkably different social environments, in which old age can mean being a powerful village elder or an infantilized has-been put out to a shuffleboard pasture.

The environmental differences can be more subtle. Periods of psychological stress involving loss of control and predictability during childhood may well predispose one toward adult depression. Two children may have had similar childhood lessons in "there's bad things out there that I can't control"— both may have seen their parents divorce, lost a grandparent, tearfully buried a pet in the backyard, faced the endless menacing of a bully. Yet the temporal pattern of their experience is unlikely to be identical, and the child who experiences all those stressors over a one-year period instead of over six years is far more likely to come with the cognitive distortion, "There's bad things out there that I can't control and, in fact, I can't control anything," that sets you up for depression. The biological factors that genes code for in the nervous system typically don't determine behavior. Instead they affect how you respond to often very subtle influences in the environment. There are genetic vulnerabilities, tendencies, predispositions—but rarely genetic inevitabilities.

Now let's go back to that first assumption about behavioral genetics— that genes always have minds of their own. It takes just two startling facts about the structure of genes to blow this one out of the water.

A chromosome is made of DNA, a vastly long string of it, a long sequence of letters coding for genetic information. People used to think that Gene 1 would comprise the first eleven letters of the DNA message. A special letter sequence would signal the end of that gene, the next eleven and a half letters would code for Gene 2, and so on, through tens of thousands of genes.

Gene 1 might specify the construction of insulin in your pancreas; Gene 2 might specify protein pigments that give eyes their color; and Gene 3, active in neurons, might make you aggressive. Ah, caught you: might make you more sensitive to aggression-provoking stimuli in the environment. Different people have different versions of Genes 1, 2, and 3, some of which work better than others. An army of biochemicals do the scut work, transcribing the genes, reading the DNA sequences, and following the instructions they contain for constructing the appropriate proteins.

As it turns out, that's not really how things work. Instead of one gene coming immediately after another, with the entire string of DNA devoted to coding for different proteins, there are long stretches of DNA that don't get transcribed. Sometimes those stretches even split up a gene into subsections. Some of the nontranscribed, noncoding DNA doesn't seem to do anything. It may have some function that we don't yet understand, or it may have none at all. But some of the noncoding DNA does something very interesting indeed. It's the instruction manual for how and when to activate genes. These stretches have many names—regulatory elements, promoters, responsive elements. Various biochemical messengers may bind to each of them, altering the activity of the gene immediately "downstream"—immediately following it in the string of DNA.

Far from being autonomous sources of information, then, genes must obey other factors that regulate when and how they function. Very often, those factors are environmental. For example, suppose something stressful happens to a primate. A drought, say, forces it to forage miles each day for food. As a result, the animal secretes a stress hormone, cortisol, from its adrenals. Cortisol molecules enter fat cells and bind to cortisol receptors. These hormone-receptor complexes find their way to the DNA and bind to a regulatory stretch of DNA. Whereupon a gene downstream is activated, which produces a protein, which indirectly inhibits that fat cell from storing fat. It's a logical thing to do—while starving and walking the grasslands in search of a meal, the primate needs fat to fuel muscles, not to laze around in fat cells.

In effect, regulatory elements introduce the possibility of environmentally modulated if-then clauses. If the environment is tough and you're working hard to find food, then make use of your genes to divert energy to exercising muscles. The environment, of course, doesn't mean just the weather. The biology is essentially the same if a human refugee travels miles from home with insufficient food because of civil strife. The behavior of one human can change the pattern of gene activity in another.

Let's look at a fancier example of how environmental factors control the regulatory elements of DNA. Suppose that Gene 4037 (not its real name—it has one, but I'll spare you the jargon), when left to its own devices, is transcriptionally active, generating its protein. However, as long as a particular messenger binds to a regulatory element that comes just before 4037 in the DNA string, Gene 4037 shuts down. Fine. Now suppose that inhibitory messenger happens to be very sensitive to temperature. In fact, if the cell gets hot, the messenger goes to pieces and comes floating off the regulatory element. Freed from the inhibitory regulation, Gene 4037 will suddenly become active.

Maybe it's a gene that works in the kidney and codes for a protein relevant to water retention. Boring—another metabolic story, this one having to do with how a warm environment triggers metabolic adaptations that stave off dehydration. But suppose, instead, Gene 4037 codes for an array of proteins that have something to do with sexual behavior. What have you just invented? Seasonal mating. Winter is waning, each day gets a little warmer, and in relevant cells in the brain, pituitary, or gonads, genes like 4037 are gradually becoming active. Finally some threshold is passed and, *wham,* everyone starts rutting and ovulating, snorting and pawing at the ground, and generally carrying on. (Actually, in most seasonal matters, the environmental signal for mating is the amount of daily light exposure, or the days are getting longer, rather than temperature, or the days are getting warmer. But the principle is the same.)

Here's a final, elegant example. Every cell in your body has a distinctive protein signature that marks it as yours. These "major histocompatability" proteins allow your immune system to tell the difference between you and some invading bacterium—that's why your body will reject a transplanted organ with a very different signature. When those signature proteins get into a mouse's urine, they help make its odor distinct. For a rodent, that's important stuff. Design receptors in olfactory cells in a rodent's nose that can distinguish signature odorant proteins similar to its own from totally novel ones. The greater the similarity, the tighter the protein will fit into the receptor. What have you just invented? A way to distinguish between the smells of relatives and strangers— something rodents do effortlessly.

Keep tinkering with this science project. Now couple those olfactory receptors to a cascade of chemical messengers inside the cell, one messenger triggering the next until you get to the DNA's regulatory elements. What might you want to construct? How about: If an olfactory receptor binds an odorant indicating the presence of a relative, *then* trigger a cascade that ultimately inhibits the activity of genes related to reproduction. You've just invented a mechanism by which animals could avoid mating with close relatives. Or you can construct a different cascade: if an olfactory receptor binds an odorant indicating a relative, then inhibit genes that are normally active and that regulate the synthesis of testosterone. There you have a means by which rodents get bristly and aggressive when a strange male stinks up their burrow but not when the scent belongs to their kid brother.

❧❀❧

In each of these examples you can begin to see the logic, an elegance that teams of engineers couldn't do much to improve. And now for the two facts about this regulation of genes that will dramatically change your view of them. First, when it comes to mammals, by the best estimates available, more than 95 percent of DNA is noncoding. Ninety-five percent. Sure, a lot of it may have no function, but your average gene comes with a huge instruction manual for how to operate it, and the operator is very often environmental. With a percentage like that, if you think about genes and behavior, you have to think about how the environment regulates genes and behavior.

The second fact involves genetic variation between individuals. A gene's DNA sequence often varies from person to person, which often translates into proteins that differ in how well they do their job. This is the grist for natural selection: Which is the most adaptive version of some (genetically influenced) trait? Given that evolutionary change occurs at the level of DNA, "survival of the fittest" really means "reproduction of individuals whose DNA sequences make for the most adaptive collection of proteins." But—here's that startling second fact—when you examine variability in DNA sequences among individuals, the noncoding regions of DNA are considerably more variable than are the regions that code for genes. Okay, a lot of that variability is attributable to DNA that doesn't do much and so is free to drift genetically over time without consequence. But there seems to be a considerable amount of variability in regulatory regions as well.

What does this mean? By now, I hope, we've gotten past "genes determine behavior" to "genes modulate how one responds to the environment." The business about 95 percent of DNA being noncoding should send us even further, to "genes can be convenient tools used by environmental factors to influence behavior." And that second fact about variability in noncoding regions means that it's less accurate to think "evolution is about natural selection for different assemblages of genes" than it is to think "evolution is about natural selection for different sensitivities and responses to environmental influences."

Sure, some behaviors are overwhelmingly under genetic control. Just consider all those mutant flies hopping into the sack with insects their parents disapprove of. And some mammalian behaviors, even human ones, are probably pretty heavily under genetic regulation as well. These are likely to code for behaviors that must be performed by everyone in much the same way for genes to be passed on. For example, all male primates have to go about the genetically based behavior of pelvic thrusting in fairly similar ways if they plan to reproduce successfully. But by the time you get to courtship, or emotions, or creativity, or mental illness, or any complex aspect of our lives, the intertwining of biological and environmental components utterly defeats any attempt to place them into separate categories, let alone to then decide that one of them has got to go.

I'm a bit hesitant to reveal the most telling example of how individuals with identical genes can nonetheless come up with very different behaviors, as I have it thirdhand through the science grapevine, and I'll probably get some of the details wrong. But what the hell, it's such an interesting finding. It concerns the very extensive opinion poll that was carried out among sheep throughout the British Isles. Apparently, the researchers managed to get data from both Dolly and her gene-donor mother. So get a load of this bombshell: Dolly's mother voted Tory, listed the Queen Mum as her favorite royal, worried about mad cow disease ("Is it good or bad for the sheep?"), enjoyed Gilbert and Sullivan, and endorsed the statement, "Behavior? It's all nature." And Dolly? Votes Green Party, thinks Harry and William are the cutest, worries about "the environment," listens to the Spice Girls, and endorsed the statement, "Behavior? Nature. Or nurture. Whatever." You see, there's more to behavior than just genes.

# POSTSCRIPT

## Does Human Cloning and Genetic Engineering Pose Evolutionary Dangers?

It is an old saying that the road to hell is paved with good intentions. Kosik's article is a cautionary tale about the complexities of doing and applying genetic science in the real world. Kosik and his colleagues were able to identify the faulty gene responsible for a form of early Alzheimer's disease among Colombians. Kosik and his team investigated this matter by interviewing family members of individuals stricken with the disease. All of the people interviewed said that they would rather take the test and find out if they had the gene than remain ignorant. However, at least one informant said that he would kill himself if the test were positive. After a great deal of soul-searching, Kosik and his colleagues "decided that the gene test will be given for research purposes only: the results will not be made available to the person tested or to anyone else. I am not fully comfortable with that arrangement, however, because I know there are, among the Colombians, people who might limit the number of children they chose to have if they knew they carried the mutation" (Kosik, 2001:35).

In contrast to Kosik, Sapolsky's article is a reassuring reminder that genes are not destiny. For example, he points out that the ability to produce clones on a wide scale is new but human clones have always existed (i.e., identical twins). Studies suggest that a twin of a schizophrenic has only a 50 percent chance of developing the same condition, despite having the same set of genes. This statistic holds true even when the twins were brought up together in the same household. Sapolsky explains this variation by reference to the environment and the fact that even identical twins do not have identical experiences.

Another interesting question is whether the personalities of clones might be different than the personalities of regular humans. Studies of identical twins suggest that clones who were raised like other humans would not develop radically different personalities from their peers. However, if clones *were* raised in different ways than other humans, then their personalities might indeed be different. Science-fiction author C.J. Cherryh envisions a future in her 1988 novel *Cyteen* where a division is drawn between "born men," or humans raised in a family household, and "azi," or humans raised in a controlled lab environment. While the infants raised in a human household must cope with intermittent reinforcement and unpredictable events, the infants raised in a controlled lab environment receive constant and consistent reinforcement and regulation that shapes their personalities in predictable ways. These two styles of child rearing—random flux vs. consistent logic—impact individual physiology and personality development differently.

46

So far azi are still science fiction. But many things that were once science fiction are common today. Take gene splicing. In the last two decades, transferring genes from the cells of one species into those of another for medical purpose has become commonplace. Insulin is now produced by genetically altered bacteria rather than from nonhuman animals. Genetically altered sheep that produce human enzymes in their milk have also been used to treat a serious form of emphysema in humans. Crops have also been altered through gene splicing. Strawberries have been made more cold resistant, and tomatoes often carry a gene that makes them less susceptible to bruising during shipment. Animals have also been given genetically engineered growth hormones to make them mature faster and grow larger. All these developments have been hailed as "improvements," and indeed many of them do have obvious advantageous. But it is becoming increasingly obvious that genetic manipulation may have hidden costs as well. How safe are genetically altered foods? Does consuming meat and dairy products from animals treated with growth hormones have ill effects on human health?

Even more disturbing is the trend toward genetically engineering uniformity in plant and animal species raised for market. In the past, diversity was maintained in crops and stock animals due to regional variation and the prevalence of small-time farmers and ranchers. Now with the move toward corporate farming and ranching, this diversity is being systematically reduced. Instead of 20 or 30 different varieties of corn, only three or four are planted. These three or four species may be the "best" in terms of ear and kernel size, maturation time, and other factors. But what happens if a blight comes along to which these species are especially suspectable? Now instead of losing only part of the year's corn crop, all harvests across the country are endangered.

Engineering artificial uniformity in human populations may be just as dangerous. Suppose Hitler had had his way and all succeeding generations of humans were blond, blue-eyed Aryans with fair skin. This phenotype is especially susceptible to the effects of ultraviolet radiation—not a good trait to have if the greenhouse effect continues and the ozone goes. Similarly, suppose the American male's current fascination for starved-looking women with itty-bitty hips was given free rein. We might end up with thousands of individuals who could not give birth naturally because their pelvis was too narrow to allow the baby's head to pass through the birth canal. Even if we approached the problem more cautiously and cloned multiple types of humans rather than one or two, we have no guarantee that the phenotypes we choose would be the most advantageous ones in the long run. In fact, we might unknowingly self-select out the very traits that might have saved us. In evolutionary terms, maintaining a diverse and genetically varied population is a species' best defense against extinction.

For an interesting overview of the eugenics movement, see "Eugenics and American Social History, 1880–1950" by Garland Allen in *Genome* (vol. 31, 1989) and "Eugenics Revisited" by John Horgan, in *Scientific American* (1993). Also see Patrick Tierney's book *Darkness in El Dorado* (Norton, 2000).

# ISSUE 3

## Is Culture Responsible for the Spread of Ethnically Related Disease?

**YES: Jared Diamond,** from "The Curse and Blessing of the Ghetto," *Discover* (March 1991)

**NO: Josie Glausiusz,** from "Unfortunate Drift," *Discover* (June 1995)

### ISSUE SUMMARY

Jared Diamond argues that the high incidence of the Tay Sachs gene among eastern European Jews was caused by cultural discrimination. He suggests that racial prejudice kept the Jewish population confined to urban ghettos. In these crowded conditions, the Tay Sachs gene may afford some protection against tuberculosis. Josie Glausiusz, on the other hand, believes that genetic drift alone is responsible for the presence of the gene in this population.

*Different ethnic groups face different health problems, for reasons of genes as well as of lifestyle (Diamond, 1991:20).*

The term *population genetics* refers to the study of how different populations within a species compare to one another genetically. It also examines the role environment plays in determining a group's genetic composition and development. Similarities between populations are often attributed to *gene flow,* or the movement of genes between populations through inbreeding. Other factors, such as geographical or behavioral isolation, inhibit gene flow and may lead to increasing differences between populations over time. This process is called *genetic drift.* This force of evolution can eventually result in speciation.

One of the most fascinating aspects of population genetics is the study of ethnically related disease. Medical research suggests that certain ethnic groups are more susceptible to some diseases than others. "Familiar examples include the prevalence of skin cancer and stroke in Japanese and diabetes in Hispanics and Pacific Islanders" (Diamond, 1991:20). In some cases, the prevalence of a disease in a particular ethnic population is not well understood. Sickle-cell anemia, for example, is a common condition in many West African countries. The disease is caused by a point mutation that produces an abnormal form of hemo-globin, the protein on the red blood cell that carries oxygen from the lungs to the body's tissues. The resulting red blood cells are often misshapen and can-not transport oxygen very well. Affected individuals thus suffer from chronic fatigue, retarded physical development as children, and increased susceptibility to infection, fever, miscarriage, and physical pain. However, heterozygote—individuals with one normal gene and one abnormal one—are protected against malaria. Malaria is an often fatal infectious disease that kills 1 to 3 million people a year. In malarial regions like West Africa, heterozygote are more likely to sur-vive to reach reproductive age and pass on their genes than individuals with normal hemoglobin. Therefore, there was strong selection for the sickle-cell gene in the heterozygote form among populations living in malarial environments.

In other situations, the evolutionary origins of ethnic disease are still being debated. The following two selections examine the high incidence of the Tay Sachs gene in eastern European Jewish populations. Josie Glausiusz proposes that genetic drift and not natural selection is responsible for Tay Sachs and other genetic diseases common to eastern European Jews. In contrast, Jared Diamond suggests that cultural and historical factors may have selected for the spread of the Tay Sachs gene in the same population.

# Curse and Blessing of the Ghetto

**M**arie and I hated her at first sight, even though she was trying hard to be helpful. As our obstetrician's genetics counselor, she was just doing her job, explaining to us the unpleasant results that might come out of the genetic tests we were about to have performed. As a scientist, though, I already knew all I wanted to know about Tay-Sachs disease, and I didn't need to be reminded that the baby sentenced to death by it could be my own.

Fortunately, the tests would reveal that my wife and I were not carriers of the Tay-Sachs gene, and our preparenthood fears on that matter at least could be put to rest. But at the time I didn't yet know that. As I glared angrily at that poor genetics counselor, so strong was my anxiety that now, four years later, I can still clearly remember what was going through my mind: If I were an evil deity, I thought, trying to devise exquisite tortures for babies and their parents, I would be proud to have designed Tay-Sachs disease.

Tay-Sachs is completely incurable, unpreventable, and preprogrammed in the genes. A Tay-Sachs infant usually appears normal for the first few months after birth, just long enough for the parents to grow to love him. An exaggerated "startle reaction" to sounds is the first ominous sign. At about six months the baby starts to lose control of his head and can't roll over or sit without support. Later he begins to drool, breaks out into unmotivated bouts of laughter, and suffers convulsions. Then his head grows abnormally large, and he becomes blind. Perhaps what's most frightening for the parents is that their baby loses all contact with his environment and becomes virtually a vegetable. By the child's third birthday, if he's still alive, his skin will turn yellow and his hands pudgy. Most likely he will die before he's four years old.

My wife and I were tested for the Tay-Sachs gene because at the time we rated as high-risk candidates, for two reasons. First, Marie was carrying twins, so we had double the usual chance to bear a Tay-Sachs baby. Second, both she and I are of Eastern European Jewish ancestry, the population with by far the world's highest Tay-Sachs frequency.

In peoples around the world Tay-Sachs appears once in every 400,000 births. But it appears a hundred times more frequently—about once in 3,600 births—among descendants of Eastern European Jews, people known as Ashkenazim. For descendants of most other groups of Jews—Oriental Jews, chiefly from the Middle East, or Sephardic Jews, from Spain and other Mediterranean countries—the frequency of Tay-Sachs disease is no higher than in non-Jews. Faced with such a clear correlation, one cannot help but wonder: What is it about this one group of people that produces such an extraordinarily high risk of this disease?

Finding the answer to this question concerns all of us, regardless of our ancestry. Every human population is especially susceptible to certain diseases, not only because of its life-style but also because of its genetic inheritance. For example, genes put European whites at high risk for cystic fibrosis, African blacks for sickle-cell disease, Pacific Islanders for diabetes—and Eastern European Jews for ten different diseases, including Tay-Sachs. It's not that Jews are notably susceptible to genetic diseases in general; but a combination of historical factors has led to Jews' being intensively studied, and so their susceptibilities are far better known than those of, say, Pacific Islanders.

Tay-Sachs exemplifies how we can deal with such diseases; it has been the object of the most successful screening program to date. Moreover, Tay-Sachs is helping us understand how ethnic diseases evolve. Within the past couple of years discoveries by molecular biologists have provided tantalizing clues to precisely how a deadly gene can persist and spread over the centuries. Tay-Sachs may be primarily a disease of Eastern European Jews, but through this affliction of one group of people, we gain a window on how our genes simultaneously curse and bless us all.

The disease's hyphenated name comes from the two physicians—British ophthalmologist W. Tay and New York neurologist B. Sachs—who independently first recognized the disease, in 1881 and 1887, respectively. By 1896 Sachs had seen enough cases to realize that the disease was most common among Jewish children.

Not until 1962, however, were researchers able to trace the cause of the affliction to a single biochemical abnormality: the excessive accumulation in nerve cells of a fatty substance called $G_{M2}$ ganglioside. Normally $G_{M2}$ ganglioside is present at only modest levels in cell membranes, because it is constantly being broken down as well as synthesized. The breakdown depends on the enzyme hexosaminidase A, which is found in the tiny structures within our cells known as lysosomes. In the unfortunate Tay-Sachs victims this enzyme is lacking, and without it the ganglioside piles up and produces all the symptoms of the disease.

We have two copies of the gene that programs our supply of hexosaminidase A, one inherited from our father, the other from our mother; each of our parents, in turn, has two copies derived from their own parents. As long as we have one good copy of the gene, we can produce enough hexosaminidase A to prevent a buildup of $G_{M2}$ ganglioside and we won't get Tay-Sachs. This genetic disease is of the sort termed recessive rather than dominant—meaning that to get it, a child must inherit a defective gene not just from one parent but from both of them. Clearly, each parent must have had one good copy of the gene along with the defective copy—if either had had two defective genes, he or she would have died of the disease long before reaching the age of reproduction. In genetic terms the diseased child is homozygous for the defective gene and both parents are heterozygous for it.

None of this yet gives any hint as to why the Tay-Sachs gene should be most common among Eastern European Jews. To come to grips with that question, we must take a short detour into history.

From their biblical home of ancient Israel, Jews spread peacefully to other Mediterranean lands, Yemen, and India. They were also dispersed violently through conquest by Assyrians, Babylonians, and Romans. Under the Carolingian kings of the eighth and ninth centuries Jews were invited to settle in France and Germany as traders and financiers. In subsequent centuries, however, persecutions triggered by the Crusades gradually drove Jews out of Western Europe; the process culminated in their total expulsion from Spain in 1492. Those Spanish Jews—called Sephardim—fled to other lands around the Mediterranean. Jews of France and Germany—the Ashkenazim—fled east to Poland and from there to Lithuania and western Russia, where they settled mostly in towns, as businessmen engaged in whatever pursuit they were allowed.

There the Jews stayed for centuries, through periods of both tolerance and oppression. But toward the end of the nineteenth century and the beginning of the twentieth, waves of murderous anti-Semitic attacks drove millions of Jews out of Eastern Europe, with most of them heading for the United States. My mother's parents, for example, fled to New York from the Lithuanian pogroms of the 1880s, while my father's parents fled from the Ukrainian pogroms of 1903–6. The more modern history of Jewish migration is probably well known to you all: most Jews who remained in Eastern Europe were exterminated during World War II, while most of the survivors immigrated to the United States and Israel. Of the 13 million Jews alive today, more than three-quarters are Ashkenazim, the descendants of the Eastern European Jews and the people most at risk for Tay-Sachs.

Have these Jews maintained their genetic distinctness through the thousands of years of wandering? Some scholars claim that there has been so much intermarriage and conversion that Ashkenazic Jews are now just Eastern Europeans who adopted Jewish culture. However, modern genetic studies refute that speculation.

First of all, there are those ten genetic diseases that the Ashkenazim have somehow acquired, by which they differ both from other Jews and from Eastern European non-Jews. In addition, many Ashkenazic genes turn out to be ones typical of Palestinian Arabs and other peoples of the eastern Mediterranean areas where Jews originated. (In fact, by genetic standards the current Arab-Israeli conflict is an internecine civil war.) Other Ashkenazic genes have indeed diverged from Mediterranean ones (including genes of Sephardic and Oriental Jews) and have evolved to converge on genes of Eastern European non-Jews subject to the same local forces of natural selection. But the degree to which Ashkenazim prove to differ genetically from Eastern European non-Jews implies an intermarriage rate of only about 15 percent.

Can history help explain why the Tay-Sachs gene in particular is so much more common in Ashkenazim than in their non-Jewish neighbors or in other Jews? At the risk of spoiling a mystery, I'll tell you now that the answer is yes, but to appreciate it, you'll have to understand the four possible explanations for the persistence of the Tay-Sachs gene.

First, new copies of the gene might be arising by mutation as fast as existing copies disappear with the death of Tay-Sachs children. That's the most likely explanation for the gene's persistence in most of the world, where the disease frequency is only one in 400,000 births—that frequency reflects a typical human mutation rate. But for this explanation to apply to the Ashkenazim would require a mutation rate of at least one per 3,600 births—far above the frequency observed for any human gene. Furthermore, there would be no precedent for one particular gene mutating so much more often in one human population than in others.

As a second possibility, the Ashkenazim might have acquired the Tay-Sachs gene from some other people who already had the gene at high frequency. Arthur Koestler's controversial book *The Thirteenth Tribe*, for example, popularized the view that the Ashkenazim are really not a Semitic people but are instead descended from the Khazar, a Turkic tribe whose rulers converted to Judaism in the eighth century. Could the Khazar have brought the Tay-Sachs gene to Eastern Europe? This speculation makes good romantic reading, but there is no good evidence to support it. Moreover, it fails to explain why deaths of Tay-Sachs children didn't eliminate the gene by natural selection in the past 1,200 years, nor how the Khazar acquired high frequencies of the gene in the first place.

The third hypothesis was the one preferred by a good many geneticists until recently. It invokes two genetic processes, termed the founder effect and genetic drift, that may operate in small populations. To understand these concepts, imagine that 100 couples settle in a new land and found a population that then increases. Imagine further that one parent among those original 100 couples happens to have some rare gene, one, say, that normally occurs at a frequency of one in a million. The gene's frequency in the new population will now be one in 200 as a result of the accidental presence of that rare founder.

Or suppose again that 100 couples found a population, but that one of the 100 men happens to have lots of kids by his wife or that he is exceptionally popular with other women, while the other 99 men are childless or have few kids or are simply less popular. That one man may thereby father 10 percent rather than a more representative one percent of the next generation's babies, and their genes will disproportionately reflect that man's genes. In other words, gene frequencies will have drifted between the first and second generation.

Through these two types of genetic accidents a rare gene may occur with an unusually high frequency in a small expanding population. Eventually, if the gene is harmful, natural selection will bring its frequency back to normal by killing off gene bearers. But if the resultant disease is recessive—if heterozygous individuals don't get the disease and only the rare, homozygous individuals die of it—the gene's high frequency may persist for many generations.

These accidents do in fact account for the astonishingly high Tay-Sachs gene frequency found in one group of Pennsylvania Dutch: out of the 333 people in this group, 98 proved to carry the Tay-Sachs gene. Those 333 are all descended from one couple who settled in the United States in the eighteenth century and had 13 children. Clearly, one of that founding couple must have carried the gene. A similar accident may explain why Tay-Sachs is also relatively common among French Canadians, who number 5 million today but are descended from fewer than 6,000 French immigrants who arrived in the New World between 1638 and 1759. In the two or three centuries since both these founding events, the high Tay-Sachs gene frequency among Pennsylvania Dutch and French Canadians has not yet had enough time to decline to normal levels.

The same mechanisms were once proposed to explain the high rate of Tay-Sachs disease among the Ashkenazim. Perhaps, the reasoning went, the gene just happened to be overrepresented in the founding Jewish population that settled in Germany or Eastern Europe. Perhaps the gene just happened to drift up in frequency in the Jewish populations scattered among the isolated towns of Eastern Europe.

But geneticists have long questioned whether the Ashkenazim population's history was really suitable for these genetic accidents to have been significant. Remember, the founder effect and genetic drift become significant only in small populations, and the founding populations of Ashkenazim may have been quite large. Moreover, Ashkenazic communities were considerably widespread; drift would have sent gene frequencies up in some towns but down in others. And, finally, natural selection has by now had a thousand years to restore gene frequencies to normal.

Granted, those doubts are based on historical data, which are not always as precise or reliable as one might want. But within the past several years the case against those accidental explanations for Tay-Sachs disease in the Ashkenazim has been bolstered by discoveries by molecular biologists.

Like all proteins, the enzyme absent in Tay-Sachs children is coded for by a piece of our DNA. Along that particular stretch of DNA there are thousands of different sites where a mutation could occur that would result in no enzyme and hence in the same set of symptoms. If molecular biologists had discovered that all cases of Tay-Sachs in Ashkenazim involved damage to DNA at the same site, that would have been strong evidence that in Ashkenazim the disease stems from a single mutation that has been multiplied by the founder effect or genetic drift—in other words, the high incidence of Tay-Sachs among Eastern European Jews is accidental.

In reality, though, several different mutations along this stretch of DNA have been identified in Ashkenazim, and two of them occur much more frequently than in non-Ashkenazim populations. It seems unlikely that genetic accidents would have pumped up the frequency of the same gene not once but twice in the same population.

And that's not the sole unlikely coincidence arguing against accidental explanations. Recall that Tay-Sachs is caused by the excessive accumulation of one fatty substance, $G_{M2}$ ganglioside, from a defect in one enzyme, hexosaminidase A. But Tay-Sachs is one of ten genetic diseases characteristic of Ashkenazim. Among those other nine, two—Gaucher's disease and Niemann-Pick disease—result from the accumulation of two other fatty substances similar to $G_{M2}$ ganglioside, as a result of defects in two other enzymes similar to hexosaminidase A. Yet our bodies contain thousands of different enzymes. It would have been an incredible roll of the genetic dice if, by nothing more than chance, Ashkenazim had independently acquired mutations in three closely related enzymes—and had acquired mutations in one of those enzymes twice.

All these facts bring us to the fourth possible explanation of why the Tay-Sachs gene is so prevalent among Ashkenazim: namely, that something about them favored accumulation of $G_{M2}$ ganglioside and related fats.

For comparison, suppose that a friend doubles her money on one stock while you are getting wiped out with your investments. Taken alone, that could just mean she was lucky on that one occasion. But suppose that she doubles her money on each of two different stocks and at the same time rings up big profits in real estate while also making a killing in bonds. That implies more than lady luck; it suggests that something about your friend—like shrewd judgment—favors financial success.

What could be the blessings of fat accumulation in Eastern European Jews? At first this question sounds weird. After all, that fat accumulation was noticed only because of the curses it bestows: Tay-Sachs, Gaucher's, or Niemann-Pick disease. But many of our common genetic diseases may persist because they bring both blessings and curses (see my article "The Cruel Logic of Our Genes" in the November 1989 issue). They kill or impair individuals who inherit two copies of the faulty gene, but they help those who receive only one defective gene by protecting them against other diseases. The best understood example is the sickle-cell gene of African blacks, which often kills homozygotes but protects heterozygotes against malaria. Natural selection sustains such genes because more heterozygotes than normal individuals survive to pass on their genes, and those extra gene copies offset the copies lost through the deaths of homozygotes.

So let us refine our question and ask, What blessing could the Tay-Sachs gene bring to those individuals who are heterozygous for it? A clue first emerged back in 1972, with the publication of the results of a questionnaire that had asked U.S. Ashkenazic parents of Tay-Sachs children what their own Eastern European–born parents had died of. Keep in mind that since these unfortunate children had to be homozygotes, with two copies of the Tay-Sachs gene, all their parents had to be heterozygotes, with one copy, and half of the parents' parents also had to be heterozygotes.

As it turned out, most of those Tay-Sachs grandparents had died of the usual causes: heart disease, stroke, cancer, and diabetes. But, strikingly, only one of the 306 grandparents had died of tuberculosis, even though TB was generally one of the big killers in these grandparents' time. Indeed, among the general population of large Eastern European cities in the early twentieth century, TB caused up to 20 percent of all deaths.

This big discrepancy suggested that Tay-Sachs heterozygotes might somehow have been protected against TB. Interestingly, it was already well known that Ashkenazim in general had some such protection: even when Jews and non-Jews were compared within the same European city, class, and occupational group (for example, Warsaw garment workers), Jews had only half the TB death rate of non-Jews, despite their being equally susceptible to infection. Perhaps, one could reason, the Tay-Sachs gene furnished part of that well-established Jewish resistance.

A second clue to a heterozygote advantage conveyed by the Tay-Sachs gene emerged in 1983, with a fresh look at the data concerning the distributions of TB and the Tay-Sachs gene within Europe. The statistics showed that the Tay-Sachs gene was nearly three times more frequent among Jews originating from Austria, Hungary, and Czechoslovakia—areas where an amazing 9 or 10 percent of the population were heterozygotes—than among Jews from Poland, Russia, and Germany. At the same time records from an old Jewish TB sanatorium in Denver in 1904 showed that among patients born in Europe between 1860 and 1910, Jews from Austria and Hungary were overrepresented.

Initially, in putting together these two pieces of information, you might be tempted to conclude that because the highest frequency of the Tay-Sachs gene appeared in the same geographic region that produced the most cases of TB, the gene in fact offers no protection whatsoever. Indeed, this was precisely the mistaken conclusion of many researchers who had looked at these data before. But you have to pay careful attention to the numbers here: even at its highest frequency the Tay-Sachs gene was carried by far fewer people than would be infected by TB. What the statistics really indicate is that where TB is the biggest threat, natural selection produces the biggest response.

Think of it this way: You arrive at an island where you find that all the inhabitants of the north end wear suits of armor, while all the inhabitants of the south end wear only cloth shirts. You'd be pretty safe in assuming that warfare is more prevalent in the north—and that war-related injuries account for far more deaths there than in the south. Thus, if the Tay-Sachs gene does indeed lend heterozygotes some protection against TB, you would expect to find the gene most often precisely where you find TB most often. Similarly, the sickle-cell gene reaches its highest frequencies in those parts of Africa where malaria is the biggest risk.

◦◦◉◦◦

But you may believe there's still a hole in the argument: If Tay-Sachs heterozygotes are protected against TB, you may be asking, why is the gene common just in the Ashkenazim? Why did it not become common in the non-Jewish populations also exposed to TB in Austria, Hungary, and Czechoslovakia?

At this point we must recall the peculiar circumstances in which the Jews of Eastern Europe were forced to live. They were unique among the world's ethnic groups in having been virtually confined to towns for most of the past 2,000 years. Being forbidden to own land, Eastern European Jews were not peasant farmers living in the countryside, but businesspeople forced to live in crowded ghettos, in an environment where tuberculosis thrived.

Of course, until recent improvements in sanitation, these towns were not very healthy places for non-Jews either. Indeed, their populations couldn't sustain themselves: deaths exceeded births, and the number of dead had to be balanced by continued emigration from the countryside. For non-Jews, therefore, there was no genetically distinct urban population. For ghetto-bound Jews, however, there could be no emigration from the countryside; thus the Jewish population was under the strongest selection to evolve genetic resistance to TB.

Those are the conditions that probably led to Jewish TB resistance, whatever particular genetic factors prove to underlie it. I'd speculate that $G_{M2}$ and related fats accumulate at slightly higher-than-normal levels in heterozygotes, although not at the lethal levels seen in homozygotes. (The fat accumulation in heterozygotes probably takes place in the cell membrane, the cell's "armor.") I'd also speculate that the accumulation provides heterozygotes with some protection against TB, and that that's why the genes for Tay-Sachs, Gaucher's, and Niemann-Pick disease reached high frequencies in the Ashkenazim.

Having thus stated the case, let me make clear that I don't want to overstate it. The evidence is still speculative. Depending on how you do the calculation, the low frequency of TB deaths in Tay-Sachs grandparents either barely reaches or doesn't quite reach the level of proof that statisticians require to accept an effect as real rather than as one that's arisen by chance. Moreover, we have no idea of the biochemical mechanism by which fat accumulation might confer resistance against TB. For the moment, I'd say that the evidence points to some selective advantage of Tay-Sachs heterozygotes among the Ashkenazim, and that TB resistance is the only plausible hypothesis yet proposed.

For now Tay-Sachs remains a speculative model for the evolution of ethnic diseases. But it's already a proven model of what to do about them. Twenty years ago a test was developed to identify Tay-Sachs heterozygotes, based on their lower-than-normal levels of hexosaminidase A. The test is simple, cheap, and accurate: all I did was to donate a small sample of my blood, pay $35, and wait a few days to receive the results.

If that test shows that at least one member of a couple is not a Tay-Sachs heterozygote, then any child of theirs can't be a Tay-Sachs homozygote. If both parents prove to be heterozygotes, there's a one-in-four chance of their child being a homozygote; that can then be determined by other tests performed on the mother early in pregnancy. If the results are positive, it's early enough for her to abort, should she choose to. That critical bit of knowledge has enabled parents who had gone through the agony of bearing a Tay-Sachs baby and watching him die to find the courage to try again.

The Tay-Sachs screening program launched in the United States in 1971 was targeted at the high-risk population: Ashkenazic Jewish couples of child-bearing age. So successful has this approach been that the number of Tay-Sachs babies born each year in this country has declined tenfold. Today, in fact, more Tay-Sachs cases appear here in non-Jews than in Jews, because only the latter couples are routinely tested. Thus, what used to be the classic genetic disease of Jews is so no longer.

There's also a broader message to the Tay-Sachs story. We commonly refer to the United States as a melting pot, and in many ways that metaphor is apt. But in other ways we're not a melting pot, and we won't be for a long time. Each ethnic group has some characteristic genes of its own, a legacy of its distinct history. Tuberculosis and malaria are not major causes of death in the United States, but the genes that some of us evolved to protect ourselves against them are still frequent. Those genes are frequent only in certain ethnic groups, though, and they'll be slow to melt through the population.

With modern advances in molecular genetics, we can expect to see more, not less, ethnically targeted practice of medicine. Genetic screening for cystic fibrosis in European whites, for example, is one program that has been much discussed recently; when it comes, it will surely be based on the Tay-Sachs experience. Of course, what that may mean someday is more anxiety-ridden parents-to-be glowering at more dedicated genetics counselors. It will also mean fewer babies doomed to the agonies of diseases we may understand but that we'll never be able to accept.

# NO ↵

Josie Glausiusz

# Unfortunate Drift

Ashkenazi Jews—those of Central and Eastern European origin, which includes most American Jews—are prey to a unique set of genetic diseases. The best known is Tay-Sachs, which kills in early infancy, but there are at least nine other inherited disorders that are especially prevalent among Ashkenazim. Why? The pattern of inheritance offers a clue: most of the diseases are caused by recessive genes, meaning that symptoms appear only if two copies of the mutant gene are inherited, one from each parent. One copy does no harm, and might even do some good—which would cause natural selection to spread the mutation through a human population instead of weeding it out. Many researchers believe the Ashkenazi burden has this sort of flip side; they argue, for instance, that the Tay-Sachs gene protects its carriers against tuberculosis, a disease that was endemic in the crowded ghettos of Eastern Europe.

But there has always been an alternative theory, says Stanford population geneticist Neil Risch: mutant genes may have become concentrated in the Ashkenazi population purely by chance or historical accident. Now Risch and his colleagues have found evidence that such "genetic drift" does indeed underlie the high incidence among Ashkenazim of idiopathic torsion dystonia (ITD), a disease that causes involuntary muscle contractions. The researchers think drift may explain or help explain the other Ashkenazi diseases as well. The mutant genes may have achieved their high frequency, says Risch, not so much because they confer a selective advantage but because they happened to arise among a relatively small number of Jews who produced a large number of descendants.

ITD, however, is a special case—as Risch and his colleagues discovered when they started analyzing its pattern of inheritance in their study group of 59 Ashkenazi families in the United States. Unlike all the other Ashkenazi diseases, they found, ITD isn't recessive—it's dominant, meaning that a single copy of the gene is enough to transmit the disease. For reasons unknown, though, it usually doesn't. Between one in 1,000 and one in 3,000 Ashkenazim carry the ITD gene, Risch estimates, but only 30 percent of them show symptoms—muscles that cramp and twist a part of the body into contorted positions—and only 10 percent have incapacitating ones. The low incidence of disease allows the gene to survive in the population; most of its carriers can still have children.

On the other hand, the gene doesn't seem to confer any type of advantage that would explain why it became so common among Ashkenazi Jews.

Another clue that genetic drift rather than natural selection might explain the spread of ITD is the history of the Ashkenazim. *Ashkenazi* is a Hebrew term for "German." Beginning in the fourteenth century, a wave of German Jews fleeing east to escape persecution established new homes in Eastern Europe. The immigrant Jews generally didn't marry members of the surrounding communities, and although historical evidence from the period is sketchy, there is some evidence that their initial population was small. If so, it was an ideal candidate for a type of genetic drift known as the founder effect: when a small group of immigrants founds a new population, isolated from others, whatever mutations the founders happen to have, good or bad, will necessarily be more concentrated in that new, smaller population than they were in the old, larger one the founders came from.

That's just what happened with ITD, says Risch. He and his colleagues have found that a single genetic mutation is responsible for most cases of the disease, and they have traced it to its source. They did so by showing that 90 percent of the families in their study had an identical pattern of genetic markers—recognizable bits of noncoding DNA—flanking the ITD gene on chromosome 9. Since chromosomes swap pieces of DNA each time a sex cell is formed by meiosis, marker patterns tend to get scrambled over time. That 90 percent of the families still had identical markers showed they had all inherited the same mutation—and also that the mutation had arisen in a single individual fairly recently.

Knowing the rate at which chromosomes swap DNA, Risch could estimate when the original ITD mutation occurred: around 1650, plus or minus a century or two—but probably after the Ashkenazi Jews migrated to Eastern Europe. When Risch started asking the people in his study about their grandparents and great-grandparents, he found that more than two-thirds of the oldest ITD carriers who could be traced hailed from Lithuania and Belorussia. The most likely scenario, Risch concludes, is that the progenitor of the ITD mutation lived in one of those two places some 350 years ago. That person's descendants spread the mutation to other parts of what came to be known as the Jewish Pale of Settlement—a region that included Poland, the Ukraine, and parts of Russia. (From the late eighteenth century on, Jews living under the Russian czar were confined to the Pale.) In the late nineteenth century, Jews fleeing pogroms in Eastern Europe carried the mutation to other parts of the world, including the United States.

By 1900 there were 5 million Jews living in the Pale of Settlement; in spite of repeated persecutions, the population had grown explosively since at least 1765, when the earliest reliable census put it at 560,000. Extrapolating that growth rate backward in time, Risch estimates that in the mid-seventeenth century, when the ITD mutation most likely appeared, the Ashkenazi population in the Pale was around 100,000. The mutation's initial frequency, then, would have been around one in 100,000. How could the frequency have risen to at least one in 3,000 among today's Ashkenazim?

The answer, Risch thinks, is a second type of genetic drift. In the seventeenth century and later, he says, not all Ashkenazi Jews left equal numbers of children. Family genealogies suggest that the more affluent classes—business and community leaders as well as scholars and rabbis, who were considered desirable marriage partners—had between four and nine children who reached adulthood. In contrast, poorer Jewish families, who were more subject to overcrowding and thus more at risk from epidemics, left fewer surviving descendants. Risch thinks the original ITD mutation just happened to arise in an affluent family, and that it spread rapidly because the affluent Jews tended to marry one another and to have many children. ITD is so common among the Ashkenazim today, he argues, because most of the world's 11 million Ashkenazim are descended from just a few thousand people who lived in the Pale of Settlement in the seventeenth century.

•◦⟨◉⟩◦•

What about the other Ashkenazi diseases? They are all recessive, which means natural selection could more easily have influenced their frequency. Typically only 1 percent or so of the carriers of a rare recessive mutation get sick (because they have two copies of the mutated gene), compared with 30 percent of the carriers of ITD. As a result, even a small selective advantage might be enough to spread a recessive mutation through the population. Risch points out that natural selection and genetic drift could have worked together to spread the Ashkenazi diseases; the two are not mutually exclusive. But he also thinks further studies will show that most or all of the diseases are, like ITD, of recent origin—too recent for the slow grind of evolution to be the main reason they have achieved such high frequency.

There is another population, Risch points out, whose history makes for an instructive comparison with the Ashkenazim. "The French Canadians have Tay-Sachs also—a different mutation, but almost at the same frequency as the Ashkenazim," he says. "I've never heard anybody arguing that Tay-Sachs gives them an advantage against tuberculosis in crowded ghettos! In fact, the French Canadians are well known for having their own, unique genetic diseases. Their demography is remarkably similar to that of the Ashkenazi Jews—there are currently about 5 million French Canadians who are descended from a relatively small founder population, in the thousands or tens of thousands, dating to 300 or 400 years ago.

"And in Eastern Europe, tuberculosis was quite common in non-Jews also, and you don't see them with these genetic diseases. But our study confirms that the conditions for the operation of genetic drift existed there. You would expect it to apply not just to the ITD gene but to others also." If Risch turns out to be right, the diseases that plague the Ashkenazim will no longer be seen as an example of the cruel beauty of evolution. They'll just be an example of bad luck.

# POSTSCRIPT

## Is Culture Responsible for the Spread of Ethnically Related Disease?

The four forces of evolution—natural selection, mutation, gene flow, and genetic drift—all impact populations in different ways. However, in particular situations, one evolutionary force may exert a greater effect than the others in determining a population's genetics. Glausiusz suggests that in the case of the Tay Sachs gene, the most important force is genetic drift. She argues persuasively that eastern European Jews are victims of the *founder effect*. When a small, founding population is effectively cut off and isolated from others, whatever mutations the founders happen to have tend to become more concentrated in the new population. Thus, eastern European Jews have a high incidence of Tay Sachs gene due to pure chance and not because of any selection for the gene. Glausiusz argues that French Canadians also have a high incidence of the Tay Sachs gene, but no one is blaming it on tuberculosis or crowded ghetto conditions. In fact, she notes that tuberculosis was quite common among non-Jews in Europe. So if the Tay Sachs gene was being selected for, it should have increased over time in many other populations in the same region.

Diamond, on the other hand, suggests that prejudice and persecution kept eastern European Jews confined to ghetto-like conditions for a long time period in ways that non-Jewish populations did not experience. He argues that they were unique in being confined to towns for 2,000 years and did not experience as many opportunities for gene flow as less-restricted populations. As a result, the Jewish population was under the strongest selection pressure to evolve genetic resistance of tuberculosis.

Both authors' arguments may have merit. However, the high incidence of the Tay Sachs gene in eastern European Jews may be caused by a combination of both the founder effect and specific socioeconomic factors targeting Jews. Other studies of ethnically related disease suggest that both forces may be at work at once. For example, research shows that hypertension among African Americans is partially due to the founder effect. Their ancestors came from a relatively small population that was brought to America via the slave trade. However, natural and cultural selection may have also played a part in determining their genetic structure. Most of the individuals captured as slaves came from regions with low-salt diets, selecting for super-efficient kidneys that retained salt. The conditions of slavery only intensified this selection. Individuals who could retain salt efficiently were less susceptible to heat stroke, diarrhea, and other debilitating conditions. Consequently, people who had the best kidneys were more likely to survive capture, transport in the holds of ships across the ocean, and finally the harshness of plantation life (Diamond, 1991). Their descendants are thus more susceptible to hypertension related to salt retention. A trait that was once a benefit to African Americans has now become a problem.

For further information on population genetics, see J. F. Crow, *Basic Concepts in Population, Quantitative, and Evolutionary Genetics* (W. H. Freeman, 1986), P. Hedrick, *Genetics of Populations* (Science Books International, 1983), M. Smith, *Evolutionary Genetics* (Oxford University Press, 1989). See also C. Scriver, "Human Genetics: Lessons from Quebec Populations," *Annual Review of Genomics and Human Genetics* (vol. 2, pp. 69–101, 2001), E. Heyer, "One Founder/One Gene Hypothesis in a New Expanding Populations: Saguenay (Quebec, Canada)," *Human Biology* (vol. 71, pp. 99–109, 1999), R. Kelley, D. Robinson, E. Puffenberger, et. al., "Amish Lethal Microcephaly," *American Journal of Medical Genetics* (vol. 112, no. 4, pp. 318–326, 2002), and M. Rosenberg, R. Argawala, G. Bouffard, et. al., "Mutant Deoxynucleotide Carrier Is Associated with Congenital Microcephaly," *Nature Genetics*, (vol. 32, no. 1, pp. 175–179, 2002) for additional articles on the effects of genetic drift and the founder effect on human populations.

# ISSUE 4

# Should the Concept of "Intelligent Design" Replace Darwin's Theory of Evolution?

**YES: William A. Dembski,** from *The Design Inference: Eliminating Chance Through Small Probabilities* (Cambridge University Press, 1998)

**NO: John Rennie,** from "15 Answers to Creationist Nonsense," *Scientific American* (July 2002)

## ISSUE SUMMARY

William Dembski argues that the theory of "intelligent design" provides a more accurate picture of the world than traditional evolutionary theory. John Rennie contends that intelligent design is really creationism in disguise and should not be taken seriously by scientists.

There is an Indian story—at least I heard it as an Indian story—about an Englishman who, having been told that the world rested on a platform which rested on the back of an elephant which rested in turn on the back of a turtle, asked (perhaps he was an ethnographer; it is the way they behave), what did the turtle rest on? Another turtle. And that turtle? "Ah Sahib, after that it is turtles all the way down" (Geertz, 1973:23–29).

This quote is more than an amusing antidote. It also depicts the age-old tension between religion and science. While a religious mind can take comfort from the explanation that "it is turtles all the way down," a scientific mind cannot. Science, like the poor Englishman, wants to get to the bottom of things. It is not simply enough to know that it is turtles all the way down. Science wants to know the turtle's size, breed, and number as well as to analyze their shell strength and other characteristics or habits. Most of all, science wants to know where it is that the turtles stop; the logical assumption being that they must stop somewhere. To a religious mind, however, where the turtles stop, or indeed if they stop at all, is not a problem. The underlying shape of reality can be felt and experienced, but it does not have to be proven. Therefore, personal and social meaning is found in being part of the world rather than in understanding your place in the world.

Whether we approach the issue from the perspective of religion or science, however, there is no doubt that many of us feel a driving need to understand who we are, where we come from, and what our relationship is with the rest of the world. All human societies everywhere are concerned with these questions and usually construct a cosmology in order to explain the origin of the universe and humans place within it. These origin stories vary widely from culture to culture and usually reflect different underlying presuppositions or assumptions about the way the world works and why people are the way they are.

In western Europe, the first origin stories arose out of the Judo-Christian tradition. According to the account in *Genesis*, God created the earth and all its inhabitants—including the original people—in a six-day period. Furthermore, humans were created in God's own image and given dominion over plants and animals. In addition to the commandment to be fruitful and multiply, the Biblical origin story also suggested that humans, plants, and animals had been created whole and perfect and did not change over time. These ideas exerted a strong influence on the development of social and scientific thought in post-Renaissance Europe. The Bible was thus seen as both the literal word of God and also as a reference point for scientific inquiry and investigation.

For example, Archbishop James Ussher used to the Bible to calculate the age of the earth in 1650. Going back through all the begats in the Bible, Ussher calculated that the year of creation was 4004 B.C., or about 6,000 years before. This date was accepted by clergyman and scientists alike. Even as new scientific discoveries began to suggest a greater antiquity for the earth and a more naturalistic explanation for events in the world, many scholars attempted to fit the new evidence into the new framework whenever possible so that the central concept of divine creation could remain valid.

A good example of this approach is found in the work of Georges Cuvier (1769–1832). A French paleontologist, Cuvier was well known for his discoveries of ancient species near Paris. Based on his excavations and reconstructions, Cuvier was able to show that at least 90 of the species he recovered were no longer living. This research provided proof for the extinction of animal species in the past. Although this finding conflicted with the Biblical origin story, supporters of Cuvier's theory (dubbed *catastrophism*) were quick to find a way around such a difficulty. Extinct plants and animals could be explained away as victims of God's past creations and destructions that occurred prior to Biblical times. Fossils could be accounted for without having to reject the idea of divine creation.

Although more sophisticated than Cuvier, proponents of intelligent design are still intent on marrying old ideas to new facts. They suggest that the complexity of the way the world works is so intricate and all encompassing that it must have been designed by a creative intelligence. This viewpoint is embraced by Dembski in his book *The Design Inference*. John Rennie's article adopts a more standard scientific perspective that evolution can and does account for complexity in the natural world without reference to a divine creator.

William A. Dembski

 **YES**

# The Design Inference: Eliminating Chance Through Small Probabilities

## Case Study: The Creation–Evolution Controversy

Design inferences occur widely in the creation–evolution controversy. Arguments by evolutionists that support biological evolution and arguments by creationists that oppose biological evolution frequently and self-consciously employ the logic of the design inference. To see this, let us consider two such arguments, one an antievolutionary argument by creationists Clifford Wilson and John Weldon, the other a proevolutionary argument by the Darwinist Richard Dawkins. First consider the antievolutionary argument by Wilson and Weldon:

> In the October, 1969, issue of *Nature* magazine, Dr. Frank Salisbury ... examined the chance of one of the most basic chemical reactions for the continuation of life taking place. This reaction involved the formation of a specific DNA molecule.... He calculated the chance of this molecule evolving on $10^{20}$ hospitable planets.... He concluded that the chances of just this one tiny DNA molecule coming into existence over four billion years ... as *one chance* in $10^{415}$.... This shows that life simply could not originate in outer space, period.
>
> [Yet] Dr. George Wald, Nobel Prize-winning biologist of Harvard University, stated several years ago: "One only has to contemplate the magnitude of [the] task to concede that spontaneous generation of a living organism is impossible. Yet here we are—as a result I believe, of spontaneous generation."
>
> [This type of reasoning] shows how far even brilliant men will go to escape the idea of God being their Creator....

Next consider the following proevolutionary argument by Richard Dawkins:

> [One in $10^{190}$] is the chance against happening to hit upon haemoglobin by luck.... It is amazing that you can still read calculations like my haemoglobin calculation, used as though they constituted arguments *against*

From *The Design Inference: Eliminating Chance Through Small Probabilities*, 1998, pp. 55–62. Copyright © 1998 by Cambridge University Press. Reprinted by permission. References and notes omitted.

Darwin's theory. The people who do this, often expert in their own field, astronomy or whatever it may be, seem sincerely to believe that Darwinism explains living organization in terms of chance—"single-step selection"— alone. This belief, that Darwinian evolution is "random," is not merely false. It is the exact opposite of the truth. Chance is a minor ingredient in the Darwinian recipe, but the most important ingredient is cumulative selection which is quintessentially *non*random.

There is a big difference, then, between cumulative selection (in which each improvement, however slight, is used as a basis for future building), and single-step selection (in which each new "try" is a fresh one). If evolutionary progress had to rely on single-step selection, it would never have got anywhere. If, however, there was any way in which the necessary conditions for *cumulative* selection could have been set up by the blind forces of nature, strange and wonderful might have been the consequences. As a matter of fact that is exactly what happened on this planet.

Both the argument by Wilson and Weldon, and the argument by Dawkins can be unpacked as design inferences—for Wilson and Weldon as a successful design inference, for Dawkins as a failed design inference. A design inference attempts to establish whether an event is due to design. If we now take the event in question to be the occurrence of life on planet Earth, and denote this event by LIFE, then the design inference assumes the following form . . . :

Premise 1:    LIFE has occurred.

Premise 2:    LIFE is specified.

Premise 3:    If LIFE is due to chance, then LIFE has small probability.

Premise 4:    Specified events of small probability do not occur by chance.

Premise 5:    LIFE is not due to a regularity.

Premise 6:    LIFE is due to regularity, chance, or design.

Conclusion: LIFE is due to design.

Since Wilson and Weldon, as well as Dawkins are attempting to explain LIFE, let us consider how their respective arguments conform to this pattern of inference. First Dawkins. Dawkins resolutely refuses to countenance design as a proper mode of explanation for LIFE. Dawkins thus rejects the conclusion of the design inference. But since the design inference constitutes a valid logical argument, for Dawkins to reject the conclusion he must reject at least one of the premises. But which one?

Let us run through the premises individually. Is Premise 1 a problem for Dawkins? Obviously not. LIFE has clearly occurred. What about Premise 2? Is LIFE specified? Dawkins is quite definite about affirming this premise: "Complicated things have some quality, specifiable in advance, that is highly unlikely to have been acquired by random chance alone. In the case of living things, the quality that is specified in advance is . . . the ability to propagate genes in reproduction." So Premise 2 isn't a problem for Dawkins either. Indeed, no evolutionist or creationist I know denies that LIFE is specified.

Consider next Premise 4, the Law of Small Probability. Here too Dawkins finds nothing objectionable. Consider, for instance, the following remark:

> We can accept a certain amount of luck in our explanations, but not too much. . . . In our theory of how we came to exist, we are allowed to postulate a certain ration of luck. This ration has, as its upper limit, the number of eligible planets in the universe. . . . We [therefore] have at our disposal, if we want to use it, odds of 1 in 100 billion billion as an upper limit (or 1 in however many available planets we think there are) to spend in our theory of the origin of life. This is the maximum amount of luck we are allowed to postulate in our theory. Suppose we want to suggest, for instance, that life began when both DNA and its protein-based replication machinery spontaneously chanced to come into existence. We can allow ourselves the luxury of such an extravagant theory, provided that the odds against this coincidence occurring on a planet do not exceed 100 billion billion to one.

Dawkins is restating the Law of Small Probability. LIFE is a specified event whose probability better not get too small. Thus, Premise 4 is not a problem for Dawkins either.

What about trichotomy, that LIFE is properly explained either by regularity, chance, or design? Here the very title of Dawkins's book—*The Blind Watchmaker*—makes clear that Premise 6 is not a problem either. Dawkins's title alludes to William Paley's famous watchmaker argument. For Dawkins, however, the watchmaker is blind, implying that the watchmaker is conditioned solely by regularity and chance. Along with most evolutionists, Dawkins holds that regularity and chance together are adequate to explain LIFE. Dawkins therefore holds to trichotomy, albeit a truncated trichotomy in which one of the disjuncts (i.e., design) is vacuous.

That leaves Premises 3 and 5. Dawkins appears to accept Premise 5—that LIFE is not due to a regularity. All the same, because Dawkins never assigns an exact probability to LIFE, he never settles whether LIFE is a high probability event and thus could legitimately be attributed to a regularity. Dawkins seems mainly interested in showing that the occurrence of life on earth is probable enough, not in determining whether this probability is so close to unity to justify calling it a high probability event. Moreover, given the importance Dawkins attaches to probabilities, it appears that chance and contingency are essential to his understanding of LIFE. Thus, we have reason to think Dawkins accepts Premise 5.

This leaves Premise 3. Dawkins rejects Premise 3. Dawkins's appeal to cumulative selection makes this clear. According to Dawkins, "Chance is a minor ingredient in the Darwinian recipe, but the most important ingredient is cumulative selection which is quintessentially *nonrandom*." The difference between cumulative selection and what Dawkins calls single-step selection can be illustrated with a coin tossing example. Suppose you want to know whether by tossing a hundred pennies you can ever expect to observe a hundred heads simultaneously. In the single-step selection scenario you put the pennies in a box, shake the box, and see if all the pennies simultaneously exhibit heads. If not, you keep repeating the process until all the pennies simultaneously exhibit heads. In the cumulative selection scenario, on the

single step →

cumulative:

other hand, you shake the box as before, but every time you look inside the box, you remove the pennies that exhibit heads. You stop when all the pennies have been removed and are exhibiting heads. . . .

Now it's clear that with the single-step selection scenario you will never observe all the pennies exhibiting heads—the odds are too much against it. On the other hand, it's equally clear that with the cumulative selection scenario you'll see all the pennies exhibiting heads very quickly. Dawkins's point, then, is that the natural processes responsible for LIFE act by cumulative selection, and therefore render LIFE reasonably probable. This he regards as the genius of Darwin, finding a naturalistic means for rendering probable what naively we take to be highly improbable. Dawkins therefore rejects Premise 3. Moreover, having rejected one of the premises in the design inference, Dawkins is under no obligation to draw the conclusion of the design inference, to wit, that the proper mode of explanation for LIFE is design. Indeed, Dawkins explicitly rejects this conclusion.

Where do Wilson and Weldon come down on the six premises of the design inference? Like Dawkins, Wilson and Weldon hold to Premises 1, 2, 4, and 6. Premises 1 and 6, though not explicitly stated, are clearly presupposed in their argument. Premises 2 and 4, on the other hand, are also presupposed, but imperfectly expressed since Wilson and Weldon do not have a well-developed notion of specification. Their version of the Law of Small Probability is Borel's Single Law of Chance: "Emile Borel . . . formulated a basic law of probability. It states that the occurrence of any event where the chances are beyond one in $10^{50}$ . . . is an event which we can state with certainty will *never* happen—no matter how much time is allotted, no matter how many conceivable opportunities could exist for the event to take place."

Wilson and Weldon are here employing a pretheoretic version of the Law of Small Probability, and one that omits specification. But since small probabilities have to combine with specifications to eliminate chance (exceedingly improbable unspecified events, after all, happen by chance all the time—see Chapter 1 and Section 2.1), a cleaned-up version of their argument would substitute Premises 2 and 4 for their pretheoretic version of the Law of Small Probability. Hence, as with Dawkins, we may regard Wilson and Weldon as affirming Premises 1, 2, 4, and 6.

But while Dawkins is not entirely clear about where he stands on Premise 5 and is perfectly clear about rejecting Premise 3, Wilson and Weldon accept both these premises. From the vast improbability of a certain DNA molecule, Wilson and Weldon infer that LIFE is vastly more improbable still, and thus conclude that it is impossible for LIFE to originate anywhere in the universe by chance. For them LIFE is therefore neither the product of a regularity of nature nor an event with anything other than a very small probability. Besides Premises 1, 2, 4, and 6, Wilson and Weldon therefore accept Premises 3 and 5 as well. And having accepted the six premises of the design inference, by force of logic they conclude that the proper mode of explanation for LIFE is design. Note, however, that their identification of design with the activity of an intelligent agent—much less the God of Scripture—does not follow by the force of this logic.

These two arguments, the one by Wilson and Weldon, and the other by Dawkins, provide an object lesson for how design inferences arise in the creation–evolution controversy. The design inference constitutes a valid logical argument. Moreover, creationists and evolutionists alike tend not to controvert Premises 1, 2, 4, and 6. Thus, when creationists and evolutionists dispute the conclusion of the design inference, the dispute is over Premises 3 and 5: *If LIFE is due to chance, how improbable was it?* and *Is LIFE due to a regularity?* If Premises 3 and 5 both hold, then the conclusion of the design inference follows. If there is reason to doubt either of these premises, then the conclusion is blocked.

One thing, however, is clear. Creationists and evolutionists alike feel the force of the design inference. At some level they are all responding to it. This is true even of those who, unlike Dawkins, think LIFE is extremely unlikely to occur by chance in the known physical universe, but who nevertheless agree with Dawkins that LIFE is properly explained without reference to design. For instance, advocates of the Anthropic Principle like Barrow and Tipler posit an ensemble of universes so that LIFE, though highly improbable in our own little universe, is nevertheless virtually certain to have arisen at least once in the many, many universes that constitute the ensemble of which our universe is a member.

On this view LIFE is the winning of a grand lottery in which our universe happens to be the lucky ticket holder: The fact that our universe was lucky enough to beget LIFE is perhaps surprising, but no reason to look for explanations other than chance—much as a lottery winner, though no doubt surprised at winning, need not look for explanations other than chance since somebody (some universe) had to win. Our sense of surprise is due to a selection effect— that we should be so lucky. The relevant probability, however, is not the vast improbability that anyone in particular should win, but the extremely high probability that some (unspecified) lottery player would be sure to win. It's the high probability that someone will be selected that transforms what started as a seeming impossibility into a virtual certainty. Thus, whereas Dawkins rejects Premise 3 and offers the standard Darwinian mechanism as grounds for his rejection, Barrow and Tipler reject Premise 5, positing an ensemble of universes so that LIFE is sure to arise somewhere in this ensemble.

Positing an ensemble of universes isn't the only way to undercut Premise 5. Some theorists think our own little universe is quite enough to render LIFE not only probable, but virtually certain. Stuart Kauffman, for instance, identifies LIFE with "the emergence of self-reproducing systems of catalytic polymers, either peptides, RNA, or others." Adopting this approach, Kauffman develops a mathematical model in which "autocatalytic polymer sets . . . are expected to form spontaneously." Kauffman attempts to lay the foundation for a theory of life's origin in which LIFE is not a lucky accident, but an event that is fully to be expected: "I believe [life] to be an expected, emergent, collective property of complex systems of polymer catalysts. Life, I suggest, 'crystallizes' in a phase transition leading to connected sequences of biochemical transformations by which polymers and simpler building blocks mutually catalyze their collective reproduction." Kauffman is not alone in explaining LIFE as a regularity of nature. Prigogine and Stengers, Wicken, Brooks and Wiley, and de Duve all share this same commitment.

To sum up, whereas creationists accept all six premises of the design inference, evolutionary biologists, to block the conclusion of the design inference, block Premises 3 and 5. Thus Darwin, to block Premises 3 and 5, had to give himself more time for variation and selection to take effect than many of his contemporaries were willing to grant (even though Lord Kelvin, the leading physicist in Darwin's day, estimated the age of the earth at 100 million years, Darwin regarded this age as too low for his theory). Thus Dawkins, to block Premises 3 and 5, and sustain his case for the blind watchmaker, not only gives himself all the time Darwin ever wanted, but also helps himself to all the conceivable planets that might exist in the known physical universe. Thus Barrow and Tipler, to block Premises 3 and 5, and give credence to their various anthropic principles, not only give themselves all the time and planets that Dawkins ever wanted, but also help themselves to a generous serving of universes (universes that are by definition causally inaccessible to us). Thus Kauffman, to block Premises 3 and 5, and explain LIFE entirely in terms of natural processes operating on the earth (and hence without recourse to an ensemble of universes), invokes laws of self-organization whereby LIFE might arise spontaneously. From the perspective of the design inference, all these moves are moves against Premises 3 and 5, and therefore moves to block the conclusion of the design inference. . . .

doesn't really do anything b/c of course Dawkins doesn't agree w/ the 6 prospects for Design. He is Evolutionary!

John Rennie                                    ◄┘ **NO**

# 15 Answers to Creationist Nonsense

**W**hen Charles Darwin introduced the theory of evolution through natural selection 143 years ago, the scientists of the day argued over it fiercely, but the massing evidence from paleontology, genetics, zoology, molecular biology and other fields gradually established evolution's truth beyond reasonable doubt. Today that battle has been won everywhere—except in the public imagination.

Embarrassingly, in the 21st century, in the most scientifically advanced nation the world has ever known, creationists can still persuade politicians, judges and ordinary citizens that evolution is a flawed, poorly supported fantasy. They lobby for creationist ideas such as "intelligent design" to be taught as alternatives to evolution in science classrooms. As this article goes to press, the Ohio Board of Education is debating whether to mandate such a change. Some antievolutionists, such as Philip E. Johnson, a law professor at the University of California at Berkeley and author of *Darwin on Trial*, admit that they intend for intelligent-design theory to serve as a "wedge" for reopening science classrooms to discussions of God.

Besieged teachers and others may increasingly find themselves on the spot to defend evolution and refute creationism. The arguments that creationists use are typically specious and based on misunderstandings of (or outright lies about) evolution, but the number and diversity of the objections can put even well-informed people at a disadvantage.

To help with answering them, the following list rebuts some of the most common "scientific" arguments raised against evolution. It also directs readers to further sources for information and explains why creation science has no place in the classroom.

*1. Evolution is only a theory. It is not a fact or a scientific law.*

Many people learned in elementary school that a theory falls in the middle of a hierarchy of certainty—above a mere hypothesis but below a law. Scientists do not use the terms that way, however. According to the National Academy of Sciences (NAS), a scientific theory is "a well-substantiated explanation of some aspect of the natural world that can incorporate facts, laws, inferences, and tested hypotheses." No amount of validation changes a theory into a law, which is a descriptive generalization about nature. So when scientists talk about the theory of evolution—or the atomic theory or the theory of relativity, for that matter—they are not expressing reservations about its truth.

In addition to the *theory* of evolution, meaning the idea of descent with modification, one may also speak of the *fact* of evolution. The NAS defines a fact as "an observation that has been repeatedly confirmed and for all practical purposes is accepted as 'true.'" The fossil record and abundant other evidence testify that organisms have evolved through time. Although no one observed those transformations, the indirect evidence is clear, unambiguous and compelling.

All sciences frequently rely on indirect evidence. Physicists cannot see sub-atomic particles directly, for instance, so they verify their existence by watching for tell-tale tracks that the particles leave in cloud chambers. The absence of direct observation does not make physicists' conclusions less certain.

> 2. *Natural selection is based on circular reasoning: the fittest are those who survive, and those who survive are deemed fittest.*

"Survival of the fittest" is a conversational way to describe natural selection, but a more technical description speaks of differential rates of survival and reproduction. That is, rather than labeling species as more or less fit, one can describe how many offspring they are likely to leave under given circum-stances. Drop a fast-breeding pair of small-beaked finches and a slower-breeding pair of large-beaked finches onto an island full of food seeds. Within a few generations the fast breeders may control more of the food resources. Yet if large beaks more easily crush seeds, the advantage may tip to the slow breed-ers. In a pioneering study of finches on the Galápagos Islands, Peter R. Grant of Princeton University observed these kinds of population shifts in the wild [see his article "Natural Selection and Darwin's Finches"; SCIENTIFIC AMERICAN, October 1991].

The key is that adaptive fitness can be defined without reference to sur-vival: large beaks are better adapted for crushing seeds, irrespective of whether that trait has survival value under the circumstances.

> 3. *Evolution is unscientific, because it is not testable or falsifiable. It makes claims about events that were not observed and can never be re-created.*

This blanket dismissal of evolution ignores important distinctions that divide the field into at least two broad areas: microevolution and macroevolution. Microevolution looks at changes within species over time—changes that may be preludes to speciation, the origin of new species. Macroevolution studies how taxonomic groups above the level of species change. Its evidence draws fre-quently from the fossil record and DNA comparisons to reconstruct how various organisms may be related.

These days even most creationists acknowledge that microevolution has been upheld by tests in the laboratory (as in studies of cells, plants and fruit flies) and in the field (as in Grant's studies of evolving beak shapes among Galápagos finches). Natural selection and other mechanisms—such as chromosomal changes, symbiosis and hybridization—can drive profound changes in populations over time.

The historical nature of macroevolutionary study involves inference from fossils and DNA rather than direct observation. Yet in the historical sciences (which include astronomy, geology and archaeology, as well as evolutionary biology), hypotheses can still be tested by checking whether they accord with physical evidence and whether they lead to verifiable predictions about future discoveries. For instance, evolution implies that between the earliest-known ancestors of humans (roughly five million years old) and the appearance of anatomically modern humans (about 100,000 years ago), one should find a succession of hominid creatures with features progressively less apelike and more modern, which is indeed what the fossil record shows. But one should not—and does not—find modern human fossils embedded in strata from the Jurassic period (65 million years ago). Evolutionary biology routinely makes predictions far more refined and precise than this, and researchers test them constantly.

Evolution could be disproved in other ways, too. If we could document the spontaneous generation of just one complex life-form from inanimate matter, then at least a few creatures seen in the fossil record might have originated this way. If superintelligent aliens appeared and claimed credit for creating life on earth (or even particular species), the purely evolutionary explanation would be cast in doubt. But no one has yet produced such evidence.

It should be noted that the idea of falsifiability as the defining characteristic of science originated with philosopher Karl Popper in the 1930s. More recent elaborations on his thinking have expanded the narrowest interpretation of his principle precisely because it would eliminate too many branches of clearly scientific endeavor.

*4. Increasingly, scientists doubt the truth of evolution.*

No evidence suggests that evolution is losing adherents. Pick up any issue of a peer-reviewed biological journal, and you will find articles that support and extend evolutionary studies or that embrace evolution as a fundamental concept.

Conversely, serious scientific publications disputing evolution are all but nonexistent. In the mid-1990s George W. Gilchrist of the University of Washington surveyed thousands of journals in the primary literature, seeking articles on intelligent design or creation science. Among those hundreds of thousands of scientific reports, he found none. In the past two years, surveys done independently by Barbara Forrest of Southeastern Louisiana University and Lawrence M. Krauss of Case Western Reserve University have been similarly fruitless.

Creationists retort that a closed-minded scientific community rejects their evidence. Yet according to the editors of *Nature, Science* and other leading journals, few antievolution manuscripts are even submitted. Some antievolution authors have published papers in serious journals. Those papers, however, rarely attack evolution directly or advance creationist arguments; at best, they identify certain evolutionary problems as unsolved and difficult (which no one disputes). In short, creationists are not giving the scientific world good reason to take them seriously.

*5. The disagreements among even evolutionary biologists show how little solid science supports evolution.*

Evolutionary biologists passionately debate diverse topics: how speciation happens, the rates of evolutionary change, the ancestral relationships of birds and dinosaurs, whether Neandertals were a species apart from modern humans, and much more. These disputes are like those found in all other branches of science. Acceptance of evolution as a factual occurrence and a guiding principle is nonetheless universal in biology.

Unfortunately, dishonest creationists have shown a willingness to take scientists' comments out of context to exaggerate and distort the disagreements. Anyone acquainted with the works of paleontologist Stephen Jay Gould of Harvard University knows that in addition to co-authoring the punctuated-equilibrium model, Gould was one of the most eloquent defenders and articulators of evolution. (Punctuated equilibrium explains patterns in the fossil record by suggesting that most evolutionary changes occur within geologically brief intervals—which may nonetheless amount to hundreds of generations.) Yet creationists delight in dissecting out phrases from Gould's voluminous prose to make him sound as though he had doubted evolution, and they present punctuated equilibrium as though it allows new species to materialize overnight or birds to be born from reptile eggs.

When confronted with a quotation from a scientific authority that seems to question evolution, insist on seeing the statement in context. Almost invariably, the attack on evolution will prove illusory.

*6. If humans descended from monkeys, why are there still monkeys?*

This surprisingly common argument reflects several levels of ignorance about evolution. The first mistake is that evolution does not teach that humans descended from monkeys; it states that both have a common ancestor.

The deeper error is that this objection is tantamount to asking, "If children descended from adults, why are there still adults?" New species evolve by splintering off from established ones, when populations of organisms become isolated from the main branch of their family and acquire sufficient differences to remain forever distinct. The parent species may survive indefinitely thereafter, or it may become extinct.

*7. Evolution cannot explain how life first appeared on earth.*

The origin of life remains very much a mystery, but biochemists have learned about how primitive nucleic acids, amino acids and other building blocks of life could have formed and organized themselves into self-replicating, self-sustaining units, laying the foundation for cellular biochemistry. Astrochemical analyses hint that quantities of these compounds might have originated in space and fallen to earth in comets, a scenario that may solve the problem of how those constituents arose under the conditions that prevailed when our planet was young.

Creationists sometimes try to invalidate all of evolution by pointing to science's current inability to explain the origin of life. But even if life on earth turned out to have a nonevolutionary origin (for instance, if aliens introduced the first cells billions of years ago), evolution since then would be robustly confirmed by countless microevolutionary and macroevolutionary studies.

>    *8. Mathematically, it is inconceivable that anything as complex as a protein, let alone a living cell or a human, could spring up by chance.*

Chance plays a part in evolution (for example, in the random mutations that can give rise to new traits), but evolution does not depend on chance to create organisms, proteins or other entities. Quite the opposite: natural selection, the principal known mechanism of evolution, harnesses nonrandom change by preserving "desirable" (adaptive) features and eliminating "undesirable" (nonadaptive) ones. As long as the forces of selection stay constant, natural selection can push evolution in one direction and produce sophisticated structures in surprisingly short times.

As an analogy, consider the 13-letter sequence "TOBEORNOTTOBE." Those hypothetical million monkeys, each pecking out one phrase a second, could take as long as 78,800 years to find it among the $26^{13}$ sequences of that length. But in the 1980s Richard Hardison of Glendale College wrote a computer program that generated phrases randomly while preserving the positions of individual letters that happened to be correctly placed (in effect, selecting for phrases more like Hamlet's). On average, the program re-created the phrase in just 336 iterations, less than 90 seconds. Even more amazing, it could reconstruct Shakespeare's entire play in just four and a half days.

>    *9. The Second Law of Thermodynamics says that systems must become more disordered over time. Living cells therefore could not have evolved from inanimate chemicals, and multicellular life could not have evolved from protozoa.*

This argument derives from a misunderstanding of the Second Law. If it were valid, mineral crystals and snowflakes would also be impossible, because they, too, are complex structures that form spontaneously from disordered parts.

The Second Law actually states that the total entropy of a closed system (one that no energy or matter leaves or enters) cannot decrease. Entropy is a physical concept often casually described as disorder, but it differs significantly from the conversational use of the word.

More important, however, the Second Law permits parts of a system to decrease in entropy as long as other parts experience an offsetting increase. Thus, our planet as a whole can grow more complex because the sun pours heat and light onto it, and the greater entropy associated with the sun's nuclear fusion more than rebalances the scales. Simple organisms can fuel their rise toward complexity by consuming other forms of life and nonliving materials.

>    *10. Mutations are essential to evolution theory, but mutations can only eliminate traits. They cannot produce new features.*

On the contrary, biology has catalogued many traits produced by point mutations (changes at precise positions in an organism's DNA)—bacterial resistance to antibiotics, for example.

Mutations that arise in the homeobox (*Hox*) family of development-regulating genes in animals can also have complex effects. *Hox* genes direct where legs, wings, antennae and body segments should grow. In fruit flies, for instance, the mutation called *Antennapedia* causes legs to sprout where antennae should grow. These abnormal limbs are not functional, but their existence demonstrates that genetic mistakes can produce complex structures, which natural selection can then test for possible uses.

Moreover, molecular biology has discovered mechanisms for genetic change that go beyond point mutations, and these expand the ways in which new traits can appear. Functional modules within genes can be spliced together in novel ways. Whole genes can be accidentally duplicated in an organism's DNA, and the duplicates are free to mutate into genes for new, complex features. Comparisons of the DNA from a wide variety of organisms indicate that this is how the globin family of blood proteins evolved over millions of years.

*11. Natural selection might explain microevolution, but it cannot explain the origin of new species and higher orders of life.*

Evolutionary biologists have written extensively about how natural selection could produce new species. For instance, in the model called allopatry, developed by Ernst Mayr of Harvard University, if a population of organisms were isolated from the rest of its species by geographical boundaries, it might be subjected to different selective pressures. Changes would accumulate in the isolated population. If those changes became so significant that the splinter group could not or routinely would not breed with the original stock, then the splinter group would be *reproductively isolated* and on its way toward becoming a new species.

Natural selection is the best studied of the evolutionary mechanisms, but biologists are open to other possibilities as well. Biologists are constantly assessing the potential of unusual genetic mechanisms for causing speciation or for producing complex features in organisms. Lynn Margulis of the University of Massachusetts at Amherst and others have persuasively argued that some cellular organelles, such as the energy-generating mitochondria, evolved through the symbiotic merger of ancient organisms. Thus, science welcomes the possibility of evolution resulting from forces beyond natural selection. Yet those forces must be natural; they cannot be attributed to the actions of mysterious creative intelligences whose existence, in scientific terms, is unproved.

*12. Nobody has ever seen a new species evolve.*

Speciation is probably fairly rare and in many cases might take centuries. Furthermore, recognizing a new species during a formative stage can be difficult, because biologists sometimes disagree about how best to define a species. The most widely used definition, Mayr's Biological Species Concept, recognizes a species as a distinct community of reproductively isolated populations—sets of organisms that normally do not or cannot breed outside their community. In practice, this standard can be difficult to apply to organisms isolated by distance or terrain or to plants (and, of course, fossils do not breed). Biologists therefore usually use organisms' physical and behavioral traits as clues to their species membership.

Nevertheless, the scientific literature does contain reports of apparent speciation events in plants, insects and worms. In most of these experiments, researchers subjected organisms to various types of selection—for anatomical differences, mating behaviors, habitat preferences and other traits—and found that they had created populations of organisms that did not breed with outsiders. For example, William R. Rice of the University of New Mexico and George W. Salt of the University of California at Davis demonstrated that if they sorted a group of fruit flies by their preference for certain environments and bred those flies separately over 35 generations, the resulting flies would refuse to breed with those from a very different environment.

13. *Evolutionists cannot point to any transitional fossils—creatures that are half reptile and half bird, for instance.*

Actually, paleontologists know of many detailed examples of fossils intermediate in form between various taxonomic groups. One of the most famous fossils of all time is *Archaeopteryx*, which combines feathers and skeletal structures peculiar to birds with features of dinosaurs. A flock's worth of other feathered fossil species, some more avian and some less, has also been found. A sequence of fossils spans the evolution of modern horses from the tiny *Eohippus*. Whales had four-legged ancestors that walked on land, and creatures known as *Ambulocetus* and *Rodhocetus* helped to make that transition [see "The Mammals That Conquered the Seas," by Kate Wong; SCIENTIFIC AMERICAN, May]. Fossil seashells trace the evolution of various mollusks through millions of years. Perhaps 20 or more hominids (not all of them our ancestors) fill the gap between Lucy the australopithecine and modern humans.

Creationists, though, dismiss these fossil studies. They argue that *Archaeopteryx* is not a missing link between reptiles and birds—it is just an extinct bird with reptilian features. They want evolutionists to produce a weird, chimeric monster that cannot be classified as belonging to any known group. Even if a creationist does accept a fossil as transitional between two species, he or she may then insist on seeing other fossils intermediate between it and the first two. These frustrating requests can proceed ad infinitum and place an unreasonable burden on the always incomplete fossil record.

Nevertheless, evolutionists can cite further supportive evidence from molecular biology. All organisms share most of the same genes, but as evolution predicts, the structures of these genes and their products diverge among species, in keeping with their evolutionary relationships. Geneticists speak of the "molecular clock" that records the passage of time. These molecular data also show how various organisms are transitional within evolution.

14. *Living things have fantastically intricate features—at the anatomical, cellular and molecular levels—that could not function if they were any less complex or sophisticated. The only prudent conclusion is that they are the products of intelligent design, not evolution.*

This "argument from design" is the backbone of most recent attacks on evolution, but it is also one of the oldest. In 1802 theologian William Paley wrote that if one finds a pocket watch in a field, the most reasonable conclusion is that someone dropped it, not that natural forces created it there. By analogy, Paley argued, the complex structures of living things must be the handiwork of direct, divine invention. Darwin wrote *On the Origin of Species* as an answer to Paley: he explained how natural forces of selection, acting on inherited features, could gradually shape the evolution of ornate organic structures.

Generations of creationists have tried to counter Darwin by citing the example of the eye as a structure that could not have evolved. The eye's ability to provide vision depends on the perfect arrangement of its parts, these critics say. Natural selection could thus never favor the transitional forms needed during the eye's evolution—what good is half an eye? Anticipating this criticism, Darwin suggested that even "incomplete" eyes might confer benefits (such as helping creatures orient toward light) and thereby survive for further evolutionary refinement. Biology has vindicated Darwin: researchers have identified primitive eyes and light-sensing organs throughout the animal kingdom and have even tracked the evolutionary history of eyes through comparative genetics. (It now appears that in various families of organisms, eyes have evolved independently.)

Today's intelligent-design advocates are more sophisticated than their predecessors, but their arguments and goals are not fundamentally different. They criticize evolution by trying to demonstrate that it could not account for life as we know it and then insist that the only tenable alternative is that life was designed by an unidentified intelligence.

15. *Recent discoveries prove that even at the microscopic level, life has a quality of complexity that could not have come about through evolution.*

"Irreducible complexity" is the battle cry of Michael J. Behe of Lehigh University, author of *Darwin's Black Box: The Biochemical Challenge to Evolution.* As a household example of irreducible complexity, Behe chooses the mousetrap—a machine that could not function if any of its pieces were missing and whose pieces have no value except as parts of the whole. What is true of the mousetrap, he says, is even truer of the bacterial flagellum, a whiplike cellular organelle used for propulsion that operates like an outboard motor. The proteins that make up a flagellum are uncannily arranged into motor components, a universal joint and other structures like those that a human engineer might specify. The possibility that this intricate array could have arisen through evolutionary modification is virtually nil, Behe argues, and that bespeaks intelligent design. He makes similar points about the blood's clotting mechanism and other molecular systems.

Yet evolutionary biologists have answers to these objections. First, there exist flagellae with forms simpler than the one that Behe cites, so it is not necessary for all those components to be present for a flagellum to work. The sophisticated components of this flagellum all have precedents elsewhere in nature, as described by Kenneth R. Miller of Brown University and others. In fact, the entire flagellum assembly is extremely similar to an organelle that *Yersinia pestis*, the bubonic plague bacterium, uses to inject toxins into cells.

The key is that the flagellum's component structures, which Behe suggests have no value apart from their role in propulsion, can serve multiple functions that would have helped favor their evolution. The final evolution of the flagellum might then have involved only the novel recombination of sophisticated parts that initially evolved for other purposes. Similarly, the blood-clotting system seems to involve the modification and elaboration of proteins that were originally used in digestion, according to studies by Russell F. Doolittle of the University of California at San Diego. So some of the complexity that Behe calls proof of intelligent design is not irreducible at all.

Complexity of a different kind—"specified complexity"—is the cornerstone of the intelligent-design arguments of William A. Dembski of Baylor University in his books *The Design Inference* and *No Free Lunch*. Essentially his argument is that living things are complex in a way that undirected, random processes could never produce. The only logical conclusion, Dembski asserts, in an echo of Paley 200 years ago, is that some superhuman intelligence created and shaped life.

Dembski's argument contains several holes. It is wrong to insinuate that the field of explanations consists only of random processes or designing intelligences. Researchers into nonlinear systems and cellular automata at the Santa Fe Institute and elsewhere have demonstrated that simple, undirected processes can yield extraordinarily complex patterns. Some of the complexity seen in organisms may therefore emerge through natural phenomena that we as yet barely understand. But that is far different from saying that the complexity could not have arisen naturally.

◦◈◦

"Creation science" is a contradiction in terms. A central tenet of modern science is methodological naturalism—it seeks to explain the universe purely in terms of observed or testable natural mechanisms. Thus, physics describes the atomic nucleus with specific concepts governing matter and energy, and it tests those descriptions experimentally. Physicists introduce new particles, such as quarks, to flesh out their theories only when data show that the previous descriptions cannot adequately explain observed phenomena. The new particles do not have arbitrary properties, moreover—their definitions are tightly constrained, because the new particles must fit within the existing framework of physics.

In contrast, intelligent-design theorists invoke shadowy entities that conveniently have whatever unconstrained abilities are needed to solve the mystery at hand. Rather than expanding scientific inquiry, such answers shut it down. (How does one disprove the existence of omnipotent intelligences?)

Intelligent design offers few answers. For instance, when and how did a designing intelligence intervene in life's history? By creating the first DNA? The first cell? The first human? Was every species designed, or just a few early ones? Proponents of intelligent-design theory frequently decline to be pinned down on these points. They do not even make real attempts to reconcile their disparate ideas about intelligent design. Instead they pursue argument by exclusion—that is, they belittle evolutionary explanations as far-fetched or incomplete and then imply that only design-based alternatives remain.

Logically, this is misleading: even if one naturalistic explanation is flawed, it does not mean that all are. Moreover, it does not make one intelligent-design theory more reasonable than another. Listeners are essentially left to fill in the blanks for themselves, and some will undoubtedly do so by substituting their religious beliefs for scientific ideas.

Time and again, science has shown that methodological naturalism can push back ignorance, finding increasingly detailed and informative answers to mysteries that once seemed impenetrable: the nature of light, the causes of disease, how the brain works. Evolution is doing the same with the riddle of how the living world took shape. Creationism, by any name, adds nothing of intellectual value to the effort.

# POSTSCRIPT

## Should the Concept of "Intelligent Design" Replace Darwin's Theory of Evolution?

**A**lthough Darwin wrote *The Origin of Species* over 160 years ago, the vehemence of the ongoing debate between the supportrs of evolution and the proponents of divine creation shows no signs of abaiting. Why is there no resolution to this argument? One reason may lie in the fact that both sides are subscribing to different paradigms. The truth of a new or different paradigm cannot be perceived unless people are willing to lay aside their old expectations and underlying presuppositions. Two individuals who have accepted different underlying presuppositions about how the world works will have difficulty finding any common ground.

For example, take a person who believes in witchcaft and another person who does not. If the first person injures his food, he is likely to explain the event in terms of witchcraft. Although he may use reason and logic to come to this conslusion, it will be a different form of reason and logic then that used by the person who does not believe in witchcraft. Just as it may be difficult for the person who believes in witchcraft to believe that it does not in fact exist, it may be equally difficult for the person who does not believe in witchcraft to "see" the logic behind the other person's conclusions. This sort of intellectual stalemate is amusingly described by E. E. Evans-Pritchard in his account of doing fieldwork among the Azande.

> *A boy knocked his foot against a small stump of wood in the center of a bush path, a frequent happening in Afaraica, and suffered pain and inconvenience in consequence. Owing to its position on his toe it was impossible to keep the cut free from dirt and it began to fester. He declared that witchcraft had made him knock his foot against the stump. I always argued with Azande and criticised their statements, and I did so on this occasion. I told the boy that he had knocked his foot against the stump of wood because he had been careless, and that witchcraft had not placed it in the path, for it had grown there naturally. He agreed that witchcraft had not placed it in the path, for it had grown there naturally. He agreed that witchraft had nothing to do with the stump of wood being in his path but added that he had kept his eyes open for stumps, as indeed every Zande does most carefully, and that if he had not been bewitched he would have seen the stump. As a conclusive argument for his view he remarked that all cuts do not take days to heal, but on the contrary, close quickly, for that is the nature of cuts. Why then had this sore festered and remained open if there were no witchcraft behind it? (1979:364).*

Intelligent design theorests and evolutionists are in somewhat of the same situation as Evans-Pritchard and the Azande. Time will tell whether both sides of

82

the debate will finally find a way to agree to disagree or whether a new paradigm will be posed that explains the world better than either of them can do alone.

For additional information on intelligent design and other creationist ideas, see *Evolution: The Challenge of the Fossil Record* by Duane T. Gish (Creation-Life Publishers, 1985), *A History of Modern Creationism* by Henry Morris (Master Book, 1984), C. Baugh, and Clifford Wilson, *Dinosaur: Scientific Evidence That Dinosaur and Men Walked Together* (Promise Publishing, 1987).

Other sources defending the traditional view of evolution include *Hen's Teeth and Horse's Toes* by Stephen Jay Gould (Norton, 1983), and "Antievolutionism and Creationism in the United States," *Annual Review of Anthropology* (vol. 2, pp. 263–289, 1997) by Eugenie Scott.

# On the Internet . . .

DUSHKIN ONLINE

## Jane Goodall Research Center

This site focuses on chimpanzee research at the Gombe National Park in Tanzania.

```
http://www.usc.edu/dept/elab/anth/
            goodall.html
```

## Bonobo Sex and Society

This site discusses bonobos and their sexual behavior and its implications for human evolution.

```
http://songweaver.com/info/bonobos.html
```

## Electronic Zoo/NetVet—Primate Page

This site covers many primates and provides a good overview of their characteristics. There are also links to many other related sites.

```
http://netvet.wustl.edu/primates.htm
```

## The African Emergence and Early Asian Dispersals of the Genus Homo

This site focuses on hominids in the Rift Valley in East Africa.

```
http://www.sigmaxi.org/amsci/subject/
            EvoBiol.html
```

# PART 2

# Primate Evolution and the Evolution of Early Hominids

*P*rimates are our closest living relatives in the animal world. We share many of the same physical and behavioral characteristics, including opposable thumbs, stereoscopic vision, strong mother-child bonds, and a large brain-to-body size ratio. By studying primate fossils and living primates, we can gain insight into the evolutionary history of our earliest ancestors. The issues discussed in this section include:

- Is Male Aggression and Competition Key to Reproductive Success?

- Are Primate Females Selected to Be Monogamous?

- Do Chimpanzees Hunt Competitively?

- Does Homosexuality or Bisexuality Have Any Evolutionary Advantage for Primates?

- Are Male and Female Relationships Based Primarily on Reproductive Sex?

- Did Bipedalism Develop as a Response to Heat Stress?

- Is *Australopithecus Africanus* on the Direct Line to Modern Humans?

# ISSUE 5

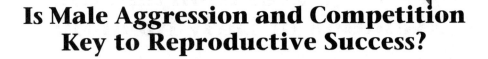

# Is Male Aggression and Competition Key to Reproductive Success?

**YES: Carl Zimmer,** from "First, Kill the Babies," *Discover* (September 1996)

**NO: Shannon Brownlee,** from "These Are Real Swinging Primates," *Discover* (April 1987)

## ISSUE SUMMARY

Carl Zimmer suggests that male aggression and competition are key to reproductive success. He describes situations in which killing infants sired by rivals increases the chances of the dominant male reproducing. In contrast, Shannon Brownlee suggests that the ability to mate longer and more frequently is a more important selective factor than aggression in some primate societies.

*Sexual selection, the evolutionary process that produces sex differences, has a lot to answer for. Without it, males wouldn't possess dangerous bodily weapons and a mindset that sanctions violence. But males who are better fighters can stop other males from mating, and they mate more successfully themselves. Better fighters tend to have more babies. That's the simple, stupid, selfish logic of sexual selection (Wrangham and Peterson 1996:47).*

The term *sexual selection* refers to an evolutionary process that selects for physical and behavioral traits that enhance the chances of successful reproduction. Sexual selection includes *intrasexual competition for mates,* as well as *intersexual mate selection.* Intrasexual competition refers to the ways members of the same sex strive to outreproduce each other, while intersexual mate selection examines how males and females pick partners to have sex with. Many researchers like Wrangham and Peterson suggest that males compete with each other vigorously for mating opportunities and that violence and aggression are key to their reproductive success. Natural selection thus accounts for the prevalence of war and territoriality among humans. Violence is innate and aggression genetic. Pride is also explained as just another way of maximizing reproductive fitness. As Wrangham and Peterson note, "Pride obviously serves as a stimulus for much interpersonal aggression in humans, and we can hypothesize confidently that this emotion evolved during countless generations in which males who achieved high status were able to turn their social success into extra reproduction. Male pride, the source of many a conflict, is reasonably seen as a mental equivalent of broad shoulders" (Wrangham and Peterson, 51).

In his book *The Selfish Gene,* Richard Dawkins suggests that even the killing of rivals and their offspring may have an adaptive value. Fewer rivals mean more opportunities for the survivors to mate. Similarly, the elimination of a rival's existing offspring increases the odds that the victor will pass on his genes. Carl Zimmer's article considers primate infanticide in this light. He suggests that males sometimes kill the offspring of their rivals as a way to enhance their own reproductive success. In contrast, Shannon Brownlee argues that intrasexual competition takes the form of "sperm wars" between the muriqui monkeys of Brazil. Instead of fighting each other or killing infants, males compete via number of copulations. The male with the most potent sperm—and usually the biggest pair of testicles—wins.

**Carl Zimmer**  **YES**

# First, Kill the Babies

Twenty-five years ago this summer a Harvard graduate student named Sarah Hrdy went to northwestern India and met the monkeys that would make her famous. The immediate impetus for the trip was a series of lectures by Stanford ecologist Paul Ehrlich on the dangers of overpopulation. Though Ehrlich was speaking about humans, what Hrdy thought of were the Indian monkeys known as Hanuman langurs. The langurs are considered sacred by many Indians and so are regularly fed by the people with whom they come into contact. Consequently, near towns, Hanuman langurs live in extremely dense populations, and apparently this unnatural density had led to unnatural, pathologically violent behavior. There had been several reports of adult males killing infants. "So there I was, listening to Ehrlich," says Hrdy, "with this adolescent desire to go do something relevant with my life, and I thought, 'I am going to go study the effects of crowding on behavior.'"

Hrdy traveled to dry, deforested Mount Abu and began to get acquainted with the sandy-bodied, dark-faced Hanumans. Before long she decided the assumption that had propelled her to India had been wrong. "It happened pretty fast. I was watching these very crowded animals, and here were these infants playing around, bouncing on these males like trampolines, pulling on their tails, and so forth. These guys were aloof but totally tolerant. They might show some annoyance occasionally, but there was nothing approaching pathological hostility toward offspring. The trouble seemed to be when males came into the troop from outside it."

The langurs of Abu are arranged into two kinds of groups. In the first, a single male—or, rarely, two—lives with a group of females and their infants. The infant females, when they grow up, stay put; the males leave to join the other kind of group, a small all-male band.

Eventually a grown male lucky enough to be in a troop of females will come under attack, either from the all-male bands or from the male of another mixed troop. Odds are that sooner or later the resident male will be chased out by a new one. Hrdy witnessed many such takeovers, and she noticed that afterward the new male would often chase after the babies in the troop, presumably all of which were offspring of the old male's. Before long some of these infants would disappear. She didn't actually see what happened to the infants, but townspeople around Abu told her that they had seen a male killing baby langurs. Soon after these takeovers, the new resident male would mate with the females.

*killing allows to mate.*

"I realized I needed a new explanatory model," says Hrdy. Her new model would become one of modern biology's most famous—and in some circles, notorious—hypotheses about animal behavior. There was nothing pathological about langur infanticide, she suggested. On the contrary, it actually made a chilling kind of sense: While a langur mother nurses, she cannot conceive; when she stops nursing, she can. Thus if a male langur kills her infant—one that is not related to him—she can bear the infanticidal male's own offspring. In Hanuman langur society, in which a male's sojourn with a harem averages a little over two years, the time saved can be critical. After all, for any offspring to survive, they should ideally be weaned before a new, potentially infanticidal male shows up. Seen in this light, infanticide could actually be an "adaptive" evolutionary strategy for fathering as many offspring as possible.

In the quarter century since Hrdy first conceived this idea, naturalists have reported cases of infanticide among a wide range of animals. Some now argue that the threat of infanticide is such a pervasive and powerful influence that it can shape animal societies. A few theorists even claim that infanticide was an important factor in human evolution.

Yet when Hrdy first published her hypothesis, she was immediately attacked, most of all by other researchers studying langurs. They contended that Hanuman langurs living in natural conditions, in remote forests, had never been observed killing infants. At Abu, they said, human feeding had crowded the langurs into conditions evolution had never prepared them for, and as a result the transfer of males into new groups became drenched with aggression. In other words, the langurs of Abu were simply not normal.

Underlying this species-specific dustup, though, was a deeper conflict. Before the 1970s most researchers viewed animal societies as smooth-running systems in which each member knew its proper role and played it for the good of the many. Animal societies—and primate societies in particular—were often portrayed as utopias that we humans would do well to emulate. But then biologists such as E. O. Wilson and Robert Trivers (both mentors of Hrdy's at Harvard) argued that such a view didn't make sense in a world shaped by evolution. Just as a bird's wing is the product of natural selection, so are the ways the individual bird interacts with other birds. Its social behavior, like its body, is ultimately designed for one purpose: to get its own genes duplicated as much as possible. Rather than being a peaceful group of community-minded role players, an animal society was made up of individuals trying to maximize their reproductive gain, with cooperation always a compromise between competing genetic interests. As a biological explanation for society, this school of thought came to be known as sociobiology.

When Hrdy hypothesized about langur infanticide, then, she wasn't just explaining the odd behavior of a few monkeys. She was pushing sociobiology to its logical extreme, in which a male's drive to reproduce was so strong that it would resort to the decidedly antisocial act of killing the young of its own species.

Over time, Hrdy added some nuances to her stark hypothesis. For example, she noted that female langurs did not passively sit by as invading males tried to rob them of their genetic legacy. Rather, females banded together to help fend off males bent on infanticide. Once an infanticidal male was in charge, however, they might choose a different tack. Female langurs can continue to have sex even after they conceive, and by mating with an invading male, they might trick him into thinking the infant was his own.

Hrdy also began noting reports of infanticide among other animals. Her "outsider male" infanticide, she realized, was clearly not the only kind of adaptive strategy practiced in the animal world. A mother might resort to infanticide if she didn't have the resources to raise all her children. Adults might also kill the infants of strangers simply for food or to eliminate the competition for limited resources.

In the decade and a half since Hrdy's work first appeared, infanticide has been reported among mice and ground squirrels, bears and deer, prairie dogs and foxes, fish and dwarf mongooses and wasps and bumblebees and dung beetles. Although the evidence from the wild has often been sketchy, most of the strategies appear to fall into one of those that Hrdy sketched out. In a few cases researchers have been able to test the hypothesis by performing natural experiments. In 1987, for example, Cornell ornithologist Stephen Emlen was studying the jacana, a Panamanian bird in which the common sex roles are switched: males sit on the eggs and raise the young alone while the females rove around their territories, mating with many males and fighting off intruding females. Essentially, if you turn Hanuman langurs into birds and switch the sex roles, you get jacanas—and theoretically, under the right conditions, you should also see infanticide. Emlen needed to shoot some birds for DNA testing, and he chose two females with male partners caring for nests of babies.

"I shot a female one night, and the next morning was just awesome. By first light a new female was already on the turf. I saw terrible things—pecking and picking up and throwing down chicks until they were dead. Within hours she was soliciting the male, and he was mounting her the same day. The next night I shot the other female, then came out the next morning and saw the whole thing again."

Among mammals, one of the best documented killers of infants has proved to be the lion. Though actual killings have only rarely been witnessed (the total is about a dozen), massive indirect evidence for the phenomenon has been gathered by the husband-and-wife team of Craig Packer and Anne Pusey, both behavioral ecologists at the University of Minnesota. From their observations of lions in the Serengeti, they've found that whenever a new male comes into the pride, the death rate of nursing cubs—and nursing cubs only—shoots up. Within six months none of the cubs are left alive.

Other primates have also joined the ranks of the infanticidal. The first reports were of only a few species such as the red howlers of Venezuela, the gorillas of Rwanda, and the blue monkeys of Uganda. But in the past few years there have been more reported instances of primate infanticide, some of which demand some expansion of Hrdy's ideas. Lemurs in Madagascar, for example, breed once a year. If a male kills another male's nursing infant, he doesn't hasten his own fatherhood, since he still has to wait until the breeding season to mate. Nonetheless, researchers have seen male lemurs sinking their fangs into babies. One observer, Michael Pereira of Bucknell University, offers an idea as to why it happens. Madagascar has a harsh climate, with a long dry season that keeps female lemurs on a knife-edge of survival. Pregnancy and the first few months of nursing take place in the harshest time of the year, and, says Pereira, successfully raising an infant one year may reduce the chances a mother will be able to raise the next year's baby. "Females who lose their infants are much fatter than females whose infants survive," Pereira explains. "If by your killing the infant she's more likely to be successful during your reign, then it's to your advantage."

In Sumatra, Dutch researchers have been studying a relative of the Hanumans known as the Thomas langur. Thomas langurs were essentially a mystery when the Utrecht University primatologists began to observe them in 1988. Now, after eight years of relentlessly tracking the animals through the forest and painstakingly recording their daily habits, the researchers are finding the langurs to be all too revealing. "Infanticide does occur. I've seen the attacks," explains Romy Steenbeek, who ran the program for four years. "We saw the body of a baby with canine slices in its belly. I saw a male attack a baby, and the baby disappeared. One baby received big wounds in an attack by a neighboring male, and she died after two very bad weeks. The males run a few hundred meters to the troop, silently attack, and when they leave they loud-call."

Like lemurs, these langurs require yet one more variation on Hrdy's grisly theme. Thomas langurs have the same all-male bands and one-male/ many-female troops of other langurs, but what distinguishes this species is that the males don't make hostile takeovers of groups of females—at least not directly. Instead outside males make harassing raids on a troop, chasing the infants and sometimes killing them. One by one the females abandon their male, the childless females first, the others as soon as their babies are weaned or die. Steenbeek suspects that the infanticidal male langurs are trying to discredit the harem male, demonstrating how incompetent he is by killing the troop's infants. The females are continually judging the contest, and if they sense that their male is getting weak, they abandon him. "Sometimes at the end of the tenure, a male stops protecting the troop," says Steenbeek. "It's like he's just given up."

If infanticide has long been a natural part of animal behavior, then so too, one would expect, has been the fight against it. Over evolutionary time, both currents would shape new behaviors and social organizations. Lionesses live in prides, according to Packer and Pusey, in large part to protect their young against murderous males. One result is that lionesses must tolerate cubs not their own stealing milk—something rarely seen in other carnivores. Female mice can somehow tell if a male approaching their litter is infanticidal or not; if he is, they leap into battle. And apparently even the babies have evolved a protection against infanticide: they call much more frequently in the presence of an infanticidal male.

Evidence is emerging that primates may face similar pressure. Female red howler monkeys in Venezuela, for example, tend to travel in small groups— generally under five members—and are hostile to new female howlers who want to join them. What determines their group size? In some animals the availability of food is the key: if the group is too big, the competition among individuals grows too intense. Yet evidently food competition isn't a problem for red howlers. What is a problem, it seems, is that the bigger a female group, the more likely it is to suffer an infanticidal attack by a male. The benefits for a male of taking over a big group make those groups good targets, and as a result females keep the groups small.

Carel van Schaik, a primatologist with Duke University and the Wildlife Conservation Society, thinks infanticide's effects may reach even further into the core of primate life. He first began thinking seriously about Hrdy's ideas in the late 1980s, while studying gibbons with Robin Dunbar, who was then at University College, London. These Asian monkeys are for the most part monogamous, although it's hard to see why. It's not that gibbon babies need the extra parental care, because the fathers don't give any. And calculations suggested that males might do better, from a genetic viewpoint, if they tried to impregnate as many females as possible rather than just one. Van Schaik and Dunbar concluded that male gibbons were staying close to home to guard their infants from other males, and the females were choosing good protectors as mates. That would explain why on the one hand gibbon couples make calls together—advertising to neighboring males that the infant is well guarded—but why on the other hand a nursing mother who becomes widowed falls silent. It doesn't matter to Van Schaik that gibbon infanticide has never been reported—it's not seen, he thinks, because the animals do such a good job of preventing it.

Van Schaik now suspects that the ever-present threat of infanticide has a similar effect on all primates. Among mammals, primate males and females are far and away the most likely to form a long-term bond. "That raises the issue: Why primates?" says Van Schaik. The answer, he thinks, is that primate babies are particularly vulnerable to infanticide. They take a long time to mature, and compared with other young mammals, they are defenseless and exposed, more often than not clinging to their mother. Female primates also tend to stay in a given territory, thereby giving males an added incentive for disposing of unrelated infants. "If you do commit infanticide, there is a good probability that you will have a future opportunity for mating," says Van Schaik. Thus the incentive and opportunity for infanticide have driven primates more than other mammals into long-term bonds, in order that males can defend their young.

If Van Schaik is right, he will add considerable weight to speculations Hrdy made in the 1980s, that protection against infanticide may have had a profound impact on primates, including early humans. Nursing is a contraceptive among humans, as it is in langurs, and it can lower a woman's fertility for up to two or three years. That could make the incentive for infanticide on the part of a new mate enormous, as would the incentives to guard against it. Such a scenario would fly in the face of the conventional view that long-term bonds between men and women evolved so that extra parental care can help their babies survive. Instead, Van Schaik suggests that infanticide may have been the prime mover behind these bonds, and only later did the added advantage of help from a father come into play.

Not surprisingly, perhaps, such ideas are not easily accepted. Most anthropologists and psychologists still view humans much as biologists once viewed animals. "Anthropology has a long history of believing that everything is for the good of the social group," says anthropologist Kim Hill of the University of New Mexico, and in that context Hrdy's ideas about infanticide don't make sense; such instances as do occur among humans can only be explained as a result of a particular cultural bias (favoring male babies over females, say) or of individual pathology. But there are a few disturbing data points. Over the past 16 years Martin Daly and Margo Wilson, both psychologists at McMaster University in Hamilton, Ontario, have collected child abuse data from governments and humane associations. One of the most startling statistics they've uncovered is this: a preschool American stepchild is 60 times more likely than a biological child to be the victim of infanticide.

Hill himself, with his studies of the Ache people of Paraguay, has gathered some of the best infanticide data available on non-Western cultures. The Ache still go on long hunting-and-foraging expeditions, as their ancestors did for 10,000 years. When a man kills an animal, he gives it to another man, who then distributes the meat to the entire band. Congenial as this may seem, natural selection creates inevitable tension: by giving most of his food away, a man allows his efforts to be diverted from his own family. This cost is outweighed by the benefits of cooperation, but when a child's father dies, the tension reveals itself. If a child loses a father, his chances of becoming the victim of infanticide at the hands of another man increase fourfold. It's not uncommon for orphaned children to be thrown into their father's grave.

But Hill does not think that the pattern is purely a cultural tradition. "If you ask them why they're killing all these babies, their first answer is 'That's our custom,'" says Hill. "And then if you push them on that, they say, 'They don't have parents, and we have to take care of them, and that makes us mad.'"

The resistance to infanticide as a reproductive strategy is still shared by many researchers. In some cases they've tested some of the predictions and found them wanting. Agustin Fuentes of the University of California at Berkeley, for example, studies the Mentawai langur, which lives on the islands of the same name, off the west coast of Sumatra. Like the gibbon, the Mentawai langur is monogamous, but it doesn't behave as Van Schaik said it should. For example, when a bonded couple are close to a solitary (and supposedly infanticidal) male, they do not become hostile or even make calls to show they are together.

Deborah Overdorff of the University of Texas at Austin studies rufous lemurs, and among these primates, at least, doubts the reality of infanticide. While rufous lemurs travel in large groups, male and female pairs will often be seen staying close together. That might seem to fit the notion of males protecting their young. Not to Overdorff. "I've found that the male is not necessarily the one the females mated with. Sometimes they turn out to be brothers. Infanticide is probably not a good explanation for pair-bonding."

Others criticize the quality of the data. They complain that most reports are inferred from indirect evidence, such as the disappearance of a baby. And except for Hanuman langurs, the few witnessed infanticides have not been followed up to see how much reproductive success the killing males have had. Given the difficulty of observing monkeys in the wild, the scrappiness of the data shouldn't be surprising, and some primatologists—including some who think that infanticide is real—worry that the theory is getting too far ahead of the data.

The biggest opposition results from the application of Hrdy's ideas to humans. Popular accounts of the theory, Hrdy complains, are "very quick to jump from the langur case to cases of strange-male-in-the-household infanticide, but the underpinnings, the groundwork for that extrapolation, aren't there." After all, a stepfather can't speed up his own reproduction through infanticide. Hrdy and Daly agree that this kind of abuse has more to do with resource competition—the resource being the mother. Moreover, they don't envision a stepfather consciously trying to eliminate that competition—rather, he may simply have a lower threshold of irritation toward the child. Such a threshold is suggested by a recent study by Daly and Wilson, in which they compared the ways in which biological fathers and stepfathers killed their children. In most cases, biological fathers shoot or suffocate their offspring (and then often kill themselves), while stepfathers kill by striking—hinting that a "lashing out" reflex is at work.

Another point of criticism is the matter of how infanticide can be carried down through the generations, and again confusion abounds. One magazine article Hrdy mentions, for example, contains a reference to an "infanticide gene." She scoffs. "I don't talk about genes." While it's true that Hrdy doesn't dabble in oversimplified genetic determinism, some of sociobiology's early pioneers did—and sometimes with great abandon. These days, however, a much suppler view exists. In any species, each individual keeps a Darwinian account book, and whenever it has to "choose" an action, it weighs the immediate and long-term costs and benefits. "Selection hasn't molded an animal that's altruistic or infanticidal," says Emlen. "It has molded an animal capable of showing a whole range of subtly different behaviors under different circumstances, but they're all predictable."

"Under one set of circumstances, a female might behave by abandoning a baby, but under another set of circumstances she would care for a baby," says Hrdy. "These are both maternal behaviors. In the first case, presumably selection has operated on her to postpone raising her young because there is the option that she might have a better chance of pulling a baby through at a future date. So it's not nonreproductive, it's not nonadaptive; it's simply a question of an animal over the course of a lifetime gauging herself." Infanticide is thus at one extreme in a spectrum of parental care. Hrdy herself has recently been exploring the ways in which European parents have historically lowered their investment in children, such as hiring a wet nurse or leaving a child at a monastery.

For animals, and to some degree ourselves, this "gauging" happens unconsciously. And while it might seem hard to believe that animals can make careful decisions, many experiments have revealed that they can. Few of these accounting experiments have been done on infanticide, though, and there isn't anywhere near enough data to test in primates, let alone humans. While almost 20 percent of Ache children fall victim to infanticide before age ten, the rate is zero among many other foraging cultures. Until researchers can explain the variation, all speculation on the role of infanticide in early human evolution must be put on hold. Our long, complex social lives and our dizzying array of cultures hide the effects of evolution as the high, obscuring leaves of the Sumatran forest hide the secrets of Thomas langurs.

Yet those who believe that infanticide is a Darwinian reality think that we need to keep looking through the foliage. "Sure, you can deny all these results—at your own peril," says Van Schaik. "What is it that makes males infanticidal, and what is it that stops males from being infanticidal? If you know these things better, you know what to do, take certain measures, counsel people. It arms us."

A look back at the infanticide hypothesis on its silver anniversary makes clear how long it takes to test and flesh out the shocking ideas of sociobiology. Hrdy herself sees this as the necessary pace of any science. She often describes her job as creating "imaginary worlds" that other scientists can then explore to see if they can help us understand the real one. "I see scientists working in different phases. Some people are better at one phase than another. Theoreticians think of other people as technicians; technicians think of theoreticians as people in outer space, not connected to the real world. But for the whole process, you need these phases, and in the initial phase, you're selecting a project, you're coming up with assumptions, you're trying to model what might be true and to generate the hypotheses that you want to look at. Then you have the actual collection of data and all the methodologies that go into that. Imaginary worlds have a place in science."

Shannon Brownlee                                    ◀ **NO**

# These Are Real Swinging Primates

**W**hen I first heard of the muriqui four years ago, I knew right away that I had
to see one. This is an unusual monkey, to say the least. To begin with, it's the largest
primate in South America; beyond that, the males have very large testicles.
We're talking gigantic, the size of billiard balls, which means that the 30-pound
muriqui has *cojones* that would look more fitting on a 400-pound gorilla.

But it wasn't prurience that lured me to Brazil. My interest in the muriqui
was intellectual, because more than this monkey's anatomy is extraordinary.
Muriqui society is untroubled by conflict: troops have no obvious pecking
order; males don't compete overtly for females; and, most un-monkeylike, these
monkeys almost never fight.

The muriqui is also one of the rarest monkeys in the world. It lives in a
single habitat, the Atlantic forest of southeastern Brazil. This mountainous
region was once blanketed with forest from São Paulo to Salvador, but several
centuries of slash-and-burn agriculture have reduced it to fragments.

In 1969 Brazilian conservationist Alvaro Coutinho Aguirre surveyed the
remaining pockets of forest and estimated that 2,000 to 3,000 muriquis survived. His data were all but ignored until Russell Mittermeier, a biologist,
trained his sights on the muriquis ten years later. Known as Russell of the Apes
to his colleagues, Mittermeier, an American, directs the primate program for
the World Wildlife Fund. He hopscotches from forest to forest around the
world looking for monkeys in trouble and setting up conservation plans for
them. In 1979 he and Brazilian zoologist Celio Valle retraced Aguirre's steps
and found even fewer muriquis. Today only 350 to 500 are left, scattered
among four state and national parks and six other privately held plots.

In 1981 Karen Strier, then a graduate student at Harvard, approached
Mittermeier for help in getting permission to observe the muriqui. He took
her to a coffee plantation called Montes Claros, near the town of Caratinga,
250 miles north of Rio de Janeiro. Over the next four years she studied the
social behavior of the muriqui there—and came up with a provocative theory
about how the monkey's unconventional behavior, as well as its colossal testicles, evolved. She reasoned that the evolution of both could be explained, at
least in part, by the muriquis' need to avoid falling out of trees.

Last June I joined Strier, now a professor at Beloit (Wis.) College, on one of
her periodic journeys to Montes Claros—clear mountains, in Portuguese. We

From *Discover*, April 1987, pp. 67–68, 70–71, 76–77. Copyright © 1987 by Shannon Brownlee.
Reprinted by permission of the author. Brownlee is a Scwartz Senior Fellow at the New America
Foundation.

arrived there after a disagreeable overnight bus trip over bad roads. As we neared the plantation, I found it difficult to believe there was a forest—much less a monkey—within miles. Through the grimy windows of the bus I saw hillsides stripped down to russet dirt and dotted with spindly coffee plants and stucco farmhouses. There wasn't anything taller than a banana tree in sight. As the bus lurched around the last curve before our stop the forest finally appeared, an island of green amid thousands of acres of coffee trees and brown pastures.

Strier was eager to start looking for the muriquis—"There's a chance we won't see them the whole four days you're here," she said—so no sooner had we dropped our bags off at a cottage on the plantation than we set out along a dirt road into the forest. The trees closed around us—and above us, where they gracefully arched to form a vault of green filigree. Parrots screeched; leaves rustled; a large butterfly flew erratically by on transparent wings. By this time Strier had guided me onto a steep trail, along which she stopped from time to time to listen for the monkeys.

They appeared soon enough, but our first meeting was less than felicitous. After we had climbed half a mile, Strier motioned for me to stop. A muffled sound, like that of a small pig grunting contentedly, came from up ahead. We moved forward a hundred yards. Putting a finger to her lips, Strier sank to her haunches and looked up.

I did the same; twelve round black eyes stared back at me. A group of six muriquis squatted, silent, 15 feet above in the branches, watching us intently. They began to grunt again. A sharp smell with undertones of cinnamon permeated the air. A light rain began to fall. I held out my palm to catch a drop. It was warm.

"Hey, this isn't rain!" I said.

Strier grinned and pointed to her head. "That's why I wear a hat," she said.

My enthusiasm for the muriquis waned slightly after that. We left them at dusk and retired to the cottage, where Strier described her arrival at Montes Claros four years earlier. Mittermeier acted as guide and interpreter during the first few days of her pilot study. He introduced her to the owner of the 5,000-acre plantation, Feliciano Miguel Abdala, then 73, who had preserved the 2,000-acre forest for more than 40 years. His is one of the only remaining tracts of Atlantic forest, and he agreed to let Strier use it as the site of her study. Then Mittermeier introduced her to the muriquis, assuring her they would be easy to see.

They weren't, and observing them closely is a little like stargazing on a rainy night: not only do you run the risk of getting wet, but you can also spend a lot of time looking up and never see a thing. Mittermeier was adept at spotting the monkeys in the forest, and helped Strier acquire this skill.

But brief glimpses of the monkeys weren't enough. "My strategy was to treat them like baboons, the only other species I'd ever studied," she says. "I thought I couldn't let them out of my sight." She tried to follow on the ground as they swung along in the trees. "They went berserk," she says. They threw branches, shrieked, urinated on her—or worse—and fled.

Even after the muriquis grew accustomed to her, keeping up with them wasn't easy. They travel as much as two miles a day, which is tough for someone picking her way through thick growth on the forest floor. As Strier and a Brazilian assistant learned the muriquis' habitual routes and daily patterns, they cleared trails. These helped, but the muriquis could still travel much faster than she could. "I've often thought the thing to have would be a jet pack," Strier says. "It would revolutionize primatology. Your National Science Foundation grant would include binoculars, pencils, and a jet pack."

The monkeys move by brachiating, swinging hand over hand from branch to branch, much like a child on a jungle gym. Only one other group of monkeys brachiates; the rest clamber along branches on all fours. The muriquis' closest relatives are two other Latin American genera, the woolly monkeys and the spider monkeys—hence woolly spider monkey, its English name. But the muriqui is so unlike them that it has its own genus, *Brachyteles*, which refers to its diminutive thumb, an adaptation for swinging through the trees. Its species name is *arachnoides*, from the Greek for spider, which the muriqui resembles when its long arms, legs, and tail are outstretched.

Brachiating is a specialization that's thought to have evolved because it enables primates to range widely to feed on fruit. Curiously, though, muriquis have a stomach designed for digesting leaves. Strier found that their diet consists of a combination of the two foods. They eat mostly foliage, low-quality food for a monkey, but prefer flowers and fruits, like figs and the *caja manga*, which is similar to the mango. Year after year they return to certain trees when they bloom and bear fruit. The rest of the time the muriquis survive on leaves by passing huge quantities of them through their elongated guts, which contain special bacteria to help them digest the foliage. By the end of the day their bellies are so distended with greenery that even the males look pregnant.

We returned to the trail the next morning just after dawn. Condensation trickled from leaves; howler monkeys roared and capuchins cooed and squeaked; a bird sang with the sweet, piercing voice of a piccolo. Then Strier had to mention snakes. "Watch out for snakes," she said blithely, scrambling on all fours up a steep bank. I followed her, treading cautiously.

The muriquis weren't where we had left them the day before. Strier led me along a ridge through a stand of bamboo, where a whisper of movement drifted up from the slope below. Maybe it was just the wind, but she thought it was the muriquis, so we sat down to wait. After a couple of hours, she confessed, "This part of research can get kind of boring."

By noon the faint noise became a distinct crashing. "That's definitely them," she said. "It's a good thing they're so noisy, or I'd never be able to find them." The monkeys, perhaps a dozen of them, swarmed uphill, breaking branches, chattering, uttering their porcine grunts as they swung along. At the crest of the ridge they paused, teetering in indecision while they peered back and forth before settling in some legume trees on the ridgetop. We crept down out of the bamboo to within a few feet of them, so close I noticed the cinnamon scent again—only this time I kept out of range.

Each monkey had its own feeding style. One hung upside down by its tail and drew the tip of a branch to its mouth; it delicately plucked the tenderest shoots with its rubbery lips. Another sat upright, grabbing leaves by the handful and stuffing its face. A female with twins—"Twins have never been seen in this species," Strier whispered as she excitedly scribbled notes—ate with one hand while hanging by the other and her tail. Her babies clung to the fur on her belly.

I had no trouble spotting the males. Their nether parts bulged unmistakably—blue-black or pink-freckled, absurd-looking monuments to monkey virility. I asked Strier what sort of obscene joke evolution was playing on the muriquis when it endowed them thus.

We were about to consider this question when a high-pitched whinnying began a few hundred yards away. Immediately a monkey just overhead pulled itself erect and let out an ear-splitting shriek, which set the entire troop to neighing like a herd of nervous horses. Then they took off down into the valley.

Strier and I had to plunge pell-mell into the underbrush or risk losing them for the rest of the day. "They're chasing the other troop," she said as we galloped downhill. A group of muriquis living on the opposite side of the forest had made a rare foray across the valley.

The monkeys we were observing swung effortlessly from tree to tree; we wrestled with thorny vines, and fell farther and farther behind. An impenetrable thicket forced us to backtrack in search of another route. By the time we caught up to the muriquis, they were lounging in a tree, chewing on unripe fruit and chuckling in a self-satisfied sort of way. The intruding troop was nowhere to be seen. "They must have scared the hell out of those other guys," said Strier, laughing.

Such confrontations occur infrequently; muriquis ordinarily tolerate another troop's incursions. Strier thinks they challenge intruders only when there's a valuable resource to defend—like the fruit tree they were sitting in.

Tolerance of another troop is odd behavior for monkeys, but not as odd as the fact that members of a muriqui troop never fight among themselves. "They're remarkably placid," said Strier. "They wait in line to dip their hands into water collected in the bole of a tree. They have no apparent pecking order or dominance hierarchy. Males and females are equal in status, and males don't squabble over females." No other primate society is known to be so free of competition, not even that of gorillas, which have lately gained a reputation for being the gentle giants of the primate world.

Strier's portrayal of the muriqui brought to mind a bizarre episode that Katharine Milton, an anthropologist at the University of California at Berkeley, once described. While studying a troop of muriquis in another patch of the Atlantic forest, she observed a female mating with a half a dozen males in succession; that a female monkey would entertain so many suitors came as no surprise, but Milton was astonished at the sight of the males lining up behind the female "like a choo-choo train" and politely taking turns copulating. They continued in this manner for two days, stopping only to rest and eat, and never even so much as bared their teeth.

Primates aren't known for their graciousness in such matters, and I found Milton's report almost unbelievable. But Strier confirms it. She says that female muriquis come into heat about every two and a half years, after weaning their latest offspring, and repeatedly copulate during that five- to seven-day period with a number of males. Copulations, "cops" in animal-behavior lingo, last as long as 18 minutes, and average six, which for most primates (including the genus *Homo*, if Masters and Johnson are correct) would be a marathon. Yet no matter how long a male muriqui takes, he's never harassed by suitors-in-waiting.

Strier has a theory to explain the muriqui's benignity, based on a paper published in 1980 by Richard Wrangham, a primatologist at the University of Michigan. He proposed that the social behavior of primates could in large part be predicted by what the females eat.

This isn't a completely new idea. For years primatologists sought correlations between ecological conditions and social structure, but few patterns emerged—until Wrangham's ingenious insight that environment constrains the behavior of each sex differently. Specifically, food affects the sociability of females more than males.

Wrangham started with the generally accepted premise that both sexes in every species have a common aim: to leave as many offspring as possible. But each sex pursues this goal in its own way. The best strategy for a male primate is to impregnate as many females as he can. All he needs, as Wrangham points out, is plenty of sperm and plenty of females. As for the female, no matter how promiscuous she is, she can't match a male's fecundity. On average, she's able to give birth to only one offspring every two years, and her success in bearing and rearing it depends in part upon the quality of food she eats. Therefore, all other things being equal, male primates will spend their time cruising for babes, while females will look for something good to eat.

Wrangham perceived that the distribution of food—that is, whether it's plentiful or scarce, clumped or evenly dispersed—will determine how gregarious the females of a particular species are. He looked at the behavior of 28 species and found that, in general, females forage together when food is plentiful and found in large clumps—conditions under which there's enough for all the members of the group and the clumps can be defended against outsiders. When clumps become temporarily depleted, the females supplement their diet with what Wrangham calls subsistence foods. He suggests that female savanna baboons, for example, live in groups because their favorite foods, fruits and flowers, grow in large clumps that are easy to defend. When these are exhausted they switch to seeds, insects, and grasses. The females form long-lasting relationships within their groups, and establish stable dominance hierarchies.

Chimpanzees provide an illustration of how females behave when their food isn't in clumps big enough to feed everybody. Female chimps eat flowers, shoots, leaves, and insects, but their diet is composed largely of fruits that are widely scattered and often not very plentiful. They may occasionally gather at a particularly abundant fruit tree, but when the fruit is gone they disperse to forage individually for other foods. Members of the troop are constantly meeting at fruit trees, splitting up, and gathering again.

These two types of female groups, the "bonded" savanna baboons and "fissioning" chimps, as Wrangham calls them, pose very different mating opportunities for the males of their species. As a consequence, the social behavior of the two species is different. For a male baboon, groups of females represent the perfect opportunity for him to get cops. All he has to do is exclude other males. A baboon troop includes a clan of females accompanied by a number of males, which compete fiercely for access to them. For baboons there are few advantages to fraternal cooperation, and many to competition.

Male chimpanzees fight far less over females than male baboons do, principally because there's little point—the females don't stick together. Instead, the males form strong alliances with their fellows. They roam in gangs looking for females in heat, and patrol their troop's borders against male interlopers.

Wrangham's theory made so much sense, Strier says, that it inspired researchers to go back into the field with a new perspective. She saw the muriqui as an excellent species for evaluating the model, since Wrangham had constructed it before anyone knew the first thing about this monkey. His idea would seem all the more reasonable if it could predict the muriqui's behavior.

It couldn't, at least not entirely. Strier has found that the females fit Wrangham's predictions: they stick together and eat a combination of preferred and subsistence foods, defending the preferred from other troops. But the males don't conform to the theory. "Considering that the females are foraging together, there should be relatively low pressure on the males to cooperate," she says. "It's odd: the males should compete, but they don't."

She thinks that limitations on male competition may explain muriqui behavior. First, the muriquis are too big to fight in trees. "I think these monkeys are at about the limit of size for rapid brachiation," she says. "If they were bigger, they couldn't travel rapidly through the trees. They fall a lot as it is, and it really shakes them up. I've seen an adult fall about sixty feet, nearly to the ground, before catching hold of a branch. That means that whatever they fight about has got to be worth the risk of falling out of a tree."

Moreover, fighting may require more energy than the muriquis can afford. Milton has estimated the caloric value of the food eaten by a muriqui each day and compared it to the amount of energy she would expect a monkey of that size to need. She concluded that the muriqui had little excess energy to burn on combat. *Environmental selections*

The restriction that rapid brachiation sets on the muriqui's size discourages competition in more subtle ways, as well. Given that muriquis are polygynous, the male should be bigger than the female, as is almost invariably the case among other polygynous species—but he's not. The link between larger males and polygyny is created by sexual selection, an evolutionary force that Darwin first recognized, and which he distinguished from natural selection by the fact that it acts exclusively on one sex. Sexual selection is responsible for the manes of male lions, for instance, and for the large canines of male baboons.

In a polygynous society, the advantages to being a large male are obvious: he who's biggest is most likely to win the battles over females—and pass on his genes for size. But sexual selection's push toward large males has been thwarted in the muriqui, says Strier. Any competitive benefits greater size might bring a male would be offset in part by the excessive demands on his energy and the costs of falling out of trees.

She believes that the constraints on the males' size have had a profound effect on the muriquis' social behavior. Most important, says Strier, with males and females being the same size, the females can't be dominated, which means they can pick their mates. Most female primates aren't so fortunate: if they copulate with subordinate males, they risk being attacked by dominant ones. But a female muriqui in heat can easily refuse a suitor, simply by sitting down or by moving away.

Fighting not only doesn't help the male muriqui in his quest for cops; it may even harm his chances, since females can shun an aggressive male. Strier believes that females may also be responsible for the male muriquis' canine teeth not being oversized. As a rule, the male's canines are the same size as the female's only in monogamous primate species, but over the generations female muriquis may have mated more readily with males whose teeth were no bigger than their own. In sum, Strier thinks, for a male muriqui the costs of competing are far outweighted by the benefits of avoiding it.

But he has the means to vie for reproductive success and still come across as Mr. Nice Guy: his sperm. Sperm competition, as it's called, is a hot new idea in sociobiology, originally proposed to explain male bonding in chimpanzees, and, as Milton was the first to suggest, it may explain why the muriqui has such enormous testicles.

The competition is something like a game of chance. Imagine a bucket with a hole in the bottom just big enough for a marble to pass through. People gather round, each with a handful of marbles. They drop their marbles in the bucket, mix them up, and one comes out the bottom. Whoever owns that marble is the winner.

In the sperm competition among male muriquis, the bucket is a female, the marbles are sperm, and winning means becoming a father. No male can be sure it will be his sperm that impregnates a female, since she mates with a number of his fellows. His chances are further complicated by the fact that the female muriqui, like all New World monkeys, gives no visible indication of ovulation; there may be nothing that signals the male (or the female) when during her heat that occurs. So it's to the male's advantage to continue mating as often as the female will have him.

This may sound like monkey heaven, but it puts the male on the horns of a dilemma. If he copulates as often as possible, he could run low on sperm just when the female is ovulating. On the other hand, if he refrains from copulating to save sperm, he may miss his chance at procreating altogether. Selection may have come to his aid, Strier reasons, by acting on his testicles.

Here's a plausible scenario. Suppose a male came along that could produce more sperm than the average muriqui because his testicles were bigger than average. That male would clean up in the reproductive arena. The ratio of testicle size to body weight has been correlated with high sperm count and repeated copulation over a short period in other mammals, and bigger testicles probably also increase the percentage of viable and motile sperm.

If the muriqui's testicles are anything like those of other species, then a male with extra big ones has a slight reproductive advantage. Like a player with more marbles to put in the bucket, a male that can produce more and better sperm has a better than average chance of impregnating females and passing on this advantageous trait to his sons. Just as important, the outsized organs probably don't cost him much in metabolic energy. Thus, over generations, the muriqui's testicles have grown larger and larger.

Strier's theory has five years of data behind it, and it's the kind of theory that will stimulate researchers to re-examine their ideas about other species. Yet it isn't her only concern; she concentrates equally on the muriqui's uncertain future. On our last day in the forest we watched the monkeys cross a six-foot gap in the canopy 60 feet above us. One by one they stood poised for a moment on the end of a branch before launching themselves. Strier counted them as they appeared in silhouette against a grey sky. The total was 33, including the twins. "They're up from twenty-two in 1982," she said. "That's a very fast increase."

The muriquis at Montes Claros make up almost one-tenth of the total population of the species, and they're critical to its survival—as are all the other isolated and widely separated troops. Each group's genetic pool is limited, and eventually the troops could suffer inbreeding depression, a decline in fecundity that often appears in populations with little genetic variability.

Strier and Mittermeier predict that one day muriquis will have to be managed, the way game species are in the U.S. They may be transported between patches of forest to provide some gene flow. But that's a dangerous proposition now. There are too few muriquis to risk it, and none has ever bred or survived for long in captivity. "Before my study, conservationists would probably have moved males between forests," Strier says. "That would've been a mistake. I have tentative evidence that in a natural situation the females may be the ones that do the transferring between groups."

For now, though, she thinks the biggest concern isn't managing the monkeys but preventing their habitat from disappearing. Preserving what remains of the Atlantic forest won't be easy, and no one knows this better than Feliciano Miguel Abdala, the man responsible for there being any forest at all at Montes Claros.

Abdala has little formal education, but he's rich; he owns nine plantations besides Montes Claros. His family lives in relative splendor in Caratinga, but he likes to spend the weekdays here. His house is just beyond the edge of the forest, and sunlight filters through the bougainvillea vine entwining the front porch. Chickens can be seen through the cracks in the floorboards, scratching in the dirt under the house. Electric cords are strung crazily from the rafters, and a bare bulb dangles in the center of his office. Abdala removes his straw hat decorously and places it on a chair before sitting at his desk.

Abdala bought the 5,000 acres of Montes-Claros in 1944. The region was barely settled then, and smoke still rose from the great burning heaps of slash left from clearing the forest. Abdala's land included one of the last stands of trees. I ask him why he saved it. "I am a conservationist," he says. "For a long time the local people thought I was crazy because I wouldn't cut the forest. I told them not to shoot the monkeys, and they stopped. Now all my workers are crazy, too."

I ask Abdala about his plans for his forest. He rubs his head distractedly and says, vaguely, "I hope it will continue."

Abdala believes the government should buy Montes Claros—plantation and rain forest—to create a nature reserve. He'll probably maintain the forest as long as he lives, but the land is quite valuable, and his heirs might not share his lofty sentiments.

   As important as the muriquis have become to understanding the evolution of primate social systems, and as much as U.S. conservationists may wish to see these monkeys preserved, Strier thinks that in the end it's up to the Brazilians to save them. She's expecting a three-year grant from the National Science Foundation; part of the money will go toward allowing her to observe the monkeys in other forest patches, watching for variation in their behavior as a test of her ideas. Studies like hers will be critical not only for proving theories but also for ensuring that plans for managing the muriquis will work. The rest of the money will permit her to train seven Brazilian graduate students, because, she says, "the future of the muriqui lies with the Brazilians."

# POSTSCRIPT

## Is Male Aggression and Competition Key to Reproductive Success?

**W**hile male aggression and infanticide do seem to be linked to reproductive success among some primates, it is clear that male violence is neither innate or inevitable. In multimale troops like the muriqui, males get farther by being nice to females and having bigger testicles. Fighting between males—as well as infanticide—seems to be more common in primate troops organized around one or a few males who are routinely disposed or replaced by younger, stronger males. Troop organization and other social and environmental factors thus play an important role in determining which behavioral traits lead to male reproductive success.

The amount of intersexual male selection also seems to be a factor in whether male aggression is linked with reproductive success. For example, Murqui females exercise a great deal of control over their choice of mates. Therefore, "fighting not only doesn't help the male murqui in his quest for cops; it may even harm his chances, since females can shun an aggressive male" (Brownlee, 1987:73). In some primate societies, females may even band together to discourage unwanted or over aggressive suitors. As Smuts notes:

> Vervet monkeys are one such species, and among these small and exceptionally feisty African monkeys, related females gang up against males. High ranking females use their dense network of female alliances to rule the troop; although smaller than males, they slap persistent suitors away like annoying flies. Researchers have observed similar alliances in many other female-bonded species, including other Old World Monkeys such as macaques, olive baboons, palas and rhesus monkeys, and gray langurs; New World Monkeys such as the capuchin; and prosimians such as the ring tailed lemur (1995:37).

Perhaps the most intriguing case of a "make love, not war society" is shown by the bonobos of Zaire. Instead of fighting or intimidation, both males and females use sex to form alliances and resolve conflicts. Homosexual contact among females also seems to cement their ability to cooperate to dominate males and avoid sexual coercion (Parish, 1994 and Smuts, 1995). Since bonobos share many other humanlike characteristics (see Issue 8), their ability to avoid conflict suggests that world peace and cooperation are also within our grasp.

Classic books on the subject of male aggression and reproductive success include *African Genesis* (Antheneum, 1961) and *The Territorial Imperative* (Antheneum, 1968), both by R. Ardrey, Charles Darwin's *The Descent of Man and His Relations to Sex*, 2nd ed. (The Henneberry Company, 1874), and Sarah Hrdy's book *The Langurs of Abu* (Harvard University Press, 1977). Important works challenging the link between male aggression and reproductive success include *The Nature of Human Aggression* by Ashley Montagu (Oxford University Press, 1976); R. Lewonlin, L. Kamin, and S. Rose's book *Not in Our Genes* (Pantheon, 1984) and Richard Sussman's articles "The Nature of Human Universals," *Reviews in Anthropology* (vol. 24, pp. 1–11, 1995) and "Exploring Our Basic Human Nature," *Anthro Notes* (vol. 19, no. 3, 1997).

# ISSUE 6

## Are Primate Females Selected to Be Monogamous?

**YES: David M. Buss,** from *The Evolution of Desire: Strategies of Human Mating* (BasicBooks, 1994)

**NO: Carol Tavris,** from *The Mismeasure of Women* (Simon and Schuster, 1992)

### ISSUE SUMMARY

**YES:** David Buss suggests that primate females have a different reproductive strategy than males. In his view, females favor monogamy because it increases the chances of male investment in them and their offspring.

**NO:** Carol Tavris argues instead that the best strategy for primate females is to get pregnant as soon as possible. Like males, females benefit from having multiple partners and engaging in promiscuous sex.

$\mathbf{A}$re females selected to be monogamous? This question has intrigued scientists since it was introduced by Charles Darwin in 1871. According to his theory, males are selected to be promiscuous because maximizing the number of sexual contacts increases their chances of reproduction. Females, on the other hand, have more to gain from being coy and selective. They size up potential suitors and eventually pick the one "Mr. Right" who will provide resources and protection for them and their offspring. Monogamy becomes a way of insuring the male's continued loyalty and parental investment. This viewpoint also assumes: (1) primate females need male help to support and protect their offspring, (2) promiscuous females receive little help or long-term support from males, and (3) females trade sex for social and economic security.

As well as insinuating its way into popular culture, the notion that females are naturally monogamous continues to be championed by scientists. For example, evolutionary psychologists like Buss argue that females have a greater investment in their offspring than males. This investment is based on the idea that females carry infants for nine months and care for them for an extended time after birth. Therefore, Buss feels that females must be choosier about selecting mates than males. Because females have fewer opportunities in their lifetime to reproduce, they must maximize the survival potential of each offspring they have by attaching themselves to a male with the stability and material resources to support them. In contrast, other researchers suggest that female promiscuity may have its own reproductive and evolutionary advantages. Carol Tavris examines this idea in detail in her book *The Mismeasure of Women*.

# YES

David M. Buss

# The Evolution of Desire: Strategies of Human Mating

## What Women Want

*We are walking archives of ancestral wisdom.*

—Helena Cronin, *The Ant and the Peacock*

What women actually want in a mate has puzzled male scientists and other men for centuries, for good reason. It is not androcentric to propose that women's preferences in a partner are more complex and enigmatic than the mate preferences of either sex of any other species. Discovering the evolutionary roots of women's desires requires going for back in time, before humans evolved as a species, before primates emerged from their mammalian ancestors, back to the origins of sexual reproduction itself.

One reason women exert choice about mates stems from the most basic fact of reproductive biology—the definition of sex. It is a remarkable circumstance that what defines biological sex is simply the size of the sex cells. Males are defined as the ones with the small sex cells, females as the ones with the large sex cells. The large female gametes remain reasonably stationary and come loaded with nutrients. The small male gametes are endowed with mobility and swimming speed. Along with differences in the size and mobility of sex cells comes a difference between the sexes in quantity. Men, for example, produce millions of sperm, which are replenished at a rate of roughly twelve million per hour, while women produce a fixed and unreplenishable lifetime supply of approximately four hundred ova.

Women's greater initial investment does not end with the egg. Fertilization and gestation, key components of human parental investment, occur internally within women. One act of sexual intercourse, which requires minimal male investment, can produce an obligatory and energy-consuming nine-month investment by the woman that forecloses other mating opportunities. Women then bear the exclusive burden of lactation, an investment that may last as long as three or four years.

No biological law of the animal world dictates that women invest more than men. Indeed, among some species, such as the Mormon cricket, pipefish seahorse, and Panamanian poison arrow frog, males invest more. The male Mormon cricket produces through great effort a large spermatophore that is loaded with nutrients. Females compete with each other for access to the males that hold the largest spermatophores. Among these so-called sex-role reversed species, it is the males who are more discriminating about mating. Among all four thousand species of mammals, including the more than two hundred species of primates, however, females bear the burden of internal fertilization, gestation, and lactation.

The great initial parental investment of women makes them a valuable, but limited, resource. Gestating, bearing, nursing, nurturing, and protecting a child are exceptional reproductive resources that cannot be allocated indiscriminately. Nor can one woman dispense them to many men.

Those who hold valuable resources do not give them away cheaply or unselectively. Because women in our evolutionary past risked enormous investment as a consequence of having sex, evolution favored women who were highly selective about their mates. Ancestral women suffered severe costs if they were indiscriminate—they experienced lower reproductive success, and fewer of their children survived to reproductive age. A man in human evolutionary history could walk away from a casual coupling having lost only a few hours of time. His reproductive success was not seriously compromised. A woman in evolutionary history could also walk away from a casual encounter, but if she got pregnant as a result, she bore the costs of that decision for months, years, and even decades afterward.

Modern birth control technology has altered these costs. In today's industrial nations, women can have short-term dalliances with less fear of pregnancy. But human sexual psychology evolved over millions of years to cope with ancestral adaptive problems. We still possess this underlying sexual psychology, even though our environment has changed.

## Components of Desire

Consider the case of an ancestral woman who is trying to decide between two men, one of whom shows great generosity with his resources to her and one of whom is stingy. Other things being equal, the generous man is more valuable to her than the stingy man. The generous man may share his meat from the hunt, aiding her survival. He may sacrifice his time, energy, and resources for the benefit of the children, furthering the woman's reproductive success. In these respects, the generous man has higher value as a mate than the stingy man. If, over evolutionary time, generosity in men provided these benefits repeatedly and the cues to a man's generosity were observable and reliable, then selection would favor the evolution of a preference for generosity in a mate.

Now consider a more complicated and realistic case in which men vary not just in their generosity but also in a bewildering variety of ways that are significant to the choice of a mate. Men vary in their physical prowess, athletic skill, ambition, industriousness, kindness, empathy, emotional stability, intelligence, social skills, sense of humor, kin network, and position in the status hierarchy. Men also differ in the costs they impose on a mating relationship: some come with children, bad debts, a quick temper, a selfish disposition, and a tendency to be promiscuous. In addition, men differ in hundreds of ways that may be irrelevant to women. Some men have navels turned in, others have navels turned out. A strong preference for a particular navel shape would be unlikely to evolve unless male navel differences were somehow adaptively relevant to ancestral women. From among the thousands of ways in which men differ, selection over hundreds of thousands of years focused women's preferences laser-like on the most adaptively valuable characteristics.

The qualities people prefer, however, are not static characteristics, Because characteristics change, mate seekers must gauge the future potential of a prospective partner. A young medical student who lacks resources now might have excellent future promise. Or a man might be very ambitious but have already reached his peak. Another man might have children from a previous marriage, but because they are about to leave the nest, they will not drain his resources. Gauging a man's mating value requires looking beyond his current position and evaluating his potential.

Evolution has favored women who prefer men who possess attributes that confer benefits and who dislike men who possess attributes that impose costs. Each separate attribute constitutes one component of a man's value to a woman as a mate. Each of her preferences tracks one component.

Preferences that favor particular components, however, do not completely solve the problem of choosing a mate. Women face further adaptive hurdles. First, a woman must evaluate her unique circumstances and personal needs. The same man might differ in value for different women. A man's willingness to do a lot of direct child care, for example, might be more valuable to a woman who does not have kin around to help her than to a woman whose mother, sisters, aunts, and uncles eagerly participate. The dangers of choosing a man with a volatile temper may be greater for a woman who is an only child than for a woman with four strapping brothers around to protect her. The value of potential males, in short, depends on the individualized, personalized, and contextualized perspective of the person doing the choosing.

In selecting a mate, women must identify and correctly evaluate the cues that signal whether a man indeed possesses a particular resource. The assessment problem becomes especially acute in areas where men are apt to deceive women, such as pretending to have higher status than they do or feigning greater commitment than they are willing to give.

Finally, women face the problem of integrating their knowledge about a prospective mate. Suppose that one man is generous but emotionally unstable. Another man is emotionally stable but stingy. Which man should a woman choose? Choosing a mate calls upon psychological mechanisms that make it possible to evaluate the relevant attributes and give each its appropriate weight in the whole. Some attributes are granted more weight than others in the final decision about whether to choose or reject a particular man. One of these heavily weighted components is the man's resources.

## Economic Capacity

The evolution of the female preference for males who offer resources may be the most ancient and pervasive basis for female choice in the animal kingdom. Consider the gray shrike, a bird that lives in the Negev Desert of Israel. Just before the start of the breeding season, male shrikes begin amassing caches of edible prey, such as snails, and other useful objects, such as feathers and pieces of cloth, in numbers ranging from 90 to 120. They impale these items on thorns and other pointed projections within their territory. Females look over the available males and prefer to mate with those having the largest caches. When the biologist Reuven Yosef arbitrarily removed portions of some males' caches and added edible objects to others, females shifted to the males with the larger bounties. Females avoided entirely males without resources, consigning them to bachelorhood. Wherever females show a mating preference, the male's resources are often the key criterion.

Among humans, the evolution of women's preference for a permanent mate with resources would have required three preconditions. First, resources would have had to be accruable, defensible, and controllable by men during human evolutionary history. Second, men would have had to differ from each other in their holdings and their willingness to invest those holdings in a woman and her children—if all men possessed the same resources and showed an equal willingness to commit them, there would be no need for women to develop the preference for them. Constants do not count in mating decisions. And third, the advantages of being with one man would have to outweigh the advantages of being with several men.

Among humans, these conditions are easily met. Territory and tools, to name just two resources, are acquired, defended, monopolized, and controlled by men worldwide. Men vary tremendously in the quantity of resources they command—from the poverty of the street bum to the riches of Trumps and Rockefellers. Men also differ widely in how willing they are to invest their time and resources in long-term mateships. Some men are cads, preferring to mate with many women while investing little in each. Other men are dads, channeling all of their resources to one woman and her children.

Women over human evolutionary history could often garner far more resources for their children through a single spouse than through several temporary sex partners. Men provide their wives and children with resources to an extent that is unprecedented among primates. Among most other primate species, for example, females must rely solely on their own efforts to acquire food, because males usually do not share food with their mates. Men, in contrast, provide food, find shelter, and defend territory. Men protect children. They tutor them in the art of hunting, the craft of war, the strategies of social influence. They transfer status, aiding offspring in forming reciprocal alliances later in life. Such benefits are unlikely to be secured by a woman from a temporary sex partner. Not all potential husbands can confer all of these benefits, but over thousands of generations, when some men were able to provide some of these benefits, women gained a powerful advantage by preferring them as mates.

So the stage was set for women to evolve a preference for men with resources. But women needed cues to signal a man's possession of those resources. These cues might be indirect, such as personality characteristics that signaled a man's upward mobility. They might be physical, such as a man's athletic ability or health. They might include reputational information, such as the esteem in which a man was held by his peers. Economic resources, however, provide the most direct cue. . . .

## Social Status

*only men?*

Traditional hunter-gatherer societies, which are our closest guide to what ancestral conditions were probably like, suggest that ancestral men had clearly defined status hierarchies, with resources flowing freely to those at the top and trickling slowly to those at the bottom. Traditional tribes today, such as the Tiwi, an aboriginal group residing on two small islands off the coast of Northern Australia; the Yanomamo of Venezuela; the Ache of Paraguay; and the !Kung tribe of Botswana, are replete with people described as "head men" and "big men" who wield great power and enjoy the resource privileges of prestige. Therefore, an ancestral man's social status would provide a powerful cue to his possession of resources.

Henry Kissinger once remarked that power is the most potent aphrodisiac. Women desire men who command a high position in society because social status is a universal cue to the control of resources. Along with status come better food, more abundant territory, and superior health care. Greater social status bestows on children social opportunities missed by the children of lower-ranked males. For male children worldwide, access to more mates and better quality mates typically accompanies families of higher social status. In one study of 186 societies ranging from the Mbuti Pygmies of Africa to the Aleut Eskimos, high-status men invariably had greater wealth, better nourishment for children, and more wives. . . .

## Age

The age of a man also provides an important cue to his access to resources. Just as young male baboons must mature before they can enter the upper ranks in the baboon social hierarchy, human adolescents and young men rarely command the respect, status, or position of more mature older men. This tendency reaches an extreme among the Tiwi tribe, a gerontocracy in which the very old men wield most of the power and prestige and control the mating system through complex networks of alliances. Even in American culture, status and wealth tend to accumulate with increasing age. . . .

In traditional societies, part of this linkage may be related to physical strength and hunting prowess. Physical strength increases in men as they get older, peaking in their late twenties and early thirties. Although there have been no systematic studies of the relationship between age and hunting ability, anthropologists believe that ability may peak when a man is in his thirties, at which point his slight decline in physical prowess is more than compensated for by his increased knowledge, patience, skill, and wisdom. So women's preference for older men may stem from our hunter-gatherer ancestors, for whom the resources derived from hunting were critical to survival. . . .

In cultures where people marry young, often the economic capacity of a man cannot be evaluated directly but must be deduced indirectly. Indeed, in hunter-gatherer groups that lack a cash economy, the target of selection cannot be financial resources per se. Among the Tiwi tribe, for example, young men are scrutinized carefully by both women and older men to evaluate which ones are "comers," destined to acquire status and resources, and which are likely to remain in the slow lane, based in part on their personality. The young men are evaluated for their promise, the key signs being good hunting skills, good fighting skills, and especially a strong proclivity to ascend the hierarchy of tribal power and influence. Women in all cultures, past and present, can select men for their apparent ability to accrue future resources, based on certain personality characteristics. And women who value the personality characteristics likely to lead to status and sustained resource acquisition are far better off than women who ignore these vital characterological cues. . . .

## Size and Strength

When the great basketball player Magic Johnson revealed that he had slept with thousands of women, he inadvertently revealed women's preference for mates who display physical and athletic prowess. The numbers may be shocking, but the preference is not. Physical characteristics, such as athleticism, size, and strength, convey important information that women use in making a mating decision.

The importance of physical characteristics in the female choice of a mate is prevalent throughout the animal world. In the species called the gladiator frog, males are responsible for creating nests and defending the eggs. In the majority of courtships, a stationary male is deliberately bumped by a female who is considering him. She strikes him with great force, sometimes enough to rock him back or even scare him away. If the male moves too much or bolts from the nest, the female hastily leaves to examine alternative mates. Most females mate with males who do not move or who move minimally when bumped. Only rarely does a female reject a male who remains firmly planted after being bumped. Bumping helps a female frog to decide how successful the male will be at defending her clutch. The bump test reveals the male's physical ability to perform the function of protection.

Women sometimes face physical domination by larger, stronger men, which can lead to injury and sexual domination by preventing them from exercising choice. Such domination undoubtedly occurred regularly during ancestral times. Indeed, studies of many nonhuman primate groups reveal that male physical and sexual domination of females has been a recurrent part of our primate heritage. The primatologist Barbara Smuts lived among baboons in the savanna plains of Africa while studying their mating patterns. She found that females frequently form enduring "special friendships" with males who offer physical protection to themselves and their infants. In return, these females grant their "friends" preferential sexual access during times of estrus. In essence, female baboons exchange sex for protection.

Analogously, one benefit to women of permanent mating is the physical protection a man can offer. A man's size, strength, and physical prowess are cues to solutions to the problem of protection. The evidence shows that women's preferences in a mate embody these cues. In the study of temporary and permanent mating. American women rated the desirability or undesirability of a series of physical traits. Women judge short men to be undesirable as a permanent mate. In contrast, they find it very desirable for a potential permanent mate to be tall, physically strong, and athletic. Another group of American women consistently indicates a preference for men of average or greater than average height, roughly five feet and eleven inches, as their ideal marriage partner. Tall men are consistently seen as more desirable dates and mates than men who are short or of average height. Furthermore, the two studies of personal ads described earlier revealed that, among women who mention height, 80 percent want a man who is six feet or taller. Perhaps even more telling is the finding that ads placed by taller men receive more responses from women than those placed by shorter men. Tall men date more often than short men and have a larger pool of potential mates. Women solve the problem of protection from aggressive men at least in part by preferring a mate who has the size, strength, and physical prowess to protect them.

Tall men tend to have a higher status in nearly all cultures. "Big men" in hunter-gatherer societies—men high in status—are literally big men physically. In Western cultures, tall men make more money, advance in their professions more rapidly, and receive more and earlier promotions. Few American presidents have been less than six feet tall. Politicians are keenly aware of voters' preference. Following the televised presidential debate in 1988, George Bush made a point of standing very close to his shorter competitor, Michael Dukakis, in a strategy of highlighting their disparity in size. As the evolutionary psychologist Bruce Ellis notes:

> Height constitutes a reliable cue to dominance in social interactions . . . shorter policemen are likely to be assaulted more than taller policemen . . . suggesting that the latter command more fear and respect from adversaries . . . taller men are more sought after in women's personal advertisements, receive more responses to their own personal advertisements, and tend to have prettier girlfriends than do shorter men.

This preference for taller men is not limited to Western cultures. Among the Mehinaku tribe of the Brazilian Amazon, the anthropologist Thomas Gregor notes the importance of men's wrestling skills as an arena where size differences become acute:

> A heavily muscled, imposingly built man is likely to accumulate many girlfriends, while a small man, deprecatingly referred to as a *perissi,* fares badly. The mere fact of height creates a measurable advantage. . . . A powerful wrestler, say the villagers, is frightening . . . he commands fear and respect. To the women, he is "beautiful" (awitsiri), in demand as a paramour and

husband. Triumphant in politics as well as in love, the champion wrestler embodies the highest qualities of manliness. Not so fortunate the vanquished! A chronic loser, no matter what his virtues, is regarded as a fool. As he wrestles, the men shout mock advice. . . . The women are less audible as they watch the matches from their doorways, but they too have their sarcastic jokes. None of them is proud of having a loser as a husband or lover.

Barbara Smuts believes that during human evolutionary history physical protection was one of the most important things a man could offer a woman. The presence of aggressive men who tried to dominate women physically and to circumvent their sexual choices may have been an important influence on women's mate selection in ancestral times. Given the alarming incidence of sexual coercion and rape in many cultures, a mate's protection value may well remain relevant to mate selection in modern environments. Many women simply do not feel safe on the streets, and a strong, tall, athletic mate acts as a deterrent for sexually aggressive men.

Attributes such as size, strength, and athletic prowess are not the only physical attributes that signal high mating value. Another physical quality critical for survival is good health.

## Good Health

Women worldwide prefer mates who are healthy. In all thirty-seven cultures included in the international study on choosing a mate, women judge good health to be anywhere from important to indispensable in a marriage partner. In another study on American women, poor physical conditions, ranging from bad grooming habits to a venereal disease, are regarded as extremely undesirable characteristics in a mate. The biologists Clelland Ford and Frank Beach found that signs of ill health, such as open sores, lesions, and unusual pallor, are universally regarded as unattractive.

In humans, good health may be signaled by behavior as well as by physical appearance. A lively mood, high energy level, and sprightly gait, for example, may be attractive precisely because they are calorically costly and can be displayed only by people brimming with good health.

The tremendous importance we place on good health is not unique to our species. Some animals display large, loud, and gaudy traits that are costly and yet signal great health and vitality. Consider the bright, flamboyant, ostentatious plumage of the peacock. It is as if the peacock is saying: "Look at me; I'm so fit that I can carry these large, cumbersome feathers, and yet still I'm thriving." The mystery of the peacock's tail, which seems so contrary to utilitarian survival, is finally on the verge of being solved. The biologists William D. Hamilton and Marlena Zuk propose that the brilliant plumage serves as a signal that the peacock carries a light load of parasites, since peacocks who carry more than the average number of parasites have duller plumage. The burdensome plumage provides a cue to health and robustness. Peahens prefer the brilliant plumage because it provides clues to the male's health.

In ancestral times, four bad consequences were likely to follow if a woman selected a mate who was unhealthy or disease-prone. First, she put herself and her family at risk of being contaminated by the disease. Second, her mate was less able to perform essential functions and provide crucial benefits to her and her children, such as food, protection, health care, and child rearing. Third, her mate was at increased risk of dying, prematurely cutting off the flow of resources and forcing her to incur the costs of searching for a new mate and courting all over again. And fourth, if health is partly heritable, she would risk passing on genes for poor health to her children. A preference for healthy mates solves the problem of mate survival and ensures that resources are likely to be delivered over the long run.

## Love and Commitment

A man's possession of such assets as health, status, and resources, however, still does not guarantee his willingness to commit them to a particular woman and her children. Indeed, some men show a tremendous reluctance to marry, preferring to play the field and to seek a series of temporary sex partners. Women deride men for this hesitancy, calling them "commitment dodgers," "commitment phobics," "paranoid about commitment," and "fearful of the M word." And women's anger is reasonable. Given the tremendous costs women incur because of sex, pregnancy, and childbirth, it is reasonable for them to require commitment from a man in return.

The weight women attach to commitment is revealed in the following true story (the names are changed). Mark and Susan had been going out with each other for two years and had been living together for six months. He was a well-off forty-two-year-old professional, she a medical student of twenty-eight. Susan pressed for a decision about marriage—they were in love, and she wanted to have children within a few years. But Mark balked. He had been married before; if he ever married again, he wanted to be absolutely sure it would be for good. As Susan continued to press for a decision, Mark raised the possibility of a prenuptial agreement. She resisted, feeling that this violated the spirit of marriage. Finally they agreed that by a date four months in the future he would have decided one way or another. The date came and went, and still Mark could not make a decision. Susan told him that she was leaving him, moved out, and started dating another man. Mark panicked. He called her up and begged her to come back, saying that he had changed his mind and would marry her. He promised a new car. He promised that there would be no prenuptial agreement. But it was too late. Mark's failure to commit was too strong a negative signal to Susan. It dealt the final blow to their relationship. She was gone forever.

Women past and present face the adaptive problem of choosing men who not only have the necessary resources but also show a willingness to commit those resources to them and their children. This problem may be more difficult than it seems at first. Although resources can often be directly observed, commitment cannot be. Instead, gauging commitment requires looking for cues that signal the likelihood of fidelity in the channeling of resources. Love is one of the most important cues to commitment. . . .

Kindness is an enduring personality characteristic that has many components, but at the core of all of them is the commitment of resources. The trait signals an empathy toward children, a willingness to put a mate's needs before one's own, and a willingness to channel energy and effort toward a mate's goals rather than exclusively and selfishly to one's own goals. Kindness, in other words, signals the ability and willingness of a potential mate to commit energy and resources selflessly to a partner.

The lack of kindness signals selfishness, an inability or unwillingness to commit, and a high likelihood that costs will be inflicted on a spouse. The study of newlyweds, for example, identified unkind men on the basis of their self-assessment, their wives' assessment, and the judgment of male and female interviewers, and then examined the wives' complaints about these husbands. Women married to unkind men complain that their spouses abuse them both verbally and physically by hitting, slapping, or spitting at them. Unkind men tend to be condescending, putting down their wife's opinions as stupid or inferior. They are selfish, monopolizing shared resources. They are inconsiderate, failing to do any housework. They are neglectful, failing to show up as promised. Finally, they have more extramarital affairs, suggesting that these men are unable or unwilling to commit to a monogamous relationship. Unkind men look out for themselves, and have trouble committing to anything much beyond that.

Because sex is one of the most valuable reproductive resources women can offer, they have evolved psychological mechanisms that cause them to resist giving it away indiscriminately. Requiring love, sincerity, and kindness is a way of securing a commitment of resources commensurate with the value of the resource that women give to men. Requiring love and kindness helps women to solve the critical adaptive mating problem of securing the commitment of resources from a man that can aid in the survival and reproduction of her offspring. . . .

## Women's Many Preferences

We now have the outlines of an answer to the enigma of what women want. Women are judicious, prudent, and discerning about the men they consent to mate with because they have so many valuable reproductive resources to offer. Those with valuable resources rarely give them away indiscriminately. The costs in reproductive currency of failing to exercise choice were too great for ancestral women, who would have risked beatings, food deprivation, disease, abuse of children, and abandonment. The benefits of choice in nourishment, protection, and paternal investment for children were abundant.

Permanent mates may bring with them a treasure trove of resources. Selecting a long-term mate who has the relevant resources is clearly an extraordinarily complex endeavor. It involves at least a dozen distinctive preferences, each corresponding to a resource that helps women to solve critical adaptive problems.

That women seek resources in a permanent mate may be obvious. But because resources cannot always be directly discerned, women's mating preferences are keyed to other qualities that signal the likely possession, or future acquisition, of resources. Indeed, women may be less influenced by money per se than by qualities that lead to resources, such as ambition, status, intelligence, and age. Women scrutinize these personal qualities carefully because they reveal a man's potential.

Potential, however, is not enough. Because many men with a high resource potential are themselves discriminating and are at times content with casual sex, women are faced with the problem of commitment. Seeking love and sincerity are two solutions to the commitment problem. Sincerity signals that the man is capable of commitment. Acts of love signal that he has in fact committed to a particular woman.

To have the love and commitment of a man who could be easily downed by other men in the physical arena, however, would have been a problematic asset for ancestral women. Women mated to small, weak men lacking in physical prowess would have risked damage from other men and loss of the couple's joint resources. Tall, strong, athletic men offered ancestral women protection. In this way, their resources and commitment could be secured against incursion. Women who selected men in part for their strength and prowess were more likely to be successful at surviving and reproducing.

Resources, commitment, and protection do a woman little good if her husband becomes diseased or dies or if the couple is so mismatched that they fail to function as an effective team. The premium that women place on a man's health ensures that husbands will be capable of providing these benefits over the long haul. And the premium that women place on similarity of interests and traits with their mate helps to ensure the convergence of mutually pursued goals. These multiple facets of current women's mating preferences thus correspond perfectly with the multiple facets of adaptive problems that were faced by our women ancestors thousands of years ago. . . .

# The Mismeasure of Woman

## The Myth of the Coy Female

> [Thus] we arrived at the important conclusion that polygamy is the natural order among human beings, just as it is in most species of the animal kingdom. . . . monogamy is responsible for the high incidence of divorce and female grievances in modern society, as well as the genetic deevolution and behavioral degeneration of civilization as a whole. . . . Culture is to blame, and fortunately *culture can be changed*. Mating is the key. [Emphasis in original.]
>
> —Sam Kash Kachigan, *The Sexual Matrix*

Sam Kash Kachigan is not a social scientist; he's just a regular fellow who thinks that the theories of sociobiology offer the best hope of improving relations between women and men. "Mating is the key," he argues. The mating he has in mind, it turns out, would (if we were truly to follow our evolutionary heritage) occur between rich old men and beautiful young girls. Among the annoying contemporary practices that Kachigan laments is the habit of beautiful young girls marrying boys their own age. To Kachigan, in any truly civilized society— that is, one in which our practices fit our sociobiological natures—girls would marry men who were old enough to demonstrate their "true potential":

> In every respect, then, it makes much more sense for young women to mate with *older* men, who will have *proven* their genetic endowment as well as their financial and emotional capacity for raising children. [Emphasis in original.]

Why do I suspect that Kachigan is such a man?

The basic ideas behind sociobiology date back to Charles Darwin, who in 1871 described what he considered to be a basic dichotomy in the sexual natures of males and females of all species. Males actively pursue females; they are promiscuous; and those who are strongest, most fit in evolutionary terms, succeed in their sexual conquest. Females, said Darwin, are "comparatively passive"; they may choose their preferred suitor, but then remain monogamous and faithful. That this dichotomy conveniently fit Victorian dating and mating patterns was, naturally, pure coincidence.

For a century after Darwin, research on sexual selection and sexual behavior was based on the belief that males are passionate and undiscriminating (any female in a storm will do), whereas females are restrained, cautious, and highly discriminating in their choice of partner (only a male who meets her shopping list of qualifications will do). According to primatologist Sarah Blaffer Hrdy, this stereotype of "the coy female" has persisted in the public mind—and she adds a phrase that by now should be familiar to us—"*despite the accumulation of abundant openly available evidence contradicting it*" [my emphasis].

The stereotype of the coy female got a major boost in an important paper published in 1948 by Angus John Bateman. Bateman was a distinguished plant geneticist who did dozens of experiments with Drosophila, the tiny fruit fly that many people remember from science experiments in junior high school. Bateman found that successful male fruit flies could, with multiple matings, produce nearly three times as many offspring as the most reproductively successful female. As Hrdy explains, "whereas a male could always gain by mating just one more time, and hence benefit from a nature that made him undiscriminatingly eager to mate, a female, already breeding near capacity after just one copulation, could gain little from multiple mating and should be quite uninterested in mating more than once or twice."

What, you may ask, does a human man have in common with a fruit fly? When it comes to sexual strategies, said Bateman, the answer is everything. Generalizing from his sixty-four experiments with Drosophila to all species, Bateman concluded that there is a universally lopsided division in the sexual natures of all creatures, apart from "a few very primitive organisms." Quite simply, males profit, evolutionarily speaking, from frequent mating, and females do not. This is why, said Bateman, "there is nearly always a combination of an undiscriminating eagerness in the males and a discriminating passivity in the females."

The modern field of sociobiology took this idea still further, attempting to account for complex human social arrangements and customs—warfare and corporate raiding, feeding infants and giving children karate lessons—in terms of the individual's basic need to reproduce his or her genes. Women and men, sociobiologists believe, adopt highly different strategies in order to do this. Males compete with other males for access to desirable females, and their goal is to inseminate as many females as possible. Females, in contrast, are motivated to attach themselves to genetically "superior" males because of the female's greater "investment" in terms of time and energy in her offspring; this, according to sociobiologists, is why females are more faithful and nurturant than males. As biologist Ruth Hubbard observes, "Thus, from the seemingly innocent asymmetries between eggs and sperm [say the sociobiologists] flow such major social consequences as female fidelity, male promiscuity, women's disproportional contribution to the care of children, and the unequal distribution of labor by sex."

Sociobiological explanations of competitive, promiscuous men and choosy, inhibited but flirtatious women fit right in with many elements within the popular culture. "And so it was," Hrdy says, "that 'coyness' came to be the single most commonly mentioned attribute of females in the literature on sociobiology."

It all seems a cruel joke of nature. Certainly many people are convinced, as the King of Siam sings in *The King and I*, that the male is like the honeybee, flitting from flower to flower, "gathering all he can," whereas the female has "honey for just one man." But notice that it is the King who sings that song; until relatively recently, no one was asking Queens for their view of things. Nor were male observers asking why, if human females were so naturally chaste, coy, and monogamous, social taboos from ostracism to death had to be placed on females who indulged in forbidden sexual relationships. For that matter, why did nonmarital affairs need to be forbidden anyway, if females have "honey for just one man"?

Sociobiologists attempt to explain human social customs by drawing on research on nonhuman animals, from the fields of primatology, evolutionary biology, anthropology, and related disciplines. In the last two decades, however, there has been an explosion of new research that casts doubt on many sociobiological assumptions, a change that is largely a result of the growing numbers of women who have entered these fields. Most of the women saw animal behavior in a different light from most of the male observers who had preceded them. Male primatologists, for example, had tended to observe and emphasize male-male competition and the number of times the male animals "got lucky"; the female animals, to the human men observing them, seemed mysterious and unpredictable. This is not unlike the ways in which human females have seemed mysterious and unpredictable to the human males who have observed *them*.

At first, women who went into these research fields saw the world as they had been taught to see it, through the academic perspective of their mentors. But after a while, they began to ask different questions and to bring different expectations to their observations. Hrdy recalls her own first glimpse of a female langur

> . . . moving away from her natal group to approach and solicit males in an all-male band. At the time, I had no context for interpreting behavior that merely seemed strange and incomprehensible to my Harvard-trained eyes. Only in time, did I come to realize that such wandering and such seemingly "wanton" behavior were recurring events in the lives of langurs.

Eventually, Hrdy learned that female langurs often leave their troops to join up with bands of males; and she also found that often a female, for reasons unknown, "simply takes a shine to the resident male of a neighboring troop." In fact, female langurs (and many other primate species) are able to shift from being in heat once a month to being continuously receptive for weeks at a time, a state not unlike the first phase of (human) love. In many primates, female receptivity is often *situation specific,* rather than being dependent exclusively on cyclical periods of being in heat.

As a result of the efforts of many pioneers like Hrdy, we now know that the females of many animal species do not behave like the patient, coy fruit fly. On the contrary, the females are sexually ardent and can even be called polyandrous (having many male partners). Further, their sexual behavior does not depend simply on the goal of being fertilized by the male, because in many cases females actively solicit males when they are not ovulating, and even when they are already pregnant. Here are a few illustrations from hundreds of research studies:

- Many species of female birds are promiscuous. In one study, researchers vasectomized the "master" of a blackbird harem . . . but the females nevertheless conceived.
- Many species of female fish are promiscuous. A female shiner perch who is not ovulating will nevertheless mate with many males, collecting sperm and storing them internally until she is ready to ovulate.
- Many species of female cats, notably leopards, lions, and pumas, are promiscuous. A lioness may mate dozens of times with many different partners during the week she is in estrus.
- Many species of female primates are promiscuous. Among savanna baboons and Barbary macaques, females initiate many different brief sexual encounters. Among chimpanzees, Hrdy reports, some females form partnerships with one male, but others engage in communal mating with all males in the vicinity. And among wild tamarin monkeys, a species long thought to be monogamous (at least in captivity), supposedly faithful females will mate with several males. So do female Hanuman langurs, blue monkeys, and redtail monkeys, all primates that were formerly believed to be one-man women. The old notion that primate females typically form "one-male breeding units," as primatologists would say, is now seriously called into question.

In spite of rapidly accumulating evidence that females of many different and varied species do mate "promiscuously" (a word that itself has evaluative overtones), it was not until 1980 or so that researchers realized that this fact threw, well, a monkey wrench into traditional evolutionary theories. Why would females have more copulations than are necessary for conception? Why would they go off with some guy from a neighboring town, whom none of their friends approves of? Why risk losing the genetic father's support by joining the baboon equivalent of Hell's Angels? And the brooding question over all of them, why did female primates develop continuous sexual receptivity?

These questions stimulated a flurry of new theories to explain why female philandering would make as much survival sense as its male counterpart. Most of these new explanations directly resulted from considering the world from the female's point of view. Traditional theories of sexual selection, after all, were based exclusively on the perspective of the male: Males compete for *access* to the female, who apparently is just hanging around waiting to go out and party with the winner. And it's only from a male point of view that multiple female matings can be considered "excessive," or that female sexual interest is even described as her time of "receptivity." Is she passively "receptive" to the active intentions of the male? The word implies that she's just putting up with his annoying lustfulness yet again.

New hypotheses argue that there are genetic benefits for the offspring of sexually adventurous mothers. According to Hrdy's review of these explanations, the "fertility backup" hypothesis assumes that females need sperm from a number of males in order to assure conception by the healthiest sperm. The "inferior cuckold" hypothesis suggests that a female who has a genetically inferior mate will sneak off with a genetically superior male when she is likely to conceive. (I suppose she knows this by the size of his income.) And the "diverse paternity" hypothesis argues that when the environment is unpredictable, females diversify. Over a reproductive lifetime, females who have numerous partners, and thus different fathers for their offspring, improve their offspring's chances for survival.

Other theories look for the social and environmental benefits of female promiscuity to the mother and her infants. The "therapeutic hypothesis" suggests that having lots of partners and multiple orgasms (in some species) makes intercourse and conception more pleasurable, and therefore more likely to occur. The "keep 'em around" hypothesis maintains that females actively solicit lower-status males (with the tacit approval of dominant males), a behavior that prevents weaker males from leaving the group. Hrdy's own favored theory is what she calls the "manipulation hypothesis," the idea that females mate with numerous males precisely because paternity becomes uncertain. The result is that male partners will be more invested in, and tolerant of, the female's infants. This idea, Hrdy explains,

> grew out of a dawning awareness that, first of all, individual females could do a great deal that would affect the survival of their offspring, and second, that males, far from mere dispensers of sperm, were critical features on the landscape where infants died or survived. That is, females were more political, males more nurturing (or at least not neutral), than some earlier versions of sexual selection theory would lead us to suppose.

Both of these points are essential: Not only are females more than passive receptacles of sperm, but also males are more than "mere dispensers of sperm." They don't just mate and run. They have a key role in determining whether infants survive or die. Among primates, there is enormous variation in the extent to which males nurture and protect offspring:

- Among the ruffed lemur, the male tends the nest while the female forages for food.
- Among New World monkeys, males directly care for offspring in half of all species; often, the male is the primary caretaker, carrying the infant on his back, sharing food with it.
- In a rare study of a monogamous species of night money, an observer found that during one infant's first week of life, the mother carried it 33 percent of the time, the father 51 percent of the time, and a juvenile member of the troop the remaining time.
- Among baboons, males do not have much direct contact with infants, but they hover nearby protectively and offer what Hrdy calls "quality" time in a very real sense: They increase the infant's chances of survival. They discourage attacks on the infant from males who are unknown, in both the literal and the Biblical sense, to the mother.

Hrdy's "manipulation hypothesis" assumes that primate males respond more benevolently to the offspring of females with whom they have mated, so the females derive obvious benefits from mating with more than one male. In numerous primate species, the mother's multiple sexual partners act like godfathers to the infant, as primatologist Jeanne Altmann calls them. Each of these males will help care for the female's offspring. Baboon males, many of whom could have served as the model for *Three Men and a Baby*, develop special relationships with the infant, carrying it on their backs on times of danger and protecting it from strangers and hazards. These affectionate bonds are possible because of the mother's closeness to the males, says Hrdy, and because the infant comes to trust these males and seek them out.

The manipulation hypothesis may or may not hold up with further research, as Hrdy acknowledges. It certainly does not apply to most human societies, where husbands do not look too kindly on their wives' "special relationships" with other men, let alone their previous lovers, husbands, and wooers. Hrdy's work, nonetheless, shows that theories depend, first and foremost, on what an observer *observes,* and then on how those observations can be blurred by unconscious expectations. Hrdy initially regarded those "wanton" female langurs as aberrations because their behavior did not fit the established theory. Not until researchers began to speculate on the potential benefits of female promiscuity did they come up with different questions and answers about female sexual behavior than had sociobiologists.

In evolutionary biology, if not in the popular press, the myth of the coy female (and, for that matter, the myth of the absent father) is dead. Hrdy is encouraged by the speed with which primatologists, once aware of the male bias that permeated their discipline, have produced "a small stampede by members of both sexes to study female reproductive strategies." This she takes to be a healthy sign, as do I. But Hrdy cautions against "substituting a new set of biases for the old ones":

> That is, among feminist scholars it is now permissible to say that males and females are different, provided one also stipulates that females are more cooperative, more nurturing, more supportive—not to mention equipped with unique moral sensibilities. . . .

Perhaps it is impossible, as biologist Donna Haraway suggests, for any of us to observe the behavior of other species, let alone our own, in a way that does not mirror the assumptions of our own way of life. It is disconcerting, says Hrdy wryly, that primatologists were finding "politically motivated females and nurturing males at roughly the same time that a woman runs for vice president of the United States and [Garry] Trudeau starts to poke fun at 'caring males' in his cartoons." Informally, scientists admit that their prejudices—such as the tendency to identify with the same sex of the species they are studying—affect their research. One woman primatologist told Hrdy, "I sometimes identify with female baboons more than I do with males of my own species."

The recognition of a male-centered bias in primatology and biology proved to be an enormous step forward, allowing scientists of both sexes to revise their theories of animal behavior. Sociobiologists (and their fans like Sam Kash

Kachigan) can no longer justify traditional sex roles, particularly male dominance and female nurturance and chastity, by appealing to the universality of such behavior in other species. Other species aren't cooperating.

But that is not the only moral of the Parable of the Primates. The female perspective is invaluable, but, as Hrdy warns, a female-centered bias will provide its own set of distortions. Cultural feminists who look to evolutionary biology to explain women's allegedly sweeter, more cooperative ways are on as shaky ground as the antifeminists they would replace.

If the sociobiological heroine is the coy female who is so different from males, the heroine of modern sexology is the lusty female who is just like them. I like her better, but I'm afraid that she, too, is (as a student of mine once inadvertently said) a fig leaf of the imagination. . . .

# POSTSCRIPT

## Are Primate Females Selected to Be Monogamous?

**S**cience is supposed to be objective. However, scientists are products of their culture. Their own cultural conditioning makes them sensitive to certain facts and blind to others that do not fit within an accepted paradigm. As we explored in Issue 2, the underlying presuppositions about inheritance prevented Mendel from receiving the recognition that he was due in his lifetime. Darwin's conviction that evolution must be gradual may also have been influenced by his Christian upbringing and the social norms of his day. Similarly, Darwin's own gender conditioning may have impacted his ideas on sexuality and mating strategies. As Tavris points out, the basic dichotomy that he proposed conveniently fit standard Victorian dating and mating patterns.

The same gender bias may have been shared by many of Darwin's peers. If so, it could account for why his basic ideas on sexual selection were not seriously questioned until the 1960s, when there was an influx of female researchers into the fields of biology and primatology. Although these women were influenced by the prevailing paradigm on sexual selection, they were not bound by it in the same way men of their generation may have been. Political and social movements such as civil rights and women's liberation may also have led these female scientists to question many of the underlying presuppositions on which the original theory of sexual selection was based.

Hrdy (1981) for example, suggests that the best way a female can maximize her reproductive potential is through mating with multiple males rather than remaining monogamous. Hrdy observed female langurs actively soliciting the sexual attention of males and sometimes even leaving their troops to pursue outside males. These behaviors would be selected for because they allow females to get pregnant as soon as possible. Promiscuity may also be an evolutionary safeguard against male sterility and tends to increase diversity in the gene pool. While American culture may socially frown on a woman who has children with different men, the behavior makes a good deal of sense from an evolutionary standpoint. Tavris also mentions the "keep'um around" hypothesis (promiscuous mating discourages males from leaving the group and insures more protection for females and their offspring) and the "manipulation" hypothesis. The latter view "assumes that primate males respond more benevolently to the offspring of females with whom they have mated, so the females derive obvious benefits from mating with more than one male" (Tavris, 1995:77). Finally, having multiple male suitors insures that a female and her offspring will not be left without protection and support should something happen to a primary mate. If Mr. Right gets eaten by a lion, there are plenty of "backups" Ms. Right can turn to.

Despite all the new research on primate societies, old ideas about female monogamy are still hard to shake. "Female promiscuity" still carries negative connotations, and most biology textbooks still talk about the "sexual receptivity" of females rather than protraying them as active sexual initiators. How deep this bias goes can even be seen in the general descriptions of human conception in college textbooks. As we noted in Issue 2, the sexual dichotomy proposed by Darwin is commonly used to describe the characteristics of egg and sperm.

> *It is remarkable how "femininely" the egg behaves and how "masculinely" the sperm. The egg is seen as large and passive. It does not move or journey, but passively "is transported," "is swept," or even "drifts" along the fallopian tube. . . . Gerald Schatten and Helen Schatten liken the egg's role to that of Sleeping Beauty: "a dormant bride awaiting her mate's magic kiss which instills the spirit that brings her to life." Sperm, by contrast, have a "mission," which is to "move through the female genital tract in quest of the ovum." One popular account has it that the sperm carry out a "perilous journey" into the "warm darkness" where some fall away "exhausted." "Survivors" "assault" the eggs, the successful candidates "surrounding the prize" (Martin, 2001:474–475).*

In addition to the dangers presented by holding on to old sexual selection paradigms due to bias, scientists must also be careful not to embrace new paradigms that are too rigid and leave no room for further refinement or discussion. As Tavris correctly observes, "The female perspective is invaluable, but, as Hrdy warns, a female-centered bias will provide its own set of distortions. Cultural feminists who look to evolutionary biology to explain women's allegedly sweeter, more cooperative ways are on as shakey gorund as the antifeminists they would replace" (1995:221).

For more information about the reproductive strategies of female primates, see Meredith Small's books *Female Choices* (1993) and *What's Love Got to Do with It? The Evolution of Human Mating* (1995). Other books that depict the evolution of the researcher's ideas as well as the complexity of primate societies, are Barbara Smut's book *Sex and Friendship in Bonobos* (1985) and Shirley Strum's book *Almost Human: A Journey into the World of Baboons* (1987). Jane Goodall's book *The Chimpanzees of Gombe* (1986) is another classic, and an interesting post-modern history of primate research is presented by Donna Haraway in her book *Primate Visions: Gender, Race and Nature in Modern Science* (1989).

# ISSUE 7

## Do Chimpanzees Hunt Competitively?

**YES: Craig B. Stanford,** from "To Catch Colobus," *Natural History* (January 1995)

**NO: Christophe Boesch and Hedwige Boesch-Achermann,** from "Dim Forest, Bright Chimps," *Natural History* (September 1991)

### ISSUE SUMMARY

**YES:** Craig Stanford argues that Gombe chimpanzees often hunt competitively in open, woodland environments. He suggests that this sort of environment was the one in which human hunting first evolved.

**NO:** Christophe Boesch and Hedwige Boesch-Achermann contend that cooperative hunting works better in a dense, rain forest environment. In their opinion, the hunting behavior of the Tai chimps provides a better model of early human evolution.

*Today, as in Darwin's time, it is once again fashionable to speak of and study the animal mind (Goodall, 1998:54).*

When Jane Goodall went into the field in the 1960s to study chimpanzees, very little was known about their behavior in the wild. Most of the studies of chimps that had been done at that time had taken place in captivity and produced a picture of chimpanzees as gentle herbivores. Most scientists were then shocked when Goodall's observations at Gombe revealed that chimpanzees not only ate meat, but that they actively hunted for it. Their prey included young baboons, monkeys, pigs, and small antelope. Further observations of hunting at Gombe suggested that older, dominant individuals often confiscated kills made by younger, subordinate animals. Males may also use hunting as a way to compete for sexual access to females. The presence of a female in estrus seems to encourage males to form a hunting party. "This finding, together with the earlier observation of Geza Teleki (formerly of George Washington University) that male hunters tend to give meat preferentially to swollen females traveling with the group, indicates that Gombe chimps sometimes hunt in order to obtain meat to offer a sexually receptive female" (Stanford, 1995: 62–63). Sharing meat strategically with allies and family members also takes place, leading Stanford to suggest that hunting among Gombe chimps is usually a competitive process.

But does competitive hunting characterize the behavior of all chimpanzees? Christophe Boesch and Hedwige Boesch-Achermann argue that the hunting behavior of chimps in the Tai forest is based more on cooperation than competition.

# YES ↵

Craig B. Stanford

# To Catch a Colobus

On a sunny July morning, I am sitting on the bank of Kakombe Stream in Gombe National Park, Tanzania. Forty feet above my head, scattered through large fig trees, is a group of red colobus monkeys. This is J group, whose twenty-five members I have come to know as individuals during several seasons of fieldwork. Gombe red colobus are large, long-tailed monkeys, with males sometimes weighing more than twenty pounds. Both sexes have a crown of red hair, a gray back, and buff underparts. The highlight of this particular morning has been the sighting of a new infant, born sometime in the previous two days. As the group feeds noisily on fruit and leaves overhead, I mull over the options for possible names for the infant.

While I watch the colobus monkeys, my attention is caught by the loud and excited pant-hoots of a party of chimpanzees farther down the valley. I judge the group to be of considerable size and traveling in my direction. As the calls come closer, the colobus males begin to give high-pitched alarm calls, and mothers gather up their infants and climb higher into the tree crowns.

A moment later, a wild chorus of pant-hoots erupts just behind me, followed by a cacophony of colobus alarm calls, and it is obvious to both J group and to me that the chimps have arrived. The male chimps immediately climb up to the higher limbs of the tall albizia tree into which most of the colobus group have retreated. Colobus females and their offspring huddle high in the crown, while a phalanx of five adult males descends to meet the advancing ranks of four adult male chimpanzees, led by seventeen-year-old, 115-pound Frodo. Frodo is the most accomplished hunter of colobus monkeys at Gombe and the only one willing to take on several colobus males simultaneously in order to catch his prey. The other hunters keep their distance while Frodo first scans the group of monkeys, then advances upon the colobus defenders. Time and again he lunges at the colobus males, attempting to race past them and into the cluster of terrified females and infants. Each time he is driven back; at one point, the two largest males of J group leap onto Frodo's back until he retreats, screaming, a few yards away.

A brief lull in the hunt follows, during which the colobus males run to one another and embrace for reassurance, then part to renew their defense. Frodo soon charges again into the midst of the colobus males, and this time manages to scatter them long enough to pluck the newborn from its mother's abdomen. In spite of fierce opposition, Frodo has caught his quarry, and he now sits calmly and eats it while the other hunters and two female chimps—their swollen pink rumps a sign that they are in estrus, a period of sexual receptivity—sit nearby begging for meat. The surviving colobus monkeys watch nervously from a few feet away. Minutes later, the mother of the dead infant attempts to approach, perhaps to try to rescue her nearly consumed offspring. She is chased, falls from the tree to the forest floor, and is pounced upon and killed by juvenile chimpanzees that have been watching the hunt from below. Seconds later, before these would-be hunters have had a chance to begin their meal, Wilkie, the chimpanzee group's dominant male, races down the tree and steals the carcass from them. He shows off his prize by charging across the forest floor, dead colobus in hand, and then, amid a frenzy of chimps eager for a morsel, he sits down to share the meat with his ally Prof and two females from the hunting party.

Until Jane Goodall observed chimpanzees eating meat in the early 1960s, they were thought to be complete vegetarians. We now know that a small but regular portion of the diet of wild chimps consists of the meat of such mammals as bush pigs, small antelopes, and a variety of monkey species. For example, chimpanzees in the Mahale Mountains of Tanzania, the Taï forest of Ivory Coast, and in Gombe all regularly hunt red colobus monkeys. Documenting the effect of such predation on wild primate populations, however, is extremely difficult because predators—whether chimps, leopards, or eagles—are generally too shy to hunt in the presence of people. The result is that even if predation is a regular occurrence, researchers are not likely to see it, let alone study it systematically.

Gombe is one of the few primate study sites where both predators and their prey have been habituated to human observers, making it possible to witness hunts. I have spent the past four field seasons at Gombe, studying the predator–prey relationship between the 45-member Kasakela chimpanzee community and the 500 red colobus monkeys that share the same twelve square miles of Gombe National Park. Gombe's rugged terrain is composed of steep slopes of open woodland, rising above stream valleys lush with riverine forest. The chimpanzees roam across these hills in territorial communities, which divide up each day into foraging parties of from one to forty animals. So far, I have clocked in more than a thousand hours with red colobus monkeys and have regularly followed the chimps on their daily rounds, observing some 150 encounters between the monkeys and chimps and more than 75 hunts. My records, together with those of my colleagues, show that the Gombe chimps may kill more than 100 red colobus each year, or nearly one-fifth of the colobus inhabiting their range. Most of the victims are immature monkeys under two years old. Also invaluable have been the data gathered daily on the chimps for the past two decades by a team of Tanzanian research assistants.

One odd outcome of my work has been that I am in the unique position of knowing both the hunters and their victims as individuals, which makes my research intriguing but a bit heart wrenching. In October 1992, for example, a party of thirty-three chimpanzees encountered my main study group, J, in upper Kakombe valley. The result was devastating from the monkeys' viewpoint. During the hour-long hunt, seven were killed; three were caught and torn apart right in front of me. Nearly four hours later, the hunters were still sharing and eating the meat they had caught, while I sat staring in disbelief at the remains of many of my study subjects.

Determined to learn more about the chimp–colobus relationship, however, I continued watching, that day and many others like it. I will need several more field seasons before I can measure the full impact of chimpanzee hunting on the Gombe red colobus, but several facts about hunting and its effects on the monkeys have already emerged. One major factor that determines the outcome of a hunt in Gombe is the number of male chimps involved. (Although females also hunt, the males are responsible for more than 90 percent of all colobus kills.) Red colobus males launch a courageous counterattack in response to their chimpanzee predators, but their ability to defend their group is directly proportional to the number of attackers and does not seem to be related to the number of defenders. The outcome of a hunt is thus almost always in the hands of the chimps, and in most instances, the best the monkeys can hope to do is limit the damage to a single group member rather than several. Chimpanzees have a highly fluid social grouping pattern in which males tend to travel together while females travel alone with their infants. At times, however, twenty or more male and female chimpanzees forage together. When ten or more male chimps hunt together, they are successful nine times out of ten, and the colobus have little hope of escape.

Hunting success depends on other factors as well. Unlike the shy red-tailed and blue monkeys with which they share the forest (and which are rarely hunted by the chimps), red colobus do not flee the moment they hear or see chimps approaching. Instead, the red colobus give alarm calls and adopt a vigilant wait-and-see strategy, with males positioned nearest the potential attackers. The alarm calls increase in frequency and intensity as the chimpanzees draw closer and cease only when the chimps are sighted beneath the tree. Then, the colobus sit quietly, watching intently, and only if the chimps decide to hunt do the colobus males launch a counterattack. The monkeys' decision to stand and fight rather than flee may seem maladaptive given their low rate of successful defense. I observed, however, that when the monkeys scatter or try to flee, the chimps nearly always pursue and catch one or more of them.

Fleeing red colobus monkeys are most likely to be caught when they have been feeding on the tasty new leaves of the tallest trees, the "emergents," which rise above the canopy. When these trees are surrounded by low plant growth, they frequently become death traps because the only way colobus can escape from attacking chimps is to leap out of the tree—often into the waiting arms of more chimpanzees on the ground below.

One of my primary goals has been to learn why a party of chimps will eagerly hunt a colobus group one day while ignoring the same group under seemingly identical circumstances on another. One determinant is the number of males in the chimp party: the more males, the more likely the group will hunt. Hunts are also undertaken mainly when a mother colobus carrying a small infant is visible, probably because of the Gombe chimps' preference for baby red colobus, which make up 75 percent of all kills. The situation is quite different in the Taï forest, where half of the chimp kills are adult colobus males (*see* "Dim Forest, Bright Chimps," *Natural History,* September 1991). Christophe and Hedwige Boesch have shown that the Taï chimps hunt cooperatively, perhaps because red colobus monkeys are harder to catch in the much taller canopy of the Taï rain forest. Successful Taï chimp hunters also regularly share the spoils. In contrast, each chimp in Gombe appears to have his own hunting strategy.

The single best predictor of when Gombe chimps will hunt is the presence of one or more estrous females in the party. This finding, together with the earlier observation by Geza Teleki (formerly of George Washington University) that male hunters tend to give meat preferentially to swollen females traveling with the group, indicates that Gombe chimps sometimes hunt in order to obtain meat to offer a sexually receptive female. Since hunts also occur when no estrous females are present, this trade of sex for meat cannot be the exclusive explanation, but the implications are nonetheless intriguing. Gombe chimps use meat not only for nutrition; they also share it with their allies and withhold it from their rivals. Meat is thus a social, political, and even reproductive tool. These "selfish" goals may help explain why the Gombe chimps do not cooperate during a hunt as often as do Taï chimps.

Whatever the chimps want the monkey meat for, their predation has a severe effect on the red colobus population. Part of my work involves taking repeated censuses of the red colobus groups living in the different valleys that form the hunting range of our chimpanzees. In the core area of the range, where hunting is most intense, predation by chimps is certainly the limiting factor on colobus population growth: red colobus group size in this area is half that at the periphery of the chimps' hunting range. The number of infant and juvenile red colobus monkeys is particularly low in the core area; most of the babies there are destined to become chimpanzee food.

The proportion of the red colobus population eaten by chimps appears to fluctuate greatly from year to year, and probably from decade to decade, as the number of male hunters in the chimpanzee community changes. In the early 1980s, for instance, there were five adult and adolescent males in the Kasakela chimp community, while today there are eleven; the number of colobus kills per year has risen as the number of hunters in the community has grown.

Furthermore, a single avid hunter may have a dramatic effect. I estimate that Frodo has single-handedly killed up to 10 percent of the entire red colobus population within his hunting range. I now want to learn if chimps living in forests elsewhere in Africa are also taking a heavy toll of red colobus monkeys. If they are, then they will add support to the theory that predation is an important limiting factor on wild primate populations and may also influence some aspects of behavior. Meanwhile, I will continue to watch in awe as Frodo and his fellow hunters attack my colobus monkeys and to marvel at the courageousness of the colobus males that risk their lives to protect the other members of their group.

**Christophe Boesch and
Hedwige Boesch-Achermann**

# Dim Forest, Bright Chimps

Taï National Park, Ivory Coast, December 3, 1985. Drumming, barking, and screaming, chimps rush through the undergrowth, little more than black shadows. Their goal is to join a group of other chimps noisily clustering around Brutus, the dominant male of this seventy-member chimpanzee community. For a few moments, Brutus, proud and self-confident, stands fairly still, holding a shocked, barely moving red colobus monkey in his hand. Then he begins to move through the group, followed closely by his favorite females and most of the adult males. He seems to savor this moment of uncontested superiority, the culmination of a hunt high up in the canopy. But the victory is not his alone. Cooperation is essential to capturing one of these monkeys, and Brutus will break apart and share this highly prized delicacy with most of the main participants of the hunt and with the females. Recipients of large portions will, in turn, share more or less generously with their offspring, relatives, and friends.

In 1979, we began a long-term study of the previously unknown chimpanzees of Taï National Park, 1,600 square miles of tropical rain forest in the Republic of the Ivory Coast (Côte d'Ivoire). Early on, we were most interested in the chimps' use of natural hammers—branches and stones—to crack open the five species of hard-shelled nuts that are abundant here. A sea otter lying on its back, cracking an abalone shell with a rock, is a familiar picture, but no primate had ever before been observed in the wild using stones as hammers. East Africa's savanna chimps, studied for decades by Jane Goodall in Gombe, Tanzania, use twigs to extract ants and termites from their nests or honey from a bees' nest, but they have never been seen using hammerstones.

As our work progressed, we were surprised by the many ways in which the life of the Taï forest chimpanzees differs from that of their savanna counterparts, and as evidence accumulated, differences in how the two populations hunt proved the most intriguing. Jane Goodall had found that chimpanzees hunt monkeys, antelope, and wild pigs, findings confirmed by Japanese biologist Toshida Nishida, who conducted a long-term study 120 miles south of Gombe, in the Mahale Mountains. So we were not surprised to discover that the Taï chimps eat meat. What intrigued us was the degree to which they hunt cooperatively. In 1953 Raymond Dart proposed that group hunting and cooperation were key ingredients in the evolution of *Homo sapiens*. The argument has been modified considerably since Dart first put it forward, and group hunting has also been observed in some social carnivores (lions and African wild dogs, for instance), and even some birds of prey. Nevertheless, many anthropologists still hold that hunting cooperatively and sharing food played a central role in the drama that enabled early hominids, some 1.8 million years ago, to develop the social systems that are so typically human.

We hoped that what we learned about the behavior of forest chimpanzees would shed new light on prevailing theories of human evolution. Before we could even begin, however, we had to habituate a community of chimps to our presence. Five long years passed before we were able to move with them on their daily trips through the forest, of which "our" group appeared to claim some twelve square miles. Chimpanzees are alert and shy animals, and the limited field of view in the rain forest—about sixty-five feet at best—made finding them more difficult. We had to rely on sound, mostly their vocalizations and drumming on trees. Males often drum regularly while moving through the forest: pant-hooting, they draw near a big buttress tree; then, at full speed they fly over the buttress, hitting it repeatedly with their hands and feet. Such drumming may resound more than half a mile in the forest. In the beginning, our ignorance about how they moved and who was drumming led to failure more often than not, but eventually we learned that the dominant males drummed during the day to let other group members know the direction of travel. On some days, however, intermittent drumming about dawn was the only signal for the whole day. If we were out of earshot at the time, we were often reduced to guessing.

During these difficult early days, one feature of the chimps' routine proved to be our salvation: nut cracking is a noisy business. So noisy, in fact, that in the early days of French colonial rule, one officer apparently even proposed the theory that some unknown tribe was forging iron in the impenetrable and dangerous jungle.

Guided by the sounds made by the chimps as they cracked open nuts, which they often did for hours at a time, we were gradually able to get within sixty feet of the animals. We still seldom saw the chimps themselves (they fled if we came too close), but even so, the evidence left after a session of nut cracking taught us a great deal about what types of nuts they were eating, what sorts of hammer and anvil tools they were using, and—thanks to the very distinctive noise a nut makes when it finally splits open—how many hits were needed to crack a nut and how many nuts could be opened per minute.

After some months, we began catching glimpses of the chimpanzees before they fled, and after a little more time, we were able to draw close enough to watch them at work. The chimps gather nuts from the ground. Some nuts are tougher to crack than others. Nuts of the *Panda oleosa* tree are the most demanding, harder than any of the foods processed by present-day hunter-gatherers and breaking open only when a force of 3,500 pounds is applied. The stone hammers used by the Taï chimps range from stones of ten ounces to granite blocks of four to forty-five pounds. Stones of any size, however, are a rarity in the forest and are seldom conveniently placed near a nut-bearing tree. By observing closely, and in some cases imitating the way the chimps handle hammerstones, we learned that they have an impressive ability to find just the right tool for the job at hand. Taï chimps could remember the positions of many of the stones scattered, often out of sight, around a panda tree. Without having to run around rechecking the stones, they would select one of appropriate size that was closest to the tree. These mental abilities in spatial representation compare with some of those of nine-year-old humans.

To extract the four kernels from inside a panda nut, a chimp must use a hammer with extreme precision. Time and time again, we have been impressed to see a chimpanzee raise a twenty-pound stone above its head, strike a nut with ten or more powerful blows, and then, using the same hammer, switch to delicate little taps from a height of only four inches. To finish the job, the chimps often break off a small piece of twig and use it to extract the last tiny fragments of kernel from the shell. Intriguingly, females crack panda nuts more often than males, a gender difference in tool use that seems to be more pronounced in the forest chimps than in their savanna counterparts.

After five years of fieldwork, we were finally able to follow the chimpanzees at close range, and gradually, we gained insights into their way of hunting. One morning, for example, we followed a group of six male chimps on a three-hour patrol that had taken them into foreign territory to the north. (Our study group is one of five chimpanzee groups more or less evenly distributed in the Taï forest.) As always during these approximately monthly incursions, which seem to be for the purpose of territorial defense, the chimps were totally silent, clearly on edge and on the lookout for trouble. Once the patrol was over, however, and they were back within their own borders, the chimps shifted their attention to hunting. They were after monkeys, the most abundant mammals in the forest. Traveling in large, multispecies groups, some of the forest's ten species of monkeys are more apt than others to wind up as a meal for the chimps. The relatively sluggish and large (almost thirty pounds) red colobus monkeys are the chimps' usual fare. (Antelope also live in the forest, but in our ten years at Taï, we have never seen a chimp catch, or even pursue, one. In contrast, Gombe chimps at times do come across fawns, and when they do, they seize the opportunity—and the fawn.)

The six males moved on silently, peering up into the vegetation and stopping from time to time to listen for the sound of monkeys. None fed or groomed; all focused on the hunt. We followed one old male, Falstaff, closely, for he tolerates us completely and is one of the keenest and most experienced hunters. Even from the rear, Falstaff set the pace; whenever he stopped, the others paused to wait for him. After thirty minutes, we heard the unmistakable noises of monkeys jumping from branch to branch. Silently, the chimps turned in the direction of the sounds, scanning the canopy. Just then, a diana monkey spotted them and gave an alarm call. Dianas are very alert and fast; they are also about half the weight of colobus monkeys. The chimps quickly gave up and continued their search for easier, meatier prey.

Shortly after, we heard the characteristic cough of a red colobus monkey. Suddenly Rousseau and Macho, two twenty-year-olds, burst into action, running toward the cough. Falstaff seemed surprised by their precipitousness, but after a moment's hesitation, he also ran. Now the hunting barks of the chimps mixed with the sharp alarm calls of the monkeys. Hurrying behind Falstaff, we saw him climb up a conveniently situated tree. His position, combined with those of Schubert and Ulysse, two mature chimps in their prime, effectively blocked off three of the monkeys' possible escape routes. But in another tree, nowhere near any escape route and thus useless, waited the last of the hunters, Kendo, eighteen years old and the least experienced of the group. The monkeys, taking advantage of Falstaff's delay and Kendo's error, escaped.

The six males moved on and within five minutes picked up the sounds of another group of red colobus. This time, the chimps approached cautiously, nobody hurrying. They screened the canopy intently to locate the monkeys, which were still unaware of the approaching danger. Macho and Schubert chose two adjacent trees, both full of monkeys, and started climbing very quietly, taking care not to move any branches. Meanwhile, the other four chimps blocked off anticipated escape routes. When Schubert was halfway up, the monkeys finally detected the two chimps. As we watched the colobus monkeys take off in literal panic, the appropriateness of the chimpanzees' scientific name—*Pan*—came to mind: with a certain stretch of the imagination, the fleeing monkeys could be shepherds and shepherdesses frightened at the sudden appearance of Pan, the wild Greek god of the woods, shepherds, and their flocks.

Taking off in the expected direction, the monkeys were trailed by Macho and Schubert. The chimps let go with loud hunting barks. Trying to escape, two colobus monkeys jumped into smaller trees lower in the canopy. With this, Rousseau and Kendo, who had been watching from the ground, sped up into the trees and tried to grab them. Only a third of the weight of the chimps, however, the monkeys managed to make it to the next tree along branches too small for their pursuers. But Falstaff had anticipated this move and was waiting for them. In the following confusion, Falstaff seized a juvenile and killed it with a bite to the neck. As the chimps met in a rush on the ground, Falstaff began to eat, sharing with Schubert and Rousseau. A juvenile colobus does not provide much meat, however, and this time, not all the chimps got a share. Frustrated individuals soon started off on another hunt, and relative calm returned fairly quickly: this sort of hunt, by a small band of chimps acting on their own at the edge of their territory, does not generate the kind of high excitement that prevails when more members of the community are involved.

So far we have observed some 200 monkey hunts and have concluded that success requires a minimum of three motivated hunters acting cooperatively. Alone or in pairs, chimps succeed less than 15 percent of the time, but when three or four act as a group, more than half the hunts result in a kill. The chimps seem well aware of the odds; 92 percent of all the hunts we observed were group affairs.

Gombe chimps also hunt red colobus monkeys, but the percentage of group hunts is much lower: only 36 percent. In addition, we learned from Jane Goodall that even when Gombe chimps do hunt in groups, their strategies are different. When Taï chimps arrive under a group of monkeys, the hunters scatter, often silently, usually out of sight of one another but each aware of the others' positions. As the hunt progresses, they gradually close in, encircling the quarry. Such movements require that each chimp coordinate his movements with those of the other hunters, as well as with those of the prey, at all times.

Coordinated hunts account for 63 percent of all those observed at Taï but only 7 percent of those at Gombe. Jane Goodall says that in a Gombe group hunt, the chimpanzees typically travel together until they arrive at a tree with monkeys. Then, as the chimps begin climbing nearby trees, they scatter as each pursues a different target. Goodall gained the impression that Gombe chimps boost their success by hunting independently but simultaneously, thereby disorganizing their prey; our impression is that the Taï chimps owe their success to being organized themselves.

Just why the Gombe and Taï chimps have developed such different hunting strategies is difficult to explain, and we plan to spend some time at Gombe in the hope of finding out. In the meantime, the mere existence of differences is interesting enough and may perhaps force changes in our understanding of human evolution. Most currently accepted theories propose that some three million years ago, a dramatic climate change in Africa east of the Rift Valley turned dense forest into open, drier habitat. Adapting to the difficulties of life under these new conditions, our ancestors supposedly evolved into cooperative hunters and began sharing food they caught. Supporters of this idea point out that plant and animal remains indicative of dry, open environments have been found at all early hominid excavation sites in Tanzania, Kenya, South Africa, and Ethiopia. That the large majority of apes in Africa today live west of the Rift Valley appears to many anthropologists to lend further support to the idea that a change in environment caused the common ancestor of apes and humans to evolve along a different line from those remaining in the forest.

Our observations, however, suggest quite another line of thought. Life in dense, dim forest may require more sophisticated behavior than is commonly assumed: compared with their savanna relatives, Taï chimps show greater complexity in both hunting and tool use. Taï chimps use tools in nineteen different ways and have six different ways of making them, compared with sixteen uses and three methods of manufacture at Gombe.

Anthropologist colleagues of mine have told me that the discovery that some chimpanzees are accomplished users of hammerstones forces them to look with a fresh eye at stone tools turned up at excavation sites. The important role played by female Taï chimps in tool use also raises the possibility that in the course of human evolution, women may have been decisive in the development of many of the sophisticated manipulative skills characteristic of our species. Taï mothers also appear to pass on their skills by actively teaching their offspring. We have observed mothers providing their young with hammers and then stepping in to help when the inexperienced youngsters encounter difficulty. This help may include carefully showing how to position the nut or hold the hammer properly. Such behavior has never been observed at Gombe.

Similarly, food sharing, for a long time said to be unique to humans, seems more general in forest than in savanna chimpanzees. Taï chimp mothers share with their young up to 60 percent of the nuts they open, at least until the latter become sufficiently adept, generally at about six years old. They also share other foods acquired with tools, including honey, ants, and bone marrow. Gombe mothers share such foods much less often, even with their infants. Taï chimps also share meat more frequently than do their Gombe relatives, sometimes dividing a chunk up and giving portions away, sometimes simply allowing beggars to grab pieces.

Any comparison between chimpanzees and our hominid ancestors can only be suggestive, not definitive. But our studies lead us to believe that the process of hominization may have begun independently of the drying of the environment. Savanna life could even have delayed the process; many anthropologists have been struck by how slowly hominid-associated remains, such as the hand ax, changed after their first appearance in the Olduvai age.

Will we have the time to discover more about the hunting strategies or other, perhaps as yet undiscovered abilities of these forest chimpanzees? Africa's tropical rain forests, and their inhabitants, are threatened with extinction by extensive logging, largely to provide the Western world with tropical timber and such products as coffee, cocoa, and rubber. Ivory Coast has lost 90 percent of its original forest, and less than 5 percent of the remainder can be considered pristine. The climate has changed dramatically. The harmattan, a cold, dry wind from the Sahara previously unknown in the forest, has now swept through the Taï forest every year since 1986. Rainfall has diminished; all the rivulets in our study region are now dry for several months of the year.

In addition, the chimpanzee, biologically very close to humans, is in demand for research on AIDS and hepatitis vaccines. Captive-bred chimps are available, but they cost about twenty times more than wild-caught animals. Chimps taken from the wild for these purposes are generally young, their mothers having been shot during capture. For every chimp arriving at its sad destination, nine others may well have died in the forest or on the way. Such priorities—cheap coffee and cocoa and chimpanzees—do not do the economies of Third World countries any good in the long run, and they bring suffering and death to innocent victims in the forest. Our hope is that Brutus, Falstaff, and their families will survive, and that we and others will have the opportunity to learn about them well into the future. But there is no denying that modern times work against them and us.

# POSTSCRIPT

## Do Chimpanzees Hunt Competitively?

In addition to physiology, natural selection also works on behavior. Certain behavioral traits, just like biological ones, may give one individual an evolutionary advantage over another. Chimpanzees, like humans, show the ability to adapt culturally as well as physically to their environment. Competitive hunting seems to prevail among savanna chimpanzees because the trees are farther apart, allowing males to hunt more independently and selfishly. In the Tai forest, however, competitive behavior is not selected for due to the dense canopy and the closeness of trees. It takes several chimps working together to strategically surround and capture a colobus monkey. The difficulty of hunting in the Tai forest also seems to effect how the kill is distributed. Access to the ill is based on right—who participated in the hunt—rather than in social dominance.

The impact of different environments on chimpanzee behavior and hunting styles is intriguing. Traditionally, most scientists had thought that human hunting began when hominids left the forests and moved out into the savanna. Boesch and Boesch-Achermann's work suggests that hunting behavior may have evolved first in the forest. With movement from the forest into the grasslands, however, the style of hunting may have become more competitive. Sadly, we may be given a chance to test this hypothesis through continuing observations of the Tai chimps. Logging and other human activities leading to deforestation have seriously diminished the forest size, and climatic changes have also reduced rainfall in the area. As the region becomes drier and more open, scientists will be able to observe if it has any effect on the Tai chimps and their hunting strategies. Will they become more competitive like the Gombe chimps? Only time and further research will tell.

For more information on chimpanzee hunting and it's implications for human evolution, see T. Nishida, *The Chimpanzees of the Mahale Mountains* (1990), C. Stanford, "The Hunting Ecology of Wild Chimpanzees: Implications for the Evolutionary Ecology of Pliocene Hominids," *American Anthropologist* (1996); H. Boesch-Achermann and C. Boesch, "Hominization in the Rainforest: The Chimpanzees Piece of the Puzzle," *Evolutionary Anthropology* (1994). Jane Goodall's books on her research among the Gombe chimpanzees are also excellent reads. See *In the Shadow of Man* (1971) and *The Chimpanzees of Gombe: Patterns of Behavior* (1986).

# ISSUE 8

# Does Homosexuality or Bisexuality Have Any Evolutionary Advantage for Primates?

**YES: Meredith F. Small,** from "What's Love Got to Do With It?" *Discover* (June 1992)

**NO: Melvin Konner,** from "Homosexuality: Who and Why?" *The New York Times Magazine* (April 2, 1989)

## ISSUE SUMMARY

Meredith Small suggests that homosexuality and bisexuality may have important evolutionary advantages for bonobos. Although these behaviors do not directly lead to reproduction, they do serve to increase social cohesion and bonding among group members. In contrast, Melvin Konner suggests that homosexuality is primarily the product of social conditioning and enculturation and not biological factors.

*To us a man is what nature, or his dreams, make him. We accept him for what he wants to be. That's up to him. (Lame Deer, Lakota shaman quoted in Williams, 1986:25).*

In many cultures, homosexuals and bisexuals are not only accepted but they are given equal rights with other individuals. Among these rights is the ability to marry members of the same biological sex. In mainstream America, however, gays and lesbians are treated differently than heterosexuals socially and legally. Consequently, the recent decision by judges in Multinomah County in Portland, Oregon, to allow homosexual as well as heterosexual unions caused a stir among church officials, political conservatives, and other advocates of heterosexual-only marriage. The debate raged until finally it was decided that the judges had exceeded their authority and the whole process as shut down. While many critics emphasized religious objectives to the idea of homosexual marriage, others argued that it was "unnatural" and should be banned on that basis. Heterosexuality, the argument runs, is something selected for by nature because it insures reproduction. Homosexuality and bisexuality, on the other hand, are selected against because such sexual contact produces no offspring.

But does this viewpoint represent scientific fact or simply social bias? Charles Darwin may have unwittingly interjected evolutionary theory with a gender bias when he suggested that sexual selection in all species followed Victorian dating and mating patterns. As a devout Christian, he may have also introduced a homophobic bias as well. It may be that homosexuality and bisexuality have hidden evolutionary advantages that researchers are only beginning to discover.

Small's article on the bonobos suggests that homosexuality and bisexuality increase survivability by promoting social cohesion and strengthening bonds among all troop members. In contrast, Konner argues that homosexuality has no survival value and removes fertile individuals from the breeding population.

 **YES**

# What's Love Got to Do With It?

**M**aiko and Lana are having sex. Maiko is on top, and Lana's arms and legs are wrapped tightly around his waist. Lina, a friend of Lana's, approaches from the right and taps Maiko on the back, nudging him to finish. As he moves away, Lina enfolds Lana in her arms, and they roll over so that Lana is now on top. The two females rub their genitals together, grinning and screaming in pleasure.

This is no orgy staged for an X-rated movie. It doesn't even involve people—or rather, it involves them only as observers. Lana, Maiko, and Lina are bonobos, a rare species of chimplike ape in which frequent couplings and casual sex play characterize every social relationship—between males and females, members of the same sex, closely related animals, and total strangers. Primatologists are beginning to study the bonobos' unrestrained sexual behavior for tantalizing clues to the origins of our own sexuality.

In reconstructing how early man and woman behaved, researchers have generally looked not to bonobos but to common chimpanzees. Only about 5 million years ago human beings and chimps shared a common ancestor, and we still have much behavior in common: namely, a long period of infant dependency, a reliance on learning what to eat and how to obtain food, social bonds that persist over generations, and the need to deal as a group with many everyday conflicts. The assumption has been that chimp behavior today may be similar to the behavior of human ancestors.

Bonobo behavior, however, offers another window on the past because they, too, shared our 5-million-year-old ancestor, diverging from chimps just 2 million years ago. Bonobos have been less studied than chimps for the simple reason that they are difficult to find. They live only on a small patch of land in Zaire, in central Africa. They were first identified, on the basis of skeletal material, in the 1920s, but it wasn't until the 1970s that their behavior in the wild was studied, and then only sporadically.

Bonobos, also known as pygmy chimpanzees, are not really pygmies but welterweights. The largest males are as big as chimps, and the females of the two species are the same size. But bonobos are more delicate in build, and their arms and legs are long and slender.

On the ground, moving from fruit tree to fruit tree, bonobos often stand and walk on two legs—behavior that makes them seem more like humans than chimps. In some ways their sexual behavior seems more human as well, suggesting that in the sexual arena, at least, bonobos are the more appropriate ancestral model. Males and females frequently copulate face-to-face, which is an uncommon position in animals other than humans. Males usually mount females from behind, but females seem to prefer sex face-to-face. "Sometimes the female will let a male start to mount from behind," says Amy Parish, a graduate student at the University of California at Davis who's been watching female bonobo sexual behavior in several zoo colonies around the world. "And then she'll stop, and of course he's really excited, and then she continues face-to-face." Primatologists assume the female preference is dictated by her anatomy: her enlarged clitoris and sexual swellings are oriented far forward. Females presumably prefer face-to-face contact because it feels better.

Like humans but unlike chimps and most other animals, bonobos separate sex from reproduction. They seem to treat sex as a pleasurable activity, and they rely on it as a sort of social glue, to make or break all sorts of relationships. "Ancestral humans behaved like this," proposes Frans de Waal, an ethologist at the Yerkes Regional Primate Research Center at Emory University. "Later, when we developed the family system, the use of sex for this sort of purpose became more limited, mainly occurring within families. A lot of the things we see, like pedophilia and homosexuality, may be leftovers that some now consider unacceptable in our particular society."

Depending on your morals, watching bonobo sex play may be like watching humans at their most extreme and perverse. Bonobos seem to have sex more often and in more combinations than the average person in any culture, and most of the time bonobo sex has nothing to do with making babies. Males mount females and females sometimes mount them back; females rub against other females just for fun; males stand rump to rump and press their scrotal areas together. Even juveniles participate by rubbing their genital areas against adults, although ethologists don't think that males actually insert their penises into juvenile females. Very young animals also have sex with each other: little males suck on each other's penises or French-kiss. When two animals initiate sex, others freely join in by poking their fingers and toes into the moving parts.

One thing sex does for bonobos is decrease tensions caused by potential competition, often competition for food. Japanese primatologists observing bonobos in Zaire were the first to notice that when bonobos come across a large fruiting tree or encounter piles of provisioned sugarcane, the sight of food triggers a binge of sex. The atmosphere of this sexual free-for-all is decidedly friendly, and it eventually calms the group down. "What's striking is how rapidly the sex drops off," says Nancy Thompson-Handler of the State University of New York at Stony Brook, who has observed bonobos at a site in Zaire called Lomako." After ten minutes, sexual behavior decreases by fifty percent." Soon the group turns from sex to feeding.

But it's tension rather than food that causes the sexual excitement. "I'm sure the more food you give them, the more sex you'll get," says De Waal. "But it's not really the food, it's competition that triggers this. You can throw in a cardboard box and you'll get sexual behavior." Sex is just the way bonobos deal with competition over limited resources and with the normal tensions caused by living in a group. Anthropologist Frances White of Duke University, a bonobo observer at Lomako since 1983, puts it simply: "Sex is fun. Sex makes them feel good and therefore keeps the group together."

Sexual behavior also occurs after aggressive encounters, especially among males. After two males fight, one may reconcile with his opponent by presenting his rump and backing up against the other's testicles. He might grab the penis of the other male and stroke it. It's the male bonobo's way of shaking hands and letting everyone know that the conflict has ended amicably.

Researchers also note that female bonobo sexuality, like the sexuality of female humans, isn't locked into a monthly cycle. In most other animals, including chimps, the female's interest in sex is tied to her ovulation cycle. Chimp females sport pink swellings on their hind ends for about two weeks, signaling their fertility, and they're only approachable for sex during that time. That's not the case with humans, who show no outward signs that they are ovulating, and who can mate at all phases of the cycle. Female bonobos take the reverse tack, but with similar results. Their large swellings are visible for weeks before and after their fertile periods, and there is never any discernibly wrong time to mate. Like humans, they have sex whether or not they are ovulating.

What's fascinating is that female bonobos use this boundless sexuality in all their relationships. "Females rule the business—sex and food," says De Waal. "It's a good species for feminists, I think." For instance, females regularly use sex to cement relationships with other females. A genital-genital rub, better known as GG-rubbing by observers, is the most frequent behavior used by bonobo females to reinforce social ties or relieve tension. GG-rubbing takes a variety of forms. Often one female rolls on her back and extends her arms and legs. The other female mounts her and they rub their swellings right and left for several seconds, massaging their clitorises against each other. GG-rubbing occurs in the presence of food because food causes tension and excitement, but the intimate contact has the effect of making close friends.

Sometimes females would rather GG-rub with each other than copulate with a male. Parish filmed a 15-minute scene at a bonobo colony at the San Diego Wild Animal Park in which a male, Vernon, repeatedly solicited two females, Lisa and Loretta. Again and again he arched his back and displayed his erect penis—the bonobo request for sex. The females moved away from him, tactfully turning him down until they crept behind a tree and GG-rubbed with each other.

Unlike most primate species, in which males usually take on the dangerous task of leaving home, among bonobos females are the ones who leave the group when they reach sexual maturity, around the age of eight, and work their way into unfamiliar groups. To aid in their assimilation into a new community, the female bonobos make good use of their endless sexual favors. While watching a bonobo group at a feeding tree, White saw a young female systematically have sex with each member before feeding. "An adolescent female, presumably a recent transfer female, came up to the tree, mated with all five males, went into the tree, and solicited GG-rubbing from all the females present," says White.

Once inside the new group, a female bonobo must build a sisterhood from scratch. In groups of humans or chimps, unrelated females construct friendships through the rituals of shopping together or grooming. Bonobos do it sexually. Although pleasure may be the motivation behind a female-female assignation, the function is to form an alliance.

These alliances are serious business, because they determine the pecking order at food sites. Females with powerful friends eat first, and subordinate females may not get any food at all if the resource is small. When times are rough, then, it pays to have close female friends. White describes a scene at Lomako in which an adolescent female, Blanche, benefited from her established friendship with Freda. "I was following Freda and her boyfriend, and they found a tree that they didn't expect to be there. It was a small tree, heavily in fruit with one of their favorites. Freda went straight up the tree and made a food call to Blanche. Blanche came tearing over—she was quite far away—and went tearing up the tree to join Freda, and they GG-rubbed like crazy."

Alliances also give females leverage over larger, stronger males who otherwise would push them around. Females have discovered there is strength in numbers. Unlike other species of primates, such as chimpanzees or baboons (or, all too often, humans), where tensions run high between males and females, bonobo females are not afraid of males, and the sexes mingle peacefully. "What is consistently different from chimps," says Thompson-Handler, "is the composition of parties. The vast majority are mixed, so there are males and females of all different ages."

Female bonobos cannot be coerced into anything, including sex. Parish recounts an interaction between Lana and a male called Akili at the San Diego Wild Animal Park. "Lana had just been introduced into the group. For a long time she lay on the grass with a huge swelling. Akili would approach her with a big erection and hover over her. It would have been easy for him to do a mount. But he wouldn't. He just kept trying to catch her eye, hovering around her, and she would scoot around the ground, avoiding him. And then he'd try again. She went around full circle." Akili was big enough to force himself on her. Yet he refrained.

In another encounter, a male bonobo was carrying a large clump of branches. He moved up to a female and presented his erect penis by spreading his legs and arching his back. She rolled onto her back and they copulated. In the midst of their joint ecstasy, she reached out and grabbed a branch from the male. When he pulled back, finished and satisfied, she moved away, clutching the branch to her chest. There was no tension between them, and she essentially traded copulation for food. But the key here is that the male allowed her to move away with the branch—it didn't occur to him to threaten her, because their status was virtually equal.

Although the results of sexual liberation are clear among bonobos, no one is sure why sex has been elevated to such a high position in this species and why it is restricted merely to reproduction among chimpanzees. "The puzzle for me," says De Waal, "is that chimps do all this bonding with kissing and embracing, with body contact. Why do bonobos do it in a sexual manner?" He speculates that the use of sex as a standard way to underscore relationships began between adult males and adult females as an extension of the mating process and later spread to all members of the group. But no one is sure exactly how this happened.

It is also unclear whether bonobo sexually became exaggerated only after their split from the human lineage or whether the behavior they exhibit today is the modern version of our common ancestor's sex play. Anthropologist Adrienne Zihlman of the University of California at Santa Cruz, who has used the evidence of fossil bones to argue that our earliest known non-ape ancestors, the australopithecines, had body proportions similar to those of bonobos, says, "The path of evolution is not a straight line from either species, but what I think is important is that the bonobo information gives us more possibilities for looking at human origins."

Some anthropologists, however, are reluctant to include the details of bonobo life, such as wide-ranging sexuality and a strong sisterhood, into scenarios of human evolution. "The researchers have all these commitments to male dominance [as in chimpanzees], and yet bonobos have egalitarian relationships," says De Waal. "They also want to see humans as unique, yet bonobos fit very nicely into many of the scenarios, making humans appear less unique."

Our divergent, non-ape path has led us away from sex and toward a culture that denies the connection between sex and social cohesion. But bonobos, with their versatile sexuality, are here to remind us that our heritage may very well include a primordial urge to make love, not war.

# NO ↵

# Homosexuality: Who and Why?

**I**n the bad old days, when homosexuality was considered a mental illness, a friend of mine was trying to go straight. He was seeing a distinguished psychoanalyst who believed (and still believes) that what some call a life style and still others call a crime is a psychiatrically treatable disorder. Through six years of anguished analysis, my friend changed his sexual orientation and married. His wife was wonderful—they had been friends for years—but he died unexpectedly of a heart attack at the age of 42, six months after the wedding. I am not superstitious, and I don't blame anyone, least of all his wife; he was happy with her. But a nagging question remains: Is it possible that my friend's doctor was trying to change something that should have been left alone?

He had been homosexual for years, and had had at least one stable long-term relationship. But he lived in a society that condemned him on religious and medical grounds. He "freely" chose to change through psychoanalysis. But this was a limited sort of freedom, and though he in fact did change—as some have—he did not live to find out how the change would work.

Those bad old days are over; yet a rising tide of bigotry against gay people has followed the AIDS epidemic. Religious fanatics point to AIDS as proof of God's wrath. Some gay men and women have begun to ponder again the nature of their sexual orientation, and parents wonder: Who becomes gay?

Neither science nor art has yet produced a single answer. Yet perhaps that in itself is an answer: that anything so complicated and various and interesting could have a single origin seems wrongheaded. Socrates and Tennessee Williams, Sappho and Adrienne Rich, to take only four people, representing only two cultures, seem certain to have come to their homosexuality in four such different ways as to make generalizations useless. In the further reaches of the anthropological universe, we find variations that knock most folk theories for a loop.

Consider the Sambia of New Guinea, described by Gilbert Herdt in "Guardians of the Flutes." They belong to a group of cultures in which homosexual practices are actually *required* of boys for several years as rites of passage into adulthood. After adolescence, the young men abandon homosexual practices, marry women, father children and continue as heterosexuals for the rest of their lives.

The lesson is threefold: first, a culture can make such a rule and get every person to conform; second, years of obligatory homosexuality apparently do

From *New York Times Magazine*, April 2, 1989, pp. 60–61. Copyright © 1989 by New York Times Syndicate. Reprinted by permission.

not commit the average man to a lifetime of homoerotic desires. The third lesson may be drawn from the life of Kalutwo, a Sambia. He grew up stigmatized as the illegitimate son of an older widow and had no contact with his father. He showed unacceptably strong homoerotic attachments, and never adjusted to a heterosexual relationship, having four marriages without issue—possibly unconsummated—by his mid-30's. According to Herdt and the psychoanalyst Robert Stoller, Kalutwo would have been homosexual anywhere.

The conclusion is reasonable. In every population, some men—most estimates say 5 to 10 percent—are drawn to homoerotic pursuits, whether they are punished, allowed or required. The percentage of strongly homoerotic women is generally estimated to be smaller, though in bisexuality women are said to outnumber men. But it should be remembered, definitions vary, and biases in such estimates are inevitable.

Some homosexuality was said to be present in all of 76 societies examined in one cross-cultural study, including the Tahitians, the Mohave Indians and a number of Amazonian tribes. In 48 (64 percent), it was condoned; in no society was it the dominant mode. Thus, all the societies had homosexuality, and the majority accepted its inevitability.

Not so our society. The Judeo-Christian tradition condemned homosexuality unequivocally, ending Greco-Roman tolerance. Yet centuries of condemnation, culminating in the Nazi attempt to physically exterminate homosexuals along with Jews and other "undesirables," have failed to make this minority acquiesce. Where do homosexuals come from, and how do they persist in the face of such persecution? In April 1935, with the Nazis' noose tightening around homosexuals, Sigmund Freud wrote to the mother of a gay man, "Homosexuality is assuredly no advantage, but it is nothing to be ashamed of, no vice, no degradation, it cannot be classified as an illness." Yet he went on to attribute it to "a certain arrest of sexual development," and then to deny that successful reorientation through psychoanalysis was possible, at least not "in the majority of cases."

Freud's sensitive formulation is remarkably close to the one we would give today. Although few accept his notion about arrested sexual development, most psychiatrists agree that sexual orientation is difficult to change, and that change is not intrinsically desirable. But a person's sexual orientation may be linked in some poorly understood way with anxiety, depression and other medically defined symptoms that can be treated, regardless of what may happen to sexual orientation.

Extensive research on the psychological development of homosexuals, by Allan Bell and others at the Kinsey Institute, found no support for most theories. The only factor implicating parents was (for both sexes) a poor relationship with the father—something shared by Kalutwo.

Yet some characteristics of the child could be predictive. For both sexes, but especially for males, gender nonconformity in childhood predicted homoerotic adaptation in adulthood. Other studies have drawn the same conclusion. The most dramatic, called "The 'Sissy Boy Syndrome' and the Development of Homosexuality," was published in 1987 by Richard Green, a psychiatrist at the University of California at Los Angeles. His was the first study starting with childhood and following through to adulthood, rather than asking adults about their memories. Boys dissatisfied with being boys—cross-dressing, avidly pursuing traditional girls' games to the exclusion of boys' games, and the like—had a high likelihood of growing up gay. Two-thirds to three-fourths became homosexuals. No homosexuality appeared in a control group.

·⟨◉⟩·

Green's unexpectedly strong findings have been variously interpreted as showing that male homosexuality is innate or that early childhood environment is key. Either way, some gay men are *intrinsically* homoerotic. Some studies have pointed to genes. For example, identical twins are more likely to share the same sexual orientation than nonidentical twins. And in a recent study by Richard Pillard and James Weinrich, homosexual men were four times as likely to have a homosexual brother (21 percent) as were heterosexual men. Although these familial patterns could be interpreted as stemming from shared early experiences, it is at least equally likely that they are due to shared genes.

Nevertheless, the rare "sissy boy" syndrome cannot account for the majority of even male homosexuals, and for females the predictive power of "tomboyishness" is less strong. Frequently, homosexual orientation is not accompanied by these or any other departure from typical gender roles. In the last decade, one study after another—as well as the expressive literature that followed the increased tolerance of the 1970's—has shown that homosexuals differ enormously from one another. As Bell and Martin Weinberg concluded in another book: "We do not do justice to people's sexual orientation when we refer to it by a singular noun. There are 'homosexualities' and there are 'heterosexualities.'" Life styles, personalities, behaviors, hopes and dreams all show tremendous variation among people who share either of those labels. No uniformity, psychological, hormonal or genetic has been found.

Bell and Weinberg write that their "least ambiguous finding . . . is that homosexuality is not necessarily related to pathology." In 1974, the American Psychiatric Association conceded the truth of this observation, essentially made by Freud. In that year—three years after my friend's death—homosexuality was removed from the association's list of diagnostic categories. In the current official diagnostic manual, it is represented by only a vestige: "persistent and marked distress about one's sexual orientation," a subcategory under "Sexual Disorder Not Otherwise Specified." This allows homosexuals who are distressed by their sexual orientation to seek psychiatric help to change it. A good therapist will understand that the distress is not necessarily intrinsic, but may be the product of continued social prejudice. As Freud put it in his 1935 letter to the mother about her homosexual son, if he "is unhappy, neurotic, torn by conflicts, inhibited in his social life, analysis may bring him harmony, peace of mind, full efficiency, whether he remains a homosexual or gets changed."

In fact, if the psychiatrist is fair-minded, the same diagnostic subcategory will admit patients dissatisfied with their heterosexual orientation and wanting to become gay. Adrienne Rich—whose lesbian poems are perhaps the most beautiful recent love poetry—has described a syndrome she calls "compulsory heterosexuality." It refers to the requirement of universal heterosexual adaptation imposed on American women, who she believes are, like all other women, naturally bisexual.

In this realm, diagnoses will not help much. The most common recent answer to the main questions about sexual orientation has been something like "I'm O.K.; you're O.K." But, better, is the reply to that bit of psychobabble provided by Fritz Perls, the founder of Gestalt psychotherapy: "I'm not O.K.; you're not O.K.—and that's O.K." As for religious pieties, they are even less helpful than diagnoses. Fear of AIDS is understandable, but it's really beside the point. If AIDS were God's punishment for gay men, then gay women would presumably be God's chosen people, for they have the lowest rates of AIDS and other sexually transmitted diseases. Perhaps in an atmosphere of tolerance and compassion, we can all do better at finding out—and becoming—who we really are.

# POSTSCRIPT

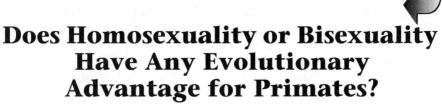

## Does Homosexuality or Bisexuality Have Any Evolutionary Advantage for Primates?

**M**any researchers believe that the bonobos are a good model for what our early human ancestors may have been like 5 to 6 million years ago. Studies suggest that the bonobos walk upright more often than chimpanzees, share food regularly within the troop, have longer estrus periods, and engage in face-to-face sex at least 25–30 percent of the time. In addition to reproduction, they also use sex for a variety of other purposes—to mediate tension, create alliances, improve their status, and for self-pleasuring and recreation; all sexual activities humans also engage in. Given these many similarities to humans, it seems probable that the bonobos use of homosexual and bisexual sex may also be characteristic of early humans. If one of the primary functions of sex is to resolve conflicts and create alliances between group members, then homosexual and bisexual sex seems very adaptive. It allows individuals to create and maintain social bonds with all group members instead of just those of one gender.

Certainly, the prominence of homosexuality and bisexuality in contemporary societies suggests that these traits may be the result of natural selection. It's estimated that one in ten people are gay or lesbian, while many others have had some sort of bisexual experience at some point in their lives. Studies of other cultures show that homosexual and bisexual behavior is quite common. Among the Ju-hoansi of S. Africa children frequently engage in sex play with both boys and girls (Shotak, 1981). Homosexual and bisexual experiences also tend to occur among adults, even those who are married to people of the opposite sex (Lee, 1993). In some societies bisexual or homosexual individuals are even awarded special status or spiritual powers. The Dagara of West, Africa, for example, believe that homosexuals are spiritual gatekeepers; they mediate between men and women or between life in this world and the realm of the ancestors (Som'e, 1998). Many Native American cultures also honor "two-spirited" individuals who assumed both male and female roles. These individuals were frequently shaman and were usually held in high esteem (Whitehead, 1981; Williams, 1986; Medicine 1983).

For more information on the bonobos and their significance for human evolution, see T. Furuichi, "The Prolonged Estrus of Females and Factors Influencing Mating in a Wild Group of Bonobos (Pan Paniscus) in Wamba Zaire," in N. Itougawa et. al., eds., *Topics in Primatology*, vol. 2 (1992); T. Nishida and M. Horaiwa-Hasigawa, "Chimpanzees and Bonobos: Cooperative Relationships among Males," in B. Smuts, et. al., eds., *Primate Societies* (1987); A. Parish, "Sex and Food Control in the 'Uncommon Chimpanzee': How Bonobo Females

Overcame a Phylogenetic Legacy of Male Dominance," *Ethnology and Sociobiology* (1994); C. Stanford, "The Social Behaviors of Chimpanzees and Bonobos," *Current Anthropology* (1998); F. de Waal, "Bonobo Sex and Society," *Scientific American* (vol. 4, 1995, pp. 82–85); F. de Waal and F. Lanting, *Bonobo: The Forgotten Ape* (1997); T. Kano, "The Bonobo's Peaceable Kingdom," *Natural History* (vol. 11, 1990, pp. 62–71); E. Ingmanson and T. Kano, "Waging Peace," *International Wildlife* (November/December 1993, pp. 30–37); F. White, "Pan Paniscus 1973 to 1996: Twenty-Three Years of Field Research," *Evolutionary Anthropology* (vol. 5, no. 1, 1996, pp. 11–17).

# ISSUE 9

## Are Male and Female Relationships Based Primarily on Reproductive Sex?

**YES: C. Owen Lovejoy,** from "The Origin of Man," *Science* (January 1981)

**NO: Barbara Smuts,** from "What Are Friends For?" *Natural History* (February 1987)

### ISSUE SUMMARY

Owen Lovejoy suggests that pair-bonding between males and females insures greater reproductive success. Thus, sex is the main reason they associate together. In contrast, Barbara Smuts argues that primate males and females associate together for many other reasons besides reproduction.

> *Men and women can't be friends because the sex thing always gets in the way.*
>
> —*Billy Crystal in When Harry Met Sally*

A charming little romantic comedy of the 1980s, *When Harry Met Sally* suggests that when it comes right down to it, the real reason men and women associate together has to do with sex. All other reasons are secondary or superfluous. While the two main characters in the movie do become friends, their friendship ultimately leads to a sexual relationship and marriage. Male and female friendship is thus portrayed as a stepping stone to pair-bonding and not as an end in itself.

This same viewpoint also echoes through much of the anthropological literature on primates and human evolution. As we discussed in Issue 6, females have been traditionally portrayed as needing male help and support to raise their infants to maturity. Sex, especially exclusive sex, is thus used by the female to lure and keep a permanent mate. Without sex, males have no reason to hang around to invest in any resulting offspring. While recent research has raised questions about the validity of this traditional viewpoint, the power of sexual pair-bonding is still seen as a driving force behind much of human cultural and biological evolution.

*conservative*

C. Owen Lovejoy adopts this premise in his article "The Origin of Man." He links the development of bipedalism, or upright walking, to male provisioning of females and the creation of exclusive pair-bonds. He also argues that this development sets the stage for population growth and cultural developments such as marriage and the family. In contrast, Smuts' article explores the evolutionary advantages of primate friendships in a wider context. While male and female friendships obviously often involve reproduction, Smuts suggests that factors such as companionship, political support, and protection are equally important.

# YES

C. Owen Lovejoy

# The Origin of Man

## A Behavioral Model for Early Hominid Evolution

Any behavioral change that increases reproductive rate, survivorship, or both, is under selection of maximum intensity. Higher primates rely on social behavioral mechanisms to promote survivorship during all phases of the life cycle, and one could cite numerous methods by which it theoretically could be increased. Avoidance of dietary toxins, use of more reliable food sources, and increased competence in arboreal locomotion are obvious examples. Yet these are among many that have remained under strong selection throughout much of the course of primate evolution, and it is therefore unlikely that early hominid adaptation was a product of intensified selection for adaptations almost universal to anthropoid primates. For early hominids we must look beyond such common variables to novel forms of behavioral change. The tendency has been to concentrate on singular, extraordinary traits of later human evolution such as intense technology, organized hunting, and the massive human brain. Yet these adaptations were not likely to have arisen de novo from elemental behaviors seen in extant nonhuman primates, such as the primitive tool using of the chimpanzee, in the absence of a broad selective milieu. It is more probable that significant preadaptations were present in early hominids that served as a behavioral base from which the "breakthrough" adaptations of later hominids could progressively develop. We are therefore in search of a novel behavioral pattern in Miocene hominoids that could evolve from typical primate survival strategies, but that might also include important elements of other mammalian strategies, that is, a behavioral pattern that arose by recombination of common mammalian behavioral elements and that increased survivorship and birthrate.

In her essay on mother-infant relationships among chimpanzees, van Lawick-Goodall noted two primary causes of mortality among infants: "inadequacy" of the mother-infant relationship and "injuries caused by falling from the mother." An intensification of both the quality and quantity of parenting would unquestionably improve survivorship of the altricial chimpanzee infant. The feeding and reproductive strategies of higher primates, however, largely prevent such an advancement. The mother must both care for the infant and forage for herself. A common method of altricial infant care in other mammals is sequestration of offspring at locations of maximum safety. Nests, lodges, setts, warrens, dreys, dens, lairs, and burrows are examples of this strategy. A similar adaptation in primates is usually not possible, however, because the need to forage requires both mother and infant to remain mobile. The requirement of mother-infant mobility is a significant cause of mortality and is at the same time the most important restriction on primate birth spacing.

Many primates display significant sex differences in foraging. Diet composition, selection of food items, feeding time, and canopy levels and sites differ in some species. In at least *Pongo pygmaeus* and *Colobus badius,* males often feed at lower canopy levels than females. In the gelada baboon, all-male groups "tended not to exploit quite the same areas as the reproductive units thus reducing indirect competition for food." Clutton-Brock notes that an increased separation of males from female-offspring foraging sites is advantageous where (i) animals feed outward from a fixed base, (ii) the adult sex ratio is close to parity, and (iii) feeding rate is limited by search time rather than by handling time, which is the time spent both preparing and consuming food. Similar feeding differences by sex are found in birds and other mammals.

It is reasonable to assume that Miocene hominoids traveled between food sources on the ground and that these primates would be best characterized as omnivores. These are ecologically sound assumptions. Increased seasonality coupled with already occurring local biotic variation (edaphic grasslands, savannah, woodland, forest) would have presented variable and mosaic conditions. Occupation of heterogeneous ("patchy") environments and use of variable food sources favors a generalist strategy, where as reliance on a homogeneous diet requires high food concentrations. The time spent searching for food is greatest among generalists who live in food-sparse environments. In short, Miocene ecological conditions support the view that feeding rate would have been more dependent on search time than handling time.

Greater seasonality and the need to increase both birthrate and survivorship would also favor at least partial separation of male and female day ranges since this strategy would increase carrying capacity and improve the protein and calorie supply of females and their offspring. Terrestriality, however, would require a centrifugal or linear displacement of males, as opposed to vertical stratification in canopy feeding. Given the Miocene conditions described above, such separation could become marked especially in the dry season. If such separation were primarily due only to an increase in the male day range, moreover, the range of the female-offspring group could be proportionately reduced by progressive elimination of male competition for local resources. This separation would be under strong positive selection. Lowered mobility of females would reduce accident rate during travel, maximize familiarity with the core area, reduce exposure to predators, and allow intensification of parenting behavior, thus elevating survivorship. Such a division of feeding areas, however, would not genetically favor males unless it specifically reduced competition with their own biological offspring and did not reduce their opportunities for consort relationships. Polygynous mating would not be favored by this adaptive strategy because the advantage of feeding divergence is reduced as the number of males is reduced. Conversely, a sex ratio close to parity would select for the proposed feeding strategy. Such a ratio would obtain if the mating pattern were monogamous pair bonding. In this case, males would avoid competition with their bonded mates and biological offspring (by using alternative feeding sites) and not be disadvantaged by physical separation, that is, there would be no loss of consort opportunity. In short, monogamous pair bonding would favor feeding divergence by "assuring" males of biological paternity and by reducing feeding competition with their own offspring and mates.

Such a system would increase survivorship and would also favor any increase in the reproductive rate of a monogamous pair so long as feeding strategy was sufficient to meet the increased load on the sources of protein and calories. One element of feeding among forest chimpanzees is the "food call" sometimes made by males upon discovery of a new food source. In the proposed system, however, selection would not favor this behavior; instead, selection would favor a behavior that would benefit only the male's own reproductive unit. The simple alternative to the food call would involve collecting the available food item or items and returning them to the mate and offspring. Contrary to the opinion that such behavior would be altruistic, it would not be so in the proposed system, because it would only benefit the biological offspring of the male carrying out the provisioning and thus would be under powerful, direct selection. If this behavior were to become a regular component of the male's behavioral repertoire, it would directly increase his reproductive rate by correspondingly improving the protein and calories supply of the female who could then accommodate greater gestational and lactation loads and intensify parenting. The behavior would thus achieve both an increase in survivorship and a reduction in birth space. It would allow a progressive increase in the number of dependent offspring because their nutritional and supervisory requirements could be met more adequately. . . .

*Table 1*

### Relative Reproductive Values of Old World Primates . . . and Multiplied by 10 for Clarity

| | Reproductive values | | |
| Annual survivorship | Old World monkeys* | Chimpanzees† | Man‡ |
| --- | --- | --- | --- |
| .90 | 17 | 4 | 2 |
| .92 | 23 | 7 | 4 |
| .94 | 31 | 13 | 9 |
| .96 | 42 | 25 | 24 |
| .98 | 58 | 50 | 64 |

*Maximum life potential = 20; sexual maturity = 4; birth space = 2 (49, 50, 103).
†Maximum life potential = 40; sexual maturity = 10; birth space = 3 (46, 54, 103).
‡Maximum life potential = 60; sexual maturity = 15; birth space = 2.5.

# Human Sexual Behavior and Anatomy

The highly unusual sexual behavior of man may now be brought into focus. Human females are continually sexually receptive and have essentially no externally recognizable estrous cycle; male approach may be considered equally stable. Copulation shows little or no synchronization with ovulation. As was pointed out above, the selective emergence of a monogamous mating structure and male provisioning would require that males not be disadvantaged in obtaining consorts. Provisioning in birds and canids is normally made possible by highly restricted breeding seasons and discrete generations—the female normally is impregnable for only brief periods during which parental care is not required. The menstrual cycle of higher primates, however, requires regular male proximity for reproductive success. The progressive elimination of external manifestations of ovulation and the establishment of continual receptivity would require copulatory vigilance in both sexes in order to ensure fertilization. Moreover, copulation would increase pair-bond adhesion and serve as a social display asserting that bond. Indeed, any sequestration of ovulation would seem to directly imply both regular copulatory behavior and monogamous mating structure. . . .

Since man displays a highly unusual mating structure, it is perhaps not surprising that his epigamic, or perhaps parasexual, anatomy is equally unusual and fully explicable by that mating structure. If pair bonding was fundamental and crucial to early hominid reproductive strategy, the anatomical characters that could reinforce pair bonds would also be under strong positive selection. Thus the body and facial hair, distinctive somatotype, the conspicuous penis of human males, and the prominent and permanently enlarged mammae of human females are not surprising in light of Mayr's observation that in "monogamous species such as herons (egrets) in which the pair bond is continuously tested and strengthened by mutual displays, there has been a 'transference' of the display characters from the males to the females with the result that both sexes have elaborate display plumes." In man, however, marked epigamic dimorphism is achieved by elaboration of parasexual characters in both males and females, rather than in males alone. Their display value is clearly cross-sexual and not intrasexual as in other primates. It should be stressed that these epigamic characters are highly variable and can thus be viewed as a mechanism for establishing and displaying individual sexual uniqueness, and that such uniqueness would play a major role in the maintenance of pair bonds. This is especially important when other epigamic features of man (public, axillary, and scalp hair), which have been elaborated in both sexes, are considered. Such characters may also contribute to individual sexual uniqueness. Redolent individuality is clearly the most probable role of axillary and urogenital scent "organs" (eccrine and apocrine glands plus hair), which are unique among mammals. An objection that might be voiced in response to these suggestions is that such auxiliary pair-bond "enhancers" are eclipsed by the paramount role of culture in the mating practices of nontechnological societies. Quite the contrary, the more that culture can be shown to dominate the mating structure and process of recent man, the more ancient must be the anatomical-physiological mechanisms involved in the formation and maintainence of pair bonds. . . .

It is of interest to explore one further effect of the proposed model on early hominid social structure. The strong maternal and sibling ties of higher primates are now well documented. The matrifocal unit of chimpanzees continues throughout the life of the mother, as do sibling ties. In the proposed hominid reproductive strategy, the process of pair bonding would not only lead to the direct involvement of males in the survivorship of offspring, in primates as intelligent as extant hominoids, it would establish paternity and thus lead to a gradual replacement of the matrifocal group by a "bifocal" one—the primitive nuclear family. The effects of such a social unit on survivorship and species success could be profound. It could lead to a further shortening of birth space, which would accelerate the reproductive rate and amplify sibling bonds. Reduction of birth space would allow coincident protraction of the subadult (learning) period. Behaviors that in other primates are common causes of infant death (for example, agonistic buffering) would be largely eliminated, while those that might improve survivorship (for example, adoption) would be facilitated. The age until which an orphaned chimpanzee does not survive the death of its mother is "around 5 years of age, but may stretch another 3 to 4 in special circumstances." Survival of a second parent may have been a crucial reproductive advance in early hominids. Primiparous females are much less adept than multiparous mothers. Drickamer found that in free-ranging *Macaca mullata* "between 40 and 50% of the infants born first or second to a female did not survive their first year, but by the fourth infant born to the same female only 9% died during the first 12 months." Lancaster notes that: "Recent field and laboratory workers have shown that in many species of mammals, and especially in monkeys and apes, learning and experience play vital roles in the development of the behavior patterns used in mating and maternal care." The effect of intensified parenting, protracted learning, and enhanced sibling relationships would have a markedly beneficial effect upon survivorship. Such projections of the behavior of developing hominids are certainly not new, but they have not received their due emphasis. Can the nuclear family not be viewed as a prodigious adaptation central to the success of early hominids? It may certainly be considered as being within the behavior repertoire of hominoid primates, provided that the reproductive and feeding strategies commensurate to its development were themselves under strong selection. This brief review of the fossil record and some primate behavioral and ecological adaptations would seem to strongly favor the correctness of this view.

## Conclusion

It is a truism to say that even late Pliocene hominids must have been unusual mammals, both behaviorally and anatomically. As was pointed out above, emphasis in models of human origin has traditionally been on singular, extraordinary traits of later human evolution. The model proposed in this article has placed greater emphasis on a fundamental behavioral base from which these unusual adaptations could be directionally selected.

The proposed model accounts for the early origin of bipedality as a locomotor behavior directly enhancing reproductive fitness, not as a behavior resulting from occasional upright feeding posture. It accounts for the origin of the home base in the same fashion as it has been acquired by numerous other mammals. It accounts for the human nuclear family, for the distinctive human sexual epigamic features, and the species' unique sexual behavior. It accounts for a functional, rudimentary material culture of long-standing, and it accounts for the greater proportion of r-selected characters in hominids relative to other hominoids. It accounts for these characters with simple behavioral changes common to both primates and other mammals and in relatively favorable environments, rather than by rapid or forced occupation of habitats for which early hominoids were clearly not adaptively or demographically equipped. It is fully consistent with primate paleogeography, present knowledge of higher primate behavior patterns (as well as those of other mammals), and the hominid fossil record.

If the model is correct, the conventional concept that material culture is pivotal to the differentiation and origin of the primary characters of the Hominidae is probably incorrect. Rather, both advanced material culture and the Pleistocene acceleration in brain development are sequelae to an already established hominid character system, which included intensified parenting and social relationships, monogamous pair bonding, specialized sexual-reproductive behavior, and bipedality. It implies that the nuclear family and human sexual behavior may have their ultimate origin long before the dawn of the Pleistocene.

# NO ⤶

**Barbara Smuts**

# What Are Friends For?

**V**irgil, a burly adult male olive baboon, closely followed Zizi, a middle-aged female easily distinguished by her grizzled coat and square muzzle. On her rump Zizi sported a bright pink swelling, indicating that she was sexually receptive and probably fertile. Virgil's extreme attentiveness to Zizi suggested to me—and all rival males in the troop—that he was her current and exclusive mate.

Zizi, however, apparently had something else in mind. She broke away from Virgil, moved rapidly through the troop, and presented her alluring sexual swelling to one male after another. Before Virgil caught up with her, she had managed to announce her receptive condition to several of his rivals. When Virgil tried to grab her, Zizi screamed and dashed into the bushes with Virgil in hot pursuit. I heard sounds of chasing and fighting coming from the thicket. Moments later Zizi emerged from the bushes with an older male named Cyclops. They remained together for several days, copulating often. In Cyclops's presence, Zizi no longer approached or even glanced at other males.

Primatologists describe Zizi and other olive baboons (*Papio cynocephalus anubis*) as promiscuous, meaning that both males and females usually mate with several members of the opposite sex within a short period of time. Promiscuous mating behavior characterizes many of the larger, more familiar primates, including chimpanzees, rhesus macaques, and gray langurs, as well as olive, yellow, and chacma baboons, the three subspecies of savanna baboon. In colloquial usage, promiscuity often connotes wanton and random sex, and several early studies of primates supported this stereotype. However, after years of laboriously recording thousands of copulations under natural conditions, the Peeping Toms of primate fieldwork have shown that, even in promiscuous species, sexual pairings are far from random.

Some adult males, for example, typically copulate much more often than others. Primatologists have explained these differences in terms of competition: the most dominant males monopolize females and prevent lower-ranking rivals from mating. But exceptions are frequent. Among baboons, the exceptions often involve scruffy, older males who mate in full view of younger, more dominant rivals.

A clue to the reason for these puzzling exceptions emerged when primatologists began to question an implicit assumption of the dominance hypothesis—that females were merely passive objects of male competition. But what if females were active arbiters in this system? If females preferred some males over others and were able to express these preferences, then models of mating activity based on male dominance alone would be far too simple.

Once researchers recognized the possibility of female choice, evidence for it turned up in species after species. The story of Zizi, Virgil, and Cyclops is one of hundreds of examples of female primates rejecting the sexual advances of particular males and enthusiastically cooperating with others. But what is the basis for female choice? Why might they prefer some males over others?

This question guided my research on the Eburru Cliffs troop of olive baboons, named after one of their favorite sleeping sites, a sheer rocky outcrop rising several hundred feet above the floor of the Great Rift Valley, about 100 miles northwest of Nairobi, Kenya. The 120 members of Eburru Cliffs spent their days wandering through open grassland studded with occasional acacia thorn trees. Each night they retired to one of a dozen sets of cliffs that provided protection from nocturnal predators such as leopards.

Most previous studies of baboon sexuality had focused on females who, like Zizi, were at the peak of sexual receptivity. A female baboon does not mate when she is pregnant or lactating, a period of abstinence lasting about eighteen months. The female then goes into estrus, and for about two weeks out of every thirty-five-day cycle, she mates. Toward the end of this two week period she may ovulate, but usually the female undergoes four or five estrous cycles before she conceives. During pregnancy, she once again resumes a chaste existence. As a result, the typical female baboon is sexually active for less than 10 percent of her adult life. I thought that by focusing on the other 90 percent, I might learn something new. In particular, I suspected that routine, day-to-day relationships between males and pregnant or lactating (nonestrous) females might provide clues to female mating preferences.

Nearly every day for sixteen months, I joined the Eburru Cliffs baboons at their sleeping cliffs at dawn and traveled several miles with them while they foraged for roots, seeds, grass, and occasionally, small prey items, such as baby gazelles or hares (see "Predatory Baboons of Kekopey," *Natural History*, March 1976). Like all savanna baboon troops, Eburru Cliffs functioned as a cohesive unit organized around a core of related females, all of whom were born in the troop. Unlike the females, male savanna baboons leave their natal troop to join another where they may remain for many years, so most of the Eburru Cliffs adult males were immigrants. Since membership in the troop remained relatively constant during the period of my study, I learned to identify each individual. I relied on differences in size, posture, gait, and especially, facial features. To the practiced observer, baboons look as different from one another as human beings do.

As soon as I could recognize individuals, I noticed that particular females tended to turn up near particular males again and again. I came to think of these pairs as friends. Friendship among animals is not a well-documented phenomenon, so to convince skeptical colleagues that baboon friendship was real, I needed to develop objective criteria for distinguishing friendly pairs.

I began by investigating grooming, the amiable simian habit of picking through a companion's fur to remove dead skin and ectoparasites (see "Little

Things That Tick Off Baboons," *Natural History*, February 1984). Baboons spend much more time grooming than is necessary for hygiene, and previous research had indicated that it is a good measure of social bonds. Although eighteen adult males lived in the troop, each nonestrous female performed most of her grooming with just one, two, or occasionally, three males. For example, of Zizi's twenty-four grooming bouts with males, Cyclops accounted for thirteen, and a second male, Sherlock, accounted for all the rest. Different females tended to favor different males as grooming partners.

Another measure of social bonds was simply who was observed near whom. When foraging, traveling, or resting, each pregnant or lactating female spent a lot of time near a few males and associated with the others no more often than expected by chance. When I compared the identities of favorite grooming partners and frequent companions, they overlapped almost completely. This enabled me to develop a formal definition of friendship: any male that scored high on both grooming and proximity measures was considered a friend.

Virtually all baboons made friends; only one female and the three males who had most recently joined the troop lacked such companions. Out of more than 600 possible adult female–adult male pairs in the troop, however, only about one in ten qualified as friends; these really were special relationships.

Several factors seemed to influence which baboons paired up. In most cases, friends were unrelated to each other, since the male had immigrated from another troop. (Four friendships, however, involved a female and an adolescent son who had not yet emigrated. Unlike other friends, these related pairs never mated.) Older females tended to be friends with older males; younger females with younger males. I witnessed occasional May-December romances, usually involving older females and young adult males. Adolescent males and females were strongly rule-bound, and with the exception of mother–son pairs, they formed friendships only with one another.

Regardless of age or dominance rank, most females had just one or two male friends. But among males, the number of female friends varied greatly from none to eight. Although high-ranking males enjoyed priority of access to food and sometimes mates, dominant males did not have more female friends than low-ranking males. Instead it was the older males who had lived in the troop for many years who had the most friends. When a male had several female friends, the females were often closely related to one another. Since female baboons spend a lot of time near their kin, it is probably easier for a male to maintain bonds with several related females at once.

When collecting data, I focused on one nonestrous female at a time and kept track of her every movement toward or away from any male; similarly, I noted every male who moved toward or away from her. Whenever the female and a male moved close enough to exchange intimacies, I wrote down exactly what happened. When foraging together, friends tended to remain a few yards apart. Males more often wandered away from females than the reverse, and females, more often than males, closed the gap. The female behaved as if she wanted to keep the male within calling distance, in case she needed his protection. The male, however, was more likely to make approaches that brought them within actual touching distance. Often, he would plunk himself down right next to his friend and ask her to groom him by holding a pose with exaggerated stillness. The female sometimes responded by grooming, but more often, she exhibited the most reliable sign of true intimacy: she ignored her friend and simply continued whatever she was doing.

In sharp contrast, when a male who was not a friend moved close to a female, she dared not ignore him. She stopped whatever she was doing and held still, often glancing surreptitiously at the intruder. If he did not move away, she sometimes lifted her tail and presented her rump. When a female is not in estrus, this is a gesture of appeasement, not sexual enticement. Immediately after this respectful acknowledgement of his presence, the female would slip away. But such tense interactions with nonfriend males were rare, because females usually moved away before the males came too close.

These observations suggest that females were afraid of most of the males in their troop, which is not surprising: male baboons are twice the size of females, and their canines are longer and sharper than those of a lion. All Eburru Cliffs males directed both mild and severe aggression toward females. Mild aggression, which usually involved threats and chases but no body contact, occurred most often during feeding competition or when the male redirected aggression toward a female after losing a fight with another male. Females and juveniles showed aggression toward other females and juveniles in similar circumstances and occasionally inflicted superficial wounds. Severe aggression by males, which involved body contact and sometimes biting, was less common and also more puzzling, since there was no apparent cause.

An explanation for at least some of these attacks emerged one day when I was watching Pegasus, a young adult male, and his friend Cicily, sitting together in the middle of a small clearing. Cicily moved to the edge of the clearing to feed, and a higher-ranking female, Zora, suddenly attacked her. Pegasus stood up and looked as if he were about to intervene when both females disappeared into the bushes. He sat back down, and I remained with him. A full ten minutes later, Zora appeared at the edge of the clearing; this was the first time she had come into view since her attack on Cicily. Pegasus instantly pounced on Zora, repeatedly grabbed her neck in his mouth and lifted her off the ground, shook her whole body, and then dropped her. Zora screamed continuously and tried to escape. Each time, Pegasus caught her and continued his brutal attack. When he finally released her five minutes later she had a deep canine gash on the palm of her hand that made her limp for several days.

This attack was similar in form and intensity to those I had seen before and labeled "unprovoked." Certainly, had I come upon the scene after Zora's aggression toward Cicily, I would not have understood why Pegasus attacked Zora. This suggested that some, perhaps many, severe attacks by males actually represented punishment for actions that had occurred some time before.

Whatever the reasons for male attacks on females, they represent a serious threat. Records of fresh injuries indicated that Eburru Cliffs adult females received canine slash wounds from males at the rate of one for every female each year, and during my study, one female died of her injuries. Males probably pose an even greater threat to infants. Although only one infant was killed during my study, observers in Botswana and Tanzania have seen recent male immigrants kill several young infants.

Protection from male aggression, and from the less injurious but more frequent aggression of other females and juveniles, seems to be one of the main advantages of friendship for a female baboon. Seventy times I observed an adult male defend a female or her offspring against aggression by another troop member, not infrequently a high-ranking male. In all but six of these cases, the defender was a friend. Very few of these confrontations involved actual fighting; no male baboon, subordinate or dominant, is anxious to risk injury by the sharp canines of another.

Males are particularly solicitous guardians of their friends' youngest infants. If another male gets too close to an infant or if a juvenile female plays with it too roughly, the friend may intervene. Other troop members soon learn to be cautious when the mother's friend is nearby, and his presence provides the mother with a welcome respite from the annoying pokes and prods of curious females and juveniles obsessed with the new baby. Male baboons at Gombe Park in Tanzania and Amboseli Park in Kenya have also been seen rescuing infants from chimpanzees and lions. These several forms of male protection help to explain why females in Eburru Cliffs stuck closer to their friends in the first few months after giving birth than at any other time.

The male–infant relationship develops out of the male's friendship with the mother, but as the infant matures, this new bond takes on a life of its own. My co-worker Nancy Nicolson found that by about nine months of age, infants actively sought out their male friends when the mother was a few yards away, suggesting that the male may function as an alternative caregiver. This seemed to be especially true for infants undergoing unusually early or severe weaning. (Weaning is generally a gradual, prolonged process, but there is tremendous variation among mothers in the timing and intensity of weaning. See "Mother Baboons," *Natural History*, September 1980.) After being rejected by the mother, the crying infant often approached the male friend and sat huddled against him until its whimpers subsided. Two of the infants in Eburru Cliffs lost their mothers when they were still quite young. In each case, their bond with the mother's friend subsequently intensified, and—perhaps as a result—both infants survived.

A close bond with a male may also improve the infant's nutrition. Larger than all other troop members, adult males monopolize the best feeding sites. In general, the personal space surrounding a feeding male is inviolate, but he usually tolerates intrusions by the infants of his female friends, giving them access to choice feeding spots.

Although infants follow their male friends around rather than the reverse, the males seem genuinely attached to their tiny companions. During feeding, the male and infant express their pleasure in each other's company by sharing spirited, antiphonal grunting duets. If the infant whimpers in distress, the male friend is likely to cease feeding, look at the infant, and grunt softly, as if in sympathy, until the whimpers cease. When the male rests, the infants of his female friends may huddle behind him, one after the other, forming a "train," or, if feeling energetic, they may use his body as a trampoline.

When I returned to Eburru Cliffs four years after my initial study ended, several of the bonds formed between males and the infants of their female friends were still intact (in other cases, either the male or the infant or both had disappeared). When these bonds involved recently matured females, their long-time male associates showed no sexual interest in them, even though the females mated with other adult males. Mothers and sons, and usually maternal siblings, show similar sexual inhibitions in baboons and many other primate species.

The development of an intimate relationship between a male and the infant of his female friend raises an obvious question: Is the male the infant's father? To answer this question definitely we would need to conduct genetic analysis, which was not possible for these baboons. Instead, I estimated paternity probabilities from observations of the temporary (a few hours or days) exclusive mating relationships, or consortships, that estrous females form with a series of different males. These estimates were apt to be fairly accurate, since changes in the female's sexual swelling allow one to pinpoint the timing of conception to within a few days. Most females consorted with only two or three males during this period, and these males were termed likely fathers.

In about half the friendships, the male was indeed likely to be the father of his friend's most recent infant, but in the other half he was not—in fact, he had never been seen mating with the female. Interestingly, males who were friends with the mother but not likely fathers nearly always developed a relationship with her infant, while males who had mated with the female but were not her friend usually did not. Thus friendship with the mother, rather than paternity, seems to mediate the development of male–infant bonds. Recently, a similar pattern was documented for South American capuchin monkeys in a laboratory study in which paternity was determined genetically.

These results fly in the face of a prominent theory that claims males will invest in infants only when they are closely related. If males are not fostering the survival of their own genes by caring for the infant, then why do they do so? I suspected that the key was female choice. If females preferred to mate with males who had already demonstrated friendly behavior, then friendships with mothers and their infants might pay off in the future when the mothers were ready to mate again.

To find out if this was the case, I examined each male's sexual behavior with females he had befriended before they resumed estrus. In most cases, males consorted considerably more often with their friends than with other females. Baboon females typically mate with several different males, including both friends and nonfriends, but prior friendship increased a male's probability of mating with a female above what it would have been otherwise.

This increased probability seemed to reflect female preferences. Females occasionally overtly advertised their disdain for certain males and their desire for others. Zizi's behavior, described above, is a good example. Virgil was not one of her friends, but Cyclops was. Usually, however, females expressed preferences and aversions more subtly. For example, Delphi, a petite adolescent female, found herself pursued by Hector, a middle-aged adult male. She did not run away or refuse to mate with him, but whenever he wasn't watching, she looked around for her friend Homer, an adolescent male. When she succeeded in catching Homer's eye, she narrowed her eyes and flattened her ears against her skull, the friendliest face one baboon can send another. This told Homer she would rather be with him. Females expressed satisfaction with a current consort partner by staying close to him, initiating copulations, and not making advances toward other males. Baboons are very sensitive to such cues, as indicated by an experimental study in which rival hamadryas baboons rarely challenged a male–female pair if the female strongly preferred her current partner. Similarly, in Eburru Cliffs, males were less apt to challenge consorts involving a pair that shared a long-term friendship.

Even though females usually consorted with their friends, they also mated with other males, so it is not surprising that friendships were most vulnerable during periods of sexual activity. In a few cases, the female consorted with another male more often than with her friend, but the friendship survived nevertheless. One female, however, formed a strong sexual bond with a new male. This bond persisted after conception, replacing her previous friendship. My observations suggest that adolescent and young adult females tend to have shorter, less stable friendships than do older females. Some friendships, however, last a very long time. When I returned to Eburru Cliffs six years after my study began, five couples were still together. It is possible that friendships occasionally last for life (baboons probably live twenty to thirty years in the wild), but it will require longer studies, and some very patient scientists, to find out.

By increasing both the male's chances of mating in the future and the likelihood that a female's infant will survive, friendship contributes to the reproductive success of both partners. This clarifies the evolutionary basis of friendship-forming tendencies in baboons, but what does friendship mean to a baboon? To answer this question we need to view baboons as sentient beings with feelings and goals not unlike our own in similar circumstances. Consider, for example, the friendship between Thalia and Alexander.

The affair began one evening as Alex and Thalia sat about fifteen feet apart on the sleeping cliffs. It was like watching two novices in a singles bar. Alex stared at Thalia until she turned and almost caught him looking at her. He glanced away immediately, and then she stared at him until his head began to turn toward her. She suddenly became engrossed in grooming her toes. But as soon as Alex looked away, her gaze returned to him. They went on like this for more than fifteen minutes, always with split-second timing. Finally, Alex managed to catch Thalia looking at him. He made the friendly eyes-narrowed, ears-back face and smacked his lips together rhythmically. Thalia froze, and for a second she looked into his eyes. Alex approached, and Thalia, still nervous, groomed him. Soon she calmed down, and I found them still together on the cliffs the next morning. Looking back on this event months later, I realized that it marked the beginning of their friendship. Six years later, when I returned to Eburru Cliffs, they were still friends.

If flirtation forms an integral part of baboon friendship, so does jealousy. Overt displays of jealousy, such as chasing a friend away from a potential rival, occur occasionally, but like humans, baboons often express their emotions in more subtle ways. One evening a colleague and I climbed the cliffs and settled down near Sherlock, who was friends with Cybelle, a middle-aged female still foraging on the ground below the cliffs. I observed Cybelle while my colleague watched Sherlock, and we kept up a running commentary. As long as Cybelle was feeding or interacting with females, Sherlock was relaxed, but each time she approached another male, his body would stiffen, and he would stare intently at the scene below. When Cybelle presented politely to a male who had recently tried to befriend her, Sherlock even made threatening sounds under his breath. Cybelle was not in estrus at the time, indicating that male baboon jealousy extends beyond the sexual arena to include affiliative interactions between a female friend and other males.

Because baboon friendships are embedded in a network of friendly and antagonistic relationships, they inevitably lead to repercussions extending beyond the pair. For example, Virgil once provoked his weaker rival Cyclops into a fight by first attacking Cyclops's friend Phoebe. On another occasion, Sherlock chased Circe, Hector's best friend, just after Hector had chased Antigone, Sherlock's friend.

In another incident, the prime adult male Triton challenged Cyclops's possession of meat. Cyclops grew increasingly tense and seemed about to abandon the prey to the younger male. Then Cyclops's friend Phoebe appeared with her infant Phyllis. Phyllis wandered over to Cyclops. He immediately grabbed her, held her close, and threatened Triton away from the prey. Because any challenge to Cyclops now involved a threat to Phyllis as well, Triton risked being mobbed by Phoebe and her relatives and friends. For this reason, he backed down. Males frequently use the infants of their female friends as buffers in this way. Thus, friendship involves costs as well as benefits because it makes the participants vulnerable to social manipulation or redirected aggression by others.

Finally, as with humans, friendship seems to mean something different to each baboon. Several females in Eburru Cliffs had only one friend. They were devoted companions. Louise and Pandora, for example, groomed their friend Virgil and no other male. Then there was Leda, who, with five friends, spread herself more thinly than any other female. These contrasting patterns of friendship were associated with striking personality differences. Louise and Pandora were unobtrusive females who hung around quietly with Virgil and their close relatives. Leda seemed to be everywhere at once, playing with infants, fighting with juveniles, and making friends with males. Similar differences were apparent among the males. Some devoted a great deal of time and energy to cultivating friendships with females, while others focused more on challenging other males. Although we probably will never fully understand the basis of these individual differences, they contribute immeasurably to the richness and complexity of baboon society.

Male–female friendships may be widespread among primates. They have been reported for many other groups of savanna baboons, and they also occur in rhesus and Japanese macaques, capuchin monkeys, and perhaps in bonobos (pygmy chimpanzees). These relationships should give us pause when considering popular scenarios for the evolution of male–female relationships in humans. Most of these scenarios assume that, except for mating, males and females had little to do with one another until the development of a sexual division of labor, when, the story goes, females began to rely on males to provide meat in exchange for gathered food. This, it has been argued, set up new selection pressures favoring the development of long-term bonds between individual males and females, female sexual fidelity, and as paternity certainty increased, greater male investment in the offspring of these unions. In other words, once women began to gather and men to hunt, presto—we had the nuclear family.

This scenario may have more to do with cultural biases about women's economic dependence on men and idealized views of the nuclear family than with the actual behavior of our hominid ancestors. The nonhuman primate evidence challenges this story in at least three ways.

First, long-term bonds between the sexes can evolve in the absence of a sexual division of labor or food sharing. In our primate relatives, such relationships rest on exchanges of social, not economic, benefits.

Second, primate research shows that highly differentiated, emotionally intense male–female relationships can occur without sexual exclusivity. Ancestral men and women may have experienced intimate friendships long before they invented marriage and norms of sexual fidelity.

Third, among our closest primate relatives, males clearly provide mothers and infants with social benefits even when they are unlikely to be the fathers of those infants. In return, females provide a variety of benefits to the friendly males, including acceptance into the group and, at least in baboons, increased mating opportunities in the future. This suggests that efforts to reconstruct the evolution of hominid societies may have overemphasized what the female must supposedly do (restrict her mating to just one male) in order to obtain male parental investment.

Maybe it is time to pay more attention to what the male must do (provide benefits to females and young) in order to obtain female cooperation. Perhaps among our ancestors, as in baboons today, sex and friendship went hand in hand. As for marriage—well, that's another story.

# POSTSCRIPT

## Are Male and Female Relationships Based Primarily on Reproductive Sex?

One of the more compelling aspects of Lovejoy's theory is the way he links locomotion, loss of estrus, and reproduction together. All other primate females experience a definite estrus period marked by increased sexual interest and visible physical changes (such as swollen bottoms). Estrus serves a double function of making sure that most mating takes place during the female's fertile time and leaves no doubt in the minds of males when that time is. The lengthening and eventual loss of estrus in humans, Lovejoy suggests, evolved as a way to increase the amount and intensity of male provisioning. While most primate males do not regularly provision females, provisioning behavior has been observed when the female is in estrus (see Issue 7). In this sort of situation, the females with the longer estrus periods would receive the most provisioning. Over time, there could be simultaneous selection for longer estrus periods and more male provisioning until both became perpetual and ongoing.

Selection for male provisioning and a lengthened estrus period among females, however, does not necessarily select for exclusive pair-bonding. As Smuts' article describes, males and females who maintain multiple "friendships" with members of the opposite sex have a better chance of passing on their genes. These friendships also offer other benefits. Females can call on their male friends for protection from other males, use male friends to intimidate female rivals, or get males to watch over their offspring. Males also gain important advantages from their friendships with females that are not related to sex. Baboon males leave the troop of their birth during adolescence and must wander about until they find a new troop to take them in. In order to be admitted to a new troop, adolescent males must be befriended by at least one resident female. She serves as his sponsor and eases his transition into the troop. Observations also suggest that friendships with high-status females in a troop also favorably impact a male's position in his own gender hierarchy.

Natural selection, therefore, seems to favor promiscuity over pair-bonding for both males and females. "This suggests that efforts to reconstruct the evolution of human societies may have overemphasized what the female must supposedly do (restrict her mating to just one male) in order to obtain male parental investment. Maybe its time to pay more attention to what the male must do (provide benefits to females and young) in order to obtain female cooperation" (Smuts, 1987:50).

Cross-cultural studies of contemporary humans also indicate that exclusive pair-bonding between males and females is not common. About 85 percent of the world's cultures allow polygamy, and adultery is frequently an issue. Human societies also vary in how much value is given to paternity. In patrilineal societies, where descent and inheritance are passed down through the male line, a woman's chances for sexual contacts and friendships with men other than her husband are limited and dangerous. On the other hand, in many matrilineal societies, women enjoy the freedom to change husbands or to maintain a variety of male friendships without social censure. Iroquois women declared themselves divorced by simply placing their husband's belongings outside the house and often took lovers when their husbands were away (Brown, 1978). Nayar women in India also entered into "side marriages" or *sambandhan* relationships when their husbands were away. Any resulting children belonged to her linage (Mencher, 1965; Fuller 1976). Other cultures, such as the Nuer in Africa, even allow woman/woman marriage under special circumstances. An older, usually menopausal woman is ritually changed into a man and "marries" wives of reproductive age. While other male kinsmen biologically father the children, the *female husband* functions as the father and husband in the household (Evans-Pritchard, 1951).

Clearly, males and females can be friends as well as lovers. Exclusive pair-bonding is not very common or particularly adaptive among primates. So the preference for monogamous mating in our own society seems to be culturally rather than biologically determined. For more information on the varieties of male and female relationships, see William Crocker and Jean Crocker, *The Canela: Kinships, Ritual and Sex in an Amazonian Tribe* (Thomson 2004); M. Goldstein, "When Brothers Share a Wife," *Natural History* (1987); M. Small, "How Many Fathers Are Best for a Child?" *Discover* (2003); and C. Hua, *A Society Without Fathers or Husbands: The Na of China* (Zone Books, 2001).

# ISSUE 10

# Did Bipedalism Develop
# as a Response to Heat Stress?

**YES: Pete Wheeler,** from "Human Ancestors Walked Tall, Stayed
Cool," *Natural History* (August 1993)

**NO: Pat Shipman,** from "Scavenger Hunt," *Natural History* (April
1984)

### ISSUE SUMMARY

Pete Wheeler contends that climatic changes in Africa forced
early hominids to walk upright in order to cope with the resulting heat stress. Pat Shipman suggests that changes in diet rather
than changes in climate were responsible for the evolution of
bipedalism. She suggests that scavenging may have been the
decisive factor leading to this change.

*It's a wonderful story. Once upon a time, there was an ape who lived in the
middle of a dark forest. It spent most of its days in the trees, munching lan-
guidly on fruits and berries. But then one day the ape decided to leave the forest for the savanna nearby, or perhaps it was the savanna that moved,
licking away at the edge of the forest one tree at a time until the fruits and
berries all the apes had found so easily weren't so easy to find any more
(Shreeve, 1996:116).*

How did bipedalism, or upright walking, first develop? Although long considered a major factor in human evolution, scientists have disagreed about
when and how bipedalism came about. Archaeological finds suggest that
hominids living 3 to 4 million years ago moved bipedally. Many of the physiological features we associate with bipedalism—wider pelvis, shorter arms and
longer legs, and the rotation of the spine underneath the skull—were all in
place. Although some researchers such as Falk (1990, 1992) have suggested that
bipedalism continued to be refined over time, most scientists agree that the
transition from bipedalism occurred somewhere between 4 to 7 million years
ago. At that time, the human line also diverged from the other apes, and bipedalism may have been an important part of this process.

So what would select for bipedalism in humans and not in apes? Over
100 years ago, Charles Darwin suggested that early humans moved from the

forest into the open grasslands due to either climate change or the adoption of new patterns of subsistence. One early scenario, described in Shreeve's opening story, hypothesized that as the grasslands expanded and the forests reduced in size, there would be a "competition for the trees." The losers would be forced out into the savanna and compelled to develop new traits in order to survive. Other theorists favored the view of early hominids as opportunistic entrepreneurs. Instead of being forced out of the forest, they actively left it in order to exploit the new resources they found in the grasslands. Both camps agreed on one point, however: Movement out into the savanna and adaptation to life there was absolutely critical to the development of bipedalism. "Bipedalism allowed hominids to see over tall savanna grass, perhaps, or escape predators, or walk more efficiently over long distances. In other scenarios, it freed the hands to make tools for hunting or gathering plants" (Shreeve, 1996:116).

Physiologist Pete Wheeler also suggests that an erect posture exposes less surface area to the sun and lifts the body above the ground, which keep the body temperature cooler and reduce the dangers of dehydration and sunstroke on the savanna. In contrast, Pat Shipman argues that bipedalism developed due to the evolution of a new subsistence strategy—scavenging.

Pete Wheeler

 **YES**

# Human Ancestors Walked Tall, Stayed Cool

**H**ominids, or humanlike primates, first appeared in Africa five to seven million years ago, when that continent's climate was becoming increasingly arid and large tracts of woodland and savanna were replacing the unbroken canopy of the equatorial rain forest. While the ancestors of chimpanzees and gorillas remained in the moist forests, the hominids started to exploit the more open, drier habitats. The exact nature of the transition remains hidden, because the oldest-known hominid fossils (*Australopithecus afarensis*) are only four million years old. But the intense sunshine in the new environment, combined with a scarcity of drinking water, must have severely challenged the ability of early hominids to regulate their body temperature.

Many savanna mammals do not even attempt to dissipate all the additional heat they absorb during the day, allowing it instead to accumulate within their bodies until nightfall, when they can cool off without expending precious water. But this strategy works only if delicate tissues, such as the central nervous system, are protected from surges in body temperature. Most savanna mammals possess special physiological mechanisms to cool the brain—notably the carotid rete, a network of fine arteries near the base of the brain, coupled with venous circulation through the muzzle.

Humans, apes, and monkeys, however, lack these features. Although humans appear to have eventually evolved an alternative mechanism to help cool the surface of their enlarged brains, the first hominids could have prevented damaging elevations of brain temperature only by keeping their entire body cool. Any adaptations that either reduced the amount of heat absorbed from the environment or facilitated its rapid dissipation would have proved highly advantageous.

Walking on two feet—the unique mode of terrestrial locomotion that is widely recognized as the first key development in hominid evolution—conferred precisely these benefits. Bipedalism dramatically reduces exposure to direct solar radiation during the middle of the equatorial day. I have placed scale models of early australopithecines in quadrupedal and bipedal postures to measure how the sun would hit them. These experiments show that when the sun is high, bombarding the earth's surface with intense radiation (because the

From *Natural History Magazine*, vol. 102, no. 8, August 1993, pp. 65–67. Copyright © 1993 by Natural History Magazine. Reprinted by permission.

rays pass through less atmosphere), far less body surface is exposed on a biped than on a quadruped. When the sun is directly overhead, the heat load on an upright hominid is only about 40 percent of that received by a quadruped of similar size.

Bipedalism also raises most of the body well above the ground, so that the skin contacts cooler and faster-moving air currents. This favors heat dissipation through convection. Allowing for variation in environmental conditions and vegetation, I calculate that hominids would have lost about one-third more heat through convection by adopting a bipedal posture.

Finally, human bipedalism at low speeds uses less energy than does either true quadrupedalism or the knuckle walking used by African apes. This reduces both dietary requirements (and the time and effort spent foraging) and the rate at which heat is generated internally as a byproduct of muscular activity.

Taking these factors into account in calculating the overall energy and water budgets of the early hominids, I conclude that bipedalism significantly decreased early hominids' dependence on shade, allowing them to forage in the open for longer periods and at higher temperatures. Bipedalism also greatly reduced the amount of drinking water they needed for evaporative cooling through sweating. I estimate that a knuckle-walking ape, active throughout the day on the savanna, would typically need to drink about five pints of water. Just by assuming bipedal posture and locomotion, a hominid of similar size would get by with three pints daily.

Bipedalism appears to be an ideal mode of terrestrial locomotion for a mammal foraging in the equatorial savanna, where food and water resources are dispersed and far from abundant. But if so, why do we find bipedalism only in humans? Probably because all other mammals of the African savanna, including monkeys such as baboons, are descended from ancestors that were already true quadrupeds.

In contrast, humans, along with chimpanzees and gorillas, probably descended from tree-dwelling primates that brachiated, or swung from branches using their arms. These ancestors were not strongly committed to one particular mode of terrestrial locomotion and may have been predisposed to walking upright. As they moved into more open habitats, the overheating problems they encountered may have tipped the balance in favor of bipedalism. (An alternative possibility is that bipedalism was first perfected in the forest habitat for some entirely different reason, and that our ancestors just happened to be preadapted for the problems they would encounter on the expanding savanna.)

Following the acquisition of an upright posture, humans evolved in other ways that enabled them to keep cool. Average body weight rose, slowing dehydration under savanna conditions. Larger hominids would have been able to forage for longer periods, and across greater distances, before needing to drink.

Later hominids—members of our own genus, *Homo*—are also taller for their body weight than their stockier and rather more apelike ancestors, the australopithecines. By at least 1.6 million years ago, *H. erectus* had acquired the tall, linear physique, with relatively narrow shoulders and hips, characteristic of many human populations inhabiting hot, arid regions of the tropics today.

A tall, thin body maximizes the skin area available for heat dissipation, while minimizing the exposure of these surfaces to the overhead sun. Longer legs help by raising the body still farther above the hot ground.

Scientists have long reasoned that one of the most obvious and unusual human features, the loss of insulating body hair, is an adaptation to the hot savanna. Although follicles are still densely distributed over most of the human body, the hairs they produce are so short and fine that the underlying skin is exposed directly to the flow of air, promoting the shedding of excess heat by convection and, when necessary, enhancing the effectiveness of sweating.

The problem with this hypothesis has always been explaining why humans differ from other savanna mammals, which have retained dense coats of hair. In environments where mammals are exposed to strong solar radiation, the coat acts as a shield, reflecting and reradiating heat before it reaches the skin. For most mammals, the loss of this insulation would create more problems that it would solve: I calculate that on the savanna, naked quadrupeds would actually need to drink additional water to cope with the extra heat load. For a biped, in contrast, a naked skin saves water because so little skin surface is exposed to the sun. Mainly the head and upper shoulders are exposed, and these can be protected by the retention of a relatively small amount of hair cover. Bipedalism and the strategy of cooling the whole body (rather than just the brain) probably explain why humans evolved a naked skin, while other savanna mammals of comparable size did not.

The stability in body temperature provided by bipedalism and a naked skin may have been an essential step in allowing our large, heat-sensitive brains to evolve further. A parallel to this can be seen in the development of modern computers. Information-processing systems—semiconductor as well as biological—generate substantial heat and are vulnerable to damage from over-heating. This presents a major obstacle to electronics engineers attempting to build ever more capable machines. The circuits of the Cray 2 supercomputer, for example, are so densely packed that they must be immersed in a tank of flu-orocarbon liquid maintained at about 65° F. As in the case of the evolution of the human brain, the development of such an elaborate cooling system does not inevitably lead to higher-performance machines, but it does make them possible.

As humans spread outward from Africa, they encountered different levels of heat, exposure, and moisture. Many studies suggest that these factors deter-mined, at least in part, the variation we now observe in features as diverse as nose shape, limb proportions, hair structure, skin pigmentation, and eye color. Modern humans inhabiting savanna and desert environments near the equa-tor, such as the Nilotic peoples of Africa and the Australian aborigines, com-monly have tall, thin physiques resembling that of early *Homo erectus*. Their skin, especially among groups that have traditionally worn little clothing, is generally very dark, owing to the high concentration of melanin pigment that protects underlying tissues from sunburn and the carcinogenic effects of ultra-violet radiation.

As humans migrated north into colder regions, where retaining heat became more vital, they evolved proportionately shorter limbs, a trend seen in many other groups of mammals. In these populations the skin has lost most of its pigmentation, apparently because of the milder impact of ultraviolet radiation at high latitudes. The reduction in pigment may simply reflect the relaxation of the need for it, or it may have been demanded to allow sufficient penetration of ultraviolet radiation (which humans need to synthesize essential vitamin D).

As they colonized—or recolonized—tropical rain forests, humans faced another obstacle. Although the canopy affords shade, the humidity inhibits the evaporation of sweat. The resultant dependence on convective heat loss favors a body form with a large surface area relative to volume. Unfortunately, the tall, linear physique that works so well in open equatorial habitats is not practical when negotiating dense vegetation. A better solution may be a small body, exemplified by the Mbuti Pygmies of the Congo Basin, who benefit from a high surface-to-volume ratio and can move with agility across the forest floor.

Pat Shipman

↵ **NO**

# Scavenger Hunt

**I**n both textbooks and films, ancestral humans (hominids) have been portrayed as hunters. Small-brained, big-browed, upright, and usually mildly furry, early hominid males gaze with keen eyes across the golden savanna, searching for prey. Skillfully wielding a few crude stone tools, they kill and dismember everything from small gazelles to elephants, while females care for young and gather roots, tubers, and berries. The food is shared by group members at temporary camps. This familiar image of Man the Hunter has been bolstered by the finding of stone tools in association with fossil animal bones. But the role of hunting in early hominid life cannot be determined in the absence of more direct evidence.

I discovered one means of testing the hunting hypothesis almost by accident. In 1978, I began documenting the microscopic damage produced on bones by different events. I hoped to develop a diagnostic key for identifying the post-mortem history of specific fossil bones, useful for understanding how fossil assemblages were formed. Using a scanning electron microscope (SEM) because of its excellent resolution and superb depth of field, I inspected high-fidelity replicas of modern bones that had been subjected to known events or conditions. (I had to use replicas, rather than real bones, because specimens must fit into the SEM's small vacuum chamber.) I soon established that such common events as weathering, root etching, sedimentary abrasion, and carnivore chewing produced microscopically distinctive features.

In 1980, my SEM study took an unexpected turn. Richard Potts (now of Yale University), Henry Bunn (now of the University of Wisconsin at Madison), and I almost simultaneously found what appeared to be stone-tool cut marks on fossils from Olduvai Gorge, Tanzania, and Koobi Fora, Kenya. We were working almost side by side at the National Museums of Kenya, in Nairobi, where the fossils are stored. The possibility of cut marks was exciting, since both sites preserve some of the oldest known archaeological materials. Potts and I returned to the United States, manufactured some stone tools, and started "butchering" bones and joints begged from our local butchers. Under the SEM, replicas of these cut marks looked very different from replicas of carnivore tooth scratches, regardless of the species of carnivore or the type of tool involved. By comparing the marks on the fossils with our hundreds of modern bones of known history, we were able to demonstrate convincingly that hominids using stone tools had processed carcasses of many different animals nearly two million years ago. For the first time, there was a firm link between stone tools and at least some of the early fossil animal bones.

This initial discovery persuaded some paleoanthropologists that the hominid hunter scenario was correct. Potts and I were not so sure. Our study had shown that many of the cut-marked fossils also bore carnivore tooth marks and that some of the cut marks were in places we hadn't expected—on bones that bore little meat in life. More work was needed.

In addition to more data about the Olduvai cut marks and tooth marks, I needed specific information about the patterns of cut marks left by known hunters performing typical activities associated with hunting. If similar patterns occurred on the fossils, then the early hominids probably behaved similarly to more modern hunters; if the patterns were different, then the behavior was probably also different. Three activities related to hunting occur often enough in peoples around the world and leave consistent enough traces to be used for such a test.

First, human hunters systematically disarticulate their kills, unless the animals are small enough to be eaten on the spot. Disarticulation leaves cut marks in a predictable pattern on the skeleton. Such marks cluster near the major joints of the limbs: shoulder, elbow, carpal joint (wrist), hip, knee, and hock (ankle). Taking a carcass apart at the joints is much easier than breaking or cutting through bones. Disarticulation enables hunters to carry food back to a central place or camp, so that they can share it with others or cook it or even store it by placing portions in trees, away from the reach of carnivores. If early hominids were hunters who transported and shared their kills, disarticulation marks would occur near joints in frequencies comparable to those produced by modern human hunters.

Second, human hunters often butcher carcasses, in the sense of removing meat from the bones. Butchery marks are usually found on the shafts of bones from the upper part of the front or hind limb, since this is where the big muscle masses lie. Butchery may be carried out at the kill site—especially if the animal is very large and its bones very heavy—or it may take place at the base camp, during the process of sharing food with others. Compared with disarticulation, butchery leaves relatively few marks. It is hard for a hunter to locate an animal's joints without leaving cut marks on the bone. In contrast, it is easier to cut the meat away from the midshaft of the bone without making such marks. If early hominids shared their food, however, there ought to be a number of cut marks located on the midshaft of some fossil bones.

Finally, human hunters often remove skin or tendons from carcasses, to be used for clothing, bags, thongs, and so on. Hide or tendon must be separated from the bones in many areas where there is little flesh, such as the lower limb bones of pigs, giraffes, antelopes, and zebras. In such cases, it is difficult to cut the skin without leaving a cut mark on the bone. Therefore, one expects to find many more cut marks on such bones than on the flesh-covered bones of the upper part of the limbs.

Unfortunately, although accounts of butchery and disarticulation by modern human hunters are remarkably consistent, quantitative studies are rare. Further, virtually all modern hunter-gatherers use metal tools, which leave more cut marks than stone tools. For these reasons I hesitated to compare the fossil evidence with data on modern hunters. Fortunately, Diane Gifford of the University of California, Santa Cruz, and her colleagues had recently completed a quantitative study of marks and damage on thousands of antelope bones processed by Neolithic (Stone Age) hunters in Kenya some 2,300 years ago. The data from Prolonged Drift, as the site is called, were perfect for comparison with the Olduvai material.

Assisted by my technician, Jennie Rose, I carefully inspected more than 2,500 antelope bones from Bed I at Olduvai Gorge, which is dated to between 1.9 and 1.7 million years ago. We made high-fidelity replicas of every mark that we thought might be either a cut mark or a carnivore tooth mark. Back in the United States, we used the SEM to make positive identifications of the marks. (The replication and SEM inspection was time consuming, but necessary: only about half of the marks were correctly identified by eye or by light microscope.) I then compared the patterns of cut mark and tooth mark distributions on Olduvai fossils with those made by Stone Age hunters at Prolonged Drift.

By their location, I identified marks caused either by disarticulation or meat removal and then compared their frequencies with those from Prolonged Drift. More than 90 percent of the Neolithic marks in these two categories were from disarticulation, but to my surprise, only about 45 percent of the corresponding Olduvai cut marks were from disarticulation. This difference is too great to have occurred by chance; the Olduvai bones did not show the predicted pattern. In fact, the Olduvai cut marks attributable to meat removal and disarticulation showed essentially the same pattern of distribution as the carnivore tooth marks. Apparently, the early hominids were not regularly disarticulating carcasses. This finding casts serious doubt on the idea that early hominids carried their kills back to camp to share with others, since both transport and sharing are difficult unless carcasses are cut up.

When I looked for cut marks attributable to skinning or tendon removal, a more modern pattern emerged. On both the Neolithic and Olduvai bones, nearly 75 percent of all cut marks occurred on bones that bore little meat; these cut marks probably came from skinning. Carnivore tooth marks were much less common on such bones. Hominids were using carcasses as a source of skin and tendon. This made it seem more surprising that they disarticulated carcasses so rarely.

A third line of evidence provided the most tantalizing clue. Occasionally, sets of overlapping marks occur on the Olduvai fossils. Sometimes, these sets include both cut marks and carnivore tooth marks. Still more rarely, I could see under the SEM which mark had been made first, because its features were overlaid by those of the later mark, in much the same way as old tire tracks on a dirt road are obscured by fresh ones. Although only thirteen such sets of marks were found, in eight cases the hominids made the cut marks *after* the carnivores made their tooth marks. This finding suggested a new hypothesis. Instead of hunting for prey and leaving the remains behind for carnivores to scavenge, perhaps hominids were scavenging from the carnivores. This might explain the hominids' apparently unsystematic use of carcasses: they took what they could get, be it skin, tendon, or meat.

Man the Scavenger is not nearly as attractive an image as Man the Hunter, but it is worth examining. Actually, although hunting and scavenging are different ecological strategies, many mammals do both. The only pure scavengers alive in Africa today are vultures; not one of the modern African mammalian carnivores is a pure scavenger. Even spotted hyenas, which have massive, bone-crushing teeth well adapted for eating the bones left behind by others, only scavenge about 33 percent of their food. Other carnivores that scavenge when there are enough carcasses around include lions, leopards, striped hyenas, and jackals. Long-term behavioral studies suggest that these carnivores scavenge when they can and kill when they must. There are only two nearly pure predators, or hunters—the cheetah and the wild dog—that rarely, if ever, scavenge.

What are the costs and benefits of scavenging compared with those of predation? First of all, the scavenger avoids the task of making sure its meal is dead: a predator has already endured the energetically costly business of chasing or stalking animal after animal until one is killed. But while scavenging may be cheap, it's risky. Predators rarely give up their prey to scavengers without defending it. In such disputes, the larger animal, whether a scavenger or a predator, usually wins, although smaller animals in a pack may defeat a lone, larger animal. Both predators and scavengers suffer the dangers inherent in fighting for possession of a carcass. Smaller scavengers such as jackals or striped hyenas avoid disputes to some extent by specializing in darting in and removing a piece of a carcass without trying to take possession of the whole thing. These two strategies can be characterized as that of the bully or that of the sneak: bullies need to be large to be successful, sneaks need to be small and quick.

Because carcasses are almost always much rarer than live prey, the major cost peculiar to scavenging is that scavengers must survey much larger areas than predators to find food. They can travel slowly, since their "prey" is already dead, but endurance is important. Many predators specialize in speed at the expense of endurance, while scavengers do the opposite.

The more committed predators among the East African carnivores (wild dogs and cheetahs) can achieve great top speeds when running, although not for long. Perhaps as a consequence, these "pure" hunters enjoy a much higher success rate in hunting (about three-fourths of their chases end in kills) than any of the scavenger-hunters do (less than half of their chases are successful). Wild dogs and cheetahs are efficient hunters, but they are neither big enough nor efficient enough in their locomotion to make good scavengers. In fact, the cheetah's teeth are so specialized for meat slicing that they probably cannot withstand the stresses of bone crunching and carcass dismembering carried out by scavengers. Other carnivores are less successful at hunting, but have specializations of size, endurance, or (in the case of the hyenas) dentition that make successful scavenging possible. The small carnivores seem to have a somewhat higher hunting success rate than the large ones, which balances out their difficulties in asserting possession of carcasses.

In addition to endurance, scavengers need an efficient means of locating carcasses, which, unlike live animals, don't move or make noises. Vultures, for example, solve both problems by flying. The soaring, gliding flight of vultures expends much less energy than walking or cantering as performed by the part-time mammalian scavengers. Flight enables vultures to maintain a foraging radius two to three times larger than that of spotted hyenas, while providing a better vantage point. This explains why vultures can scavenge all of their food in the same habitat in which it is impossible for any mammal to be a pure scavenger. (In fact, many mammals learn where carcasses are located from the presence of vultures.)

Since mammals can't succeed as fulltime scavengers, they must have another source of food to provide the bulk of their diet. The large carnivores rely on hunting large animals to obtain food when scavenging doesn't work. Their size enables them to defend a carcass against others. Since the small carnivores—jackals and striped hyenas—often can't defend carcasses successfully, most of their diet is composed of fruit and insects. When they do hunt, they usually prey on very small animals, such as rats or hares, that can be consumed in their entirety before the larger competitors arrive.

The ancient habitat associated with the fossils of Olduvai and Koobi Fora would have supported many herbivores and carnivores. Among the latter were two species of large saber-toothed cats, whose teeth show extreme adaptations for meat slicing. These were predators with primary access to carcasses. Since their teeth were unsuitable for bone crushing, the saber-toothed cats must have left behind many bones covered with scraps of meat, skin, and tendon. Were early hominids among the scavengers that exploited such carcasses?

All three hominid species that were present in Bed I times (*Homo habilis, Australopithecus africanus, A. robustus*) were adapted for habitual, upright bipedalism. Many anatomists see evidence that these hominids were agile tree climbers as well. Although upright bipedalism is a notoriously peculiar mode of locomotion, the adaptive value of which has been argued for years (See Matt Cartmill's article, "Four Legs Good, Two Legs Bad," *Natural History*, November 1983), there are three general points of agreement.

First, bipedal running is neither fast nor efficient compared to quadrupedal gaits. However, at moderate speeds of 2.5 to 3.5 miles per hour, bipedal *walking* is more energetically efficient than quadrupedal walking. Thus, bipedal walking is an excellent means of covering large areas slowly, making it an unlikely adaptation for a hunter but an appropriate and useful adaptation for a scavenger. Second, bipedalism elevates the head, thus improving the hominid's ability to spot items on the ground—an advantage both to scavengers and to those trying to avoid becoming a carcass. Combining bipedalism with agile tree climbing improves the vantage point still further. Third, bipedalism frees the hands from locomotive duties, making it possible to carry items. What would early hominids have carried? Meat makes a nutritious, easy-to-carry package; the problem is that carrying meat attracts scavengers. Richard Potts suggests that carrying stone tools or unworked stones for toolmaking to caches would be a more efficient and less dangerous activity under many circumstances.

In short, bipedalism is compatible with a scavenging strategy. I am tempted to argue that bipedalism evolved because it provided a substantial advantage to scavenging hominids. But I doubt hominids could scavenge effectively without tools, and bipedalism predates the oldest known stone tools by more than a million years.

Is there evidence that, like modern mammalian scavengers, early hominids had an alternative food source, such as either hunting or eating fruits and insects? My husband, Alan Walker, has shown that the microscopic wear on an animal's teeth reflects its diet. Early hominid teeth have microscopic wear more like that of chimpanzees and other modern fruit eaters than that of carnivores. Apparently, early hominids ate mostly fruit, as the smaller, modern scavengers do. This accords with the estimated body weight of early hominids, which was only about forty to eighty pounds—less than that of any of the modern carnivores that combine scavenging and hunting but comparable to the striped hyena, which eats fruits and insects as well as meat.

Would early hominids have been able to compete for carcasses with other carnivores? They were too small to use a bully strategy, but if they scavenged in groups, a combined bully-sneak strategy might have been possible. Perhaps they were able to drive off a primary predator long enough to grab some meat, skin, or marrow-filled bone before relinquishing the carcass. The effectiveness of this strategy would have been vastly improved by using tools to remove meat or parts of limbs, a task at which hominid teeth are poor. As agile climbers, early hominids may have retreated into the trees to eat their scavenged trophies, thus avoiding competition from large terrestrial carnivores.

In sum, the evidence on cut marks, tooth wear, and bipedalism, together with our knowledge of scavenger adaptation in general, is consistent with the hypothesis that two million years ago hominids were scavengers rather than accomplished hunters. Animal carcasses, which contributed relatively little to the hominid diet, were not systematically cut up and transported for sharing at base camps. Man the Hunter may not have appeared until 1.5 to 0.7 million years ago, when we do see a shift toward omnivory, with a greater proportion of meat in the diet. This more heroic ancestor may have been *Homo erectus*, equipped with Acheulean-style stone tools and, increasingly, fire. If we wish to look further back, we may have to become accustomed to a less flattering image of our heritage.

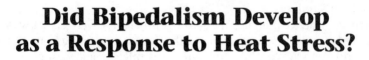

# POSTSCRIPT

## Did Bipedalism Develop as a Response to Heat Stress?

**B**oth Wheeler and Shipman offer intriguing explanations of how life on the savanna might select for bipedalism. However, recent archaeological finds suggest that bipedalism may have begun *before* hominids began to move out into the savanna. Dated at 4.4 million years ago, *Ardipithicus ramidus* seems to be a partial biped who was still living in a forest environment (White, Suwa and Asfaw, 1994). Other discoveries also suggest that the environments in which the later *Australiopithicines* lived were not always as arid and treeless as scientists had first supposed (Brunet, Beauvillian, Coppens and Heintz, 1995). Rather, the environment may have been made up of a "heterogeneous mosaic" (Kingston et. al., 1994) of ecozones in which hominids were selected to live in both wooded and open habitats (Potts, 1986, 1998).

As a result of these finds, physical anthropologists have been sent scrambling to come up with forest-based explanations of bipedalism. Among them are the provisioning hypothesis (Lovejoy, 1981, 1988), the display model (Jabonski and Chaplin, 2000), and the carrying hypothesis (Videan and McGrew, 2000). Although forest-based theories may end up explaining the *origins* of bipedalism better than savanna-based ones, it still remains probable that life on the open grasslands also selected for bipedalism. Certainly, factors such as heat stress and scavenging may have contributed to this process. So in the end, it is perhaps better not to discard savanna-based theories entirely, but instead reframe them as theories explaining how bipedalism came to be refined over time. In fact, the speed at which bipedalism appears and becomes established in hominids suggests that a variety of selective pressures may be involved.

For more information on other theories of bipedalism, see C. Jolly, "The Seed Eaters," *Man* (1970); S. Washburn, *The Social Life of Early Man* (Aldine, 1961); L. Isbell and T. Young, "The Evolution of Bipedalism in Hominids and Reduced Group Size in Chimpanzees," *Journal of Human Evolution* (1996); W. Leonard and M. Robertson, "Energetic Efficiency of Human Bipedality," *American Journal of Physical Anthropology* (1995); and K. Steudel, "Limb Morphology, Bipedal Gait, and the Energetics of Hominid Locomotion," *American Journal of Physical Anthropology* (1996).

# ISSUE 11

## Is *Australopithecus Africanus* on the Direct Line to Modern Humans?

**YES: Meave Leakey and Alan Walker,** from "Early Hominid Fossils from Africa," *Scientific American* (June 1997)

**NO: Bernard Wood,** from "The Oldest Hominid Yet," *Nature* (September 1994)

### ISSUE SUMMARY

Meave Leakey and Alan Walker argue that there is good archaeological evidence to support the claim that later hominids evolved from *Australopithecus Africanus*. In contrast, Bernard Wood favors the idea that *Australopithecus Africanus* was an evolutionary dead end. In his view, *Africanus* should not be considered an ancestor of modern humans.

*One species rarely turns into another by total transformation over its entire geographic range. Rather, a small population becomes geographically isolated from the rest of the species—and this fragment changes to become a new species while the bulk of the parental population does not alter (Gould, 1992:77).*

In Issue 1, we discussed how the proponents of gradual evolution tend to see natural selection as a linear process with one form gradually evolving into another. Rapid evolutionists also tend to emphasize the power of genetic drift in creating new species, while gradual evolutionists favor mutation and natural selection. The latter camp also tend to refer to different types of early hominids as *forms*, rather than species. Called *lumpers*, they argue that gene flow through inbreeding tended to discourage speciation in the past just like it does among human populations in the present. In contrast, supporters of rapid evolution are more comfortable with the idea of multiple species coexisting in the same space and time. Called *splitters*, they tend to see human evolution as a colorful profusion of hominid species all vying for inclusion into the direct line leading to modern humans.

As a result of this philosophical division within the discipline, physical anthropologists rarely agree about the significance of any new archaeological find. In fact, fervent debates about the status of most discoveries are common.

Donald Johansen and Yves Coppens argued for years over whether one or two species of *Australopithecus Afarensis* existed 3 to 4 million years ago. A more recent controversy concerns the origin of modern humans. This debate can also be viewed from a lumper vs. splitter perspective.

Historically, the status of *Australopithecus Africanus* has also been the subject of much debate. *Australopithecus Africanus*—also known as gracile australiopithicines—lived 2 to 3 million years ago. They were good bipeds with brains slightly larger than chimpanzees. Analysis of their dentition suggests that they were omnivores, may have scavenged or hunted small game, and probably used tools. By about 1.9 million years ago, *A. Africanus* had either evolved into early *Homo* or been replaced by them. Wood favors the second view. He adopts a splitter perspective and suggests that *A. Africanus* was not on the direct line to modern humans. Wood also thinks that the *Homo* line evolved directly from *A. Afarensis* much earlier than 1.9 million years ago. According to his scenario, early *Homo* would have co-existed with *A. Africanus* and probably replaced them. Meave Leakey and Alan Walker, on the other hand, suggest that *A. Africanus* may have been ancestral to early *Homo* and see early *Homo* appearing around 2 million years ago.

# YES ⬅

**Meave Leakey and
Alan Walker**

# Early Hominid Fossils from Africa

The year was 1965. Bryan Patterson, a paleoanthropologist from Harvard University, unearthed a fragment of a fossil arm bone at a site called Kanapoi in northern Kenya. He and his colleagues knew it would be hard to make a great deal of anatomic or evolutionary sense out of a small piece of elbow joint. Nevertheless, they did recognize some features reminiscent of a species of early hominid (a hominid is any upright-walking primate) known as *Australopithecus*, first discovered 40 years earlier in South Africa by Raymond Dart of the University of the Witwatersrand. In most details, however, Patterson and his team considered the fragment of arm bone to be more like those of modern humans than the one other *Australopithecus* humerus known at the time.

The age of the Kanapoi fossil proved somewhat surprising. Although the techniques for dating the rocks where the fossil was uncovered were still fairly rudimentary, the group working in Kenya was able to show that the bone was probably older than the various *Australopithecus* specimens previously found. Despite this unusual result, however, the significance of Patterson's discovery was not to be confirmed for another 30 years. In the interim, researchers identified the remains of so many important early hominids that the humerus from Kanapoi was rather forgotten.

Yet Patterson's fossil would eventually help establish the existence of a new species of *Australopithecus*—the oldest yet to be identified—and push back the origins of upright walking to more than four million years (Myr) ago. But to see how this happened, we need to trace the steps that paleoanthropologists have taken in constructing an outline for the story of hominid evolution.

## Evolving Story of Early Hominids

Scientists classify the immediate ancestors of the genus *Homo* (which includes our own species, *Homo sapiens*) in the genus *Australopithecus*. For several decades, it was believed that these ancient hominids first inhabited the earth at least three and a half million years ago. The specimens found in South Africa by Dart and others indicated that there were at least two types of *Australopithecus*— *A. africanus* and *A. robustus*. The leg bones of both species suggested that they had the striding, bipedal locomotion that is a hallmark of humans among living mammals. (The upright posture of these creatures was vividly confirmed in

1978 at the Laetoli site in Tanzania, where a team led by archaeologist Mary Leakey discovered a spectacular series of footprints made 3.6 Myr ago by three *Australopithecus* individuals as they walked across wet volcanic ash.) Both *A. africanus* and *A. robustus* were relatively small-brained and had canine teeth that differed from those of modern apes in that they hardly projected past the rest of the tooth row. The younger of the two species, *A. robustus*, had bizarre adaptations for chewing—huge molar and premolar teeth combined with bony crests on the skull where powerful chewing muscles would have been attached.

Paleoanthropologists identified more species of *Australopithecus* over the next several decades. In 1959 Mary Leakey unearthed a skull from yet another East African species closely related to *robustus*. Skulls of these species uncovered during the past 40 years in the northeastern part of Africa, in Ethiopia and Kenya, differed considerably from those found in South Africa; as a result, researchers think that two separate *robustus*-like species—a northern one and a southern one—existed.

In 1978 Donald C. Johanson, now at the Institute of Human Origins in Berkeley, Calif., along with his colleagues, identified still another species of *Australopithecus*. Johanson and his team had been studying a small number of hominid bones and teeth discovered at Laetoli, as well as a large and very important collection of specimens from the Hadar region of Ethiopia (including the famous "Lucy" skeleton). The group named the new species *afarensis*. Radiometric dating revealed that the species had lived between 3.6 and 2.9 Myr ago, making it the oldest *Australopithecus* known at the time.

This early species is probably the best studied of all the *Australopithecus* recognized so far, and it is certainly the one that has generated the most controversy over the past 20 years. The debates have ranged over many issues: whether the *afarensis* fossils were truly distinct from the *africanus* fossils from South Africa; whether there was one or several species at Hadar; whether the Tanzanian and Ethiopian fossils were of the same species; whether the fossils had been dated correctly.

But the most divisive debate concerns the issue of how extensively the bipedal *afarensis* climbed in trees. Fossils of *afarensis* include various bone and joint structures typical of tree climbers. Some scientists argue that such characteristics indicate that these hominids must have spent at least some time in the trees. But others view these features as simply evolutionary baggage, left over from arboreal ancestors. Underlying this discussion is the question of where *Australopithecus* lived—in forests or on the open savanna.

By the beginning of the 1990s, researchers knew a fair amount about the various species of *Australopithecus* and how each had adapted to its environmental niche. A description of any one of the species would mention that the creatures were bipedal and that they had ape-size brains and large, thickly enameled teeth in strong jaws, with nonprojecting canines. Males were typically larger than females, and individuals grew and matured rapidly. But the origins of *Australopithecus* were only hinted at, because the gap between the earliest well-known species in the group (*afarensis*, from about 3.6 Myr ago) and the postulated time of the last common ancestor of chimpanzees and humans (between 5 and 6 Myr ago) was still very great. Fossil hunters had unearthed only a few older fragments of bone, tooth and jaw from the inter-vening 1.5 million years to indicate the anatomy and course of evolution of the very earliest hominids.

# Filling the Gap

Discoveries in Kenya over the past several years have filled in some of the miss-ing interval between 3.5 and 5 Myr ago. Beginning in 1982, expeditions run by the National Museums of Kenya to the Lake Turkana basin in northern Kenya began finding hominid fossils nearly 4 Myr old. But because these fossils were mainly isolated teeth—no jawbones or skulls were preserved—very little could be said about them except that they resembled the remains of *afarensis* from Laetoli. But our recent excavations at an unusual site, just inland from Allia Bay on the east side of Lake Turkana yielded more complete fossils.

The site at Allia Bay is a bone bed, where millions of fragments of weathered tooth and bone from a wide variety of animals, including hominids, spill out of the hillside. Exposed at the top of the hill lies a layer of hardened volcanic ash called the Moiti Tuff, which has been dated radiometrically to just over 3.9 Myr old. The fossil fragments lie several meters below the tuff, indicating that the remains are older than the tuff. We do not yet understand fully why so many fossils are concentrated in this spot, but we can be certain that they were deposited by the precursor of the present-day Omo River.

Today the Omo drains the Ethiopian highlands located to the north, emptying into Lake Turkana, which has no outlet. But this has not always been so. Our colleagues Frank Brown of the University of Utah and Craig Feibel of Rutgers University have shown that the ancient Omo River dominated the Turkana area for much of the Pliocene (roughly 5.3 to 1.6 Myr ago) and the early Pleistocene (1.6 to 0.7 Myr ago). Only infrequently was a lake present in the area at all. Instead, for most of the past four million years, an extensive river system flowed across the broad floodplain, proceeding to the Indian Ocean without dumping its sediments into a lake.

The Allia Bay fossils are located in one of the channels of this ancient river system. Most of the fossils collected from Allia Bay are rolled and weath-ered bones and teeth of aquatic animals—fish, crocodiles, hippopotamuses and the like—that were damaged during transport down the river from some distance away. But some of the fossils are much better preserved; these come from the animals that lived on or near the riverbanks. Among these creatures are several different species of leaf-eating monkeys, related to modern colobus monkeys, as well as antelopes whose living relatives favor closely wooded areas. Reasonably well preserved hominid fossils can also be found here, suggesting that, at least occasionally, early hominids inhabited a riparian habitat.

Where do these *Australopithecus* fossils fit in the evolutionary history of hominids? The jaws and teeth from Allia Bay, as well as a nearly complete radius (the outside bone of the forearm) from the nearby sediments of Sibilot just to the north, show an interesting mixture of characteristics. Some of the traits are primitive ones—that is, they are ancestral features thought to be present before the split occurred between the chimpanzee and human lineages. Yet these bones also share characteristics seen in later hominids and are therefore said to have more advanced features. As our team continues to unearth more bones and teeth at Allia Bay, these new fossils add to our knowledge of the wide range of traits present in early hominids.

# Return to Kanapoi

Across Lake Turkana, some 145 kilometers (about 90 miles) south of Allia Bay, lies the site of Kanapoi, where our story began. One of us (Leakey) has mounted expeditions from the National Museums of Kenya to explore the sediments located southwest of Lake Turkana and to document the faunas present during the earliest stages of the basin's history. Kanapoi, virtually unexplored since Patterson's day, has proved to be one of the most rewarding sites in the Turkana region.

A series of deep erosion gullies, known as badlands, has exposed the sediments at Kanapoi. Fossil hunting is difficult here, though, because of a carapace of lava pebbles and gravel that makes it hard to spot small bones and teeth. Studies of the layers of sediment, also carried out by Feibel, reveal that the fossils here have been preserved by deposits from a river ancestral to the present-day Kerio River, which once flowed into the Turkana basin and emptied into an ancient lake we call Lonyumun. This lake reached its maximum size about 4.1 Myr ago and thereafter shrank as it filled with sediments.

Excavations at Kanapoi have primarily yielded the remains of carnivore meals, so the fossils are rather fragmentary. But workers at the site have also recovered two nearly complete lower jaws, one complete upper jaw and lower face, the upper and lower thirds of a tibia (the larger bone of the lower leg), bits of skull and several sets of isolated teeth. After careful study of the fossils from both Allia Bay and Kanapoi—including Patterson's fragment of an arm bone—we felt that in details of anatomy, these specimens were different enough from previously known hominids to warrant designating a new species. So in 1995, in collaboration with both Feibel and Ian McDougall of the Australian National University, we named this new species *Australopithecus anamensis*, drawing on the Turkana word for lake (*anam*) to refer to both the present and ancient lakes.

To establish the age of these fossils, we relied on the extensive efforts of Brown, Feibel and McDougall, who have been investigating the paleogeographic history of the entire lake basin. If their study of the basin's development is correct, the *anamensis* fossils should be between 4.2 and 3.9 Myr old. Currently McDougall is working to determine the age of the so-called Kanapoi Tuff—the layer of volcanic ash that covers most of the fossils at this site. We expect that once McDougall successfully ascertains the age of the tuff, we will be confident in both the age of the fossils and Brown's and Feibel's understanding of the history of the lake basin.

A major question in paleoanthropology today is how the anatomic mosaic of the early hominids evolved. By comparing the nearly contemporaneous Allia Bay and Kanapoi collections of *anamensis*, we can piece together a fairly accurate picture of certain aspects of the species, even though we have not yet uncovered a complete skull.

The jaws of *anamensis* are primitive—the sides sit close together and parallel to each other (as in modern apes), rather than widening at the back of the mouth (as in later hominids, including humans). In its lower jaw, *anamensis* is also chimp-like in terms of the shape of the region where the left and right sides of the jaw meet (technically known as the mandibular symphysis).

Teeth from *anamensis*, however, appear more advanced. The enamel is relatively thick, as it is in all other species of *Australopithecus*; in contrast, the tooth enamel of African great apes is much thinner. The thickened enamel suggests *anamensis* had already adapted to a changed diet—possibly much harder food—even though its jaws and some skull features were still very apelike. We also know that *anamensis* had only a tiny external ear canal. In this regard, it is more like chimpanzees and unlike all later hominids, including humans, which have large external ear canals. (The size of the external canal is unrelated to the size of the fleshy ear.)

The most informative bone of all the ones we have uncovered from this new hominid is the nearly complete tibia—the larger of the two bones in the lower leg. The tibia is revealing because of its important role in weight bearing: the tibia of a biped is distinctly different from the tibia of an animal that walks on all four legs. In size and practically all details of the knee and ankle joints, the tibia found at Kanapoi closely resembles the one from the fully bipedal *afarensis* found at Hadar, even though the latter specimen is nearly a million years younger.

Fossils of other animals collected at Kanapoi point to a somewhat different paleoecological scenario from the setting across the lake at Allia Bay. The channels of the river that laid down the sediments at Kanapoi were probably lined with narrow stretches of forest that grew close to the riverbanks in otherwise open country. Researchers have recovered the remains of the same spiral-horned antelope found at Allia Bay that very likely lived in dense thickets. But open-country antelopes and hartebeest appear to have lived at Kanapoi as well, suggesting that more open savanna prevailed away from the rivers. These results offer equivocal evidence regarding the preferred habitat of *anamensis:* we know that bushland was present at both sites that have yielded fossils of the species, but there are clear signs of more diverse habitats at Kanapoi.

# An Even Older Hominid?

At about the same time that we were finding new hominids at Allia Bay and Kanapoi, a team led by our colleague Tim D. White of the University of California at Berkeley discovered fossil hominids in Ethiopia that are even older than *anamensis*. In 1992 and 1993 White led an expedition to the Middle Awash area of Ethiopia, where his team uncovered hominid fossils at a site known as Aramis. The group's finds include isolated teeth, a piece of baby's mandible (the lower jaw), fragments from an adult's skull and some arm bones, all of which have been dated to around 4.4 Myr ago. In 1994, together with his colleagues Berhane Asfaw of the Paleoanthropology Laboratory in Addis Ababa and Gen Suwa of the University of Tokyo, White gave these fossils a new name: *Australopithecus ramidus*. In 1995 the group renamed the fossils, moving them to a new genus,

*Ardipithecus*. Other fossils buried near the hominids, such as seeds and the bones of forest monkeys and antelopes, strongly imply that these hominids, too, lived in a closed-canopy woodland.

This new species represents the most primitive hominid known—a link between the African apes and *Australopithecus*. Many of the *Ardipithecus ramidus* fossils display similarities to the anatomy of the modern African great apes, such as thin dental enamel and strongly built arm bones. In other features, though—such as the opening at the base of the skull, technically known as the foramen magnum, through which the spinal cord connects to the brain—the fossils resemble later hominids.

Describing early hominids as either primitive or more advanced is a complex issue. Scientists now have almost decisive molecular evidence that humans and chimpanzees once had a common ancestor and that this lineage had previously split from gorillas. This is why we often use the two living species of chimpanzee (*Pan troglodytes* and *P. paniscus*) to illustrate ancestral traits. But we must remember that since their last common ancestor with humans, chimpanzees have had exactly the same amount of time to evolve as humans have. Determining which features were present in the last common ancestor of humans and chimpanzees is not easy.

But *Ardipithecus*, with its numerous chimplike features, appears to have taken the human fossil record back close to the time of the chimp-human split. More recently, White and his group have found parts of a single *Ardipithecus* skeleton in the Middle Awash region. As White and his team extract these exciting new fossils from the enclosing stone, reconstruct them and prepare them for study, the paleoanthropological community eagerly anticipates the publication of the group's analysis of these astonishing finds.

But even pending White's results, new *Australopithecus* fossil discoveries are offering other surprises, particularly about where these creatures lived. In 1995 a team led by Michel Brunet of the University of Poitiers announced the identification in Chad of *Australopithecus* fossils believed to be about 3.5 Myr old. The new fossils are very fragmentary—only the front part of a lower jaw and an isolated tooth. In 1996, however, Brunet and his colleagues designated a new species for their specimen: *A. bahrelghazali*. Surprisingly, these fossils were recovered far from either eastern or southern Africa, the only areas where *Australopithecus* had been found until now. The site, in the Bahr el Ghazal region of Chad, lies 2,500 kilometers west of the western part of the Rift Valley, thus extending the range of *Australopithecus* well into the center of Africa.

The *bahrelghazali* fossils debunk a hypothesis about human evolution postulated in the pages of *Scientific American* by Yves Coppens of the College of France [see "East Side Story: The Origin of Humankind," May 1994]; ironically, Coppens is now a member of Brunet's team. Coppens's article proposed that the formation of Africa's Rift Valley subdivided a single ancient species, isolating the ancestors of hominids on the east side from the ancestors of modern apes on the west side. In general, scientists believe such geographical isolation can foster the development of new species by prohibiting continued interbreeding among the original populations. But the new Chad fossils show that early hominids did live west of the Rift Valley. The geographical separation of apes and hominids previously apparent in the fossil record may be more the result of accidental circumstances of geology and discovery than the species' actual ranges.

The fossils of *anamensis* that we have identified should also provide some answers in the long-standing debate over whether early *Australopithecus* species lived in wooded areas or on the open savanna. The outcome of this discussion has important implications: for many years, paleoanthropologists have accepted that upright-walking behavior originated on the savanna, where it most likely provided benefits such as keeping the hot sun off the back or freeing hands for carrying food. Yet our evidence suggests that the earliest bipedal hominid known to date lived at least part of the time in wooded areas. The discoveries of the past several years represent a remarkable spurt in the sometimes painfully slow process of uncovering human evolutionary past. But clearly there is still much more to learn.

# NO

# The Oldest Hominid Yet

. . . Tim White and his co-workers present compelling fossil evidence that they have found the oldest hominid species yet. The fossils, largely of dentition, are almost 4.5 million years old. They represent the remains of a species that lies so close to the divergence between the lineages leading to the African apes and modern humans that its attribution to the human line is metaphorically—and literally—by the skin of its teeth.

Charles Darwin predicted that the deepest roots of human evolutionary history would be found in Africa. Since then an impressive body of fossil, comparative and genomic evidence has confirmed the close relationship between modern humans and the African apes. Three-score and ten years ago Raymond Dart had the perspicacity to recognize that a child's skull from Taung, in southern Africa, was neither ape nor human, but a hominid, an ancient ape-like human ancestor. He named it *Australopithecus africanus*, and for half a century it retained the distinction of being the most primitive hominid species known. This position was usurped in 1978 by the announcement of the discovery in Ethiopia and Tanzania of an even more primitive hominid species, *A. afarensis*, represented among other evidence by the remains of 'Lucy'. With their discovery of a new and yet-more primitive species of australopithecine, White and his colleagues now push back our knowledge of the human lineage by more than half a million years.

The remains of this species, *A. ramidus*, were recovered from the region known as the Middle Awash, which lies either side of the Awash river in Ethiopia. Its northern boundary extends to within 20 kilometers of the Hadar area, where *A. afarensis* was discovered. Research by the team has been conducted in the Middle Awash since 1981, and remains attributed to *A. afarensis*, dated to between 3.4 and 3.8 million years old (Myr), have already been recovered from two other localities, Maka and Belohdelie, in the region. The latest discoveries were made in the drainage of the Aramis river which lies a few kilometres to the west of the Awash river, due west of Maka. Special mention should be made of the contribution of the Ethiopian prospectors and field crew; without their skills work such as this would not be nearly so fruitful.

The geological context of the fossils is described by WoldeGabriel and his colleagues. They have been able to identify a layer of volcanic ash, the VT-1/Moiti tuff, in the south-east corner of the Aramis drainage area, and both field observation and laboratory studies suggest that the bulk of the sediments exposed in the Aramis locality lie beneath the VT-1/Moiti horizon, which is reliably dated at around 3.9 Myr. Two tuff horizons lower in the section were crucial for locating the hominid fossils, as well as the other faunal and floral remains recovered by the group. The higher of the two horizons is a distinctive dark layer of basaltic tuff, referred to as DABT. No more than 4 metres or so below it is the second reference horizon which is a characteristic, paler, vitric tuff called the GATC. All but one of the 17 hominid fossils recovered by the team were surface finds from sediments sandwiched between the DABT and the GATC tuff horizons.

Not surprisingly, intensive efforts have been made to date the two crucial ash layers. Unfortunately, both tuffs are heavily contaminated by the remains of Miocene rocks of about 23 Myr. These much older sanidine grains were so common in the samples from the DABT horizon that no reliable dates could be obtained, even with the advantages of the single-crystal laser fusion $^{40}$Ar/$^{39}$Ar method. But at least one sample, MA92-37, of the underlying GATC vitric tuff yielded enough contemporary feldspar crystals to give an age of around 4.4 Myr. Using this reliable date, and the known age of the VT-1/Moiti tuff, it is possible to use the magnetic polarity record preserved in the rocks to place the Aramis section on the magnetostratigraphic timescale. The unambiguous reversed polarity of the DABT horizon suggests that the hominid-bearing sediments correspond to the reversed interval between the top of the Ninivak and the bottom of the Cochiti subchrons. This implies that the hominid fossils are between 4.5 and 4.3 Myr.

The preliminary palaeogeographic reconstruction of the Aramis locality suggests that the hominid-bearing sediments were deposited on a flat landscape. The abundance of fossil wood and seeds, including the seeds of a genus common in forests and woodland, and the high proportion of monkey remains, which make up more than 30 per cent of the vertebrates in the faunal collection, have prompted WoldeGabriel and his colleagues to propose that the Aramis hominids "lived and died in a woodland setting." On the face of it, their suggestion appears to be well founded. But, to be substantiated, the 'woodland hypothesis' will need to be subjected to scrutiny by researchers well versed in the biases that occur before, during and after the deposition of animal and plant remains. These taphonomic biases can so distort the fossil record that it is conceivable that the impression of woodland is the result of *post mortem* transport or the influence of predators. Even if their palaeoecological interpretation is substantiated, the authors are not the first to suggest a woodland setting for early African hominids, and there is increasing evidence from later in the fossil hominid record that the abandonment of some element of arboreality may have occurred as recently as around 2 Myr.

Of the 17 hominid specimens, all but two, VP-1/4 and VP-7/2, are cranial. Teeth predominate in the cranial remains, with the non-dental specimens restricted to a mandible fragment, VP-1/129, and the remains of a cranial base, VP-1/500. The taxonomic and functional questions arising when fossils are recovered from any fresh location are well rehearsed. Does the material belong to any existing species group? If not, can it be assigned to existing genera?

What were the physical characteristics of the new species? What size was it? What was its posture, locomotion, feeding strategy and so on?

With respect to the need to recognize a new species, the taxonomic conclusions of White and colleagues are soundly based. The Aramis remains are morphologically distinct from *A. afarensis*. These distinctions are starkest for a lower first deciduous molar ($dm_1$) which is much more primitive in its crown morphology than the $dm_1$ of *A. afarensis*. Indeed, in nearly all the features that differ between *A. ramidus* and *A. afarensis*, the morphology of the former is more like that of the chimpanzee. Does this mean that it would have been more appropriate to allocate the new species to *Pan?*

In fact, the 'fit' into *Pan* is no more comfortable—indeed it is marginally less comfortable—than into *Australopithecus*. In either case homoplasies, evidence of convergent evolution, are implied. On balance the evidence of the reorganization of the cranial base with respect to that of the African apes, and the reduction in the size of the canine, together with modifications to the ulna, suggests that the hominid-like features are more likely to be derived, with the African ape-like features more likely to be either primitive retentions or examples of convergence. The evidence from the cranial base is particularly remarkable, for if the anterior border of the foramen magnum, which is the opening that transmits the spinal cord, is level with the plane that bisects the two openings that transmit the carotid arteries, then it implies a substantial shortening of the cranial base, specifically the part known as the basioccipital, comparable to that seen in *Paranthropus boisei*. So derived a cranial-base configuration is unexpected in a hominid that is otherwise so primitive.

A more radical taxonomic solution would have been to erect a new genus for the Aramis remains; only material from other parts of the skeleton will confirm whether that would be justified. My own prejudice is that, even on the present evidence, the differences between the Aramis species and *A. afarensis* are more profound, and are more likely to reflect the sort of grade distinction that is most usefully reflected in generic distinctions, than are the differences between, say, *A. afarensis* and *A. africanus*.

The likely body size of the creatures to which the Aramis remains belong is somewhat of a puzzle, and may be another indication of the distinctive nature and adaptation of the new species. The size of the humeral head would suggest animals at least as large as the smaller individuals belonging to *A. afarensis* (that is, in excess of 30 kilograms), yet the size of the molar tooth crowns is small. Does this mean that *A. ramidus* had relatively small molar crown areas for its body mass? If so, this would distinguish it from all other australopithecines, and indeed from all other early hominids until early African *Homo erectus* or *H. ergaster*. Only in the latter species does relative molar size return to the low levels that are characteristic of living species of *Pan*. Likewise, the preliminary observations about the thickness of the enamel of the molar teeth suggests that, in this character too, the Aramis hominid shows evidence of an adaptive grade different from that of the later australopithecines.

Most significant discoveries of hominid fossils are usually, but not always justifiably, announced with the implication that they will necessitate a radical reappraisal of hypotheses of human evolutionary history. It is a sign of the growing maturity of palaeoanthropological research that, important as the discovery of *A. ramidus* is, the presence of a hominid much like it had been predicted. Since the discovery of *A. afarensis* two decades ago, opinions have been divided about its significance. Some held *A. afarensis* to be so primitive that it was treated as if it were the common hominid ancestor, or the epitome of australopithecine primitiveness. However, in other cladistic studies, in which no assumptions were made about its primitiveness, it was apparent that *A. afarensis* showed evidence of sufficient derived features to preclude it, in all likelihood, from being ancestral to all later hominids. There was, therefore, enough 'morphological space' between the hypothetical common ancestor of African apes and hominids, on the one hand, and *A. afarensis* on the other, to predict that a hominid, as yet undiscovered, would occupy it.

The finds at Aramis are a vindication of proposals, based on protein morphology, that modern humans share a close and relatively recent ancestry with the African apes. Evidence from molecular biology has since provided powerful confirmation of that relationship, but there is no consensus about whether the closest relationship is with *Pan*, or whether the relationship between *Pan*, *Gorilla* and the hominids is so close that its details cannot be resolved. The wheel has come full circle—on this occasion the palaeontologists can assist the molecular biologists, for the evidence from *A. ramidus* would predict that the lineage that includes modern humans is more closely related to *Pan* than to *Gorilla*. The metaphor of a 'missing link' has often been misused, but it is a suitable epithet for the hominid from Aramis.

# POSTSCRIPT

## Is *Australopithecus Africanus* on the Direct Line to Modern Humans?

**M**uch of the controversy over the status of *A. Africanus* stems from its relationship to *A. Afarensis* and the earlier hominids (*Australopithecus Anamensis* and *Ardipithecus Ramidus*) that have been discovered more recently. Splitters like Wood tend to favor the emergence of the *Homo* line much earlier than lumpers like Leakey and Walker. However, research by paleontologist Elisabeth Vrba (1993) suggests that a dramatic climatic change began to occur 2 to 2.5 million years ago. Many species that were adapted to wooded environments suddenly disappeared from the fossil record, while species suited to grassy regions appeared and multiplied. This time also "marks the appearance of stone tools and the arrival on the scene of new hominid species, some with brains big enough to merit inclusion in the genus *Homo*" (Shreeve, 1997:105).

Among the different *Australopithecines* existing at this time, *Africanus* seems to be the only one that adapted to the changing environment. Falk (1992) has CAT-scanned brain casts from fossil skulls for *A. Africanus* and found that they have the modern blood flow patterns associated with later *Homo*. In contrast, *A. Robustus* has a more primitive blood flow pattern that is also associated with casts of skulls of *A. Afarensis*. The implications are that *A. Afarensis* and *Robustus* lived in more wooded environments than *A. Africanus*, who developed more efficient patterns of blood flow in order to live in the hotter, more open grasslands. Falk also contends that the number of *foramina*, small veins passing through the skull that allows the brain to cool, are also more numerous in *A. Africanus* than in *A. Robustus* or earlier hominids. The increase the number of foramina correlates with significant increases in brain size beginning about two million years ago. Within a 200,000-year time period, the cranial capacity of hominids jumps from 400 to 500 ccs (*Africanus*), to 600 to 700 ccs (*H. Hablis*) to 900 to 1200 ccs for later *Homo* like *Homo Erectus*. These increases are especially impressive if you consider that for two million years previous, hominid brains had remained roughly the same size.

For more information about *A. Africanus* and earlier *Australopithecines*, see R. Leakey and R. Lewin, *Origins Reconsidered* (Doubleday, 1992), M. Simons, "New Species of Early Human Reported Found in Africa," *New York Times* (1996), R. Dart, "Australopithecus Africanus, the Man-Ape of South Africa," *Nature* (1925), M. Brunet, et. al., "The First Skull and Other New Discoveries of Australopithicus Afarensis at Hadar, Ethiopia," *Nature* (1994, pp. 449–451), M. Brunet, et. al., "The First Australopithecine 2500 kilometers West of the Rift Valley (Chad)," *Nature* (1995, pp. 273–275), D. Johansen and M. Edey, *Lucy: The Beginnings of Humankind* (Simon and Schuster, 1981), and D. Johansen and J. Shreeve, *Lucy's Child* (William Morrow, 1989).

## Human Prehistory

This site provides information on *Australopithecus*, *Homo Hablis*, *Homo Erectus*, and *Homo Sapiens* as well as people during paleolithic and neolithic times.

> http://users.hol.gr/-dilos/prehis.htm

## Fossil Evidence for Human Evolution in China

This site includes a catalog of chinese fossil remains and provides links to other sites on paleontology, human evolution, and chinese prehistory.

> http://www.chineseprehistory.org

## Shamanism

This excellent site provides a list of worldwide workshops on shamanism provided by the Foundation for Shamanic studies, as well as information on shamanic supplies, books, videos, and CDs.

> http://www.shamanism.org

## Cult Archaeoogy Topics

This site focuses on interesting pseudoscientific theories that have attracted scholarly attention such as the Lost Tribes, Big Foot, and the Loch Ness Monster.

> http://www.usd.edu/ath/cultarch/
> culttopics.html

# PART 3

# The Evolution of Later Humans

*I*n the later stages of human evolution, culture becomes increasingly important to human adaptation. The invention of stone tools, big game hunting, clothing, art, verbal language, and more complex social roles may have been instrumental in allowing our ancestors to migrate out of Africa and eventually populate the whole world. In this section, the following issues are examined:

- Is Hominid Brain Expansion Linked to the Invention of Stone Tools?

- Is Hunting More Critical Than Gathering to Cultural Development?

- Does Biology Limit a Woman's Ability to Hunt?

- Is Cannibalism a Prominent Feature of Prehistoric Societies?

- Does Cave Art Depict Shamanism?

- Is "Race" an Outdated Concept?

# ISSUE 12

# Is Hominid Brain Expansion Linked to the Invention of Stone Tools?

**YES: Kenneth P. Oakley,** from "On Man's Use of Fire, with Comments on Tool-Making and Hunting," in Sherwood L. Washburn, ed., *Social Life of Early Man* (Aldine Publishing, 1961)

**NO: Dean Falk,** from *Braindance* (Henry Holt, 1992)

### ISSUE SUMMARY

Kenneth Oakley suggests that the development of tools led to selection for intelligence among early hominids. Dean Falk opposes this perspective. Falk contends that hominid brain expansion is linked to the body's ability to effectively diffuse heat.

*The abundant evidence shows very clearly that human evolutionary history is characterized by the precedence of upright posture and the tardy development of the brain (Feder, 2000:39).*

What makes us human—our body or our brain? This question has been at the forefront of evolutionary discussions since the days of Charles Darwin. Although Darwin suggested that the original human ancestor would be found in Africa, many other scientists did not agree. Most of the early archaeological discoveries that supported the idea of human evolution were found in Europe or Asia. This assumption was comfortable and well-received because most signs of early civilizations were found in these areas. Most countries were also ethnocentric enough to believe that their culture had preceded the rest. There was also the matter of ethnicity. Many Europeans did not find the idea that they might have descended from a dark-skinned ancestor very pleasant. Indeed, many people do not like to think so today! As a result, discovering the oldest human became a matter of national interest and pride, as well as an assertion of ethnic superiority.

By the early 1900s, English scientists were simply itching to come up with an important discovery of their own to rival the finds of other countries. In addition to these concerns, many scientists were uncomfortable with the picture of human evolution that had been painted so far. All the evidence suggested that ancient human ancestors had more primitive heads—and by implication more primitive brains—that sat atop modern-looking bodies.

Such a picture was precisely the opposite of what many people had expected and hoped for. After all, it was argued, it is intelligence that most clearly and absolutely differentiates humanity from the rest of the animal kingdom. It is in our ability to think, to communicate, and to invent that we are the most distant from our animal cousins. This being the case, it was assumed that such abilities must have been evolving the longest; in other words, the human brain and the ability to think, must have evolved first. Thus the argument went, fossil evidence for evolution should show that the brain had expanded first, followed by the modernization of the body (Feder, 2000:30).

The "discovery" of Piltdown Man in a gravel deposit near Sussex, England, in 1908 was thus eagerly accepted by the scientific community for several reasons. First, it gave the English the ancient human ancestor whom they had coveted. Second, the specimen seemed to support the preferred bias that brain development came first. The size and shape of the skull cap found was large and modern, while the jaw found in association with it was primitive and apelike. Piltdown Man was dubbed "the missing link" between apes and humans and used to suggest that earlier discoveries were evolutionary dead ends. "By paleontological standards the implications were breathtaking. In one sweeping blow Piltdown had presented England with its first ancestral human fossil, it had shown that human fossils found elsewhere in the world were either primitive evolutionary offshoots or later throwbacks to a more primitive type, and it had forced the rewriting of the entire story of human evolution" (Feder, 2000:32–33).

The desire for a human ancestor with a large brain and apelike body was so strong that subsequent discoveries of *Homo Erectus* in China and earlier *Australiopithicines* in Africa in the 1920s and 1930s were often dismissed as unimportant. It was not until the 1940s that scientists began to seriously wonder about Piltdown Man's validity. Finally, in 1949 the specimen was subjected to chemical tests that showed that the bones were no more than 50,000 years old. A more precise test in 1953 revealed that the skull and jaw were of entirely different ages and could not belong to the same individual. At this point, a detailed re-examination of the fossil was conducted, and Piltdown Man was shown to be a hoax. The skull was of a modern human that had been chemically stained to look old; the jaw probably belonged to an orangutan. The teeth showed clear evidence of being filed down. Many of the other artifacts associated with the bones also showed evidence of being "planted" in the original site. Clearly, someone had had a grand joke at science's expense!

Today science accepts the fact that bipedalism proceeds brain expansion. What is not yet agreed upon is why the brain should grow when it did and what selective pressures were responsible for this change. Oakley suggests that it was tool making and tool use that selected for greater intelligence. In contrast, Dean Falk links hominid brain expansion with the body's ability to diffuse heat.

Kenneth P. Oakley  **YES**

# On Man's Use of Fire, with Comments on Tool-Making and Hunting

## Man as Tool-Maker

The ancestral stock of apes and man was probably not highly adapted to forest life. Some of the monkey-like apes, such as *Proconsul,* lived in woodlands and could brachiate but could also probably run short distances bipedally on the ground. During Miocene times in East Africa they inhabited a mixed environment of corridor forests along streams and lakes, separated by bushy grassland. It has been suggested that members of the group were sometimes forced to move through the tall grass between forest areas and that, since this necessitated raising their level of vision, bipedal abilities would have had selective advantages. Supposedly, some members of the group moved into permanent forest and became solely arboreal, with hands specialized for hooking onto or hanging from boughs, while other members became adapted to more open country and evolved into bipeds.

In these latter—one might call them protohominids—the feet became rigid supporting organs, with pelvic changes accompanying bipedalism. The hands were freed as manipulative organs. It seems a mistake to think that tool-making depended upon any evolution of the hand; probably a generalized pongid hand could make tools if enough brain capacity were present. As Wood-Jones has indicated, manual skill depends upon initiation and co-ordination in the cerebral system. Men have developed manual skill even when their hands and limbs were maimed. Refined stereoscopic-color vision and erect posture with a vertical position of the skull are probably important. These allow close visual concentration over a wide field. The earliest hominids would have been anatomically equipped to use tools. It is a question of when they did, and why.

Tools are additions to the body that supplement the hands and teeth. In the arboreal prosimians, hands are climbing and feeding organs. These hands could have been used for other activities whenever such animals became ground-dwellers. Even baboons, partly ground-dwelling but adapted for quadrupedal

From *Social Life of Early Man*, Sherwood Washburn, ed., Viking Fund Publications in Anthropology #31, New York, NY, 1961, pp. 186–191. Copyright © 1961 by Wenner-Gren Foundation for Anthropological Research, Inc. Reprinted by permission. Notes omitted.

progression, occasionally use a pebble to kill a scorpion needed as food (observation by Professor D. M. S. Watson). Chimpanzees are rarely known to use tools in the wild but will do so in capitivity when they are forced to live on the ground.

When did tool-using begin? If the protohominids inhabiting the edge of the forest spent much time on the open ground, it is conceivable that they began picking up things to use. Life in the open is more precarious than life in the trees, and tool-using would offer a selective advantage. An increased period of learning would also be an important factor; the mother would assist and teach the child for a protracted period if adult status was retarded (as it may well have been) through the acquisition of bipedal habit and through continuing operation of the principle of pedomorphism.

Tool-making requires a higher order of intelligence than does tool-using. Chimpanzees are the only reported animals that *make* tools, and then only in captivity. Sultan, the chimpanzee observed by Kohler, was capable of improvising tools in certain situations. Tool-making occurred only in the presence of a visible reward, and never without it. In the chimpanzee the mental range seems to be limited to present situations, with little conception of past or future. The power of conceptual thought is basic to tool-making but is only "incipient" in apes. For instance, a chimpanzee can learn to make fine discriminations in color shading but retains the learning for only a short time; a chimpanzee, through constant exploratory activity, will see possible single sticks to use as tools in a broken box but not in a whole box. Man can see a tool in a formless lump of stone. This ability of conceptual thought may have been present in a few individuals in a group, becoming extended by selection when conditions demanded. The range of tool types already present in the oldest industries includes *tools for making other tools* (e.g., hammerstones), illustrating that what we regard as the unique foresight of man was present at a very early stage in his evolution.

By the end of Lower Pleistocene times, the human level of cerebral development had certainly been reached, and stone artifacts of crudely standardized types were being made (e.g., Oldowan pebble tools). The incipient standardization shows that the manufacture of such tools (e.g., at Sterkfontein) was not an isolated occurrence but was already a tradition that served certain permanent needs of the earliest human beings. What were these needs? The use of tools and weapons was surely the means whereby the Hominidae kept themselves alive after they had abandoned the protection and sustenance provided by forests.

The tree-climbing primates had no use for tools. Tool-using arose in connection with adaptation to life on open ground away from forests. In the evolution of the primates the forelimbs have continually showed a tendency to take on functions performed in their ancestors by the teeth. The use of tools is evidently an extension of this trend, and we may suppose that tools were largely substitutes for teeth.

The apes of today are forest creatures, subsisting almost exclusively on fruits, leaves, shoots, and insects. All known races of man, on the other hand, include a substantial proportion of mammalian flesh in their diet. We have ample evidence that Peking man, Neanderthal man, and Late Paleolithic races of *Homo sapiens* were meat-eaters. I suggest that meat-eating is as old as man the tool-maker, that with adaptation to partly open forest margins the diet of proto-men inevitably became more varied, and that they changed from being eaters largely of plants and the fruits of plants to being in part meat-eaters.

It seems probable, on the important analogy of the baboons, that early Hominidae living in such country (savanna) may have become increasingly addicted to flesh-eating as a result of the intensification of the struggle for existence by excessive drought. It may be recalled that baboons, which in day-time range into grassland away from trees, occasionally prey on lambs and other animals of similar size, using their powerful canine teeth as offensive weapons, and, moreover, that this habit is likely to become more prevalent when conditions of existence are hard. Owing to the extensive folklore associated with baboons, reports of the carnivorous habits of those in South Africa have been discounted by some zoölogists, but information from many different observers, collected by my friend Mr. F. E. Hiley in 1950, leaves no doubt that such reports are substantially true. A report from Captain H. B. Potter, with long experience as a game conservator in Zululand, is typical of those received:

> The following are my personal observations over a period of twenty years' wardenship in the Hluhluwe Game Reserve: I have seen full-grown poultry killed and actually eaten by baboons, mostly however by aged individuals. Eggs and chickens are taken by the dozen, by old and young baboons. I have on many occasions actually witnessed apparently organized hunts which often result in the death of the intended victim. The baboons, usually led by a veteran of the troop, surround an unsuspecting three-parts-grown Mountain Reedbuck, or Duiker, as the case may be, and on one occasion a young Reedbuck doe was the victim. It would appear that on a given signal the baboons close in on their quarry, catch it and tear it asunder. As a matter of interest I have refrained from interference in these grim encounters so that I would be in a position authentically to record the results. In nine cases out of ten the game animal is devoured limb by limb and after the affair is over all that is to be found are the skull and leg bones.

Baboons, like some other monkeys, and apes too, have powerful canine teeth, serving mainly for defense against carnivores and, in males, for gaining dominance. It has been suggested that the reduction in the size of the canine teeth in hominids was an outcome of functional replacement by hand weapons. The canine teeth may have been reduced in the Hominidae at an evolutionary stage below that of systematic tool-making. That australopithecines, with small canines, must surely have been at least tool-*users*. Certainly the protohominids would have needed some means of defending themselves in the open and, having their hands free, may well have used stones as missiles and sticks or animal long bones as clubs.

In dry, open country the protohominids, like baboons, might readily have taken to eating flesh, particularly in times of drought or scarcity of food. Although they lacked teeth suited to carnivorous habits, they could easily have killed small mammals. Life in the open set a premium on co-operation. Drawing on our knowledge of the mentality and social life of other primates, particularly baboons, it seems not unreasonable to suppose that, hunting in groups, the proto-hominids could have killed medium-sized mammals, say, by cornering them and using improvised hand weapons such as they might earlier have *learned to improvise in the first instance for their own defense.* The protohominids could certainly have killed small mammals.

It should not be forgotten that in the wild, after a kill by one of the larger carnivores, there is a scavenging food queue; when the lions, for instance, have had their fill, the hyenas and then the vultures enter the scene of slaughter. The protohominids may have first obtained the meat of larger mammals by entering this queue at an early stage. It has been reported that African children have been known to drive lions from their kill by beating tins. It is certainly conceivable that the protohominids used tactics of intimidation to facilitate their scavenging and that this preceded the hunting of larger wild game.

This is frankly speculation, for there is still no direct evidence that the earliest Hominidae were semicarnivorous or that they passed through a tool-using stage before becoming tool-makers. It is true that Dart has claimed that the quantities of broken animal bones found at Makapan in association with *Australopithecus* represent the food refuse of this creature and that some of the bones had been *used* as weapons, but other authorities are unconvinced and consider that the Makapan "bone statistics" can be satisfactorily explained as representing the product of *several* selective agencies, notably hyenas. The few pieces of mammalian bone found in the tool-bearing layer at Sterkfontein may yield some important clues bearing on this problem. Although there is a strong probability that all australopithecines were tool-users, and that some at least were tool-makers, the evidence remains *sub judice*.

By the time that the Hominidae had evolved into tool-makers, they were evidently largely carnivorous—quantities of meat bones were associated with the remains of *Pithecanthropus pekinensis*. It is easy to see how the one habit led to the other. Although the killing of game may have been accomplished easily enough in some such way as that suggested above, the early hominids must often have encountered difficulty in removing skin and fur and in dividing the flesh. In the absence of strong canine teeth, the solution would have been overcome most readily by using sharp pieces of stone. Here, surely, was the origin of the tradition of tool-making. Where no naturally sharp pieces of stone lay readily to hand, some of the more intelligent individuals saw that pebbles, which broke on the ground when thrown, provided the solution. By breaking pebbles, fresh sharp edges were produced. Once the tradition of tool-making had begun, the manifold uses of chipped stones became obvious. They were useful for sharpening sticks for digging out burrowing mammals; for making spears sharp enough to be effective weapons in hunting larger game; for scraping meat from bones, splitting them to get at the marrow; and for chopping the meat into convenient mouthfuls. All the main uses of stone tools were, I suggest, connected in the first place with adoption of semicarnivorous habits.

From the endowment of nature we should be vegetarians. We lack the teeth evolved by true carnivores, and we have the long gut associated with a herbivorous diet. Furthermore, we are the only members of the Hominoidea accustomed to eating meat on any considerable scale. It is true that anthropoid apes, like most herbivores, consume small quantities of animal protein; some of them occasionally rob birds' nests of eggs and fledglings, but by and large they are fruit and plant eaters.

One can well imagine that a changing environment, for instance during a period of desiccation, may have produced an abnormal appetite in the early hominids. Gorillas in captivity quickly develop a liking for meat, and this appears to be due to a change in the flora and fauna of their intestines. Normally, their intestines are richly supplied with ciliate protozoa (Infusoria), which serve to digest cellulose. According to Reichenow, under the abnormal conditions of captivity the Infusoria are ingested, and, with their disappearance from the intestines, the animal develops an abnormal appetite and readily takes to eating meat—and may even prefer meat to its normal fare.

By widening his diet and becoming a tool-maker, man became the most adaptable of all primates. The change from herbivorous to semicarnivorous habits was important from the point of view of the use of energy. To obtain a given amount of energy, a carnivore subsists on a smaller quantity of food than does a herbivore. Instead of eating almost continually, like their ancestors, the Hominidae spent must of their time hunting. This led to increased interdependence. New skills and aptitudes were developed through this new way of life, and with increasing control of environment through the use of manufactured tools, man became the most adaptable of all creatures, free to spread into every climatic zone.

An important step in the control of environment in northern climes was the making of fire. This could have been discovered only as an outcome of tool-making.

To sum up: I think it may fairly be claimed that tool-making is one of man's fundamental characteristics from a biological point of view. But the definition of man as the tool-*making* primate carries the implication that the term "human" should be applied only to the later members of the family Hominidae.

# NO ↵

Dean Falk

# The Radiator Theory of
# Brain Evolution

## Of Car Radiators and Letters from France

It was an "aha" experience, if ever I've had one, and the weirdest combination of events led to it. First, the engine in my 1970 Mercedes needed major surgery. I took it to Walter Anwander (a whiz) in Lafayette, Indiana, who completely rebuilt the engine. One day, while enumerating the wonders beneath the hood (about which I definitely needed schooling), Walter pointed to the radiator and told me "the engine can only be as big as that can cool." I didn't think much about it at the time.

During the period when my car was in the shop, I received a letter (dated January 13, 1987) from Michel Cabanac, a French physiologist who is now at the School of Medicine at Laval University in Québec. He said that my publication on the evolution of emissary veins was of interest to his research team because they had been doing research on exactly the same veins. To my surprise, Cabanac's group had shown that the mastoid and parietal emissary veins help to cool the brain when people are overheated.

The brain is an exquisitely heat-sensitive organ. According to the noted vascular physiologist, Mary Ann Baker:

> A rise of only four or five degrees C above normal begins to disturb brain functions. For example, high fevers in children are sometimes accompanied by convulsions; these are manifestations of the abnormal functioning of the nerve cells of the overheated brain. Indeed, it may be that the temperature of the brain is the single most important factor limiting the survival of man and other animals in hot environments.

Cabanac and his colleague Heiner Brinnel (of the Hôpital-Maternité L'Arbresle, France) wanted to know how the human brain keeps cool when everything else heats up, such as occurs during intense physical exercise. Accordingly, they studied the relationship between different temperature states and the direction of blood flow in cranial veins (which lack valves) by carrying out intriguing physiological experiments on six healthy adult men. To achieve the cold state (hypothermia), the subjects occupied a turbulent climatic chamber set at 0°C for half an hour. Their blood vessels constricted, they shivered, and their oral temperature dropped to 36.3°C 0.05°. To attain the heated condition (hyperthermia), the men pedaled on a cycle for twenty to thirty minutes, by which time they were sweating profusely and had an oral temperature of 37.6°C 0.18°.

In the minutes following cold exposure or exercise, the direction of blood flow was recorded for the parietal and mastoid emissary veins. This was done by placing an instrument called a Doppler probe directly on the scalp at the point where the vein passes through the cranium. (Four of the men were conveniently bald.) The results were startling. In cold subjects, blood flow was slow and flowed out from the cranium, i.e., from the brain to the skin. In overheated subjects, however, blood rapidly drained from the skin *into* the braincase. Further, these findings were identical to those determined earlier for a third emissary vein, the ophthalmic vein of the face. Thus, when subjects became overheated, blood flow reversed from the normal direction in all three of these emissary veins. Consequently, blood that had been cooled by evaporation from the sweating face and scalp was delivered into the braincase.

Whereas I had merely speculated that the mastoid and parietal emissary veins provided windows into a wider, more complicated network of cranial veins, Cabanac and Brinnel had actually demonstrated this to be the case. They noted that innumerable, microscopic emissary veins exist in humans and that the network of veins found within the bones of the skull itself (diploic veins) opens both externally and internally. By gently massaging the outside surface of the skullcap from a fresh cadaver, Cabanac and Brinnel showed that blood is capable of flowing through this entire network of emissary and diploic veins from the outside to the inside of the cranium.

The three relatively large emissary veins that were used to record direction of blood flow are located at dispersed points throughout the network of cranial veins—at the face (ophthalmic), the back of the ear (mastoid), and the top, back part of the skull (parietal). Cabanac and Brinnel therefore took these three veins to be representative of the wider network and concluded that when blood flows into the braincase in the ophthalmic, mastoid, and parietal veins, it also flows inward in the innumerable other veins that comprise the cranial network. Apparently, cool blood from the entire surface of the human head participates in cooling the brain—but only when a person is overheated. Physiologists call this phenomenon "selective brain cooling." Since Cabanac and Brinnel's original paper, other experimental evidence has accumulated that supports their conclusion (although it still remains controversial). Just like my car, the brain has a radiator!

You can see these cranial radiators at work in any gymnasium. Take where I work out, the Sweat Shop in Albany. Every Sunday, Judy Torel (the owner) teaches a 105-minute endurance aerobics class. The class begins with a moderately paced warm-up. Everybody stays cool. Most people are not even wearing headbands. The warm-up is followed by one hour of nonstop, high-impact aerobics (done to music, something like fast dancing). A ways into it, small sweat spots start to appear on torsos (whole-body cooling has kicked in). Further into the hour, sweat marks are bigger. Headbands go on. At about the forty-five-minute mark, even Judy (who seems not to sweat) puts on a headband. Near the end of the high-impact portion of the class, cranial radiators are in full throttle causing faces to flush as surface vessels dilate and assimilate the cooling effects of evaporation. Some heads are actually dripping. In vessels of a dozen bouncing crania, cooled surface blood flows inward to soothe exhilarated brains. These people are now ready to do weights!

Cabanac's letter had a profound influence on me. In a key portion, he wrote:

> It is possible that emissary veins were developed for the defense of brain temperature. Brain size has increased with bipedalism. The brain's thermolytic (cooling) needs have increased with its increasing size. . . . This hypothesis does not contradict yours but might complement it. I would be interested in hearing from you.

Cabanac enclosed reprints of his scientific articles with his letter. I read them right away and should have seen their implications immediately, but it took three days for the light bulb to go on.

The impact of Cabanac's research hit me in the middle of the night, when I awoke thinking something to the extent of: "Ye gods! Cabanac's work might be the key for understanding why bipedalism preceded the increase in brain size." There was only one thing to do. I got up, got dressed, and went to my lab to plot hominid cranial capacities against the data for emissary veins. It turned out to be worth the trip.

It was beautiful. For the past two million years, the increase in frequencies of emissary foramina kept *exact* pace with the sharp increase in brain size in *Homo*. Clearly, the brain and the veins had evolved rapidly and together. I saw that Cabanac's letter was right and that I had unwittingly charted the evolution of a radiator for the brain in my earlier work on emissary foramina. As Anwander had said about my car, the engine can only be as big as the radiator can cool. Apparently, the same is true for heat-sensitive brains.

But the engine, or brain, and the radiator increased in only one lineage of hominids—that leading to *Homo*. Why? And what about bipedalism and gravity? If the above reasoning is correct, heat stress (or thermoregulation) would have been a key factor in the evolution, and possibly the origin, of *Homo*. As it turns out, there is plenty of speculation, and even some evidence, that suggests just that.

## Hot Times on the Savanna

The protohominids who gave rise to the CA around five million years ago were presumably already semierect or preadapted for bipedalism because of their primate ancestry. Like living pygmy chimpanzees, they would have been capable of spurts of bipedalism on the ground or even in the trees. But the shift to full bipedal locomotion would take some time. And during this process, vascular systems would be reshaped through natural selection because of the changed hydrostatic pressures associated with erect posture. Whatever else was demanded of the cranial veins, they had to be able, by hook or by crook, to sustain delivery of blood to the vertebral plexus of veins. Further, because of gravity, this would be true forever after, for all hominids, in all types of environments.

Apparently, robust australopithecines kept cool throughout their evolution. The early ones from Hadar had curved finger and toe bones which were handy for hanging in the shady trees that grew in Hadar's evergreen bushland habitat. According to Elisabeth Vrba of Yale University, the more recent robust australopithecines from East Africa also lived in wooded areas near water. (Unfortunately, the environments occupied by South African robust australopithecines are, for various reasons, difficult to assess.) Further, all robust australopithecines were strict vegetarians, just as Robinson suggested years ago. No need for them to chase down animals during the heat of the day! They had it made in the shade. Except, of course, for the fact that their brains never got very big, and they eventually became extinct.

It's another story for gracile australopithecines, however. Both their teeth and their cranial vascular systems show that these creatures were completely different from robust australopithecines. For example, of six scorable gracile australopithecines, only Taung had an O/M sinus system like that found in robust australopithecines. (And remember, Taung might actually have been an immature robust australopithecine.) Further, the data for emissary veins indicate that unlike robust australopithecines, gracile australopithecines had the floor plan for a radiator network of veins. These are excellent reasons for believing that by the time we pick up their fossil records, robust and gracile australopithecines had been separated for a relatively long time—long enough to evolve distinctly different systems for cranial blood flow.

But how did the division between robust and gracile australopithecines occur? These so-called speciation events generally happen when one subgroup of a population settles down somewhere else. If the new environment (which doesn't have to be far away) is different enough from the original environment and if the pioneers remain isolated from the original group, then the two groups will go their own evolutionary directions. Given enough time, the two populations will become more and more different, until, eventually, they would no longer be able to interbreed with each other (if, that is, they were so inclined, which they probably wouldn't be anyway). At that point, speciation has occurred.

Now, I can think of no better way for a hominid to go somewhere else than to walk there. In fact, by its very nature, any new form of locomotion (be it bipedalism or airplanes) should open up new territory (niches) for more-adventurous souls. Further, we know that a variety of patchy environments were available to hominids during the Plio-Pleistocene. It again appears that Robinson had it right: While robust australopithecines kept cool among the trees, gracile australopithecines ventured afield on foot. Like savanna baboons, graciles spent most of their waking hours away from the forests and woodlands, and on the hot African savanna. It was *there* that full-fledged bipedalism was refined.

And it was on the savanna that hominids experienced the double whammy of changed gravitational pressures on their vascular systems and heat stress on their whole bodies. Presumably, both sexes spent a good deal of time exploiting the scattered resources of open African grasslands that were subject to hot temperatures and intense solar radiation during the day. Many workers, including Zihlman and Cohn, have argued convincingly that sweat glands, reduced body hair, and dark skin evolved as a functional complex in response to the thermal stress associated with living on the African savanna.

Pete Wheeler, as was discussed earlier, takes the topic of savanna-adapted hominid responses to thermal stress a step further. According to Wheeler, early hominids foraging in patchy habitats reduced their heat loads by postural means, i.e., by engaging in increased amounts of bipedal locomotion, especially during the heat of the day, which reduced the amount of body surface exposed to direct hits of solar radiation. In other words, Wheeler sees bipedalism itself as an adaptive response to heat stress. His theory also incorporates ideas about the evolution of sweat glands, hair loss, and even body fat.

Whenever I read Wheeler's papers, I have a flashback to an experience that I had on the island of La Parguera, off the southwest coast of Puerto Rico. During the early 1980s, the island, which is uninhabited by people, provided a refuge for a large group of beautiful, strawberry blond Old World patas monkeys. In their native African habitats, patas monkeys are quadrupedal animals that live in open savanna grasslands. Although well known for being silent, extremely swift runners, patas monkeys frequently assume bipedal stances in the wild. Primatologists have traditionally attributed this proclivity for uprightness to sentinel behavior, i.e., standing up to look out (over the high grass) for predators.

When I visited La Parguera, it was extremely hot. So much so that I could barely function. During the middle of the day, I positioned myself (and a good water supply) on a shaded observation deck that overlooked a large corral containing dozens of patas monkeys. The corral was encircled by high corrugated metal sheeting and, unfortunately, there were no trees within it to shade the monkeys. Although I had read about sentinel behavior in patas monkeys, I was amazed at the amount of bipedalism I saw that day. At the time, I guessed that the monkeys might be trying to see over the tops of the metal enclosure, although it did seem odd because the sides were much too high to allow that. Years later, after reading Wheeler's work, I now suspect that the monkeys were standing up simply because they were more comfortable absorbing less sunshine. (Incidentally, I also think it was inhumane to place the monkeys in such a horrid situation.)

# The Radiator Theory in a Nutshell

Put all this information together and you have the radiator theory of hominid brain evolution. This theory explains why bipedalism preceded the increase in brain size in *Homo* and why brain size never got very big in australopithecines. Beginning with the latter, brain size never got above 600 cm$^3$ because an organism's ability to cool its cranial blood places a limiting factor, or constraint, on its brain size. Australopithecines simply did not have vascular systems that were able to regulate temperature in brains that were any larger. Although robust australopithecines evolved a dramatic, enlarged O/M sinus that delivered blood from the cranium when they were bipedal, this system did not provide a cooling net of veins that could function as a radiator for an enlarging brain. Thus, brain size remained relatively conservative in this group of hominids.

Bipedalism in early gracile australopithecines preceded the takeoff in brain size in their descendants, *Homo*, for two reasons. First, because of the constraints of gravity, bipedalism necessitated a rearrangement in cranial blood vessels. (Since this was also true for robust australopithecines, it was a necessary but not sufficient condition for the subsequent evolution in brain size.) Second, bipedalism allowed the ancestors of gracile australopithecines to "go over there" to thermally stressful savanna habitats. And if Wheeler is right, thermally stressful habitats themselves may have contributed to an increase in the frequency of bipedal behavior. (This is a cyclical, yet logical, notion.) Thus, the vascular systems of gracile australopithecines became modified in response to both gravitational and temperature pressures that were associated with refinement of bipedalism on the savanna. One result was the beginnings of a cranial radiator system of veins in gracile australopithecines. It could do two things: help deliver blood to the vertebral plexus of veins and help cool the brain under conditions of intense exercise. More important, once in place, this system was modifiable. It, therefore, released thermal constraints that had previously kept brain size in check. The engine (brain) could and did get bigger in *Homo*, but only after *Homo*'s australopithecine ancestors had refined bipedalism in a savanna environment that facilitated development of a prototype radiator. That is why the feet went first. . . .

# POSTSCRIPT

## Is Hominid Brain Expansion Linked to the Invention of Stone Tools?

**S**herwood Washburn's theories were developed during the 1960s when the icon of "Man the Toolmaker" was being overturned by Jane Goodall's studies of tool use and tool making among the Gombe chimps. Washburn suggested that tool making and the use of weapons for defense would have facilitated the movement of early hominids out into the savannas and encouraged the development of bipedalism. He also suggested a connection between increasing intelligence and more sophisticated tools. Although his ideas that making tools sparked bipedalism (at least in the savanna) has not stood the test of time, his other idea that greater intelligence and more complex tools are linked is still popular. Labeled as "the 2001 theory" by Dean Falk, this view of human evolution suggests that the full adaptation to savanna life that started occurring 2 to 2.5 million years ago simultaneously selected for the development of enlarged brains and the first production of stone tools. These stone tools gave humans an advantage in hunting, allowing them to kill large game for the first time. Prior to this time, hominids presumably spent more of their time in forest and woodland environments where the selection for large brains and more sophisticated tools was less intense.

Many physical anthropologists still find this explanation compelling despite evidence by Boesche and Boesche-Achermann that forest-dwelling chimps at Tai "show greater complexity in both hunting and tool use. Tai chimps use tools in nineteen different ways and have six different ways of making them, compared with sixteen uses and three methods of manufacture at Gombe" (1991:59). Other studies suggest that the *Australiopithicines* may have also used a variety of tools in woodland environments. Ragir (2000) suggests that they may have dug up rootstocks with bone tools, and Holden (2001) makes a case for their use in opening termite mounds. Sussman (1984) also made comparisons of the hands of fossil hominds with those of contemporary humans, chimps, and bonobos. He suggests that *Robustus* may have been capable of a precision grip like modern humans, something that would have facilitated tool making. Shipman (1987) also notes indirect evidence of stone tools being used to slice meat off bones that had also been chewed by carnivores. Even more intriguing is the discovery of hominid cranial and postcranial bones associated with the bones of antelope, horses, and other animals that exhibit cut marks made by stone tools (Asfaw et al., 1999; Culotta, 1999; de Heinzdin et al., 1999). These finds have been dated at around 2.5 million years ago and suggests that at least some hominids had made the transition to using stone tools.

So with all this tool use and manufacture going on, why did the brain remain small until about 2 million years ago? Besides Falk's "radiator theory," another possibility may be the increase in available protein. The brain is a metabolically expensive organ, and it can grow only as large as the amount of protein in the diet would allow. Prior to 2.5 million years ago, the consumption of protein by hominids may not have been great enough to facilitate sustained brain growth. Limits were then placed upon how large the brain could grow. However, after 2.5 million years ago, hominids may have begun spending more time in the grasslands, and their access to meat from large game animals— either by hunting or scavenging—could have increased dramatically. As protein consumption went up, so did brain size.

Another possibility is "the social brain hypothesis" proposed by Robin Dunbar (1998). Dunbar notes that, among living primates, there is a positive relationship between brain size and the size of the species social groups. Larger social groups require larger brains to keep track of the complexities of relationships. Dunbar argues that socially skillful animals would probably survive better and have more opportunities to reproduce. Thus, larger brains began to be selected for as hominids adapted to the more open savanna environment— especially if this adaptation caused them to increase their territories and brought them frequently into contact with other wandering bands. Using an equation relating brain size and group size for primates, Dunbar calculates that *Homo-Hablis* may have kept track of a cognitive group of about 80 individuals, or approximately three bands of 25 to 30 people.

For more information on hominid brain development and factors influencing it, see R. Holloway "The Evolution of the Primate Brain," *Brain Research* (vol. 7, 1968), P. Greenfield, "Language, Tools and Brain: The Ontogeny and Phylogeny of Hierarchically Organized Segregated Behavior," *Behavioral and Brain Sciences* (vol. 14, 1991), L. Aiello and R. Dunbar, "Neocortex Size, Group Size and the Evolution of Language," *Current Anthropology* (vol. 34, 1993), P. Tobias, *The Brain in Human Evolution* (1991).

# ISSUE 13

## Is Hunting More Critical Than Gathering to Cultural Development?

**YES: Sherwood L. Washburn and C. S. Lancaster,** from "The Evolution of Hunting," in Richard B. Lee and Irven DeVore, eds., *Man the Hunter* (Aldine Publishing, 1968)

**NO: Sally Slocum,** from "Woman the Gatherer: Male Bias in Anthropology," in Rayna R. Reiter, ed., *Toward an Anthropology of Women* (Monthly Review Press, 1975)

### ISSUE SUMMARY

Sherwood Washburn and C.S. Lancaster propose that hunting stimulates cultural development among early humans. In contrast, Sally Slocum contends that gathering is just as important as hunting to cultural development. She cites male bias in anthropology as the reason that this factor has been often overlooked in the study of human evolution.

*Higher evolution, one would think was something reserved for the primate who had the guts and wits to go out there and grab it (Shreeve, 1996:117).*

In addition to physiology, natural selection also acts upon behavior. Behaviors that promote survival or increase reproductive rates in a species are selected for and may be passed from parent to offspring through social learning. For example, studies of chimpanzees suggest that the daughters of dominant females are apt to grow to be dominant females themselves and that they learned how to be dominant from their mothers. The chimpanzee Flo was the alpha female in the Gombe research group when Jane Goodall began her studies in the 1960s. Jane described Flo as "aggressive, tough as nails, and easily the most dominant of all the females at that time" (1971:92). Flo's daughter FiFi followed in her footsteps. She dominated the other females in her age group and after Flo's death, succeeded her as the alpha female. In highly social species, such as apes and humans, adaptive behaviors also become part of established cultural traditions. These traditions are passed not only from mother to child, but from troop to troop as individuals move between them.

Higher primates also seem capable of *cultural invention*. On Koshima Island, Japan, primatologists introduced sweet potatoes as a food source to facilitate their study of a resident troop of macaques. Normally, macaques rub dirt off their food with their hands. However, one day a young female took her sweet potato to a stream and washed it. Other members of her play group picked up this behavior, and it soon spread to the mothers of these young monkeys and eventually to the other adults in the troop. Four years later, over 80 percent of the monkeys in the troop were washing sweet potatoes.

Like other higher primates, early humans may have also used social learning, the passing of cultural traditions and cultural invention, as ways to adapt to their environment. Over time, human cultural adaptation increased in both scope and complexity. Our abilities not only outstripped those of other primates, but eventually our command of culture became so great that we were able to use it to help buffer ourselves from the effects of natural selection. At this point, the pace of physical evolution slowed. Biologically, we are essentially the same as people living thousands of years ago. But culturally, we are vastly different. In fact, the speed at which culture moves is so swift today that significant changes can and do take place within a single lifetime.

So how do we account for this phenomenon? Why does human cultural development exceed those of other primates? Some researchers suggest that the answer lies in hunting. Although other primates do hunt (see Issue 7), none of them hunt big game or use sophisticated weapons and hunting strategies as humans do. Washburn and Lancaster suggest that the evolution of hunting was the primary factor separating early humans from other primates and that it had a vital role in shaping the rest of human nature and culture. In contrast, Sally Slocum makes a case for the importance of gathering and other female activities as factors stimulating cultural development. She cites male bias and cautions that the image of "Man the Hunter" minimizes the importance of women and women's contributions to human evolution.

# YES

**Sherwood L. Washburn
and C. S. Lancaster**

# The Evolution of Hunting

It is significant that the title of this symposium is Man the Hunter for, in contrast to carnivores, human hunting, if done by males, is based on a division of labor and is a social and technical adaptation quite different from that of other mammals. Human hunting is made possible by tools, but it is far more than a technique or even a variety of techniques. It is a way of life, and the success of this adaptation (in its total social, technical, and psychological dimensions) has dominated the course of human evolution for hundreds of thousands of years. In a very real sense our intellect, interests, emotions, and basic social life—all are evolutionary products of the success of the hunting adaptation. When anthropologists speak of the unity of mankind, they are stating that the selection pressures of the hunting and gathering way of life were so similar and the result so successful that populations of *Homo sapiens* are still fundamentally the same everywhere. In this essay we are concerned with the general characteristics of man that we believe can be attributed to the hunting way of life.

Perhaps the importance of the hunting way of life in producing man is best shown by the length of time hunting has dominated human history. The genus *Homo* has existed for some 600,000 years, and agriculture has been important only during the last few thousand years. Even 6,000 years ago large parts of the world's population were nonagricultural, and the entire evolution of man from the earliest populations of *Homo erectus* to the existing races took place during the period in which man was a hunter. The common factors that dominated human evolution and produced *Homo sapiens* were preagricultural. Agricultural ways of life have dominated less than 1 percent of human history, and there is no evidence of major biological changes during that period of time. The kind of minor biological changes that occurred and which are used to characterize modern races were not common to *Homo sapiens*. The origin of all common characteristics must be sought in preagricultural times. Probably all experts would agree that hunting was a part of the social adaptation of all populations of the genus *Homo*, and many would regard *Australopithecus* as a still earlier hominid who was already a hunter, although possibly much less efficient than the later forms. If this is true and if the Pleistocene period had a duration of three million years, then pre-*Homo erectus* human tool using and hunting lasted for at least four times as long as the duration of the genus *Homo* (Lancaster, MS.). No matter how the earlier times may ultimately be interpreted, the observation of more hunting among apes than was previously suspected and increasing evidence for hunting by *Australopithecus* strengthens the position that less than 1 percent of human history has been dominated by agriculture. It is for this reason that the consideration of hunting is so important for the understanding of human evolution. . . .

Hunting by members of the genus *Homo* throughout the 600,000 years that the genus has persisted has included the killing of large numbers of big animals. This implies the efficient use of tools, as Birdsell stressed at the symposium. The adaptive value of hunting large animals has been shown by Bourlière, who demonstrated that 75 percent of the meat available to human hunters in the eastern Congo was in elephant, buffalo, and hippopotamus. It is some measure of the success of human hunting that when these large species are protected in game reserves (as in the Murchison Falls or Queen Elizabeth Parks in Uganda), they multiply rapidly and destroy the vegetation. Elephants alone can destroy trees more rapidly than they are replaced naturally, as they do in the Masai Amboseli Reserve in Kenya. Since the predators are also protected in reserves, it appears that human hunters have been killing enough large game to maintain the balance of nature for many thousands of years. It is tempting to think that man replaced the saber-toothed tiger as the major predator of large game, both controlling the numbers of the game and causing the extinction of Old World saber-tooths. We think that hunting and butchering large animals put a maximum premium on cooperation among males, a behavior that is at an absolute minimum among the nonhuman primates. It is difficult to imagine the killing of creatures such as cave bears, mastodons, mammoths—or *Dinotherium* at a much earlier time—without highly coordinated, cooperative action among males. It may be that the origin of male-male associations lies in the necessities of cooperation in hunting, butchering, and war. Certainly butchering sites, such as described by F. Clark Howell in Spain, imply that the organization of the community for hunting large animals goes back for many, many thousands of years. From the biological point of view, the development of such organizations would have been paralleled by selection for an ability to plan and cooperate (or reduction of rage). Because females and juveniles may be involved in hunting small creatures, the social organization of big-game hunting would also lead to an intensification of a sexual division of labor.

It is important to stress, as noted before, that human hunting is a set of ways of life. It involves divisions of labor between male and female, sharing according to custom, cooperation among males, planning, knowledge of many species and large areas, and technical skill. Goldschmidt has stressed the uniqueness and importance of human sharing, both in the family and in the wider society, and Lee emphasizes orderly sharing as fundamental to human hunting society. The importance of seeing human hunting as a whole social pattern is well illustrated by the old idea, recently revived, that the way of life of our ancestors was similar to that of wolves rather than that of apes or monkeys. But this completely misses the special nature of the human adaptation.

Human females do not go out and hunt and then regurgitate to their young when they return. Human young do not stay in dens but are carried by mothers. Male wolves do not kill with tools, butcher, and share with females who have been gathering. In an evolutionary sense the whole human pattern is new, and it is the success of this particularly human way that dominated human evolution and determined the relation of biology and culture for thousands of years. Judging from the archeological record, it is probable that the major features of this human way, possibly even including the beginnings of language, had evolved by the time of *Homo erectus*. . . .

Moving over long distances creates problems of carrying food and water. Lee has pointed out that the sharing of food even in one locality implies that food is carried, and there is no use in gathering quantities of fruit or nuts unless they can be moved. If women are to gather while men hunt, the results of the labors of both sexes must be carried back to some agreed upon location. Meat can be carried away easily, but the development of some sort of receptacles for carrying vegetable products may have been one of the most fundamental advances in human evolution. Without a means of carrying, the advantages of a large area are greatly reduced, and sharing implies that a person carries much more than one can use. However that may be, the whole human pattern of gathering and hunting to share—indeed, the whole complex of economic reciprocity that dominates so much of human life—is unique to man. In its small range, a monkey gathers only what it itself needs to eat at that moment. Wherever archeological evidence can suggest the beginnings of movement over large ranges, cooperation, and sharing, it is dating the origin of some of the most fundamental aspects of human behavior—the human world view. We believe that hunting large animals may demand all these aspects of human behavior which separate man so sharply from the other primates. If this is so, then the human way appears to be as old as *Homo erectus*. . . .

A large territory not only provides a much wider range of possible foods but also a greater variety of potentially useful materials. With tool use this variety takes on meaning, and even the earliest pebble tools show selection in size, form, and material. When wood ceases to be just something to climb on, hardness, texture, and form become important. Availability of materials is critical to the tool user, and early men must have had a very different interest in their environment from that of monkeys or apes. Thus, the presence of tools in the archeological record is not only an indication of technical progress but also an index of interest in inanimate objects and in a much larger part of the environment than is the case with non-human primates.

The tools of the hunters include the earliest beautiful manmade objects, the symmetrical bifaces, especially those of the Acheulian tradition. Just how they were used is still a matter of debate, but, as contemporary attempts to copy them show, their manufacture is technically difficult, taking much time and practice and a high degree of skill. The symmetry of these tools may indicate that they were swung with great speed and force, presumably attached to some sort of handle. A tool that is moved slowly does not have to be symmetrical, but balance becomes important when an object is swung rapidly or thrown with speed. Irregularities will lead to deviations in the course of the blow or the trajectory of flight. An axe or spear to be used with speed and power is subject to very different technical limitations from those of scrapers or digging sticks, and it may well be that it was the attempt to produce efficient high-speed weapons that first produced beautiful, symmetrical objects.

When the selective advantage of a finely worked point over an irregular one is considered, it must be remembered that a small difference might give a very large advantage. A population in which hunters hit the game 5 percent more frequently, more accurately, or at greater distance would bring back much more meat. There must have been strong selection for greater skill in manufacture and use, and it is no accident that the bones of small-brained men (*Australopithecus*) are never found with beautiful, symmetrical tools. If the brains of contemporary apes and men are compared, the areas associated with manual skills (both in cerebellum and cortex) are at least three times as large in man. Clearly, the success of tools has exerted a great influence on the evolution of the brain, and has created the skills that make art possible. The evolution of the capacity to appreciate the product must evolve along with the skills of manufacture and use, and the biological capacities that the individual inherits must be developed in play and practiced in games. In this way, the beautiful, symmetrical tool becomes a symbol of a level of human intellectual achievement, representing far more than just the tool itself.

In a small group like the hunting band, which is devoted to one or two major cooperative activities, the necessity for long practice in developing skills to a very high level restricts the number of useful arts, and social organization is relatively simple. Where there is little division of labor, all men learn the same activities, such as skill in the hunt or in war. In sports (like the decathlon) we take it for granted that no one individual can achieve record levels of performance in more than a limited set of skills. This kind of limitation is partially biological but it is also a matter of culture. In warfare, for example, a wide variety of weapons is useful only if there are enough men to permit a division of labor so that different groups can practice different skills. Handedness, a feature that separates man from ape, is a part of this biology of skill. To be ambidextrous might seem to be ideal, but in fact the highest level of skill is attained by concentrating both biological ability and practice primarily on one hand. The evolution of handedness reflects the importance of skill, rather than mere use. . . .

Behind this human view that the flight of animals from man is natural lie some aspects of human psychology. Men enjoy hunting and killing, and these activities are continued as sports even when they are no longer economically necessary. If a behavior is important to the survival of a species (as hunting was for man throughout most of human history), then it must be both easily learned and pleasurable. Part of the motivation for hunting is the immediate pleasure it gives the hunter, and the human killer can no more afford to be sorry for the game than a cat can for its intended victim. Evolution builds a relation between biology, psychology, and behavior, and, therefore, the evolutionary success of hunting exerted a profound effect on human psychology. Perhaps, this is most easily shown by the extent of the efforts devoted to maintain killing as a sport. In former times royalty and nobility maintained parks where they could enjoy the sport of killing, and today the United States government spends many millions of dollars to supply game for hunters. Many people dislike the notion that man is naturally aggressive and that he naturally enjoys the destruction of other creatures. Yet we all know people who use the lightest fishing tackle to prolong the fish's futile struggle, in order to maximize the personal sense of mastery and skill. And until recently war was viewed in much the same way as hunting. Other human beings were simply the most dangerous game. War has been far too important in human history for it to be other than pleasurable for the males involved. It is only recently, with the entire change in the nature and conditions or war, that this institution has been challenged, that the wisdom of war as a normal part of national policy or as an approved road to personal social glory has been questioned. . . .

The extent to which the biological bases for killing have been incorporated into human psychology may be measured by the ease with which boys can be interested in hunting, fishing, fighting, and games of war. It is not that these behaviors are inevitable, but they are easily learned, satisfying, and have been socially rewarded in most cultures. The skills for killing and the pleasures of killing are normally developed in play, and the patterns of play prepare the children for their adult roles. At the conference Woodburn's excellent motion pictures showed Hadza boys killing small mammals, and Laughlin described how Aleuts train boys from early childhood so that they would be able to throw harpoons with accuracy and power while seated in kayaks. The whole youth of the hunter is dominated by practice and appreciation of the skills of the adult males, and the pleasure of the games motivates the practice that is necessary to develop the skills of weaponry. Even in monkeys, rougher play and play fighting are largely the activities of the males, and the young females explore less and show a greater interest in infants at an early age. These basic biological differences are reinforced in man by a division of labor which makes adult sex roles differ far more in humans than they do in nonhuman primates. Again, hunting must be seen as a whole pattern of activities, a wide variety of ways of life, the psychobiological roots of which are reinforced by play and by a clear identification with adult roles. Hunting is more than a part of the economic system, and the animal bones in Choukoutien are evidence of the patterns of play and pleasure of our ancestors. . . .

To see how radically hunting changed the economic situation, it is necessary to remember that in monkeys and apes an individual simply eats what it needs. After an infant is weaned, it is on its own economically and is not dependent on adults. This means that adult males never have economic responsibility for any other animal, and adult females do only when they are nursing. In such a system, there is no economic gain in delaying any kind of social relationship. But when hunting makes females and young dependent on the success of male skills, there is a great gain to the family members in establishing behaviors which prevent the addition of infants, unless these can be supported. . . .

That family organization may be attributed to the hunting way of life is supported by ethnography. Since the same economic and social problems as those under hunting continue under agriculture, the institution continued. The data on the behavior of contemporary monkeys and apes also show why this institution was not necessary in a society in which each individual gets its own food. Obviously the origin of the custom cannot be dated, and we cannot prove *Homo erectus* had a family organized in the human way. But it can be shown that the conditions that make the family adaptive existed at the time of *Homo erectus*. The evidence of hunting is clear in the archeological record. A further suggestion that the human kind of family is old comes from physiology; the loss of estrus is essential to the human family organization, and it is unlikely that this physiology, which is universal in contemporary mankind, evolved recently. . . .

# NO

**Sally Slocum**

# Woman the Gatherer:
# Male Bias in Anthropology

**L**ittle systematic attention has been given in our discipline to an "anthropology of knowledge." While some anthropologists have concerned themselves with knowledge in general, as seen through the varieties of human cultures, few have examined anthropological knowledge itself. . . .

We are human beings studying other human beings, and we cannot leave ourselves out of the equation. We choose to ask certain questions, *and not others.* Our choice grows out of the cultural context in which anthropology and anthropologists exist. Anthropology, as an academic discipline, has been developed primarily by white Western males, during a specific period in history. Our questions are shaped by the particulars of our historical situation, and by unconscious cultural assumptions.

Given the cultural and ethnic background of the majority of anthropologists, it is not surprising that the discipline has been biased. There are signs, however, that this selective blindness is beginning to come under scrutiny. . . . We have always encouraged members of American minority groups, and other "foreigners," to take up anthropology because of the perspective on the world that they can supply. The invitation is increasingly being accepted. As we had both hoped and feared, repercussions from this new participation are being felt in theory, method, interpretation, and problem choice, shaking anthropology to the roots.

The perspective of women is, in many ways, equally foreign to an anthropology that has been developed and pursued primarily by males. There is a strong male bias in the questions asked, and the interpretations given. This bias has hindered the full development of our discipline as "the study of the human animal" (I don't want to call it "the study of man" for reasons that will become evident). I am going to demonstrate the Western male bias by reexamining the matter of evolution of Homo sapiens from our nonhuman primate ancestors. In particular, the concept of "Man the Hunter" as developed by Sherwood Washburn and C. Lancaster and others is my focus. This critique is offered in hopes of transcending the male bias that limits our knowledge by limiting the questions we ask.

Though male bias could be shown in other areas, hominid evolution is particularly convenient for my purpose because it involves speculations and inferences from a rather small amount of data. In such a case, hidden assumptions and premises that lie behind the speculations and inferences are more easily demonstrated. Male bias exists not only in the ways in which the scanty data are interpreted, but in the very language used. All too often the word "man" is used in such an ambiguous fashion that it is impossible to decide whether it refers to males or to the human species in general, including both males and females. In fact, one frequently is led to suspect that in the minds of many anthropologists, "man," supposedly meaning the human species, is actually exactly synonymous with "males."

This ambiguous use of language is particularly evident in the writing that surrounds the concept of Man the Hunter. Washburn and Lancaster make it clear that it is specifically males who hunt, that hunting is much more than simply an economic activity, and that most of the characteristics which we think of as specifically human can be causally related to hunting. They tell us that hunting is a whole pattern of activity and way of life: "The biology, psychology, and customs that separate us from the apes—all these we owe to the hunters of time past." If this line of reasoning is followed to its logical conclusion, one must agree with Jane Kephart when she says:

> Since only males hunt, and the psychology of the species was set by hunting, we are forced to conclude that females are scarcely human, that is, do not have built-in the basic psychology of the species: to kill and hunt and ultimately to kill others of the same species. The argument implies built-in aggression in human males, as well as the assumed passivity of human females and their exclusion from the mainstream of human development.

To support their argument that hunting is important to human males, Washburn and Lancaster point to the fact that many modern males still hunt, though it is no longer economically necessary. I could point out that many modern males play golf, play the violin, or tend gardens: these, as well as hunting, are things their culture teaches them. Using a "survival" as evidence to demonstrate an important fact of cultural evolution can be accorded no more validity when proposed by a modern anthropologist than when proposed by Tylor.

Regardless of its status as a survival, hunting, by implication as well as direct statement, is pictured as a male activity to the exclusion of females. This activity, on which we are told depends the psychology, biology, and customs of our species, is strictly male. A theory that leaves out half the human species is unbalanced. The theory of Man the Hunter is not only unbalanced; it leads to the conclusion that the basic human adaptation was the desire of males to hunt and kill. This not only gives too much importance to aggression, which is after all only one factor of human life, but it derives culture from killing. I am going to suggest a less biased reading of the evidence, which gives a more valid and logical picture of human evolution, and at the same time a more hopeful one. First I will note the evidence, discuss the more traditional reading of it, and then offer an alternative reconstruction. . . .

As I was taught anthropology, the story goes something like this. Obscure selection pressures pushed the protohominid in the direction of erect bipedalism—perhaps the advantages of freeing the hands for food carrying or for tool use. Freeing the hands allowed more manipulation of the environment in the direction of tools for gathering and hunting food. Through a hand-eye-brain feedback process, coordination, efficiency, and skill were increased. The new behavior was adaptive, and selection pressure pushed the protohominid further along the same lines of development. Diet changed as the increase in skill allowed the addition of more animal protein. Larger brains were selected for, making possible transmission of information concerned tool making, and organizing cooperative hunting. It is assumed that as increased brain size was selected for, so also was neoteny—immaturity of infants at birth with a corresponding increase in their period of dependency, allowing more time for learning at the same time as this learning became necessary through the further reduction of instinctual behaviors and their replacement by symbolically invented ones.

Here is where one may discover a large logical gap. From the difficult-to-explain beginning trends toward neoteny and increased brain size, the story jumps to Man the Hunter. The statement is made that the females were more burdened with dependent infants and could not follow the rigorous hunt. Therefore they stayed at a "home base," gathering what food they could, while the males developed cooperative hunting techniques, increased their communicative and organizational skills through hunting, and brought the meat back to the dependent females and young. Incest prohibitions, marriage, and the family (so the story goes) grew out of the need to eliminate competition between males for females. A pattern developed of a male hunter becoming the main support of "his" dependent females and young (in other words, the development of the nuclear family for no apparent reason). Thus the peculiarly human social and emotional bonds can be traced to the hunter bringing back the food to share. Hunting, according to Washburn and Lancaster, involved "cooperation among males, planning, knowledge of many species and large areas, and technical skill." They even profess to discover the beginnings of art in the weapons of the hunter. They point out that the symmetrical Acheulian biface tools are the earliest beautiful man-made objects. Though we don't know what these tools were used for, they argue somewhat tautologically that the symmetry indicates they may have been swung, because symmetry only makes a difference when irregularities might lead to deviations in the line of flight. "It may well be that it was the attempt to produce efficient high-speed weapons that first produced beautiful, symmetrical objects."

So, while the males were out hunting, developing all their skills, learning to cooperate, inventing language, inventing art, creating tools and weapons, the poor dependent females were sitting back at the home base having one child after another (many of them dying in the process), and waiting for the males to bring home the bacon. While this reconstruction is certainly ingenious, it gives one the decided impression that only half the species—the male half—did any evolving. In addition to containing a number of logical gaps, the argument becomes somewhat doubtful in the light of modern knowledge of genetics and primate behavior.

The skills usually spoken of as being necessary to, or developed through, hunting are things like coordination, endurance, good vision, and the ability to plan, communicate, and cooperate. I have heard of no evidence to indicate that these skills are either carried on the Y chromosome, or are triggered into existence by the influence of the Y chromosome. In fact, on just about any test we can design (psychological, aptitude, intelligence, etc.) males and females score just about the same. The variation is on an individual, not a sex, basis. . . .

Hunting does not deserve the primary place it has been given in the reconstruction of human evolution, as I will demonstrate by offering the following alternate version.

Picture the primate band: each individual gathers its own food, and the major enduring relationship is the mother-infant bond. It is in similar circumstances that we imagine the evolving protohominids. We don't know what started them in the direction of neoteny and increased brain size, but once begun the trends would prove adaptive. To explain the shift from the primate individual gathering to human food sharing, we cannot simply jump to hunting. Hunting cannot explain its own origin. It is much more logical to assume that as the period of infant dependency began to lengthen, *the mothers would begin to increase the scope of their gathering to provide food for their still-dependent infants.* The already strong primate mother-infant bond would begin to extend over a longer time period, increasing the depth and scope of social relationships, and giving rise to the first sharing of food.

It is an example of male bias to picture these females with young as totally or even mainly dependent on males for food. Among modern hunter-gatherers, even in the marginal environments where most live, the females can usually gather enough to support themselves and their families. In these groups gathering provides the major portion of the diet, and there is no reason to assume that this was not also the case in the Pliocene or early Pleistocene. In the modern groups women and children both gather and hunt small animals, though they usually do not go on the longer hunts. So, we can assume a group of evolving protohominids, gathering and perhaps beginning to hunt small animals, with the mothers gathering quite efficiently both for themselves and for their offspring.

It is equally biased, and quite unreasonable, to assume an early or rapid development of a pattern in which one male was responsible for "his" female(s) and young. In most primate groups when a female comes into estrus she initiates coitus or signals her readiness by presenting. The idea that a male would have much voice in "choosing" a female, or maintain any sort of individual, long-term control over her or her offspring, is surely a modern invention which could have had no place in early hominid life. (Sexual control over females through rape or the threat of rape seems to be a modern human invention. Primate females are not raped because they are willing throughout estrus, and primate males appear not to attempt coitus at other times, regardless of physiological ability.) In fact, there seems to me no reason for suggesting the development of male-female adult pair-bonding until much later. Long-term monogamy is a fairly rare pattern even among modern humans—I think it is a peculiarly Western male bias to suppose its existence in protohuman society.

An argument has been made that traces the development of male-female pair-bonding to the shift of sexual characteristics to the front of the body, the importance of the face in communication, and the development of face-to-face coitus. This argument is insufficient in the first place because of the assumption that face-to-face coitus is the "normal," "natural," or even the most common position among humans (historical evidence casts grave doubt on this assumption). It is much more probable that the coitus position was invented *after* pair-bonding had developed for other reasons. . . .

Food sharing and the family developed from the mother-infant bond. The techniques of hunting large animals were probably much later developments, after the mother-children family pattern was established. When hunting did begin, and the adult males brought back food to share, the most likely recipients would be first their mothers, and second their siblings. In other words, a hunter would share food not with a wife or sexual partner, but with those who had shared food with him: his mother and siblings.

It is frequently suggested or implied that the first tools were, in fact, the weapons of the hunters. Modern humans have become so accustomed to the thought of tools and weapons that it is easy for us to imagine the first manlike creature who picked up a stone or club. However, since we don't really know what the early stone tools such as hand-axes were used for, it is equally probable that they were not weapons at all, but rather *aids in gathering.* We know that gathering was important long before much animal protein was added to the diet, and continued to be important. Bones, sticks, and hand-axes could be used for digging up tubers or roots, or to pulverize tough vegetable matter for easier eating. If, however, instead of thinking in terms of tools and weapons, we think in terms of *cultural inventions,* a new aspect is presented. I suggest that two of the *earliest and most important* cultural inventions were containers to hold the products of gathering, and some sort of sling or net to carry babies. The latter in particular must have been extremely important with the loss of body hair and the increasing immaturity of neonates, who could not cling and had less and less to cling to. Plenty of material was available—vines, hides, human hair. If the infant could be securely fastened to the mother's body, she could go about her tasks much more efficiently. Once a technique for carrying babies was developed, it could be extended to the idea of carrying food, and eventually to other sorts of cultural inventions—choppers and grinders for food preparation, and even weapons. Among modern hunter-gatherers, regardless of the poverty of their material culture, food carriers and baby carriers are always important items in their equipment.

A major point in the Man the Hunter argument is that cooperative hunting among males demanded more skill in social organization and communication, and thus provided selection pressure for increased brain size. I suggest that longer periods of infant dependency, more difficult births, and longer gestation periods also demanded more skills in social organization and communication—creating selective pressure for increased brain size without looking to hunting as an explanation. The need to organize for feeding after weaning, learning to handle the more complex social-emotional bonds that were developing, the new skills and cultural inventions surrounding more extensive gathering—all would demand larger brains. Too much attention has been given to the skills required by hunting, and too little to the skills required for gathering and the raising of dependent young. The techniques required for efficient gathering include location and identification of plant varieties, seasonal and geographical knowledge, containers for carrying the food, and tools for its preparation. Among modern hunting-gathering groups this knowledge is an extremely complex, well-developed, and important part of their cultural equipment. Caring for a curious, energetic, but still dependent human infant is difficult and demanding. Not only must the infant be watched, it must be taught the customs, dangers, and knowledge of its group. For the early hominids, as their cultural equipment and symbolic communication increased, the job of training the young would demand more skill. Selection pressure for better brains came from many directions.

Much has been made of the argument that cooperation among males demanded by hunting acted as a force to reduce competition for females. I suggest that competition for females has been greatly exaggerated. It could easily have been handled in the usual way for primates—according to male status relationships already worked out—and need not be pictured as particularly violent or extreme. The seeds of male cooperation already exist in primates when they act to protect the band from predators. Such dangers may well have increased with a shift to savannah living, and the longer dependency of infants. If biological roots are sought to explain the greater aggressiveness of males, it would be more fruitful to look toward their function as protectors, rather than any supposedly basic hunting adaptation. The only division of labor that regularly exists in primate groups is the females caring for infants and the males protecting the group from predators. The possibilities for both cooperation and aggression in males lies in this protective function.

The emphasis on hunting as a prime moving factor in hominid evolution distorts the data. It is simply too big a jump to go from the primate individual gathering pattern to a hominid cooperative hunting-sharing pattern without some intervening changes. Cooperative hunting of big game animals could only have developed *after* the trends toward neoteny and increased brain size had begun. Big-game hunting becomes a more logical development when it is viewed as growing out of a complex of changes which included sharing the products of gathering among mothers and children, deepening social bonds over time, increase in brain size, and the beginnings of cultural invention for purposes such as baby carrying, food carrying, and food preparation. Such hunting not only needed the prior development of some skills in social organization and communication; it probably also had to await the development of the "home base." It is difficult to imagine that most or all of the adult primate males in a group would go off on a hunting expedition, leaving the females and young exposed to the danger of predators, without some way of communicating to arrange for their defense, or at least a way of saying, "Don't worry, we'll be back in two days." Until that degree of communicative skill developed, we must assume either that the whole band traveled *and hunted* together, or that the males simply did not go off on large cooperative hunts.

The development of cooperative hunting requires, as a prior condition, an increase in brain size. Once such a trend is established, hunting skills would take part in a feedback process of selection for better brains just as would other cultural inventions and developments such as gathering skills. By itself, hunting fails to explain any part of human evolution and fails to explain itself. . . .

# POSTSCRIPT

## Is Hunting More Critical Than Gathering to Cultural Development?

**B**oth hunting and gathering behaviors have been observed in other primates. Some species—such as the bonobo—also regularly share food within the troop. Early hominids probably engaged in all of these behaviors. But with the invention of stone tools and the advent of big game hunting around 2 million years ago, these behaviors intensified and fused into what we now recognize as a *hunting and gathering* or *food-foraging lifestyle*. Food foragers tend to live in nomadic bands of 25 to 30 people and share food communally. They recognize few status distinctions except those of age and sex and tend to be peaceful and non-materialistic. Studies of contemporary food foragers show that both men and women make important social and economic contributions and depend upon each other for survival. For example, among the Ju/'Hoansi of South Africa, anthropologist Richard Lee found that:

> about one-fifth of all men's working days were spent in gathering and men's gathering accounted for 22 percent of all the gathered foods. When I looked at the total contribution of all forms of activity in the diet, I saw that men provided about 45 percent of the food, and women 55 percent, even though men worked harder than women. Overall, vegetable foods provided 70 percent of the diet and meat the other 30 percent (1993:58).

Among early humans, the same patterns probably also prevailed. Men and women would have formed interdependent economic units and lived as social equals, sharing responsibilities for child rearing and decision making. This basic framework may have led to the development of customs such as marriage, kinship, and the incest taboo to facilitate family formation and interband cooperation. Migration out of Africa and into the temperate zones would have also selected for the invention of clothing and hide containers for storage and transport. All these advances probably made life easier and more comfortable for our ancestors. Given this scenario, it could be argued that both hunting and gathering were spurs to cultural development. "Man the Hunter" and "Woman and Gatherer" stand side by side as equally compelling images in prehistory.

For more information on hunting and gathering societies and their significance for human evolution, see G. Issac, "The Diet of Early Man," *World Archaeology* (1971) and T. Ingold, D. Riches, and J. Woodburn, eds., *Hunters and Gatherers, Volume 1: History, Evolution and Social Change* (Berg, 1988). *A View to a Death in the Morning* by Mark Cartmill examines the history of the hunting hypothesis in anthropology and its linked social and political implications. See also *Gender in Archaeology* (1997) by Sarah Milledge Nelson and *Engendering Archaeology* (1991) by Joan Gero and Margaret Conkey, eds., for more information on women in prehistory and their cultural contributions. Cheryl Claassen's book *Women in Archaeology* (1994) also looks at the scientific contributions of female archaeologists.

# ISSUE 14

## Does Biology Limit a Woman's Ability to Hunt?

**YES: Ernestine Friedl,** from "Society and Sex Roles," in James Spradley and David W. McCurdy, eds., *Conformity and Conflict: Readings in Cultural Anthropology* (Allyn and Bacon, 2003)

**NO: Agnes Estioko-Griffin and P. Bion Griffin,** from "Woman the Hunter: The Agta," in Caroline B. Brettell and Carolyn F. Sargent, eds., *Gender in Cross-Cultural Perspective* (Prentice Hall, 2001)

### ISSUE SUMMARY

Ernestine Friedl argues that pregnancy and nursing young infants tends to limit women's ability to hunt effectively in hunting and gathering societies. Agnes Estioko-Griffin and Bion Griffin disagree. They provide evidence that in some hunting and gathering societies, women hunt just as regularly and effectively as men.

A key aspect of the debate about the evolution of sex-role behavior centers on food collection, and the way in which females and males may have foraged for different foods (Ehrenberg, 2004:17).

Does biology determine behavior? For many years, anthropologists have argued over whether differences in male and female behavior are genetic or cultural. These debates have taken many forms. One line of thought links male aggression and competition with reproductive success (see Issue 6). Another controversy has raged over the evolutionary implications of sexual behavior: Is homosexuality and bisexuality "unnatural," or does it have any evolutionary advantages (see Issue 9)? Other researchers have argued over whether physiology and natural selection predispose men and women to adopt different reproductive strategies (see Issues 7 and 10).

The economic roles of men and women have also been scrutinized from this perspective. Archaeological investigations suggest that early humans began to live in bands of about 30 people at least a million and a half years ago. Tools, bone refuse, and other artifacts indicate that these people probably engaged in food sharing and that a division of labor based on age and sex may have started to develop (Isacc, 1969, 1978). These characteristics are also associated with contemporary hunters and gatherers. As Lee notes, "Our ancestors evolved as foragers, and all basic human institutions—language, marriage, kinship, family, exchange and human nature itself—were formed during the two-to-four-million year period when we lived by hunting and gathering. Thus the study of the surviving foragers—the San, Inuit (Eskimo), Australian Aborigines, and others—had much to teach us" (1993:2).

Using this evolutionary model, some researchers suggest that physiological factors are responsible for the sexual division of labor found in most of the world's foraging cultures. Men hunt and women gather, Ernestine Friedl argues, because hunting is incompatible with child rearing. In contrast, Agnes Estioko-Griffin and P. Bion Griffin suggest that women are frequent and effective hunters in cultures like the Agta of the Philippines.

 **YES**

# Society and Sex Roles

... As Western history and the anthropological record have told us, equality between the sexes is rare; in most known societies females are subordinate. Male dominance is so widespread that it is virtually a human universal; societies in which women are consistently dominant do not exist and have never existed.

Evidence of a society in which women control all strategic resources like food and water, and in which women's activities are the most prestigious, has never been found. The Iroquois of North America and the Lovedu of Africa came closest. Among the Iroquois, women raised food, controlled its distribution, and helped to choose male political leaders. Lovedu women ruled as queens, exchanged valuable cattle, led ceremonies, and controlled their own sex lives. But among both the Iroquois and Lovedu, men owned the land and held other positions of power and prestige. Women were equal to men; they did not have ultimate authority over them. Neither culture was a true matriarchy.

Patriarchies are prevalent, and they appear to be strongest in societies in which men control significant goods that are exchanged with people outside the family. Regardless of who produces food, the person who gives it to others creates the obligations and alliances that are at the center of all political relations. The greater the male monopoly on the distribution of scarce items, the stronger their control of women seems to be. This is most obvious in relatively simple hunter-gatherer societies.

Hunter-gatherers, or foragers, subsist on wild plants, small land animals, and small river or sea creatures gathered by hand; large land animals and sea mammals hunted with spears, bows and arrows, and blow guns; and fish caught with hooks and nets. The three hundred thousand hunter-gatherers alive in the world today include the Eskimos, the Australian aborigines, and the Pygmies of Central Africa.

Foraging has endured for two million years and was replaced by farming and animal husbandry only ten thousand years ago; it covers more than 99 percent of human history. Our foraging ancestry is not far behind us and provides a clue to our understanding of the human condition.

Hunter-gatherers are people whose ways of life are technologically simple and socially and politically egalitarian. They live in small groups of 50 to 200

From CONFORMITY AND CONFLICT: READINGS IN CULTURAL ANTHROPOLOGY, ed. by James Spradley and David W. McCurry, 2003, pp. 262–267. Copyright © 2003 by Ernestine Friedl. Reprinted by permission of the author.

and have neither kings, nor priests, nor social classes. These conditions permit anthropologists to observe the essential bases for inequalities between the sexes without the distortions induced by the complexities of contemporary industrial society.

The source of male power among hunter-gatherers lies in their control of a scarce, hard to acquire, but necessary nutrient—animal protein. When men in a hunter-gatherer society return to camp with game, they divide the meat in some customary way. Among the !Kung San of Africa, certain parts of the animal are given to the owner of the arrow that killed the beast, to the first hunter to sight the game, to the one who threw the first spear, and to all men in the hunting party. After the meat has been divided, each hunter distributes his share to his blood relatives and his in-laws, who in turn share it with others. If an animal is large enough, every member of the band will receive some meat.

Vegetable foods, in contrast, are not distributed beyond the immediate household. Women give food to their children, to their husbands, to other members of the household, and rarely, to the occasional visitor. No one outside the family regularly eats any of the wild fruits and vegetables that are gathered by the women.

The meat distributed by the men is a public gift. Its source is widely known, and the donor expects a reciprocal gift when other men return from a successful hunt. He gains honor as a supplier of a scarce item and simultaneously obligates others to him.

These obligations constitute a form of power or control over others, both men and women. The opinions of hunters play an important part in decisions to move the village; good hunters attract the most desirable women; people in other groups join camps with good hunters; and hunters, because they already participate in an internal system of exchange, control exchange with other groups for flint, salt, and steel axes. The male monopoly on hunting unites men in a system of exchange and gives them power; gathering vegetable food does not give women equal power even among foragers who live in the tropics, where the food collected by women provides more than half the hunter-gatherer diet.

If dominance arises from a monopoly on big-game hunting, why has the male monopoly remained unchallenged? Some women are strong enough to participate in the hunt and their endurance is certainly equal to that of men. Dobe San women of the Kalahari Desert in Africa walk an average of 10 miles a day carrying from 15 to 33 pounds of food plus a baby.

Women do not hunt, I believe, because of four interrelated factors: variability in the supply of game; the different skills required for hunting and gathering; the incompatibility between carrying burdens and hunting; and the small size of seminomadic foraging populations.

Because the meat supply is unstable, foragers must make frequent expeditions to provide the band with gathered food. Environmental factors such as seasonal and annual variation in rainfall often affect the size of the wildlife population. Hunters cannot always find game, and when they do encounter animals, they are not always successful in killing their prey. In northern latitudes, where meat is the primary food, periods of starvation are known in every generation. The irregularity of the game supply leads hunter-gatherers in areas where plant foods are available to depend on these predictable foods a good part of the time. Someone must gather the fruits, nuts, and roots and carry them back to camp to feed unsuccessful hunters, children, the elderly, and anyone who might not have gone foraging that day.

Foraging falls to the women because hunting and gathering cannot be combined on the same expedition. Although gatherers sometimes notice signs of game as they work, the skills required to track game are not the same as those required to find edible roots or plants. Hunters scan the horizon and the land for traces of large game; gatherers keep their eyes to the ground, studying the distribution of plants and the texture of the soil for hidden roots and animal holes. Even if a woman who was collecting plants came across the track of an antelope, she could not follow it; it is impossible to carry a load and hunt at the same time. Running with a heavy load is difficult, and should the animal be sighted, the hunter would be off balance and could neither shoot an arrow nor throw a spear accurately.

Pregnancy and child care would also present difficulties for a hunter. An unborn child affects a woman's body balance, as does a child in her arms, on her back, or slung at her side. Until they are two years old, many hunter-gatherer children are carried at all times, and until they are four, they are carried some of the time.

An observer might wonder why young women do not hunt until they become pregnant, or why mature women and men do not hunt and gather on alternate days, with some women staying in camp to act as wet nurses for the young. Apart from the effects hunting might have on a mother's milk production, there are two reasons. First, young girls begin to bear children as soon as they are physically mature and strong enough to hunt, and second, hunter-gatherer bands are so small that there are unlikely to be enough lactating women to serve as wet nurses. No hunter-gatherer group could afford to maintain a specialized female hunting force.

Because game is not always available, because hunting and gathering are specialized skills, because women carrying heavy loads cannot hunt, and because women in hunter-gatherer societies are usually either pregnant or caring for young children, for most of the last two million years of human history men have hunted and women have gathered.

If male dominance depends on controlling the supply of meat, then the degree of male dominance in a society should vary with the amount of meat available and the amount supplied by the men. Some regions, like the East African grasslands and the North American woodlands, abounded with species of large mammals; other zones, like tropical forests and semideserts, are thinly populated with prey. Many elements affect the supply of game, but theoretically, the less meat provided exclusively by the men, the more egalitarian the society.

All known hunter-gatherer societies fit into four basic types: those in which men and women work together in communal hunts and as teams gathering edible plants, as did the Washo Indians of North America; those in which men and women each collect their own plant foods although the men supply some meat to the group, as do the Hadza of Tanzania; those in which male hunters and female gatherers work apart but return to camp each evening to share their acquisitions, as do the Tiwi of North Australia; and those in which the men provide all the food by hunting large game, as do the Eskimo. In each case the extent of male dominance increases directly with the proportion of meat supplied by individual men and small hunting parties.

Among the most egalitarian of hunter-gatherer societies are the Washo Indians, who inhabited the valleys of the Sierra Nevada in what is now southern California and Nevada. In the spring they moved north to Lake Tahoe for the large fish runs of sucker and native trout. Everyone—men, women, and children—participated in the fishing. Women spent the summer gathering edible berries and seeds while the men continued to fish. In the fall some men hunted deer, but the most important source of animal protein was the jackrabbit, which was captured in communal hunts. Men and women together drove the rabbits into nets tied end to end. To provide food for the winter, husbands and wives worked as teams in the late fall to collect pine nuts.

Since everyone participated in most food-gathering activities, there were no individual distributors of food and relatively little difference in male and female rights. Men and women were not segregated from each other in daily activities; both were free to take lovers after marriage; both had the right to separate whenever they chose; menstruating women were not isolated from the rest of the group; and one of the two major Washo rituals celebrated hunting while the other celebrated gathering. Men were accorded more prestige if they had killed a deer, and men directed decisions about the seasonal movement of the group. But if no male leader stepped forward, women were permitted to lead. The distinctive feature of groups such as the Washo is the relative equality of the sexes.

The sexes are also relatively equal among the Hadza of Tanzania, but this near-equality arises because men and women tend to work alone to feed themselves. They exchange little food. The Hadza lead a leisurely life in the seemingly barren environment of the East African Rift Gorge, which is, in fact, rich in edible berries, roots, and small game. As a result of this abundance, from the time they are ten years old, Hadza men and women gather much of their own food. Women take their young children with them into the bush, eating as they forage, and collect only enough food for a light family meal in the evening. The men eat berries and roots as they hunt for small game, and should they bring down a rabbit or a hyrax, they eat the meat on the spot. Meat is carried back to the camp and shared with the rest of the group only on those rare occasions when a poisoned arrow brings down a large animal—an impala, a zebra, an eland, or a giraffe.

Because Hadza men distribute little meat, their status is only slightly higher than that of the women. People flock to the camp of a good hunter and the camp might take on his name because of his popularity, but he is in no sense a leader of the group. A Hadza man and a woman have an equal right to divorce, and each can repudiate a marriage simply by living apart for a few weeks. Couples tend to live in the same camp as the wife's mother, but they sometimes make long visits to the camp of the husband's mother. Although a man may take more than one wife, most Hadza males cannot afford to indulge in this luxury.

In order to maintain a marriage, a man must supply both his wife and his mother-in-law with some meat and trade goods, such as beads and cloth, and the Hadza economy gives few men the wealth to provide for more than one wife and mother-in-law. Washo equality is based on cooperation; Hadza equality is based on independence.

In contrast to both these groups, among the Tiwi of Melville and Bathurst Islands off the northern coast of Australia, male hunters dominate female gatherers. The Tiwi are representative of the most common form of foraging society, in which the men supply large quantities of meat, although less than half the food consumed by the group. Each morning Tiwi women, most with babies on their backs, scatter in different directions in search of vegetables, grubs, worms, and small game such as bandicoots, lizards, and opossums. To track the game, they use hunting dogs. On most days women return to camp with some meat and with baskets full of *korka,* the nut of a native palm, which is soaked and mashed to make a porridge-like dish. The Tiwi men do not hunt small game and do not hunt every day, but when they do they often return with kangaroo, large lizards, fish, and game birds.

The porridge is cooked separately by each household and rarely shared outside the family, but the meat is prepared by a volunteer cook, who can be male or female. After the cook takes one of the parts of the animal traditionally reserved for him or her, the animal's "boss," the one who caught it, distributes the rest to all near kin and then to all others residing with the band. Although the small game supplied by the women is distributed in the same way as the big game supplied by the men, Tiwi men are dominant because the game they kill provides most of the meat.

The power of Tiwi men is clearest in their betrothal practices. Among the Tiwi, a woman must always be married. To ensure this, female infants are betrothed at birth and widows are remarried at the gravesides of their late husbands. Men form alliances by exchanging daughters, sisters, and mothers in marriage, and some collect as many as twenty-five wives. Tiwi men value the quantity and quality of the food many wives can collect and the many children they can produce.

The dominance of the men is offset somewhat by the influence of adult women in selecting their next husbands. Many women are active strategists in the political careers of their male relatives, but to the exasperation of some sons attempting to promote their own futures, widowed mothers sometimes insist on selecting their own partners. Women also influence the marriages of their daughters and granddaughters, especially when the selected husband dies before the bestowed child moves to his camp.

Among the Eskimo, representative of the rarest type of forager society, inequality between the sexes is matched by inequality in supplying the group with food. Inland Eskimo men hunt caribou throughout the year to provision the entire society, and maritime Eskimo men depend on whaling, fishing, and some hunting to feed their extended families. The women process the carcasses, cut and sew skins to make clothing, cook, and care for the young; but they collect no food of their own and depend on the men to supply all the raw materials for their work. Since men provide all the meat, they also control the trade in hides, whale oil, seal oil, and other items that move between the maritime and inland Eskimos.

Eskimo women are treated almost exclusively as objects to be used, abused, and traded by men. After puberty all Eskimo girls are fair game for any interested male. A man shows his intentions by grabbing the belt of a woman, and if she protests, he cuts off her trousers and forces himself upon her. These encounters are considered unimportant by the rest of the group. Men offer their wives' sexual services to establish alliances with trading partners and members of hunting and whaling parties. . . .

Agnes Estioko-Griffin
and P. Bion Griffin

◀ **NO**

# Woman the Hunter: The Agta

**A**mong Agta Negritos of northeastern Luzon, the Philippines, women are of special interest to anthropology because of their position in the organization of subsistence. They are substantial contributors to the daily subsistence of their families and have considerable authority in decision making in the family and in residential groups. In addition, and in contradiction to one of the sacred canons of anthropology, women in one area frequently hunt game animals. They also fish in the rivers with men and barter with lowland Filipinos for goods and services.

In this chapter, we describe women's roles in Agta subsistence economy and discuss the relationship of subsistence activities, authority allocation, and egalitarianism. With this may come an indication of the importance of the Agta research to the anthropology of women and of hunter-gatherers in general. . . .

Women, especially women in hunting-gathering societies, have been a neglected domain of anthropological research. The recent volume edited by Richard Lee and Irven DeVore and the *!Kung of Nyae Nyae* begin to remedy the lack but focus solely on the !Kung San of southern Africa. Other works are either general or synthetic, or report narrowly bounded topics. Sally Slocum, writing in *Toward an Anthropology of Women*, has provided impetus for the Agta study. Slocum points out a male bias in studying hunter-gatherers, showing how approaching subsistence from a female view gives a new picture. From the insights of Slocum we have sought to focus on Agta women, to compare the several dialect groups, and to begin investigating the nature and implications of women as not "merely" gatherers but also hunters. . . .

As is typical of hunting-gathering societies, no formal, institutionalized authority base exists. The nuclear family is the decision maker concerning residence, work, and relations with other people. Older, respected individuals, often parents and grandparents of group members, may be consulted, but their opinions are not binding. Often group consensus is desired; people who disagree are free to grumble or to leave.

The settlement pattern is determined, in part, by the seasonal cycle of rains and sunny weather, and by these influences on the flora and fauna exploited for food. Rainy season flooding restricts forest travel, brings hardships in exchange, but is compensated by good condition of the game animals. The dry season permits travel over greater distances and into the remote

From GENDER IN CROSS-CULTURAL PERSPECTIVE, by Caroline B. Brettell and Carolyn F. Sargent, ed., 2001, pp. 256–259. Copyright © 2001 by Yale University Press. Reprinted by permission. Notes omitted.

mountains. Predictable fish resources enhance the advantages of human dispersal; only the need to carry trade meats to farmers inhibits distant residence placement.

# Women's Activities

Women participate in all the subsistence activities that men do. Women trade with farmers, fish in the rivers, collect forest plant foods, and may even hunt game animals. Tasks are not identical, however; a modest sexual division of labor does exist. Furthermore, considerable variation is found among the groups of Agta of Isabella and Cagayan provinces. These differences may possibly be ascribed to degree of adjustment of Agta to lowland Filipino culture. Some differences may be due to unique culture histories and to little contact.

Although in Isabela most Agta women do not hunt with bow and arrows, with machetes, or by use of traps, most are willing to assist men in the hunt. Not uncommonly, women help carry game out of the forest. Since mature pig and deer are heavy and the terrain is difficult, this is no small accomplishment. Even in areas around Palanan and Casiguran, women are known to accompany men and dogs into the forest and to guide the dogs in the game drive. Some women are famous for their abilities to handle dogs; one informant, a girl about fifteen years of age, was especially skilled. In Palanan and Casiguran, women and men laugh at the idea of women hunting. Such a practice would be a custom of wild, uncivilized Agta (*ebuked*) far in the mountains, they say. Many of the attributes of *ebuked* seem to be old-fashioned customs still practiced by interior groups.

Two groups studied as part of the present research do have women who hunt. Among the Dipagsanghang Agta, several mature women claim to have hunting skills; they learned these in their unmarried teen years. They only hunt under extreme circumstances, such as low food supplies or great distances from farmers and a supply of corn. All these Agta are found in southern Isabela between Dipagsanghang and Dinapiqui.

In the northernmost section of Isabela and well into Cagayan province, women are active and proficient hunters. While we have termed the Agta here as the Dianggu-Malibu group, we are actually referring to speakers of the southeast Cagayan dialect who live on the river drainage areas of the Dianggu and Malibu rivers. Both the dialect and women who hunt are found over a considerably greater territory, according to informants, reaching north to Baggao, Cagayan, and at least to the Taboan River.

Among the Dianggu-Malibu women some variation, perhaps localized, perhaps personal, is found. On the Dianggu, some of the women questioned, and observed hunting, carried machetes and were accompanied by dogs. They claim to prefer the machete to the bow and arrow, allowing dogs to corner and hold pigs for sticking with the knife. Our sample of actual observations is too small to argue that only immature pigs are killed, but we do know that in the dry season adult male pigs are dangerous in the extreme. Dogs may be killed during hunts. Since Agta dogs are seldom strong animals, we wonder if mature pigs are acquired only occasionally. On the other hand, so many dogs are owned by these Agta that sheer numbers may favor large kills. We have observed two Agta women with as many as fifteen dogs. Other Dianggu women prefer the bow.

On the Malibu River, Agta women are expert bow and arrow hunters. On both of our brief visits to this group, women were observed hunting. They claim to use bows always, and they seek the full range of prey animals. Wild pig is most desired, while deer are often killed. Future work must quantify the hunting details, but women seem to vary slightly from men in their hunting strategies. Informants say they hunt only with dogs. On closer questioning they admit to knowing techniques that do not involve dogs—for example, they may climb trees and lie in wait for an animal to approach to feed on fallen fruit. Among all Agta, hunting practices vary considerably between the rainy and dry seasons. Our fieldwork in Malibu has been confined to the dry season, when dogs are important. In the rainy season solitary stalking is practiced. Field observations should eventually provide quantitative data on women hunting in this season; we must stress that our data are primarily from interview and brief observation. We have not resided among Cagayan Agta long enough to advance quantitatively based generalizations.

Women not only hunt but appear to hunt frequently. Like men, some enjoy hunting more than others. The more remotely located Agta seem most to favor hunting. Even among Agta certain males and females are considered lacking in initiative, a fault that may not be confined to hunting.

Informant data indicate that while women may make their own arrows, the actual black-smithing of the metal projectile points is a male activity. More field research is necessary to confirm the universality of this detail. Other items of interest pertain to the composition of hunting parties. Most people in any one residence group are consanguineally or affinely related. We have observed several combinations of hunting parties. Men and women hunt together or among themselves. Often sisters, or mother and daughter, or aunt and niece hunt together. At Malibu, two sisters, co-wives of one male, hunt together, and either or both sisters join the husband to hunt. When young children exist, one of the two wives may stay at the residence while the husband and the other wife hunt and fish. Also, sisters and brothers cooperate on the hunt. A woman would not hunt with, for example, a cousin's husband unless the cousin were along.

The only real argument, in our opinion, that has been advanced to support the contention that women must gather and men hunt relates to childbearing and nurture. Among the Agta, during late pregnancy and for the first few months of nursing, a woman will not hunt. In spite of the small size of each residential group, however, some females seem always to be around to hunt, although one or more may be temporarily withdrawn from the activity. Women with young children hunt less than teenagers and older women. On the occasion of brief hunts—part of one day—children are cared for by older siblings, by grandparents, and by other relatives. Occasionally a father will tend a child. Only infants are closely tied to mothers.

Girls start hunting shortly after puberty. Before then they are gaining forest knowledge but are not strong. Boys are no different. We have no menopause data, but at least one woman known to us as a hunter must have passed childbearing age. She is considered an older woman, but since she is strong, she hunts. The pattern is typical of men also. As long as strength to travel and to carry game is retained, people hunt. Our best informant, a young grandmother, hunts several times a week. . . .

# POSTSCRIPT

## Does Biology Limit a Woman's Ability to Hunt?

**W**hile Friedl and Estioko-Griffin and Bion-Griffin present different perspectives on whether biology limits a woman's ability to hunt, they both agree that women tend to have a higher social status in cultures where female economic contributions and control over resources are also high. Friedl compares four different hunting and gathering societies on the basis of this criterion. The Griffins also note differences between groups of Agta. The Agta in the mountainous regions live primarily by hunting, fishing, and trading and show little sexual division of labor. Women generally hunt and fish as much as men. In the lowland areas, women hunt and fish less but play increasingly important roles in trade and farming. Although their roles differ from mens, womens' high degree of economic contributions and control they exercise over resources maintain gender equality.

Other research suggests that when womens' economic control and participation is reduced, their social status also suffers. Draper (1975) found that domestic violence and gender antagonism increased markedly among the !Kung or Ju/'Hoansi of South Africa when they were forced to give up foraging and become sedentary. This new lifestyle limited women's economic participation since most of the related subsistence activities—herding, farming and wage labor—were restricted to men. Murphy and Murphy (1985) also note a similar situation among the Mundurucu of South America. As the Mundurucu have become increasingly drawn into a commercial economy based on the rubber trade, men's control over rubber trees and the accompanying trade have resulted in greater male social and political dominance overall.

These findings may also have implications for human evolution. Archaeological research suggests that human populations began settling down about 10,000 years ago and domesticating plants and animals. One of the consequences of this change may have been the loss of gender equality and the rise of patriarchal systems based on male social and economic dominance (see Martin and Voorhies, 1975; Leacock, 1975, 1978; Boserup, 1970; Harris, 1970). Some archaeologists see the existence of Venus figurines—statues of women with exaggerated breasts and buttocks—in the later paleolithic era as evidence of a fertility or goddess cult in Europe (Gimbutas, 1982). Although Meskell (1995) has questioned this view, Venus figurines probably reflect the social importance of women during these times. As new modes of subsistence replaced foraging, new social values that reflected and justified the shifts of power would have evolved. Many patriarchal cultures today justify the social and political dominance of men over women on spiritual grounds. For example, Hutterites see their social order and the structure of gender relationships as something that was ordained by God

> *By divine order male is over the female, husband over wife, older over younger, and parent over child. Women have neither vote nor a passive participation in the formal decision. Marital relationships proceed from the divine order. God rules over the soul or spirit, the spirit rules over the body and man rules over woman. As a woman should obey the man, so also the body should obey the spirit. In creation man has lordship over woman while the woman has "weakness, humility, and submission." Woman should "heed her husband . . . and do all things with and naught without his counsel." If she does not, she forsakes the order of God. Man "should have compassion on the woman as the weaker instrument" and must care for her in temporal and spiritual things (Hostetler and Huntington, 1980:10–11).*

Other cultures see women as dangerous or polluting. "This premise renders cosmic and natural the terms of man's domination or religion and ritual, and the limited coparticipation of men and women in domestic life" (Keesing, 1982:7). The Sambia of New Guinea designate village paths as either male or female, and the sexes live separately most of the time. Young boys are also taken from their mothers at around the age of six or seven to live in the communal men's house. Subsequent initiation rituals emphasize the dangers of pollution by women and teach boys how to protect or strengthen their male essence. Oral sex and the ingestion of semen is an important part of this process, as well as minimizing all contact with women. Adult Sambia men also ritually bleed themselves after having sex with their wives to reduce the dangers of pollution. "[Nose] bleeding is done even though it is painful and the blood loss is disliked; men are that desperate to remove female contaminants from the body and blood to reinforce warrior aggressiveness" (Herdt, 1986:140).

Mainstream American culture also has its share of interesting beliefs that support male social and political supremacy as "natural." One of these is the viewpoint that a woman's place is in the home and that the country's economic difficulties is to be blamed on career women (who take jobs away from men), or that the welfare problem could be solved by requiring women to marry the fathers of their children. These ideas ignore the reality that marriage does not guarantee economic support, and that men are not the sole economic providers in most cultures. In fact, the current trend of couples both working and sharing domestic duties and child rearing is bringing us closer to the economic and social equality enjoyed by men and women in many foraging cultures. In this case, embracing our past may be a way of moving forward.

For more information on the sexual division of labor and how economic roles affect gender relationships, see Jane Goodale, *Tiwi Wives* (University of Washington Press, 1971), Tanno Tadashi, "The Mbuti Net-Hunters in the Ituri Forest, Eastern Zaire: Their Hunting Activities and Band Composition," *Kyoto University African Studies* (vol. 10, 1976, pp. 101–135), and Susan Rasmussen, "Pastoral Nomadism and Gender," in C. Brettell and C. Sargent, eds., *Gender in Cross Cultural Perspective* (Prentice-Hall, 2004, pp. 155–169). For more information on economic roles and gender relationships in prehistory, see J. Gero and M. Conkey, eds., *Engendering Archaeology: Women and Prehistory* (Oxford University Press, 1991) and P. Rice "Prehistoric Venuses," *Journal of Anthropological Research* (vol. 37, no. 4, 1981, pp. 402–414).

# ISSUE 15

## Is Cannibalism a Prominent Feature of Prehistoric Societies?

**YES: Ann Gibbons,** from "Archaeologists Rediscover Cannibals," *Science* (August 1997)

**NO: Noel T. Boaz and Russell L. Ciochon,** from "The Scavenging of 'Peking Man,'" *Natural History* (March 2001)

### ISSUE SUMMARY

Ann Gibbons contends that cannibalism was a more prominent feature in many prehistoric societies than many archaeologists initially believed. In contrast, Noel Boaz and Russell Ciochon suggest that scientists are sometimes too quick to cry cannibalism when other explanations may be more accurate. They provide evidence that the condition of the skulls and other bones found at the Peking Man site was not caused by cannibalism.

"I'm having an old friend for dinner."

—Anthony Hopkins as Hannibal Lector in *The Silence of the Lambs*

Cannibalism or the consumption of human flesh is a stock theme in horror films and thrillers for a very good reason. Most contemporary cultures have strong taboos against the practice, and the revulsion we feel is not easily over-come. Only in life-and-death situations do the taboos seem to pale. The soccer team stranded by a plane crash in the Andes during the 1970s ate the flesh of dead companions to survive, but scrupulously avoided consuming the flesh of relatives or close friends. Similarly, the Donner Party, who were snowbound in the Sierra Nevada Mountains in 1847, also resorted to cannibalism when their supplies ran out. There is even some evidence to suggest that some people were murdered for the purpose of eating them. Single men, who had no family or other close, emotional ties to other members of the Party, were especially subject to this fate. Of the 16 single men who began the trip, 13 of them perished during the winter (Diamond, 1992).

Cannibalism under other circumstances, however, is usually taken as a sign of either psychosis or savagery. As a result, some researchers believe that cannibalism may have occurred more frequently in the past than it does today. Gibbons examines this premise in light of recent archaeological excavations in the Americas and Europe. In contrast, Boaz and Ciochon suggest that cannibalism was not a prominent feature of prehistoric societies. They show how the claims that Peking Man may have practiced cannibalism may not stand up to modern scientific scrutiny.

Ann Gibbons                                    ➡ **YES**

# Archaeologists Rediscover Cannibals

**W**hen Arizona State University bioarchaeologist Christy G. Turner II first looked at the jumbled heap of bones from 30 humans in Arizona in 1967, he was convinced that he was looking at the remains of a feast. The bones of these ancient American Indians had cut marks and burns, just like animal bones that had been roasted and stripped of their flesh. "It just struck me that here was a pile of food refuse," says Turner, who proposed in *American Antiquity* in 1970 that these people from Polacca Wash, Arizona, had been the victims of cannibalism.

But his paper was met with "total disbelief," says Turner. "In the 1960s, the new paradigm about Indians was that they were all peaceful and happy. So, to find something like this was the antithesis of the new way we were supposed to be thinking about Indians"—particularly the Anasazi, thought to be the ancestors of living Pueblo Indians. Not only did Turner's proposal fly in the face of conventional wisdom about the Anasazi culture, but it was also at odds with an emerging consensus that earlier claims of cannibalism in the fossil record rested on shaky evidence. Where earlier generations of archaeologists had seen the remains of cannibalistic feasts, current researchers saw bones scarred by ancient burial practices, war, weathering, or scavenging animals.

To Turner, however, the bones from Polacca Wash told a more disturbing tale, and so he set about studying every prehistoric skeleton he could find in the Southwest and Mexico to see if it was an isolated event. Now, 30 years and 15,000 skeletons later, Turner is putting the final touches on a 1500-page book to be published next year by the University of Utah press in which he says, "Cannibalism was practiced intensively for almost four centuries" in the Four Corners region. The evidence is so strong that Turner says "I would bet a year of my salary on it."

He isn't the only one now betting on cannibalism in prehistory. In the past decade, Turner and other bioarchaeologists have put together a set of clear-cut criteria for distinguishing the marks of cannibalism from other kinds of scars. "The analytical rigor has increased across the board," says paleoanthropologist Tim D. White of the University of California, Berkeley. Armed with the new criteria, archaeologists are finding what they say are strong signs of cannibalism throughout the fossil record. This summer, archaeologists are excavating several

From *Science*, vol. 277, August 1, 1997, pp. 635–637. Copyright © 1997 by American Association for the Advancement of Science. Reprinted by permission.

sites in Europe where the practice may have occurred among our ancestors, perhaps as early as 800,000 years ago. More recently, our brawny cousins, the Neandertals, may have eaten each other. And this behavior wasn't limited to the distant past—strong new evidence suggests that in addition to the Anasazi, the Aztecs of Mexico and the people of Fiji also ate their own kind in the past 2500 years.

These claims imply a disturbing new view of human history, say Turner and others. Although cannibalism is still relatively rare in the fossil record, it is frequent enough to imply that extreme hunger was not the only driving force. Instead of being an aberration, practiced only by a few prehistoric Donner Parties, killing people for food may have been standard human behavior—a means of social control, Turner suspects, or a mob response to stress, or a form of infanticide to thin the ranks of neighboring populations.

Not surprisingly, some find these claims hard to stomach: "These people haven't explored all the alternatives," says archaeologist Paul Bahn, author of the *Cambridge Encyclopedia* entry on cannibalism. "There's no question, for example, that all kinds of weird stuff is done to human remains in mortuary practice"—and in warfare. But even the most prominent skeptic of earlier claims of cannibalism, cultural anthropologist William Arens of the State University of New York, Stony Brook, now admits the case is stronger: "I think the procedures are sounder, and there is more evidence for cannibalism than before."

White learned how weak most earlier scholarship on cannibalism was in 1981, when he first came across what he thought might be a relic of the practice—a massive skull of an early human ancestor from a site called Bodo in Ethiopia. When he got his first look at this 600,000-year-old skull on a museum table, White noticed that it had a series of fine, deep cut marks on its cheekbone and inside its eye socket, as if it had been defleshed. To confirm his suspicions, White wanted to compare the marks with a "type collection" for cannibalism—a carefully studied assemblage of bones showing how the signature of cannibalism differs from damage by animal gnawing, trampling, or excavation.

"We were naïve at the time," says White, who was working with archaeologist Nicholas Toth of Indiana University in Bloomington. They learned that although the anthropological literature was full of fantastic tales of cannibalistic feasts among early humans at Zhoukoudian in China, Krapina cave in Croatia, and elsewhere, the evidence was weak—or lost.

Indeed, the weakness of the evidence had already opened the way to a backlash, which was led by Arens. He had deconstructed the fossil and historical record for cannibalism in a book called *The Man-Eating Myth: Anthropology and Anthropophagy* (Oxford, 1979). Except for extremely rare cases of starvation or insanity, Arens said, none of the accounts of cannibalism stood up to scrutiny—not even claims that it took place among living tribes in Papua New Guinea (including the Fore, where cannibalism is thought to explain the spread of the degenerative brain disease kuru). There were no reliable eye witnesses for claims of cannibalism, and the archaeological evidence was circumstantial. "I didn't deny the existence of cannibalism," he now says, "but I found that there was no good evidence for it. It was bad science."

Physical anthropologists contributed to the backlash when they raised doubts about what little archaeological evidence there was (*Science,* 20 June 1986, p. 1497). Mary Russell, then at Case Western Reserve University in Cleveland, argued, for example, that cut marks on the bones of 20 Neandertals at Krapina Cave could have been left by Neandertal morticians who were cleaning the bones for secondary burial, and the bones could have been smashed when the roof caved in, for example. In his 1992 review in the *Cambridge Encyclopedia,* Bahn concluded that cannibalism's "very existence in prehistory is hard to swallow."

# Rising from the Ashes

But even as some anthropologists gave the ax to Krapina and other notorious cases, a new, more rigorous case for cannibalism in prehistory was emerging, starting in the American Southwest. Turner and his late wife, Jacqueline Turner, had been systematically studying tray after tray of prehistoric bones in museums and private collections in the United States and Mexico. They had identified a pattern of bone processing in several hundred specimens that showed little respect for the dead. "There's no known mortuary practice in the Southwest where the body is dismembered, the head is roasted and dumped into a pit unceremoniously, and other pieces get left all over the floor," says Turner, describing part of the pattern.

White, meanwhile, was identifying other telltale signs. To fill the gap he discovered when he looked for specimens to compare with the Bodo skull, he decided to study in depth one of the bone assemblages the Turners and others had cited. He chose Mancos, a small Anasazi pueblo on the Colorado Plateau from A.D. 1150, where archaeologists had recovered the scattered and broken remains of at least 29 individuals. The project evolved into a landmark book, *Prehistoric Cannibalism at Mancos* (Princeton, 1992). While White still doesn't know why the Bodo skull was defleshed—"it's a black box," he says—he extended the blueprint for identifying cannibalism.

In his book, White describes how he painstakingly sifted through 2106 bone fragments, often using an electron microscope to identify cut marks, burn traces, percussion and anvil damage, disarticulations, and breakages. He reviewed how to distinguish marks left by butchering from those left by animal gnawing, trampling, or other wear and tear. He also proposed a new category of bone damage, which he called "pot polish"—shiny abrasions on bone tips that come from being stirred in pots (an idea he tested by stirring deer bones in a replica of an Anasazi pot). And he outlined how to compare the remains of suspected victims with those of ordinary game animals at other sites to see if they were processed the same way.

When he applied these criteria to the Mancos remains, he concluded that they were the leavings of a feast in which 17 adults and 12 children had their heads cut off, roasted, and broken open on rock anvils. Their long bones were broken—he believes for marrow—and their vertebral bodies were missing, perhaps crushed and boiled for oil. Finally, their bones were dumped, like animal bones.

In their forthcoming book, the Turners describe a remarkably similar pattern of bone processing in 300 individuals from 40 different bone assemblages in the Four Corners area of the Southwest, dating from A.D. 900 to A.D. 1700. The strongest case, he says, comes from bones unearthed at the Peñasco Blanco great house at Chaco Canyon in New Mexico, which was the highest center of the Anasazi culture and, he argues, the home of cannibals who terrorized victims within 100 miles of Chaco Canyon, where most of the traumatized bones have been excavated. "Whatever drove the Anasazi to eat people, it happened at Chaco," says Turner.

The case for cannibalism among the Anasazi that Turner and White have put together hasn't swayed all the critics. "These folks have a nice package, but I don't think it proves cannibalism," says Museum of New Mexico archaeologist Peter Bullock. "It's still just a theory."

But even critics like Bullock acknowledge that Turner and White's studies, along with work by the University of Colorado, Boulder's, Paolo Villa and colleagues at another recent site, Fontbrégoua Cave in southeastern France (*Science*, 25 July 1986, p. 431), have raised the standards for how to investigate a case of cannibalism. In fact, White's book has become the unofficial guidebook for the field, says physical anthropologist Carmen Pijoan at the Museum of Anthropology in Mexico City, who has done a systematic review of sites in Mexico where human bones were defleshed. In a forthcoming book chapter, she singles out three sites where she applied diagnostic criteria outlined by Turner, White, and Villa to bones from Aztec and other early cultures and concludes that all "three sites, spread over 2000 years of Mexican prehistory, show a pattern of violence, cannibalism, and sacrifice through time."

White's book "is my bible," agrees paleontologist Yolanda Fernandez-Jalvo of the Museum of Natural History in Madrid, who is analyzing bones that may be the oldest example of cannibalism in the fossil record—the remains of at least six individuals who died 800,000 years ago in an ancient cave at Atapuerca in northern Spain.

## Age-Old Practices

The Spanish fossils have caused considerable excitement because they may represent a new species of human ancestor (*Science,* 30 May, pp. 1331 and 1392). But they also show a pattern familiar from the more recent sites: The bones are highly fragmented and are scored with cut marks, which Fernandez-Jalvo thinks were made when the bodies were decapitated and the bones defleshed. A large femur was also smashed open, perhaps for marrow, says Fernandez-Jalvo, and the whole assemblage had been dumped, like garbage. The treatment was no different from that accorded animal bones at the site. The pattern, says Peter Andrews, a paleoanthropologist at The Natural History Museum, London, is "pretty strong evidence for cannibalism, as opposed to ritual defleshing." He and others note, however, that the small number of individuals at the site and the absence of other sites of similar antiquity to which the bones could be compared leave room for doubt.

A stronger case is emerging at Neandertal sites in Europe, 45,000 to more than 130,000 years old. The new criteria for recognizing cannibalism have not completely vindicated the earlier claims about Krapina Cave, partly because few animal bones are left from the excavation of the site in 1899 to compare with the Neandertal remains. But nearby Vindija Cave, excavated in the 1970s, did yield both animal and human remains. When White and Toth examined the bones recently, they found that both sets showed cut marks, breakage, and disarticulation, and had been dumped on the cave floor. It's the same pattern seen at Krapina, and remarkably similar to that at Mancos, says White, who will publish his conclusions in a forthcoming book with Toth. Marseilles prehistorian Alban DeFleur is finding that Neandertals may also have feasted on their kind in the Moula-Guercy Cave in the Ardeche region of France, where animal and Neandertal bones show similar processing. Taken together, says White, "the evidence from Krapina, Vindija, and Moula is strong."

Not everyone is convinced, however. "White does terrific analysis, but he hasn't proved this is cannibalism," says Bahn. "Frankly, I don't see how he can unless you find a piece of human gut [with human bone or tissue in it]." No matter how close the resemblance to butchered animals, he says, the cut marks and other bone processing could still be the result of mortuary practices. Bullock adds that warfare, not cannibalism, could explain the damage to the bones.

White, however, says such criticism resembles President Clinton's famous claim about marijuana: "Some [although not all] of the Anasazi and Neandertals processed their colleagues. They skinned them, roasted them, cut their muscles off, severed their joints, broke their long bones on anvils with hammerstones, crushed their spongy bones, and put the pieces into pots." Borrowing a line from a review of his book, White says: "To say they didn't eat them is the archaeological equivalent of saying Clinton lit up and didn't inhale."

White's graduate student David DeGusta adds that he has compared human bones at burial sites in Fiji and at a nearby trash midden from the last 2000 years. The intentionally buried bones were less fragmentary and had no bite marks, burns, percussion pits, or other signs of food processing. The human bones in the trash midden, however, were processed like those of pigs. "This site really challenges the claim that these assemblages of bones are the result of mortuary ritual," says DeGusta.

After 30 years of research, Turner says it is a modern bias to insist that cannibalism isn't part of human nature. Many other species eat their own, and our ancestors may have had their own "good" reasons—whether to terrorize subject peoples, limit their neighbors' offspring, or for religious or medicinal purposes. "Today, the only people who eat other people outside of starving are the crazies," says Turner. "We're dealing with a world view that says this is bad and always has been bad. . . . But in the past, that view wasn't necessarily the group view. Cannibalism could have been an adaptive strategy. It has to be entertained."

# The Scavenging of "Peking Man"

China is filled with archaeological wonders, but few can rival the Peking Man Site at Zhoukoudian, which has been inscribed on UNESCO's World Heritage List. Located about thirty miles southwest of Beijing, the town of Zhoukoudian boasts several attractions, including ruins of Buddhist monasteries dating from the Ming Dynasty (1368–1644). But the town's main claim to fame is Longgushan, or Dragon Bone Hill, the site of the cave that yielded the first (and still the largest) cache of fossils of *Homo erectus pekinensis*, historically known as Peking man—a human relative who walked upright and whose thick skull bones and beetling brow housed a brain three-quarters the size of *H. sapiens*'s.

The remains of about forty-five individuals—more than half of them women and children—along with thousands of stone stools, debris from tool manufacturing, and thousands of animal bones, were contained within the hundred-foot-thick deposits that once completely filled the original cave. The task of excavation, initiated in 1921, was not completed until 1982. Some evidence unearthed at the site suggested that these creatures, who lived from about 600,000 to 300,000 years ago, had mastered the use of fire and practiced cannibalism. But despite years of excavation and analysis, little is certain about what occurred here long ago. In the past two years we have visited the cave site, reexamined the fossils, and carried out new tests in an effort to sort out the facts.

To most of the early excavators, such as anatomist Davidson Black, paleontologist Pierre Teilhard de Chardin, and archaeologist Henri Breuil, the likely scenario was that these particular early humans lived in the cave where their bones and stone tools were found and that the animal bones were the remains of meals, proof of their hunting expertise. Excavation exposed ash in horizontal patches within the deposits or in vertical patches along the cave's walls; these looked very much like the residue of hearths built up over time.

A more sensational view, first advanced by Breuil in 1929, was that the cave contained evidence of cannibalism. If the animal bones at the site were leftovers from the cave dwellers' hunting forays, he argued, why not the human bones as well? And skulls were conspicuous among the remains, suggesting to him that these might be the trophies of headhunters. Perhaps, Breuil even proposed, the dull-witted *H. erectus* had been prey to a contemporary, advanced cousin, some ancestral form of *H. sapiens*. Most paleoanthropologists rejected this final twist, but the cannibalism hypothesis received considerable support.

In the late 1930s Franz Weidenreich, an eminent German paleoanthropologist working at Peking Union Medical College, described the *H. erectus* remains in scientific detail. A trained anatomist and medical doctor, he concluded that some of the skulls showed signs of trauma, including scars and fresh injuries from attacks with both blunt and sharp instruments, such as clubs and stone tools. Most convincing to him and others was the systematic destruction of the skulls, apparently at the hands of humans who had decapitated the victims and then broken open the skull bases to retrieve the brains. Weidenreich also believed that the large longitudinal splits seen, for example, in some of the thighbones could only have been caused by humans and were probably made in an effort to extract the marrow.

Others held dissenting views. Chinese paleoanthropologist Pei Wenzhong, who codirected the early Zhoukoudian excavations, disagreed with Breuil and suggested in 1929 that the skulls had been chewed by hyenas. Some Western scientists also had doubts. In 1939 German paleontologist Helmuth Zapfe published his findings on the way hyenas at the Vienna zoo fed on cow bones. Echoing Pei's earlier observations, of which he was aware, Zapfe convincingly argued that many of the bones found at sites like Longgushan closely resembled modern bones broken up by hyenas. In fact, a new term, taphonomy, was coined shortly thereafter for the field Zapfe pioneered: the study of how, after death, animal and plant remains become modified, moved, buried, and fossilized. Franz Weidenreich soon revised his prior interpretation of several *H. erectus* bones whose condition he had attributed to human cannibalistic activity, but he continued to argue that the long-bone splinters and broken skull bases must have resulted from human action.

Following disruptions in fieldwork during World War II (including the loss of all the *H. erectus* fossils collected at Longgushan up to that time, leaving only the casts that had been made of them), Chinese paleoanthropologists resumed investigation of the site. While rejecting the idea of cannibalism, they continued to look upon the cave as a shelter used by early humans equipped with stone tools and fire, as reflected in the title of paleoanthropologist Jia Lampo's book *The Cave Home of Peking Man*, published in 1975.

About this time, Western scientists began to appreciate and develop the field of taphonomy. A few scholars, notably U.S. archaeologist Lewis R. Binford, then reexamined the Longgushan evidence, but only from a distance, concluding that the burning of accumulated bat or bird guano may have accounted for the ash in the cave. With the founding in 1993 of the Zhoukoudian International Paleoanthropological Research Center at Beijing's Institute of Vertebrate Paleontology and Paleoanthropology, a new era of multidisciplinary and international research at Longgushan began. At the institute, we have been able to collaborate with paleontologists Xu Qinqi and Liu Jinyi and with other scholars in a reassessment of the excavations.

One of taphonomy's maxims is that the most common animals at a fossil site and/or the animals whose remains there are the most complete are most likely the ones to have inhabited the area in life. Standing in the Beijing institute amid row after row of museum cases filled with mammal fossils from the cave, we were immediately struck by how few belonged to *H. erectus*—perhaps only 0.5 percent. This suggests that most of the time, this species did not live in the cave. Furthermore, none of the *H. erectus* skeletons is complete. There is a dearth of limb bones, especially of forearms, hands, lower leg bones, and feet—indicating to us that these individuals died somewhere else and that their partial remains were subsequently brought to the cave. But how?

The answer was suggested by the remains of the most common and complete animal skeletons in the cave deposit: those of the giant hyena, *Pachycrocuta brevirostris*. Had *H. erectus*, instead of being the mighty hunters of anthropological lore, simply met the same ignominious fate as the deer and other prey species in the cave? This possibility, which had been raised much earlier by Pei and Zapfe, drew backing from subsequent studies by others. In 1970, for example, British paleontologist Anthony J. Sutcliffe reported finding a modern hyena den in Kenya that contained a number of human bones, including skulls, which the animals had apparently obtained from a nearby hospital cemetery. In the same year, South African zoologist C. K. Brain published the findings of his extensive feeding experiments with captive carnivores, akin to those of Zapfe three decades earlier. One of Brain's conclusions was that carnivores tend to chew up and destroy the ends of the extremities, leaving, in the case of primates, very little of the hands and feet.

To test the giant hyena hypothesis, we examined all the fossil casts and the few actual fossils of *H. erectus* from Longgushan. We looked for both carnivore bite marks and the shallow, V-shaped straight cuts that would be left by stone tools (although we realized that cut marks would probably not be detectable on the casts). We also analyzed each sample's fracture patterns. Breaks at right angles indicate damage long after death, when the bone is fossilized or fossilizing; fractures in fresh bone tend to be irregular, following natural structural lines. Breakage due to crushing by cave rocks is usually massive, and the fracture marks characteristically match rock fragments pushed into the bone.

We were surprised by our findings. Two-thirds of Longgushan's *H. erectus* fossils display what we are convinced are one or more of the following kinds of damage: puncture marks from a carnivore's large, pointed front teeth, most likely the canines of a hyena; long, scraping bite marks, typified by U-shaped grooves along the bone; and fracture patterns comparable to those created by modern hyenas when they chew bone. Moreover, we feel that the longitudinal splitting of large bones—a feature that Weidenreich considered evidence of human activity—can also be attributed to a hyena, especially one the size of the extinct *Pachycrocuta*, the largest hyena known, whose preferred prey was giant elk and woolly rhinoceros. One of the *H. erectus* bones, part of a femur, even reveals telltale surface etchings from stomach acid, indicating it was swallowed and then disgorged.

The pattern of damage on some of the skulls sheds light on how hyenas may have handled them. Bite marks on the brow ridge above the eyes indicate that this protrusion had been grasped and bitten by an animal in the course of chewing off the face. Most animals' facial bones are quite thin, and modern hyenas frequently attack or bite the face first; similarly, their ancient predecessors would likely have discovered this vulnerable region in *H. erectus*. Practically no such facial bones, whose structure is known to us from discoveries at other sites, have been found in the Longgushan cave.

The rest of the skull is a pretty tough nut to crack, however, even for *Pachycrocuta*, since it consists of bones half again as thick as those of a modern human, with massive mounds called tori above the eyes and ears and around the back of the skull. Puncture marks and elongated bite marks around the skulls reveal that the hyenas gnawed at and grappled with them, probably in an effort to crack open the cranium and consume the tasty, lipid-rich brain. We concluded that the hyenas probably succeeded best by chewing through the face, gaining a purchase on the bone surrounding the foramen magnum (the opening in the cranium where the spinal cord enters), and then gnawing away until the skull vault cracked apart or the opening was large enough to expose the brain. This is how we believe the skull bases were destroyed—not by the actions of cannibalistic *H. erectus*.

We know from geological studies of the cave that the animal bones found there could not have been washed in by rains or carried in by streams: the sediments in which the bones are found are either very fine-grained—indicating gradual deposition by wind or slow-moving water—or they contain angular, sharp-edged shards that would not have survived in a stream or flood. Some of the bones may have belonged to animals that died inside the cave during the course of living in it or frequenting it. Other bones were probably brought in and chewed on by hyenas and other carnivores.

Cut marks we observed on several mammal bones from the cave suggest that early humans did sometimes make use of Longgushan, even if they were not responsible for accumulating most of the bones. Stone tools left near the cave entrance also attest to their presence. Given its long history, the cave may have served a variety of occupants or at times have been configured as several separate, smaller shelters. Another possibility is that, in a form of time-sharing, early humans ventured partway into the cave during the day to scavenge on what the hyenas had not eaten and to find temporary shelter. They may not have realized that the animals, which roamed at twilight and at night, were sleeping in the dark recesses a couple of hundred feet away.

What about the ash in the cave, which has been taken as evidence that *H. erectus* used fire? Recently published work by geochemist Steve Weiner and his team at the Weizmann Institute of Science in Israel suggests that the fires were not from hearths. In detailed studies of the ash levels, they discovered no silica-rich layers, which would be left by the burning of wood. Wood (as well as grass and leaves) contains silica particles known as phytoliths—heat-resistant residues that are ubiquitous in archaeological hearth sites. The results indicate that fire was present in the cave but that its controlled use in hearths was not part of the story.

Still, a human hand may somehow be implicated in these fires. One possibility we are exploring in the next phase of our research is that Longgushan was a place where *Pachycrocuta* and *H. erectus* confronted each other as the early humans sought to snatch some of the meat brought back to the cave by the large hyenas. *Pachycrocuta* would have had the home court advantage, but *H. erectus*, perhaps using fire to hold the carnivore at bay, could have quickly sliced off slivers of meat. Although today we might turn up our noses at such carrion, it may have been a dependable and highly prized source of food during the Ice Age.

# POSTSCRIPT

## Is Cannibalism a Prominent Feature of Prehistoric Societies?

**C**ould cannibalism have some adaptive advantage? Traditionally, the existence of strong taboos against cannibalism in most cultures is thought to be the result of natural selection. Preying upon other humans for food tends to reduce group size and, consequently, reproductive rates. So there would be strong selection against the practice in most situations. Anthropologist Marvin Harris (1977) suggested that cannibalism might be a way of increasing the amount of protein in the diet in regions where no large game animals exist. He argued that the Aztec sacrifices of war victims to the sun were a good example of this phenomenon. The American Southwest is another region where large game animals are scarce, so Christy Turner's discovery of cannibalism among the Anasazi may also fit this profile.

Another possibility is that cannibalism may function as a form of population control. Killing and eating other people who belong to different groups may increase the amount of resources available to the survivors. The practice of infanticide has been viewed in this light. Where resources are inadequate to support additional children, newborn babies may be neglected or allowed to die (Chagnon, 1997; Scheper-Hughes, 1989). Many anthropologists have noted that girls are often the targets of infanticide, particularly in patrilineal cultures where they are considered to be economic burdens. Rasmussen (1931) noted that among the Netsilik Eskimo, 38 out of 96 female infants born to 18 families were put to death. Female infanticide also tends to be more common in cultures like Japan and India where population pressure is often intense and resources consequently scarce (see Miller, 2001; Skinner, 1984). Reducing the number of females in the population also lowers the reproductive rate. So it may be that cannibalism—like infanticide—is a response to overpopulation in some societies.

Cross-culturally, however, *gustatory cannibalism*—eating people as a food source—is not as common as *ritual cannibalism*. The latter involves the consumption of human flesh or bones in a ceremonial context and for spiritual or social reasons. For example, the Yanomami Indians of Brazil and Venezuela believe that cannibalism is essential to release the soul of the deceased. After death, the body is burnt and the bones broken up and reduced to a fine powder. The powder is then added to a soup that everyone in the group shares, thereby releasing the person's soul (Chagnon, 1997). Other variations of ritual cannibalism include eating certain body parts of relatives as a way of honoring them, or as a method of absorbing another individual's courage or foresight. Twentieth-century headhunters, for example, frequently ate the brains of their victims in order to acquire their knowledge and wisdom (von Koeniswald, 1956). If early hominids also engaged in cannibalism, then it is likely to have been a form of ritual cannibalism. Instead of providing evidence of their greater savagery, the presence of cannibalism in prehistory may be taken as a sign of increasing spiritual or cultural complexity.

For more information investigating possible cannibalism in prehistory, see P. Villa, "Cannibalism in Prehistoric Europe," *Evolutionary Anthropology* (vol. 1, 1992), C. Turner and J. Turner, *Man Corn* (University of Utah Press, 1999), and T. White, *Prehistoric Cannibalism at Mancos 5MTUMB-2346* (Princeton University Press, 1992). See also *The Man Eating Myth* by W. Arens (1993) and "Cannibalism or Ritual Dismemberment?" by P. Bahn in S. Jones, R. Martin, and D. Pilbeam, eds., *The Cambridge Encyclopedia of Human Evolution* (Cambridge University Press, 1992) for works that question the prevalence of cannibalism.

# ISSUE 16

## Does Cave Art Depict Shamanism?

**YES: Sharon Begley,** from "Secrets of the Cave's Art," *Newsweek* (May 1999)

**NO: Pat Shipman,** from "Old Masters," *Discover* (July 1990)

### ISSUE SUMMARY

Sharon Begley suggests that cave art primarily depicts the spiritual life of humans in paleolithic times. Pat Shipman opposes this view. She argues that art had a practical rather than spiritual value. According to her view, art may have functioned as a teaching aid, a means to preserve information about animal habits, or as a description of social ritual.

*Shamanism represents the most widespread and ancient methodological system of mind-body healing known to humanity. Archaeological and ethnological evidence suggests that shamanic methods are at least twenty or thirty thousand years old (Harner, 1980:51).*

What is the function of prehistoric art? Why did paleolithic people paint images on cave walls, make sculptures, or engrave designs in rock or pieces of bone and antler? These questions have long intrigued researchers, and various hypotheses have been proposed over the years. Traditionally, one of the most popular explanations is that the art depicts *hunting magic* (Breuil, 1952; Maringer, 1960). Proponents of this view suggest that the art is often found in areas of the cave that are difficult to access or are far from the common living areas. Most of the images are of animals, many of whom are wounded, bleeding, or menaced by humans with weapons. The images are also frequently superimposed over one another. These clues could mean that paleolithic hunters sought more control over the animals they hunted, and that the art functioned as a form of *sympathetic magic* (i.e., killing an animal in a painting gave the hunter power to kill the same animal in the material world).

Other researchers favor the idea of art as a form of *fertility magic*. The art frequently depicts pairs of animals together, sometimes in the act of mating, or shows pregnant animals. A more Freudian interpretation has even been offered by French anthropologist Levoi-Gourhan (1967). He suggests that the

264

art symbolizes the dual nature of male and female and depicts early peoples' attempts to come to grips with this dichotomy.

Another intriguing theory has been proposed by Alexander Marshack (1972). He suggests that art functioned as a sort of hunter's guide to the seasons. Most of the compositions were seasonal and depicted animals, plants, birds, or fish that might be available at these times. The art, therefore, had a practical value, serving as a teaching tool or a quick reference guide. Pat Shipman favors this explanation. In contrast, Begley proposes that cave art reveals information about paleolithic spirituality.

Sharon Begley  **YES**

# Secrets of the Cave's Art

**S**tanding before the hanging rock deep inside the damp cave, archeologist
Yanik Le Guillou had a brainstorm: he would mount the digital camera on a
10-foot-long pole, maneuver it around and past the rock, turn the whole con-
traption just so, and . . . snap! capture on film whatever was hidden on the wall
behind. On the first try, the scientists cut off the head of what looked like a
painting of a bison. On the second try they cut off its feet. Finally they captured the whole animal—it was now looking more like a musk ox or a rhinoceros without horns—and the next day bagged even bigger quarry: painted next
to the beast were a lion and a mammoth, powerful animals that are almost as rare
in Paleolithic cave art as they are on the streets of Paris. It was like peering into
the inner sanctum of an art gallery where the dealer kept the best works for his
best customers. And although the Grotte Chauvet, in southeast France, was no
gathering spot for Stone Agers drinking white wine and nibbling canapés, it
came close: for thousands of years, archeologists now think, people returned to
the grotto again and again on what seems to have been a spiritual pilgrimage.

The Grotte Chauvet is one of hundreds of natural caverns cut into the
pale limestone cliffs that form the Ardèche Gorge. But it is unique. Its stone
etchings and 416 paintings—a dozen more were discovered in the 15-day expedition that began last week—are, at 32,000 years, the oldest cave art known to
science. The find consists of mural after mural of bold lions, leaping horses,
pensive owls and charging rhinoceroses that together make up a veritable Louvre
of Paleolithic art. Although Jean-Marie Chauvet and friends stumbled upon the
cave in 1994, for years exploration had been blocked by lawsuits over who
owned the rights to the grotto. Finally, archeologist Jean Clottes, a science
adviser to France's Ministry of Culture, won permission to lead a team into the
cave in 1998. Last week he and a dozen colleagues returned, seeking clues to
the social structure, mind-sets and spiritual beliefs of the ancient artists.

They certainly left behind enough clues. A string of three chambers,
1,700 feet long, as well as one connecting gallery and three vestibules, are all
covered with masterworks breathtaking in their use of perspective (as in overlapping mammoths) and shading, techniques that were supposedly not invented
until millenniums later. And eons before Seurat got the idea, Stone Age artists
had invented pointillism: one animal, probably a bison, is composed of nothing

but red dots. Most striking, however, is that the artists had a thing for rhinos, lions, cave bears and mammoths. In contrast, most cave art depicts hunted animals. "Out of these people's whole bestiary, the artists chose predatory, dangerous animals," says archeologist Margaret Conkey of the University of California, Berkeley. By painting species that virtually never wound up on the Paleolithic menu but which "symbolized danger, strength and power," says Clottes, the artists may have been attempting "to capture the essence of" the animals.

Like bemused gallery goers, Clottes's team spends long hours staring at a painting and asking, what does it mean? One clue comes from how the images are integrated into the walls. In the "Goldilocks" chamber, the missing hindquarters of a cave bear drawn in red ocher seem to lie within rather than on the rock. "The bear seems to come out of the wall," says Clottes. And last week Clottes's team discovered two painted ibexes in the same chamber. The horns of one are actually cracks in the wall which the artist scraped and enlarged. "To these people's way of thinking, those animal spirits were *in* the walls," says Clottes. Painting them, the artists may have believed, allowed the power within to seep into the real world.

Other hints of the cave's spiritual role include engravings of two large pubic triangles—symbols of fertility?—and a creature with human legs but the head and torso of a bison, suggesting that people hoped to incorporate within themselves some of the animals' power. The cave bear in particular may have had special meaning. The presence of 55 ancient bear skulls, including one carefully placed on a fallen rock as if on an altar, suggests a cult of the cave bear. And that may explain why the cave artists chose Chauvet: dozens of hollows in the floor indicate that the enormous bears hibernated there. People returned time and again to view the works. On the 30-foot-long "panel of the horses," the charcoal marks of torches being knocked against the wall were made after the paintings, says Conkey: the marks are superimposed on the mineral sheen that covers the figures. If painting was the first step in a spiritual quest, perhaps, then paying homage to the works was the second.

Doing cave archeology still means roughing it. Base camp is a 25-foot-deep cave strewn with clothes, equipment and baguettes. But since the discovery of the Lascaux painted caves in 1940, the work has gone high-tech. Clottes's team is photographing the paintings and etchings with a regular 35-mm, a digital camera and an infrared camera, which picks up the red-ocher paint better than standard optical devices. Back at the research base in the valley, the team scans or downloads the photos into computers, which can brighten the colors, pump up the contrast or manipulate the image. That technique has helped explain two arrays of red dots that seem unique to Chauvet. Using a scanner, the archeologists fed images of the dots into a computer. A program superimposed arrays of hands onto the dots. The best fit to an array of 48 dots is a sequence of handprints made by an adolescent or a short woman. A panel of 92 dots was probably the handiwork of a tall man. The presence of people of different ages and sexes suggests either a communal experience or masters passing their secrets on to apprentices. Even 32,000 years ago, art was created for more than art's sake.

**Pat Shipman**                                     ↵ **NO**

# Old Masters

**F**ifty years ago, in a green valley of the Dordogne region of southwest France, a group of teenage boys made the first claustrophobic descent into the labyrinthine caverns of Lascaux. When they reached the main chamber and held their lamps aloft, the sight that flickered into view astonished them. There were animals everywhere. A frieze of wild horses, with chunky bodies and fuzzy, crew-cut manes, galloped across the domed walls and ceiling past the massive figure of a white bull-like creature (the extinct aurochs). Running helter-skelter in the opposing direction were three little stags with delicately drawn antlers. They were followed by more bulls, cows, and calves rounding the corner of the chamber.

Thousands have since admired these paintings in Lascaux's Hall of the Bulls, probably the most magnificent example of Ice Age art known to us today. In fact, by 1963 so many tourists wanted to view the cave that officials were forced to close Lascaux to the general public; the paintings were being threatened as the huge influx of visitors warmed the air in the cave and brought in corrosive algae and pollen. (Fortunately, a nearby exhibit called Lascaux II faithfully reproduces the paintings.) After I first saw these powerful images, they haunted me for several months. I had looked at photographs of Lascaux in books, of course, so I knew that the paintings were beautiful; but what I didn't know was that they would reach across 17,000 years to grab my soul.

Lascaux is not an Ice Age anomaly. Other animal paintings, many exquisitely crafted, adorn hundreds of caves throughout the Dordogne and the French Pyrenees and the region known as Cantabria on the northern coast of Spain. All these images were created by the people we commonly call Cro-Magnons, who lived during the Upper Paleolithic Period, between 10,000 and 30,000 years ago, when Europe lay in the harsh grip of the Ice Age.

What did this wonderful art mean, and what does it tell us about the prehistoric humans who created it? These questions have been asked since the turn of the century, when cave paintings in Spain were first definitively attributed to Paleolithic humans. Until recently the dominant answers were based on rather sweeping symbolic interpretations—attempts, as it were, to read the Paleolithic psyche.

These days some anthropologists are adopting a more literal-minded approach. They are not trying to empathize with the artists' collective soul—a

From *Discover*, vol. 11, no. 7, July 1990, pp. 61–65. Copyright © 1990 by Pat Shipman. Reprinted by permission by the author.

perilous exercise in imagination, considering how remote Cro-Magnon life must have been from ours. Rather, armed with the tools of the late twentieth century—statistics, maps, computer analyses of the art's distribution patterns— the researchers are trying to make sense of the paintings by piecing together their cultural context.

This is a far cry from earlier attempts at interpretation. At the beginning of the century, with little more to go on than his intuition, the French amateur archeologist Abbé Henri Breuil suggested that the pictures were a form of hunting magic. Painting animals, in other words, was a magical way of capturing them, in the hope that it would make the beasts vulnerable to hunters. Abstract symbols painted on the walls were interpreted as hunting paraphernalia. Straight lines drawn to the animals' sides represented spears, and V and O shapes on their hides were seen as wounds. Rectangular grids, some observers thought, might have been fences or animal traps.

❧

In the 1960s this view was brushed aside for a much more complex, somewhat Freudian approach that was brought into fashion by anthropologist André Leroi-Gourhan. He saw the cave paintings as a series of mythograms, or symbolic depictions, of how Paleolithic people viewed their world—a world split between things male and female. Femaleness was represented by animals such as the bison and aurochs (which were sometimes juxtaposed with human female figures in the paintings), and maleness was embodied by such animals as the horse and ibex (which, when accompanied by human figures, were shown only with males). Female images, Leroi-Gourhan suggested, were clustered in the central parts of the dark, womblike caves, while male images either consorted with the female ones or encircled them in the more peripheral areas.

Leroi-Gourhan also ascribed sex to the geometric designs on the cave walls. Thin shapes such as straight lines, which often make up barbed, arrowlike structures, were seen as male (phallic) signs. Full shapes such as ovals, V shapes, triangles, and rectangles were female (vulval) symbols. Thus, an arrow stuck into a V-shaped wound on an animal's hide was a male symbol entering a complementary female one.

Leroi-Gourhan was the first to look for structure in the paintings systematically, and his work reinforced the notion that these cave paintings had underlying designs and were not simply idle graffiti or random doodles. Still, some scholars considered his "*perspective sexomaniaque*" rather farfetched; eventually even he played down some of the sexual interpretations. However, a far bigger problem with both his theory and Breuil's was their sheer monolithic scope: a single explanation was assumed to account for 20,000 years of paintings produced by quite widely scattered groups of people.

Yet it is at least as likely that the paintings carried a number of different messages. The images' meaning may have varied depending on who painted them and where. Increasingly, therefore, researchers have tried to relate the content of the paintings to their context—their distribution within a particular cave, the cave's location within a particular region, and the presence of other nearby dwelling sites, tools, and animal bones in the area.

Anthropologist Patricia Rice and sociologist Ann Paterson, both from West Virginia University, made good use of this principle in their study of a single river valley in the Dordogne region, an area that yielded 90 different caves containing 1,955 animal portrayals and 151 dwelling sites with animal bone deposits. They wanted to find out whether the number of times an animal was painted simply reflected how common it was or whether it revealed further information about the animals or the human artists.

By comparing the bone counts of the various animals—horses, reindeer, red deer, ibex, mammoths, bison, and aurochs—Rice and Paterson were able to score the animals according to their abundance. When they related this number to the number of times a species turned up in the art, they found an interesting relationship: Pictures of the smaller animals, such as deer, were proportionate to their bone counts. But the bigger species, such as horses and bison, were portrayed more often than you'd expect from the faunal remains. In fact, it turned out that to predict how often an animal would appear, you had to factor in not just its relative abundance but its weight as well.

A commonsense explanation of this finding was that an animal was depicted according to its usefulness as food, with the larger, meatier animals shown more often. This "grocery store" explanation of the art worked well, except for the ibex, which was portrayed as often as the red deer yet was only half its size and, according to the bone counts, not as numerous. The discrepancy led Rice and Paterson to explore the hypothesis that animals may have also been depicted more or less frequently depending on how aggressive they were to humans.

To test this idea, the researchers asked wildlife-management specialists to score the animals according to a "danger index." The feisty ibex, like the big animals, was rated as highly aggressive; and like these other dangerous animals, it was painted more often than just the numbers of its remains would suggest. Milder-tempered red deer and reindeer, on the other hand, were painted only about as often as you'd expect from their bones. Rice and Paterson concluded that the local artists may have portrayed the animals for both "grocery store" and "danger index" reasons. Maybe such art was used to impress important information on the minds of young hunters—drawing attention to the animals that were the most worthwhile to kill, yet balancing the rewards of dinner with the risks of attacking a fearsome animal.

One thing is certain: Paleolithic artists knew their animals well. Subtle physical details, characteristic poses, even seasonal changes in coat color or texture, were deftly observed. At Lascaux bison are pictured shedding their dark winter pelts. Five stags are shown swimming across a river, heads held high above the swirling tide. A stallion is depicted with its lip curled back, responding to a mare in heat. The reddish coats, stiff black manes, short legs, and potbellies of the Lascaux horses are so well recorded that they look unmistakably like the modern Przhevalsky's horses from Mongolia.

New findings at Solutré, in east-central France, the most famous horsehunting site from the Upper Paleolithic, show how intimate knowledge of the animal's habits was used to the early hunter's advantage. The study, by archeologist Sandra Olsen of the Virginia Museum of Natural History, set out to reexamine how vast numbers of horses—from tens to hundreds of thousands, according to fossil records—came to be killed in the same, isolated spot. The archeological deposits at Solutré are 27 feet thick, span 20,000 years, and provide a record of stone tools and artifacts as well as faunal remains.

The traditional interpretation of this site was lots of fun but unlikely. The Roche de Solutré is one of several high limestone ridges running east-west from the Saône River to the Massif Central plateau; narrow valleys run between the ridges. When the piles of bones were discovered, in 1866, it was proposed that the site was a "horse jump" similar to the buffalo jumps in the American West, where whole herds of bison were driven off cliffs to their death. Several nineteenth-century paintings depict Cro-Magnon hunters driving a massive herd of wild horses up and off the steep rock of Solutré. But Olsen's bone analysis has shown that the horse jump scenario is almost certainly wrong.

For one thing, the horse bones are not at the foot of the steep western end of Solutré, but in a natural cul-de-sac along the southern face of the ridge. For the horse jump hypothesis to work, one of two fairly incredible events had to occur. Either the hunters drove the horses off the western end and then dragged all the carcasses around to the southern face to butcher them or the hunters herded the animals up the steep slope and then forced them to veer off the southern side of the ridge. But behavioral studies show that, unlike bison, wild horses travel not in herds but in small, independent bands. So it would have been extremely difficult for our Cro-Magnons on foot to force lots of horses together and persuade them to jump en masse.

Instead the horse behavior studies suggested to Olsen a new hypothesis. Wild horses commonly winter in the lowlands and summer in the highlands. This migration pattern preserves their forage and lets them avoid the lowland's biting flies and heat in summer and the highland's cold and snow in winter. The Solutré horses, then, would likely have wintered in the Saône's floodplain to the east and summered in the mountains to the west, migrating through the valleys between the ridges. The kill site at Solutré, Olsen notes, lies in the widest of these valleys, the one offering the easiest passage to the horses. What's more, from the hunters' point of view the valley has a convenient cul-de-sac running off to one side. The hunters, she proposes, used a drive lane of brush, twigs, and rocks to divert the horses from their migratory path into the cul-de-sac and then speared the animals to death. Indeed, spear points found at the site support this scenario.

The bottom line in all this is that Olsen's detailed studies of this prehistoric hunting site confirm what the cave art implies: these early humans used their understanding of animals' habits, mating, and migration patterns to come up with extremely successful hunting strategies. Obviously this knowledge must have been vital to the survival of the group and essential to hand down to successive generations. Perhaps the animal friezes in the cave were used as a mnemonic device or as a visual teaching aid in rites of initiation—a means for people to recall or rehearse epic hunts, preserve information, and school their young. The emotional power of the art certainly suggests that this information was crucial to their lives and could not be forgotten.

The transmission of this knowledge may well have been assisted by more than illustration. French researchers Iégor Reznikoff and Michel Dauvois have recently shown that cave art may well have been used in rituals accompanied by songs or chants. The two studied the acoustic resonances of three caves in the French Pyrenees by singing and whistling through almost five octaves as they walked slowly through each cave. At certain points the caves resonated in response to a particular note, and these points were carefully mapped.

When Reznikoff and Dauvois compared their acoustic map with a map of the cave paintings, they found an astonishing relationship. The best resonance points were all well marked with images, while those with poor acoustics had very few pictures. Even if a resonance point offered little room for a full painting, it was marked in some way—by a set of red dots, for example. It remains to be seen if this intriguing correlation holds true for other caves. In the meantime, the image of Paleolithic humans moving by flickering lamps, singing, chanting, and drawing their knowledge of their world indelibly into their memories is so appealing that I find it hard to resist.

Yet the humans in this mental image of mine are shadowy, strangely elusive people. For all the finely observed animal pictures, we catch only the sketchiest glimpses of humans, in the form of stick figures or stylized line drawings. Still, when Rice and Paterson turned to study these human images in French and Spanish caves, a few striking patterns did emerge. Of the 67 images studied, 52 were male and a mere 15 were female. Only men were depicted as engaged in active behavior, a category that included walking, running, carrying spears, being speared, or falling. Females were a picture of passivity; they stood, sat, or lay prone. Most women were shown in close proximity to another human figure or group of figures, which were always other women. Seldom were men featured in social groups; they were much more likely to be shown facing off with an animal.

These images offer tantalizing clues to Paleolithic life. They suggest a society where males and females led very separate lives. (Male-female couples do not figure at all in Paleolithic art, for all the sexual obsessions of earlier researchers.) Males carried out the only physical activities—or at least the only ones deemed worthy of recording. Their chief preoccupation was hunting, and from all appearances, what counted most was the moment of truth between man and his prey. What women did in Paleolithic society (other than bear children and gather food) remains more obscure. But whatever they did, they mostly did it in the company of other women, which would seem to imply that social interaction, cooperation, and oral communication played an important role in female lives.

If we could learn the sex of the artists, perhaps interpreting the social significance of the art would be easier. Were women's lives so mysterious because the artists were male and chauvinistically showed only men's activities in their paintings? Or perhaps the artists were all female. Is their passive group activity the recording and encoding of the information vital to the group's survival in paintings and carvings? Did they spend their time with other women, learning the songs and chants and the artistic techniques that transmitted and preserved their knowledge? The art that brightened the caves of the Ice Age endures. But the artists who might shed light on its meaning remain as enigmatic as ever.

# POSTSCRIPT

## Does Cave Art Depict Shamanism?

**M**ithin (1996) suggests that prehistoric art reflects the emergence of the modern human mind. If that assumption is true, then the use of art and symbol by contemporary people can provide clues to artistic behavior in the past. As Shipman suggests, paleolithic hunters and gatherers needed to have detailed and complex knowledge of the animals they depended on for survival. Many historic foragers also faced the same challenges. For example, the Plains Indians of North America looked to the buffalo for most of their food, clothing, and shelter. This same animal also figures prominently in their stories and art. Ethnographic accounts, however, make it clear that the practical aspect of art did not necessarily diminish its spiritual value. The Plains Indians also considered the buffalo to be a sacred animal, and many of their ceremonies and rituals centered around it.

> The Lakota believe that they did not always have the pipe or their current form of belief system; rather, their legends hold that a figure called the White Buffalo Calf Woman brought 'the way of the pipe' to them, including prescriptions for its use and the seven sacred rites associated with it. The legendary transformation of this woman into a buffalo marked the beginning of the nomadic existence on the Plains and the fact there is no longer any real economic dependence on the buffalo, the memory of this deep relationship between the Lakota and the buffalo is recalled continually even today. It is expressed in the use of the buffalo skull as a religious altar, the dragging of the buffalo skull in one form of the Sun Dance, the use of buffalo robes as beds for Sun Dance candidates to lie upon while being pierced, and on other religious occasions where there is some historical review of Lakota life (Grobsmith, 1981:65).

The presence of animals who can shape-shift into human form, or humans who can take on the characteristics of animals, also shows up in prehistoric art. Lewis-Williams (1983) and Clottes (1989) suggest that these images depict early *shamanism* and may have been drawn by the shamans themselves. Shaman is a Tungus word that refers to "a man or woman who enters an altered state of consciousness—at will—to contact and utilize an ordinarily hidden reality in order to acquire knowledge, power and to help other persons. The shaman has at least one, and usually more, 'spirits' in his personal service" (Harner, 1980:25–26). Shaman in contemporary cultures frequently use art as a means of communicating with their spiritual helpers or to depict the content of their visions. Material objects such as drums, shields, bundles, and medicine bags are often produced and decorated for this purpose. "In many cultures shamans honor their spirit allies by depicting them on their ritual garments, either in representational or nonrepresentational form. The Huichols weave symbols of the *neirika*, the threshold to the Otherworld, into beautiful yarn pictures" (Cowan, 1996:79).

Contemporary shamans also often draw or carry images of animal spirits who are their personal helpers with them as a way of communicating with the helper or of drawing upon its power. If paleolithic shaman were doing the same thing, then it may explain why many of the animal images are of species that were not regularly eaten. Conkey (1993), for example, argues that 65 percent of the European cave images depict horses and bison, while red deer and reindeer dominate the food refuse. If animals depicted were considered to be helpers or totems and not as food, then their prominence in the art makes sense.

The out-of-the-way location of much of the cave art may also have shamanic significance. As noted by Shipman, there seems to be a relationship between the location of cave paintings and the acoustical value of that part of the cave. The areas with the best acoustics tended to have the most art work. Many shaman in contemporary cultures use song, chants, drumming, rattling, or other types of repetitive sound to help them alter their consciousness or facilitate healing (Harner, 1996; Mokelke, 2004). So it suggests that paleolithic people could have engaged in the same practices. The presence of cave art in favorable acoustical areas lends strength to Lewis-Williams and Clottes' hypothesis that shamans may have been the artists.

For more information on prehistoric art, see D. Dickson, *The Dawn of Belief* (University of Arizona Press, 1990), P. Ucko and A. Rosenfield, *Paleolithic Cave Art* (McGraw-Hill, 1967), J-M. Chauvet, et. al., *Dawn of Art: The Chauvet Cave* (1996), and A. Marshack, "Images of the Ice Age," *Archaeology* (vol. 48, 1995, pp. 28–39). For more information on shamanism cross-culturally, see M. Eliade, *Shamanism: Archaic Techniques of Ecstasy* (Princeton University Press, 1996) and J. Halefax, *Shamanic Voices* (E.P. Dutton, 1979). For more information on scientific research on the physiological and psychological effects of drumming, see Nehr, 1961, 1963; Jilek, 1974, Achterberg, 1986; Harner and Tyron, 1996; and Bittman et. al. 2001. Sandra Ingerman's book *Soul Retrieval* (1991) is also a good example of how ancient shamanic methods can be combined with modern psychotherapy. Another interesting read is *Medicine for the Earth* (2000) also by Sandra Ingerman. In it, she discusses shamanic practices to help transmute personal and environmental toxins.

# ISSUE 17

# Is "Race" an Outdated Concept?

**YES: C. Loring Brace,** from "Does Race Exist? An Antagonist's Perspective," *Nova Online* (October 12, 2000)

**NO: George W. Gill,** from "Does Race Exist? A Proponent's Perspective," *Nova Online* (October 12, 2000)

## ISSUE SUMMARY

C. Loring Brace argues that there is no evidence that biological races actually exist. Therefore, he thinks that the concept should be retired. In contrast, George Gill argues that race is a useful biological concept and should not be discarded by scientists.

. . . one evening, I turned on the TV, and there was Patric Stewart "—Captain Picard, of 'Star Trek'—" and I said, "My God, there he is! Kennewick Man!"

—James Chatters (Preston, 1997)

Since its discovery in 1996, Kennewick Man has attracted a storm of controversy. Initially, the skeleton was thought to be the remains of an early European pioneer or fur trader due to the height of the individual and the prominence of Caucasoid features such as a narrow face and a long, narrow braincase. Further study, however, revealed the presence of a stone spear point in the skeleton's hip. The spear point resembled those used by Native Americans from about 9,000 to 4,500 years ago. Radiocarbon dating also confirmed the skeleton's antiquity. Kennewick Man lived around 9,000 years ago, long before Europeans were thought to set foot on the continent.

Foreseeing trouble, the Army Corps of Engineers confiscated the skeleton and put it under lock and key. A few days later, a coalition of five Indian tribes in the Columbia River Basin formally claimed the skeleton under the provisions of the NAGPRA (Native American Graves Protection and Repatriation Act). Not everyone, however, was convinced that Kennewick Man was a Native American. The corps received more than a dozen other claims for the skeleton, including one from the Asutru Folk Assembly, a California-based following of an old Norse religion, who wanted the bones for their own religious purposes (Preston, 1997). Scientists were also split on this issue. While some anthropologists believed that Kennewick Man was a Paleo Indian and should be repatriated, others were not content to let the matter rest without further study. When it seemed that the Corps were about to repatriate the skeleton to the tribes, a group of eight anthropologists filed suit to stop the proceeding. The issue of Kennewick Man's identity was turned over to the courts, and a nasty legal battle ensued.

Even several years later, Kennewick Man still remains a "bone of contention." Was he Native American, or was he a Caucasian? The passion this question generates reflects how complicated and emotionally charged the issue of race is in America. Some scientists argue that race is an outdated concept and one that is difficult to prove convincingly. Loring Brace suggests that race is primarily a cultural and political category rather than an accurate biological classification. Gills, on the other hand, proposes that the concept of race and races still has scientific validity.

# YES ↵

C. Loring Brace

# Does Race Exist?
# An Antagonist's Perspective

**I** am going to start this essay with what may seem to many as an outrageous assertion: There is no such thing as a biological entity that warrants the term "race."

The immediate reaction of most literate people is that this is obviously nonsense. The physician will retort, "What do you mean 'there is no such thing as race'? I see it in my practice everyday!" Jane Doe and John Roe will be equally incredulous. Note carefully, however, that my opening declaration did not claim that "there is no such thing as race." What I said is that there is no "biological entity that warrants the term 'race'." "You're splitting hairs," the reader may retort. "Stop playing verbal games and tell us what you really mean!"

And so I shall, but there is another charge that has been thrown my way, which I need to dispel before explaining the basis for my statement. Given the tenor of our times at the dawn of the new millennium, some have suggested that my position is based mainly on the perception of the social inequities that have accompanied the classification of people into "races." My stance, then, has been interpreted as a manifestation of what is being called "political correctness." My answer is that it is really the defenders of the concept of "race" who are unwittingly shaped by the political reality of American history. . . .

But all of this needs explaining. First, it is perfectly true that the long-term residents of the various parts of the world have patterns of features that we can easily identify as characteristic of the areas from which they come. It should be added that they have to have resided in those places for a couple of hundred thousand years before their regional patterns became established. Well, you may ask, why can't we call those regional patterns "races"? In fact, we can and do, but it does not make them coherent biological entities. "Races" defined in such a way are products of our perceptions. "Seeing is believing" will be the retort, and, after all, aren't we seeing reality in those regional differences?

I should point out that this is the same argument that was made against Copernicus and Galileo almost half a millennium ago. To this day, few have actually made the observations and done the calculations that led those Renaissance scholars to challenge the universal perception that the sun sets in the evening to rise again at the dawn. It was just a matter of common sense to believe that the sun revolves around the Earth, just as it was common sense to "know" that the Earth was flat. Our beliefs concerning "race" are based on the same sort of common sense, and they are just as basically wrong.

# The Nature of Human Variation

I would suggest that there are very few who, of their own experience, have actually perceived at first hand the nature of human variation. What we know of the characteristics of the various regions of the world we have largely gained vicariously and in misleadingly spotty fashion. Pictures and the television camera tell us that the people of Oslo in Norway, Cairo in Egypt, and Nairobi in Kenya look very different. And when we actually meet natives of those separate places, which can indeed happen, we can see representations of those differences at first hand. But if one were to walk up beside the Nile from Cairo, across the Tropic of Cancer to Khartoum in the Sudan and on to Nairobi, there would be no visible boundary between one people and another. The same thing would be true if one were to walk north from Cairo, through the Caucasus, and on up into Russia, eventually swinging west across the northern end of the Baltic Sea to Scandinavia. The people at any adjacent stops along the way look like one another more than they look like anyone else since, after all, they are related to one another. As a rule, the boy marries the girl next door throughout the whole world, but next door goes on without stop from one region to another.

We realize that in the extremes of our transit—Moscow to Nairobi, perhaps—there is a major but gradual change in skin color from what we euphemistically call white to black, and that this is related to the latitudinal difference in the intensity of the ultraviolet component of sunlight. What we do not see, however, is the myriad other traits that are distributed in a fashion quite unrelated to the intensity of ultraviolet radiation. Where skin color is concerned, all the northern populations of the Old World are lighter than the long-term inhabitants near the equator. Although Europeans and Chinese are obviously different, in skin color they are closer to each other than either is to equatorial Africans. But if we test the distribution of the widely known ABO blood-group system, then Europeans and Africans are closer to each other than either is to Chinese.

Then if we take that scourge sickle-cell anemia, so often thought of as an African disease, we discover that, while it does reach high frequencies in some parts of sub-Saharan Africa, it did not originate there. Its distribution includes southern Italy, the eastern Mediterranean, parts of the Middle East, and over into India. In fact, it represents a kind of adaptation that aids survival in the face of a particular kind of malaria, and wherever that malaria is a prominent threat, sickle-cell anemia tends to occur in higher frequencies. It would appear that the gene that controls that trait was introduced to sub-Saharan Africa by traders from those parts of the Middle East where it had arisen in conjunction with the conditions created by the early development of agriculture.

Every time we plot the distribution of a trait possessing a survival value that is greater under some circumstances than under others, it will have a different pattern of geographical variation, and no two such patterns will coincide.

Nose form, tooth size, relative arm and leg length, and a whole series of other traits are distributed each in accordance with its particular controlling selective force. The gradient of the distribution of each is called a "cline" and those clines are completely independent of one another. This is what lies behind the aphorism, "There are no races, there are only clines." Yes, we can recognize people from a given area. What we are seeing, however, is a pattern of features derived from common ancestry in the area in question, and these are largely without different survival value. To the extent that the people in a given region look more like one another than they look like people from other regions, this can be regarded as "family resemblance writ large." And as we have seen, each region grades without break into the one next door.

There is nothing wrong with using geographic labels to designate people. Major continental terms are just fine, and sub-regional refinements such as Western European, Eastern African, Southeast Asian, and so forth carry no unintentional baggage. In contrast, terms such as "Negroid," "Caucasoid," and "Mongoloid" create more problems than they solve. Those very terms reflect a mix of narrow regional, specific ethnic, and descriptive physical components with an assumption that such separate dimensions have some kind of common tie. Biologically, such terms are worse than useless. Their continued use, then, is in social situations where people think they have some meaning.

## America and the Race Concept

The role played by America is particularly important in generating and perpetuating the concept of "race." The human inhabitants of the Western Hemisphere largely derive from three very separate regions of the world—Northeast Asia, Northwest Europe, and Western Africa—and none of them has been in the New World long enough to have been shaped by their experiences in the manner of those long-term residents in the various separate regions of the Old World.

It was the American experience of those three separate population components facing one another on a daily basis under conditions of manifest and enforced inequality that created the concept in the first place and endowed it with the assumption that those perceived "races" had very different sets of capabilities. Those thoughts are very influential and have become enshrined in laws and regulations. This is why I can conclude that, while the word "race" has no coherent biological meaning, its continued grip on the public mind is in fact a manifestation of the power of the historical continuity of the American social structure, which is assumed by all to be essentially "correct."

Finally, because of America's enormous influence on the international scene, ideas generated by the idiosyncrasies of American history have gained currency in ways that transcend American intent or control. One of those ideas is the concept of "race," which we have exported to the rest of the world without any realization that this is what we were doing. The adoption of the biologically indefensible American concept of "race" by an admiring world has to be the ultimate manifestation of political correctness.

George W. Gill

← **NO**

# Does Race Exist?
# A Proponent's Perspective

**S**lightly over half of all biological/physical anthropologists today believe in the traditional view that human races are biologically valid and real. Furthermore, they tend to see nothing wrong in defining and naming the different populations of *Homo sapiens*. The other half of the biological anthropology community believes either that the traditional racial categories for humankind are arbitrary and meaningless, or that at a minimum there are better ways to look at human variation than through the "racial lens."

Are there differences in the research concentrations of these two groups of experts? Yes, most decidedly there are. As pointed out in a recent 2000 edition of a popular physical anthropology textbook, forensic anthropologists (those who do skeletal identification for law-enforcement agencies) are overwhelmingly in support of the idea of the basic biological reality of human races, and yet those who work with blood-group data, for instance, tend to reject the biological reality of racial categories.

I happen to be one of those very few forensic physical anthropologists who actually does research on the particular traits used today in forensic racial identification (i.e., "assessing ancestry," as it is generally termed today). Partly this is because for more than a decade now U.S. national and regional forensic anthropology organizations have deemed it necessary to quantitatively test both traditional and new methods for accuracy in legal cases. I volunteered for this task of testing methods and developing new methods in the late 1980s. What have I found? Where do I now stand in the "great race debate?" Can I see truth on one side or the other—or on both sides—in this argument?

## Findings

First, I have found that forensic anthropologists attain a high degree of accuracy in determining geographic racial affinities (white, black, American Indian, etc.) by utilizing both new and traditional methods of bone analysis. Many well-conducted studies were reported in the late 1980s and 1990s that test methods objectively for percentage of correct placement. Numerous individual methods involving midfacial measurements, femur traits, and so on are over 80 percent

From *Nova Online*, October 12, 2000. Copyright © 2000 by George W. Gill. Reprinted by permission.

accurate alone, and in combination produce very high levels of accuracy. No forensic anthropologist would make a racial assessment based upon just *one* of these methods, but in combination they can make very reliable assessments, just as in determining sex or age. In other words, multiple criteria are the key to success in all of these determinations.

I have a respected colleague, the skeletal biologist C. Loring Brace, who is as skilled as any of the leading forensic anthropologists at assessing ancestry from bones, yet he does not subscribe to the concept of race. Neither does Norman Sauer, a board-certified forensic anthropologist. My students ask, "How can this be? They can identify skeletons as to racial origins but do not believe in race!" My answer is that we can often *function* within systems that we do not believe in.

As a middle-aged male, for example, I am not so sure that I believe any longer in the chronological "age" categories that many of my colleagues in skeletal biology use. Certainly parts of the skeletons of some 45-year-old people look older than corresponding portions of the skeletons of some 55-year-olds. If, however, law enforcement calls upon me to provide "age" on a skeleton, I can provide an answer that will be proven sufficiently accurate should the decedent eventually be identified. I may not believe in society's "age" categories, but I can be very effective at "aging" skeletons. The next question, of course, is how "real" is age biologically? My answer is that if one can use biological criteria to assess age with reasonable accuracy, then age has some basis in biological reality even if the particular "social construct" that defines its limits might be imperfect. I find this true not only for age and stature estimations but for sex and race identification.

The "reality of race" therefore depends more on the definition of reality than on the definition of race. If we choose to accept the system of racial taxonomy that physical anthropologists have traditionally established—major races: black, white, etc.—then one can classify human skeletons within it just as well as one can living humans. The bony traits of the nose, mouth, femur, and cranium are just as revealing to a good osteologist as skin color, hair form, nose form, and lips to the perceptive observer of living humanity. I have been able to prove to myself over the years, in actual legal cases, that I am *more* accurate at assessing race from skeletal remains than from looking at living people standing before me. So those of us in forensic anthropology know that the skeleton reflects race, whether "real" or not, just as well if not better than superficial soft tissue does. The idea that race is "only skin deep" is simply not true, as any experienced forensic anthropologist will affirm.

## Position on Race

Where I stand today in the "great race debate" after a decade and a half of pertinent skeletal research is clearly more on the side of the reality of race than on the "race denial" side. Yet I do see why many other physical anthropologists are able to ignore or deny the race concept. Blood-factor analysis, for instance, shows many traits that cut across racial boundaries in a purely *clinal* fashion with very few if any "breaks" along racial boundaries. (A cline is a gradient of change, such as from people with a high frequency of blue eyes, as in Scandinavia, to people with a high frequency of brown eyes, as in Africa.)

Morphological characteristics, however, like skin color, hair form, bone traits, eyes, and lips tend to follow geographic boundaries coinciding often with climatic zones. This is not surprising since the selective forces of climate are probably the primary forces of nature that have shaped human races with regard not only to skin color and hair form but also the underlying bony structures of the nose, cheekbones, etc. (For example, more prominent noses humidify air better.) As far as we know, blood-factor frequencies are *not* shaped by these same climatic factors.

So, serologists who work largely with blood factors will tend to see human variation as clinal and races as not a valid construct, while skeletal biologists, particularly forensic anthropologists, will see races as biologically real. The common person on the street who sees only a person's skin color, hair form, and face shape will also tend to see races as biologically real. They are not incorrect. Their perspective is just different from that of the serologist.

So, yes, I see truth on both sides of the race argument.

Those who believe that the concept of race is valid do not discredit the notion of clines, however. Yet those with the clinal perspective who believe that races are not real do try to discredit the evidence of skeletal biology. Why this bias from the "race denial" faction? This bias seems to stem largely from socio-political motivation and not science at all. For the time being at least, the people in "race denial" are in "reality denial" as well. Their motivation (a positive one) is that they have come to believe that the race concept is socially dangerous. In other words, they have convinced themselves that race promotes racism. Therefore, they have pushed the politically correct agenda that human races are not biologically real, no matter what the evidence.

Consequently, at the beginning of the 21st century, even as a majority of biological anthropologists favor the reality of the race perspective, not one introductory textbook of physical anthropology even presents that perspective as a possibility. In a case as flagrant as this, we are not dealing with science but rather with blatant, politically motivated censorship. But, you may ask, are the politically correct actually correct? Is there a relationship between thinking about race and racism?

# Race and Racism

Does discussing human variation in a framework of racial biology promote or reduce racism? This is an important question, but one that does not have a simple answer. Most social scientists over the past decade have convinced themselves that it runs the risk of promoting racism in certain quarters. Anthropologists of the 1950s, 1960s, and early 1970s, on the other hand, believed that they were combating racism by openly discussing race and by teaching courses on human races and racism. Which approach has worked best? What do the intellectuals among racial minorities believe? How do students react and respond?

Three years ago, I served on a NOVA-sponsored panel in New York, in which panelists debated the topic "Is There Such a Thing as Race?" Six of us sat on the panel, three proponents of the race concept and three antagonists. All had authored books or papers on race. Loring Brace and I were the two anthropologists "facing off" in the debate. The ethnic composition of the panel was three white and three black scholars. As our conversations developed, I was struck by how similar many of my concerns regarding racism were to those of my two black teammates. Although recognizing that embracing the race concept can have risks attached, we were (and are) more fearful of the form of racism likely to emerge if race is denied and dialogue about it lessened. We fear that the social taboo about the subject of race has served to suppress open discussion about a very important subject in need of dispassionate debate. One of my teammates, an affirmative-action lawyer, is afraid that a denial that races exist also serves to encourage a denial that racism exists. He asks, "How can we combat racism if no one is willing to talk about race?"

## Who Will Benefit?

In my experience, minority students almost invariably have been the strongest supporters of a "racial perspective" on human variation in the classroom. The first-ever black student in my human variation class several years ago came to me at the end of the course and said, "Dr. Gill, I really want to thank you for changing my life with this course." He went on to explain that, "My whole life I have wondered about why I am black, and if that is good or bad. Now I know the reasons why I am the way I am and that these traits are useful and good."

A human-variation course with another perspective would probably have accomplished the same for this student if he had ever noticed it. The truth is, innocuous contemporary human-variation classes with their politically correct titles and course descriptions do not attract the attention of minorities or those other students who could most benefit. Furthermore, the politically correct "race denial" perspective in society as a whole suppresses dialogue, allowing ignorance to replace knowledge and suspicion to replace familiarity. This encourages ethnocentrism and racism more than it discourages it.

# POSTSCRIPT

## Is "Race" an Outdated Concept?

**A**lthough anthropologists argue over the validity of race, no one disagrees that biological differences do exist among human populations. Biological variation among present-day populations may reflect a combination of genetic drift and adaptation to different regional and cultural conditions. Populations vary in terms of *anatomical features*, such as skin color, hair form, and body shape; *physiological features* such as metabolic rate, hormone activity, color blindness, growth rate, and genetic diseases; and *biochemical features* relating to characteristics of the blood.

One of the anatomical features that has received a lot of attention is skin color. This trait is controlled by the amount of melanin in the skin and correlates closely with latitude. People with darker skin color are usually found nearest to the equator with progressively lighter-skinned people appearing in regions closer to the poles. The reason for these differences has to do with temperature changes and the amount of sunlight each population is exposed to. In the tropics, dark skin protects against overexposure to ultraviolet rays (Beall and Steegman, 2000; Jablonski and Chaplin, 2000). In the more temperate zones, the reduced sunlight and colder temperatures make darker skin less advantageous. In fact, studies suggest that lighter skin may have been selected for in other latitudes because it supported the synthesis of vitamin D. Individuals who do not get enough vitamin D may be more susceptible to diseases such as rickets. So there could have been fairly rapid selection for this trait in temperate environments as humans migrated out of Africa. Other research (Post, et al., 1995; Robbins, 1991) suggests that dark-skinned people are more susceptible to cold and suffer from frostbite more frequently. This factor would be another pressure selecting for lighter skin in the temperate zones.

There are some exceptions to this rule. Inuits are dark skinned and live in the Arctic. However, archaeological evidence suggests that they migrated into the area recently and traditionally got significant amounts of vitamin D in their diet. Both factors probably account for the persistence of their darker skin tone.

Another interesting difference between populations is body build. In 1847, Carl Bergmann observed that populations in colder climates tended to be heavier in order to retain heat, while populations in hot environments tend to be slimmer. I.A. Allen later suggested that the length of the body's extremities, such as arms, legs, and fingers, tends to be longer in warm areas. This feature results in a high surface area-to-weight ratio. In cold regions, the reverse is true. Populations tend to have shorter arms and legs and a low surface area-to-weight ratio to reduce heat loss. These two rules have been combined to form *the Bergmann-Allen rule*.

In other situations, the connection between the environment and human biological variation is less clear. The distribution of ABO blood groups around

284

the world is a good example. The blood group O is found in high concentrations among indigenous populations in the Americas. It is also commonly found in Northern Asia and Siberia, suggesting that Native Americans are probably descended from prehistoric populations from those regions. The prevalence of this blood type in the Americas is also probably due to the *founder's effect* and not natural selection. In other regions, however, the O blood type may have been actively selected against. Studies show that mosquitoes may be more attracted to people with blood type O. As a result, people with this blood type have a greater chance of being exposed to diseases carried by mosquitoes. Perhaps it is no mistake that the percentage of people with O blood type is low in West Africa and other regions where the risk of malaria is high.

For more information about the concept of race and human biological variation, see A.R. Templeton, "Human Race: A Genetic and Evolutionary Perspective," *American Anthropologist* (1998); E. Shanklin, *Anthropology and Race* (Wadsworth, 1994); C. Loring Brace, "Intelligence and Race," *Natural History* (1997); and the AAPA Statement on the Biological Aspects of Race in *American Journal of Physical Anthropology* (1996). See also Matt Cartmill's article "The Third Man," *Discover* (1997), which examines how racial politics has influenced the study of fossils and prehistory. For opposing views on repatriation, see James Riding, "Repatriation: A Pawnee Perspective," *American Indian Quarterly* (1996), "Some Scholars Views on Reburial," *American Antiquity* (1992) and R. Bonnichsen and A. Schneider, "The Battle of the Bones," *The Sciences* (2000). For more information on some of the ethical issues confronting scientists, also see L. Goldstein and K. Kintagh, "Ethics and the Reburial Controversy," *American Antiquity* (1990) and T.A. Del Bene, "Take the Moral Ground: An Essay on the 'Reburial' Issue," *West Virginian Archaeologist* (vol. 42, no. 2, 1990, pp. 11–19).

# Contributors to This Volume

## EDITOR

**DR. MARY COURTIS** received her Ph.D. in anthropology from the University of Oregon in 1992. For the past 12 years, she has been teaching classes in anthropology at Portland Community College. In addition to physical anthropology, her research interests include gender roles, shamanism, East Indian spirituality, and Native North American ethnology. Dr. Courtis lives in the country with her two dogs and five cats.

## STAFF

| | |
|---|---|
| Larry Loeppke | Managing Editor |
| Jill Peter | Senior Developmental Editor |
| Nichole Altman | Developmental Editor |
| Beth Kundert | Production Manager |
| Jane Mohr | Project Manager |
| Tara McDermott | Design Coordinator |
| Bonnie Coakley | Editorial Assistant |
| Lori Church | Permissions |

# AUTHORS

**SHARON BEGLEY** is the science editor of *The Wall Street Journal* and was formerly a senior editor at *Newsweek* magazine for 20 years.

**NOEL T. BOAZ** is a professor of anatomy who co-authored the book *Dragon Bone Hill: Reinvestigating the Cave of Beijing Man* with Russell Ciochon. Recently, Boaz and Ciochon have speculated about the social life of *Homo erectus* in China. They link the presence of large thick skulls in males to sexual selection.

**CHRISTOPHE BOESCH** is a member of the department of primatology at the Max Planck Institute of Evolutionary Anthropology in Leipzig, Germany.

**HEDWIGE BOESCH-ACHERMANN** has investigated the social lives and tool-making styles of chimpanzees in the Tai forest. Her research indicates that female chimpanzees are the most active toolmakers and teachers, leading her to speculate about the role of woman the toolmaker in human evolution.

**C. LORING BRACE** is a professor of anthropology at the University of Michigan. His research addresses issues of morphological variability between human populations.

**SHANNON BROWNLEE** has been freelancing since 1999 when she left *U.S. News & World Report*. She is a senior fellow at the New America Foundation, where she focuses on the lack of scientific evidence behind many common medical practices.

**DAVID M. BUSS** is a professor of psychology at the University of Texas. He received his Ph.D. in psychology from the University of California, Berkeley, in 1981. His research interests focus on different aspects of evolutionary psychology, such as human mating strategies, the emotion of jealousy, social conflict, and stalking.

**RUSSELL CIOCHON** is a professor of anthropology at the University of Iowa. His research interests include human evolution in Asia concerning the first arrival of early *Homo* and the evolution of *Homo erectus*.

**WILLIAM A. DEMBSKI** is a mathematician and a philosopher. He is an associate research professor in the conceptual foundations of science at Baylor University and a senior fellow with Discovery Institute's Center for Science and Culture in Seattle.

**JARED DIAMOND** is a professor of geography at the University of California, Los Angeles. He is the Pulitzer Prize–winning author of the widely acclaimed *Guns, Germs, and Steel: The Fates of Human Societies*.

**AGNES ESTIOKO-GRIFFIN** conducted research in the Phillipines with P. Bion Griffin on female roles among the Agata. She was influential in showing ethnographic evidence that women can and do take part in significant hunting in some cultures.

**DEAN FALK** is a physical anthropologist and is a professor of anthropology at Florida State University. His works include *Constraints on Brain Size: The Radiator Hypothesis* and *Braindance, Revised and Expanded Edition* (University Press of Florida).

**ERNESTINE FRIEDL** is a James B. Duke Professor Emerita and taught at Wellesley College before going to Duke in 1973. Her major publication is *Vasilika: A Village in Mo Greece* (1962).

**DOUGLAS J. FUTUYMA** received his Ph.D. from the University of Michigan in 1969. He has been a Guggenheim and Fulbright Fellow, the president of the Society for the Study of Evolution and the American Society of Naturalists, and the editor of *Evolution*. He is also the author of a successful textbook, *Evolutionary Biology*.

**ANN GIBBONS** writes about paleoanthropology, anthropology, and biological sciences.

**GEORGE W. GILL** is professor of anthropology at the University of Wyoming. He also serves as the forensic anthropologist for Wyoming law-enforcement agencies and the Wyoming state crime laboratory.

**JOSIE GLAUSIUSZ** has written on a wide range of scientific subjects. A senior editor at *Discover* magazine, she lives in New York.

**STEPHEN JAY GOULD** was a monthly columnist for *Natural History* magazine from 1974–2001 and has written over 300 essays. He received his B.A. degree in geology from Antioch College and earned his Ph.D. at Columbia University. He became a full professor at Harvard in 1973. His works include *The Structure of Evolutionary Theory* and *Questioning the Millennium: A Rationalist's Guide to Precisely Arbitrary Countdown*.

**P. BION GRIFFIN** is a professor and an acting associate dean at the University of Hawaii. He is also Co-P.I. on the East Cambodia Archaeological Survey project.

**MELVIN KONNER** is Samuel Candler Dobbs Professor of Anthropology and associate professor of psychiatry and neurology at Emory University. He spent two years doing fieldwork among the Kalahari San or Bushmen.

**KENNETH KOSIK** is a professor of neurology at Harvard Medical School and an attending physician at Brigham and Women's Hospital in Boston, where he was cofounder of the Memory Disorders Clinic.

**MAUVE LEAKEY** is head of the division of paleontology at the National Museums of Kenya in Nairobi.

**C. OWEN LOVEJOY** joined the department of anthropology of Kent State University in 1972 and was appointed university professor in 1993. His present interests are in developmental biology and the earliest human fossil record.

**KENNETH P. OAKLEY** is a British archaeologist best known for exposing Piltdown Man as a hoax in 1953. Much of his research revolved around the connection between toolmaking and human evolution as described in his classic work *Man the Toolmaker*.

**JOHN RENNIE** has been editor in chief of *Scientific American* magazine since 1994. He has been a recipient of the Sagan Award from the Council of Scientific Society Presidents for excellence in advancing the public understanding of science.

**ROBERT SAPOLSKY** is a professor of biological sciences at Stanford University and of neurology at Stanford's School of Medicine. His latest book, *A Primate's Memoir*, grew out of his year spent in Africa.

**PAT SHIPMAN** studied fossil assemblages from early Pleistocene sites in Kenya and Tanzania and has examined purported worked bones from Europe and North and South America. Her books include *The Evolution of Racism* (Simon and Schuster).

**SALLY SLOCUM** is the executive director of the Helena Symphony. She holds a Ph.D. in anthropology and taught for several years before joining the Foreign Service.

**MEREDITH F. SMALL** is a professor of anthropology at Cornell University and is the author of *Our Babies, Ourselves: What's Love Got to Do with It?* She writes frequently for *Natural History Magazine* and *Discover,* and is a commentator for National Public Radio's *All Things Considered.*

**BARBARA SMUTS** received her Ph.D. from Stanford University, and is currently a professor at the University of Michigan. Her research includes the evolution of social behavior.

**CRAIG STANFORD** is a specialist in the fields of great ape behavior and human origins. He is chair of anthropology and co-director of the Jane Goodall Research Center at the University of Southern California.

**CAROL TAVRIS** is a social psychologist and writer. Her books include *The Mismeasure of Woman* (Touchstone).

**ALAN WALKER** is a physical anthropologist. He taught at Harvard University from 1973–1978, then joined Johns Hopkins University in 1978.

**SHERWOOD L. WASHBURN** is a U.S. biological anthropologist. He is a leading authority on primate and human evolution. He has edited *Social Life of Early Man* (1962) and numerous other publications.

**PETER WHEELER** is a professor of evolutionary biology. His research interests include the evolution of the human brain and the influence of thermoregulatory selection pressures on human evolution.

**BERNARD WOOD** is presently the Henry R. Luce Professor of Human Origins in the department of anthropology at George Washington University and adjunct senior scientist at the National Museum of Natural History, the Smithsonian Institution.

**CARL ZIMMER** is the author of several popular science books and writes frequently for magazines including *The New York Times Magazine, National Geographic,* and *Discover.* His books include *Parasite Rex and Evolution: The Triumph of an Idea.*